# Lessons Learned in Disaster Mental Health:
# The Earthquake in Armenia and Beyond

**Figure 0.1** A clock in Central Gumri Square frozen at the moment the earthquake struck on a chilly Wednesday morning while workers and school children were indoors, December 7, 1988.
Photographer Roman Poderni (TASS)

# Lessons Learned in Disaster Mental Health: The Earthquake in Armenia and Beyond

Edited by

## Armen Goenjian, MD, LDFAPA.
Full Research Psychiatrist, UCLA/Duke University National Center for Child Traumatic Stress, Geffen School of Medicine at UCLA
and
Director of the Psychiatric Outreach Program of Armenia

## Alan Steinberg, PhD
Associate Director, UCLA/Duke University National Center for Child Traumatic Stress, Geffen School of Medicine at UCLA

## Robert Pynoos, MD, MPH
Co-Director, UCLA/Duke University National Center for Child Traumatic Stress, Geffen School of Medicine at UCLA

CAMBRIDGE
UNIVERSITY PRESS

# CAMBRIDGE
## UNIVERSITY PRESS

University Printing House, Cambridge CB2 8BS, United Kingdom

One Liberty Plaza, 20th Floor, New York, NY 10006, USA

477 Williamstown Road, Port Melbourne, VIC 3207, Australia

314–321, 3rd Floor, Plot 3, Splendor Forum, Jasola District Centre,
New Delhi – 110025, India

103 Penang Road, #05–06/07, Visioncrest Commercial, Singapore 238467

Cambridge University Press is part of the University of Cambridge.

It furthers the University's mission by disseminating knowledge in the pursuit of
education, learning, and research at the highest international levels of excellence.

www.cambridge.org
Information on this title: www.cambridge.org/9781108813143
DOI: 10.1017/9781108877992

First published 2022

Printed in the United Kingdom by TJ Books Limited, Padstow Cornwall

*A catalogue record for this publication is available from the British Library.*

*Library of Congress Cataloging-in-Publication Data*
Names: Goenjian, Armen, editor. | Steinberg, Alan (Alan M.), editor. | Pynoos, Robert S., editor.
Title: Lessons learned in disaster mental health : the earthquake in Armenia and beyond / edited by Armen
Goenjian, Alan Steinberg, Robert Pynoos.
Description: New York, NY : Cambridge University Press, 2022. | Includes index.
Identifiers: LCCN 2021032164 (print) | LCCN 2021032165 (ebook) | ISBN 9781108813143 (paperback) |
ISBN 9781108877992 (ebook)
Subjects: MESH: Stress Disorders, Post-Traumatic – therapy | Earthquakes | Mental Health Services –
organization & administration | Relief Work – organization & administration | Armenia
Classification: LCC RC552.P67 (print) | LCC RC552.P67 (ebook) | NLM WM 172.5 | DDC 616.85/
210094756–dc23
LC record available at https://lccn.loc.gov/2021032164
LC ebook record available at https://lccn.loc.gov/2021032165

ISBN 978-1-108-81314-3 Paperback

........................................................................................................................

# Contents

*We pay homage to the victims of the Spitak earthquake and dedicate this book to traumatized children everywhere.*

# Preface

**Armen Goenjian, MD, DFAPA**

This book is based on our collective, long-term experience in implementing a major post-disaster mental health response and recovery program in the aftermath of the catastrophic 1988 earthquake in Soviet Armenia. The Psychiatric Outreach Program represents one of the most intensive and sustained recovery efforts after a natural disaster. The chapters describe the initiation of the program by Dr. Armen Goenjian and colleagues on a limited budget, and its expansion to include sixty highly dedicated Armenian speaking mental health clinicians who volunteered to go to the earthquake zone from the United States and Europe to provide practical assistance and psychological treatment to the survivors. It describes the evolution of the program from the initial acute phase, when clinical fieldwork was carried out in makeshift structures, tents, and mobile clinics, to its growth as a three-year teaching/training program for local psychologists, psychiatrists, and teachers, to the building of two clinics that provided services for over twenty years to the populace of two cities, Gumri and Spitak, and villages in the vicinity.

When the program began, school-aged children and adolescents were the main targets for intervention. Adults were also treated in hospitals, factories, and mobile clinics. With the support of the Armenian Relief Society of the Western United States, two clinics were built in the earthquake zone operated by the newly trained mental health workers under the supervision of expert psychologists and psychiatrists from the United States and Europe. After the first year, studies were conducted to examine the performance of the staff the course of stress reactions among survivors, including PTSD, depression, and anxiety; and the contribution of a variety of pre- and post-earthquake variables to the severity of ongoing post-earthquake reactions.

This book describes the background conditions of the earthquake, the widespread devastation it caused the inception of the program, the organizational challenges of working with the Soviet government and school personnel in the devastated cities, and the clinicians from the diaspora who came to work in the earthquake zone. This work could not have been accomplished without the involvement and support of many local partners, including the Ministries of Health and Education, school headmasters and teachers in the earthquake zone, and local political officials. It also describes the process of decision-making regarding achieving a balance of services and research, including preliminary needs assessment, case finding, outreach strategies, and clinical work with the affected population.

We have also included chapters by several experts, also from UCLA and other universities, with whom we have collaborated on different topics, including moral development and pathological interference with conscience functioning among traumatized youth from Spitak; the effects of relocation on children and their mothers after the earthquake; the longitudinal epidemiology of mental health consequences after disasters; the heritability of vulnerability to PTSD, depression, and anxiety among multigenerational families; and candidate gene studies. The genetic study is the only multigenerational family study that demonstrates the significant heritability and pleiotropy (sharing of genes) of PTSD, depression, and anxiety. An important feature of this volume is its focus on children and adolescents, an understudied population in the aftermath of a natural disaster. In most chapters we have included significant findings from other major disasters.

This volume covers a comprehensive set of disaster-related clinically relevant topics that we have examined over the past thirty years; including the course of PTSD, depression, and anxiety among children, adolescents, and adults differentially exposed to the earthquake in Gumri, Spitak, and Yerevan; long-term risk and protective factors associated with stress reactions; and treatment outcome. An important contribution of this project has been the demonstration of the efficacy of the UCLA Trauma and Grief Focused Psychotherapy intervention in several prospective long-term studies among children and early adolescents.

Another important longitudinal finding was the substantial detrimental effect of post-earthquake adversities in increasing depression and impeding the remediation of PTSD symptoms. The paucity of long-term follow-up studies among children and adolescents after disasters highlights the importance of these findings.

Other studies examined the effect of exposure to double trauma (prior exposure to political violence in Azerbaijan followed by exposure to the Spitak earthquake); parental loss, comparing stress reactions among orphans versus those who lost either a father or a mother during the earthquake; and the course of PTSD among adults conducted two, five and twenty-three years post-earthquake. For each of the topic areas, we provide a discussion of research methods, draw implications for theory building, consider directions for future research and application for the delivery for the delivery of post-disaster mental health services. In addition to discussing our findings from Armenia, we have also included findings from our other disaster-related studies, including the Parnitha earthquake in Greece and Hurricane Mitch in Nicaragua.

In the final chapter, we discuss lessons learned from our experiences in the trenches and those of others involved in other disasters, including China, Japan, the United States, Honduras, and Haiti. Many of these studies conducted after major disasters during the past decade have expanded our knowledge of the mental health impact of disasters and effective response and recovery strategies. In addition to describing lessons learned, clinical and organizational recommendations are provided, including ways to improve the outcome of therapy, minimize burn-out or vicarious traumatization of therapists, and build a working alliance with headmasters, teachers, and government officials. We have also included a chapter that describes the evolving conceptual framework that guided our intervention and research approach.

We have added the human perspective in describing the many challenges faced in implementing the program from ground zero during the Soviet era and maintaining it thereafter for two decades. We describe the emotional difficulties experienced by some therapists from the diaspora and strategies to address them. We have also included a chapter of earthquake memoirs, one from a senior psychologist from Glendale, California, who treated many survivors and trained the local therapists in the earthquake zone, a second from the Spitak clinic head therapist, and a third from a housewife, also from Spitak, who was a preadolescent at the time of the earthquake.

This book is intended to be a useful compendium of our published findings and subsequent literature in the field. We hope that it will provide much-needed evidence-based practical guidelines for developing and implementing public mental health recovery and research programs after catastrophic disasters globally, especially in developing countries where morbidity and mortality are high and resources sparse. We believe that what is discussed in this book has broad implications that extend beyond earthquakes to other types of natural and man-made disasters and large-scale mass violence events.

The intended audience includes a wide range of professionals, including psychologists, psychiatrists, social workers, school psychologists and counselors, community religious professionals, epidemiologists, sociologists, primary care physicians, and nurses, historians, and professionals who work for both public and private relief organizations after disasters and mass violence in the United States and around the world. We envision its use by educators in graduate schools and training programs across these many fields.

We want to acknowledge support and assistance from the many agencies, organizations, and individuals who contributed significantly to the implementation of this program. These include the Officials of Ministry of Health and Education of the Soviet Republic of Armenia, the Armenian Relief Society of the Western United States (the sponsor of the relief program), the Psychiatric Outreach Program therapists, the Earthquake Relief Fund for Armenia, the Armenian Missionary Association of America, the United States Agency for International Development, Dr. Garo Aivazian, Dr. Mousegh L. Najarian, Dr. Ida Karaian, Reverend Berdj Jambazian, Reverend Movses Janbazian, Dr. Samvel Torosian, Dr. Norair Tarpinian, Roupen Sarkissian, Professor Garlen Darlakyan, Gumri Party Secretary Spartak Petrosian, Dr. Meline Karakashian, Dr. Madeline Tashjian, Dr. Haigaz Grigorian, Shakeh Yegavian, Aram Manukyan, Pavagan Petrosian, Gagik Manukyan, Susana Poghosian, Dr. Julieta Markarian, Hasmig Garabedyan, Dr. Angela Boghosian, Raffi Manjikian, Suzanna Maranjian, Artyom Manukian, Dr. David Walling, Dr. Louis Fauve-Hovanessian, Dr. Sarikis Arevian, Sarkis Ghazarian, Hermine Mahseredjian, Margaret Avedissian, Dr. Alice Kassabian, Dr. Hagop Papazian, Rosalie Kerbekian, Sira Dermen, Dr. Ani Kaladjian, Artyom Shamamyan, Karine Armen, Dr. Anahid Oghanian, Dr. Shoghig Aroyan, Adiane Cody, Garine Ghaplanian, Gayane Markaryan-Stepanyan, Marlene Dersarkissian, Dr. Diane Zakarian, Dr. Avedis Panajian, Arpy Injejikian, Garbis Moushigian, Dr. Jack Chelebian, Zabel Alahaydoian, Roozan Varteresian, Dr. Armand Vartanian, Dr. Viken Movsessian, Dr. Armen Sarkissian, Manoug Kaprielian, Dr. Ernie Nobel (Babikian), Antranig Mkrtchyan, Dr. Edmond Guergerian, Dr. Carolann Najarian, Magda Bechar, Dr. Simon Kochakian, Dr. George Bezirganian, Dr. Julia Bailey, Dr. Sheryl Bishop, Dr. Barbara Stillwell, Dr. Lynn Fairbanks, Dr. David Pelcovitz, Dr. Matt Galvin, Seta Manoukian, Dr. Rachel Yehuda, Dr. Araxi Arganian, Dr. Ruben Khachadourian, and Joe Barbera of Hanna-Barbera Productions Inc., Finally, we are indebted to the many teachers and principals in Gumri and Spitak for their dedication to the recovery of their students.

# Contributors

Haroutune K. Armenian, MD, DrPH: Professor of Epidemiology, UCLA Fielding School of Public Health; and American University of Armenia, Turpanjian School of Public Health

Mathew Galvin, MD: Clinical Associate Professor, Faculty Department of Psychiatry, Indiana University School of Medicine, Indianapolis

Ida Karayan PsyD, LMFT, CBT: Director of the Armenian Relief Society Child Youth Family Guidance Center; Private practice

Vahe Khachadourian, MD, MPH, PhD: Postdoctoral Fellow, Department of Psychiatry, Icahn School of Medicine at Mount Sinai

Louis M. Najarian, MD, DFAPA: Clinical Professor of Psychiatry, Zucker School of Medicine at Hofstra. Northwell

Pavagan Petrosyan, Director and Head Psychotherapist of Spitak Mental Health Clinic, Armenia

David Pelcovitz, PhD: Professor, Straus Chair in Psychology and Education, Azrieli Graduate school of Jewish Education and Administration, Yeshiva University, New York

Barbara Stillwell, MD: Associate Professor Emeritus, Department of Psychiatry, Indiana University School of Medicine, Indianapolis

Chapter

# 1

# The 1988 Spitak Earthquake in Armenia and the Implementation of the Psychiatric Outreach Program

Armen Goenjian

## 1.1 The Ravages of the Spitak Earthquake and the Faltered Recovery

On December 7, 1988, at 11:37 a.m., a strong trembler of magnitude 6.9 on the Richter scale and maximum intensity of X (classified as "Devastating" on the Medvedev–Sponheuer–Karnik scale) shook northwestern Armenia (Figure 1.1). The epicenter was the town of Nalband near the city of Spitak, after which the earthquake was named. Four minutes later, an aftershock of magnitude 5.8 caused further destruction, killing many of those who were trapped and those who were trying to rescue survivors who were trapped. Swarms of aftershocks, some as large as magnitude 5.0, continued for months in the area around Spitak (Figure 1.2).

There was widespread destruction in two cities. In Gumri, known as Leninakan during the Soviet era (population 250,000), the second largest city in Armenia, 16.8 miles from the epicenter of the earthquake, more than half of the structures were severely damaged or destroyed. The city of Spitak, 6.6 miles from the epicenter, population 30,000, was nearly leveled. In Gumri, sixty-one of sixty-six nursery schools and thirty-seven of forty-six primary/secondary schools were either destroyed or substantially damaged. And, in Spitak, eleven of twelve nursery schools and five of seven primary/secondary schools were destroyed or severely damaged. Surveys commissioned by the World Bank four years after the earthquake indicated that over 100,000 people were still residing in emergency accommodations called *domigs* (makeshift homes), 87% of which were located in Gumri and Spitak.

According to official government reports, the number of deaths due to the earthquake was approximately 25,000. However, by other estimates the death toll was around 35,000. The death toll in Gumri comprised 7% of the population and in Spitak 16%. Many of those people who were injured during the earthquake died subsequently because of a lack of medical resources such as dialysis machines and antibiotics.

Assistance in rebuilding the earthquake zone came from many countries, including Uzbekistan, Switzerland, Russia, Austria, Finland, Norway, Italy, Germany, Czechoslovakia, and Estonia. However, in the face of the enormity of the devastation, the assistance was insufficient, and as a result, the region remained devastated for years. The President of the Soviet Union at the time, Mikhail Gorbachev, promised that reconstruction would be completed in two years. But that promise was not fulfilled. Rebuilding and retrofitting proceeded extremely slowly. Two and a half decades after the earthquake, thousands of people who had lost their homes during the earthquake were still living in makeshift dwellings.

**Figure 1.1** Gumri (Leninakan), December 1988.
Photographer Martin Shakhbazyan (TASS).

**Figure 1.2** "Boundless Desperation." Dead bodies after the Spitak Earthquake, December 7, 1988.
Photographer Aleksander Kopachev.

In 1988, two major geopolitical events occurred that shaped the psyche and socioeconomic conditions of the populace in Armenia and Nagorno-Karabagh, an Armenian enclave in Azerbaijan. The first event was the war with neighboring Azerbaijan, which began when Armenians, the majority of the population of Nagorno-Karabagh, demanded self-determination. The reaction by the Azeris was brutal. Many Armenian residents throughout Azerbaijan were killed or deported, abandoning most of their belongings. Some of the displaced refugees settled in what later was to become the earthquake zone.

Fearing the break-up of the Soviet Union, President Gorbachev resorted to force in order to suppress the demands for self-determination by Armenians in Nagorno-Karabagh. The Soviet military occupied Yerevan, the capital of Armenia, and supported the Azeris in their relentless bombardment of Nagorno-Karabagh. Both neighboring countries to Armenia, Azerbaijan and Turkey, imposed a blockade, making it extremely difficult for Armenia to conduct international commerce and import essential goods such as food, medicines, and construction materials. Against this backdrop, the earthquake occurred on December 7, 1988, just before noon.

Recovery proceeded slowly due to a lack of funding and resources such as gas, electricity, and construction materials. Compounding the existing problems was the Soviet Union's meltdown and the subsequent chaos in Armenia, with inexperienced leaders trying to manage the enormous difficulties in the earthquake zone. Additionally, rampant corruption in the government and market manipulation by the oligarchs for profiteering compounded the already existing shortages of food, medicine, fuel, and electricity. These shortages continued for a good part of the next two decades.

After the earthquake, the homeless were placed in poorly insulated makeshift dwellings, where multiple family members shared limited living spaces. At the time of our twenty-five-year follow-up study, thousands in the earthquake zone were still living in dilapidated makeshift structures. According to government figures, unemployment and poverty in Gumri as of 2015 was about 45%, and in Spitak, where recovery proceeded at a relatively faster pace, partially attributed to more dedicated mayors, it was about 34%.

In general, Armenians place a strong emphasis on family ties. They make great efforts to keep families closely knit. During stressful times, family members support one another. After the earthquake, family lives were disrupted, and the support that existed before abated. For many families, the only way to survive financially was for a member, usually the father or son, to go to a neighboring country to work and send money home. Often these departures lasted many years. Another reason for the disruption of family life included earthquake- or war-related psychological and physical disabilities. Many of the disabled could not work and provide financial or emotional support to other family members. Finally, there was the permanent departure of family members who did not want to live in the dismal conditions of the earthquake zone. They had relatives and friends in other countries who helped them leave Armenia. Usually, these were young people who had the means to travel and found employment elsewhere in other countries. This lack of support from the missing or disabled family members hampered the recovery of those who had PTSD and depression.

## 1.2  Mental Health Delivery System in Soviet Armenia

Before the earthquake, mental health services in Armenia were provided by psychiatrists, primarily to individuals with severe mental disorders that often required hospitalization. Some psychologists treated patients; most taught and conducted research. There were only a few mental health clinics in Yerevan that provided psychotherapy, and virtually none existed outside Yerevan. The treatment offered in clinics included pharmacotherapy, supportive psychotherapy, and in some centers, behavior therapy. There was a stigma associated with having psychological problems. Consequently, families concealed their psychological issues.

In 1989, only four psychologists in Armenia were certified by the Ministry of Health to provide treatment. There were no marriage and family counselors nor clinical social workers who offered primary psychological care to clients. Very few therapists were knowledgeable enough about Posttraumatic Stress Disorder (PTSD). In addition to the dearth of experts on trauma psychiatry, local psychiatrists and psychologists were overwhelmed by their own problems and unable to provide adequate care to their patients. In summary, the existing mental health delivery system was inadequate to meet the earthquake survivors' psychological needs, both in quality and quantity. The introduction of our therapeutic modalities, which encouraged the free expression of feelings and thoughts between client and therapist, was well received.

## 1.3 The Clergy

The majority of Armenians in Armenia are Apostolic Christians, and a minority are Evangelical and Catholic. There are also Yazidis (an ethnoreligious group), Jews, and several other religious groups. The clergy in Armenia had no training in dealing with mental health problems. Additionally, the clergy were not trusted because they were regarded as subservient (with good reason) to the whims of the communist government. This contrasted with the major supportive role clergy had played historically during and after the Armenian Genocide in the Middle-East, and in Armenia before the Soviet regime.

After the earthquake, many had an insatiable thirst for religious/spiritual support. Non-Armenian Christian groups belonging to various denominations such as Mormons and Jehovha's witnesses and non-Christians such as Hindus came to Armenia to help the survivors and convert them to their denominations or religion. They provided spiritual and material support, such as church services, clothing, and housing. The emotional support they provided was well received, and many people proselytized.

## 1.4 Initiation of an Intervention Program in Soviet Armenia

On December 7, 1988, on my way to see my patients in Los Angeles, there was a news flash on the radio that said: "A devastating earthquake has effaced the city of Spitak in Armenia, thousands had died, and many were homeless in freezing temperatures." I had difficulty concentrating at work. My patients recognized it and were forgiving. That evening we saw television footage depicting the widespread destruction in Spitak with dead bodies lying all over. I had flashbacks to my youth when Armenian Genocide survivors used to tell us harrowing stories of the decimation of innocent women and children. These indelible memories had not gone away; they resurfaced. I thought that this time I might have a choice to do something helpful for the survivors. In the ensuing weeks, I tried to go to Armenia. It was not easy to get a visa to go to a Soviet country from the United States. A few weeks after the earthquake, the deputy mayor of Yerevan was visiting Los Angeles. I thought he might be able to help me get a visa. I asked him about help being provided to the children who were relocated from the earthquake zone to Yerevan. He dismissed my concern with a harsh response, "They have no problems. We don't need help." He then turned his back on me, picked up an English language magazine, and started flipping the pages. Once again, I tried to engage him in the conversation. Again, he snubbed me.

After a few more unsuccessful attempts to get a visa, I met a great humanitarian, Reverend Berdj Jambazian, who was back from the earthquake zone. He had gone there on a humanitarian mission to help the survivors. There he had cultivated a good relationship with Professor Garlen Darlakin, the head of the committee for diaspora Armenians called "Spyurkahai Gabi Committee" (SGB). His office was in charge of vetting the visitors from the diaspora. Soon after the Reverend intervened, I was issued a visa to go to Armenia.

After a tortuous journey via Finland to Moscow, I made it to Yerevan, Armenia's capital. An employee of the SGB took me to its headquarters, where I met Professor Darlakian, a dignified gray-haired refined intellectual. He was a shrewd and astute man. He questioned me briefly, thanked me, and then called in Dr. Norair Tarpinian, Chief of Psychiatry of Yerevan, who was assigned to help me with my plans. Dr. Tarpinian was a charismatic man who had little experience with trauma psychiatry but was willing to help. He also enjoyed good food and cognac. Dinners gave us the opportunity to nurture a good relationship. He was very curious about my background, life in the United States, and how I compared Middle-Eastern and Soviet Armenians.

My initial intent was to assess the psychological condition of children from the earthquake zone, sum up my findings, and make recommendations to Professor Darlakian and the Ministry of Health representatives to convince them to pave the way for my main objective, which was to provide psychological intervention to the children as they were the country's future. I thought, if we were going to make an impact as diaspora therapists, the most efficient way would be working with children in schools. I requested to visit the schools in Yerevan, where there were children relocated from the earthquake zone, and then go to the earthquake zone for more meetings. Access to the schools was granted by the Deputy Minister of Education, who understood well the survivors' suffering. His daughter, who lived in Gumri with her husband and two children, had only just escaped the collapse of their apartment. They were now living with him and his wife in Yerevan.

The following day, Dr. Ani Kaladjian, a dedicated and respected psychologist from New York whom I had asked to accompany me on this trip, joined us. First, we went to a Yerevan school where there were numerous students from the earthquake zone. There we met with the principal and teachers. Almost two months had passed since the earthquake. What surprised us at the meeting was the extent and intensity of the teachers' emotions. At the time of the earthquake, these teachers had been in Yerevan, where the earthquake's impact was much less compared to cities in the earthquake zone. After a brief introduction, I asked the teachers an open-ended question about the earthquake's effect on them. As if the walls of a dam had broken, there was wailing by many of the teachers. They talked about their grief and that of the relocated children from the earthquake zone. In addition to being educators, these teachers had to deal with the emotional problems of the children as well as their own. What I experienced during the meeting portended the daunting task that laid ahead of us in the earthquake zone.

The next day, we headed to Gumri and Spitak, two of the most severely earthquake-impacted cities. On our way, we passed the village of Nalband, a desolate place at the epicenter of the earthquake. All the cinderblock homes around the highway were destroyed. Almost two months had passed since the earthquake, and still, there were no people in sight. Finally, we saw a middle-aged man, unshaven, unkempt, wandering by the highway. We parked the car nearby and introduced ourselves. He was pleased that we showed interest in him. He seemed to be in a daze and preoccupied. He said he had left his children with relatives in Yerevan and came alone back to Nalband, trying to find his wife's body to bury her. People would tell him, to no avail, to stop searching for her. His grief was unbearable. He said his two boys were in Yerevan "yearning to see their mother." As tears started flowing down his cheeks, he mumbled, "I have no answer for them. I have to find her." I had no answer, either. My eyes welled. I gave him a hug, wished him well, and headed to Gumri with my colleagues.

During numerous stopovers, we saw sadness and fear. We saw an elderly couple digging through rubble to find some of their buried belongings; classes held under tents next to a demolished school; jumpy children were ducking under their desks every time a noisy truck passed. We saw exhausted teachers overwhelmed by their problems and those of their students. Students had become inattentive, restless, unruly. Parents and administrators had become less tolerant and demanding. Most were grieving the loss of someone close to them. They feared the recurrence of another earthquake. They were grieving the loss of loved ones, their homes, their beloved city, the comfort they used to enjoy. All had vanished.

When we entered Gumri, we passed by the ruins of a high-rise building where the Deputy Minister's daughter and her family lived. The Deputy Minister, who was accompanying us, brokedown and began sobbing. From there on, he hardly spoke a word until we were on our way back to Yerevan late at night. The internist who was accompanying us avoided getting out of the car with the rest of us in Spitak to look at the ruins; instead, he read a book he had brought with him. During our meetings with teachers, he kept interrupting by asking irrelevant questions while they were recounting their painful memories of the earthquake. This was his way of dealing with stress. In one day, we had witnessed a condensed version of a trauma textbook, including PTSD symptoms, dissociative states, intense grief, depression, and separation anxiety. I was exhausted and tried to deal with my sadness by overworking and planning.

In Yerevan, we were asked to see relocated families from Gumri and Spitak and refugees from Azerbaijan. These were refugees who had fled the pogroms in Azerbaijan. Between February 18–26, 1988, demonstrations were held in Yerevan for the unification of Nagorno-Karabakh (an Armenian enclave in Azerbaijan) with Armenia. What followed was the torture, killing, and looting of Armenians living in Azerbaijan. These refugees fled; some settled in the earthquake zone and others on the outskirts of Yerevan.

At the end of my tenure, I gave a summary report to Professor Darlakyan and the Head of Psychiatry for Armenia, Dr. Samvel Torosian, about the ubiquity of post-traumatic psychological problems among the survivors of the earthquake and the pogroms, and offered them mental health intervention by experts from the diaspora. They accepted the recommendation and agreed to support us.

In February 1989, after returning to California, I presented a plan to the Earthquake Relief Fund for Armenia (ERFA) to send teams of mental health workers to Armenia for the next six months. ERFA was a coalition of various Armenian organizations that had raised money to help the earthquake victims. They accepted the proposal and agreed to pay for the travel expenses. The Ministry of Health decided to pay for the hotel and food costs in Yerevan. As to the chaotic earthquake zone, where there were no functioning hotels, we relied on the goodwill of residents for housing or slept in a mobile clinic, hospital wards, or tents.

## 1.5  The Psychiatric Outreach Program

During the subsequent months, the Psychiatric Outreach Program (POP) was initiated. The participants were all volunteers that included psychologists, psychiatrists, social workers, and marriage and family counselors from the United States and Europe. Initially the funding for travel expenses were provided by the the Earthquake Relief Fund for Armenia. Eventually, the Armenian Relief Society (ARS) of the Western United States took over the responsibility of managing the funding of the program. The ARS is highly regarded independent, philanthropic organization serving the humanitarian, social, and educational needs of Armenians and non-Armenians alike for over one hundred years. It operates as a non-governmental organization and has entities in twenty-seven countries. I had great trust in this organization's ability to deliver assistance to the needy based on its impeccable record.

We received constructive input from two highly qualified, experienced psychiatrists. These experts included Dr. Garo Aivazian, the Chairman of the Psychiatry Department at the University of Tennessee, a superb clinician and teacher, and Dr. John Yacoubian, an eminent child psychiatrist from Washington.

Our primary target population for intervention was the children. Posttraumatic Stress Disorder, depression, grief reactions, and separation anxiety symptoms were ubiquitous among children. These reactions were understandable, given the severity of the trauma, death, and destruction that had been pervasive. Even if a student had not lost an immediate family member or had their house destroyed, someone close (a relative, friend, or teacher) had lost a family member, was homeless, or physically handicapped due to injuries. Such widespread losses depleted the potential support of many students. We provided them with psychoeducation, supportive therapy, and trauma-grief-focused psychotherapy, and refrained from use of pharmacotherapy except in severe cases. Among adults, we used psychotherapy and pharmacotherapy primarily when needed. Besides the severity of, stress reactions, and comorbidities, another striking problem that hindered recovery was the omnipresence of reminders such as destroyed buildings, the physically disabled, and the makeshift shacks. For years, destroyed buildings were left untouched. Compounding matters was the war with neighboring Azerbaijan. The stream of refugees made it harder for the government to provide resources to victims of both tragedies.

## 1.6  Teaching and Training Program

We lacked the human resources to deal with the enormity of this challenge. Volunteer mental health workers from the diaspora continued working in the earthquake zone. Six months had passed since the earthquake. Still, many children were highly symptomatic. We decided to move to another phase which included building two clinics and training local professionals and paraprofessionals by Western treatment standards. The ARS financed the building of the clinic in Gumri. In Spitak, the government allocated a prefabricated building that we converted to a clinic. The structure was part of the "Villagio Italiano" housing complex donated by the Italian government. Twenty local psychologists, psychiatrists, logotherapists, and teachers were selected from Spitak, Gumri, and Yerevan for the three-year program funded by the ARS and the United States Agency for International Development (USAID). The training was similar to clinically oriented psychiatry residency programs in the United States. Dr. Luis M. Najarian, a prominent child psychiatrist and Clinical Professor of psychiatry from Northshore Medical Center in New York, was the

Clinical Director in charge of teaching and training. And with the support of highly qualified academics and clinicians (from the United States) who spent weeks and months every year teaching and supervising the candidates, the three-year program was completed.

At mid-term of the program, USAID sent three academics from American universities to evaluate the program. They rated it as excellent. Their recommendation was to continue the program and for USAID to use the Psychiatric Outreach Program model as a prototype for future disasters, including for the war-stricken Bosnia-Herzegovina. They also recommended that we conduct studies for the benefit of victims of future disasters. After completing the courses and clinical training, the candidates took a final exam. Those who passed the exam were certified as psychotherapists by the Ministry of Health and were employed at both of our clinics.

During the first year after the earthquake, we refrained from doing research, as our primary objective was to provide direct psychological care to the survivors. We could not spare our meager resources for research, as this would have had a detrimental effect on our clinical work. Up to that time, we had conducted periodic, cross-sectional studies, gathering and analyzing data at different locations in the earthquake zone to better gauge what was needed for the implementation of our program. After the USAID consultants' recommendation to do more research, we began to gather data more rigorously, while remaining aware that our primary mission was to help the survivors clinically.

During the first few years, the intervention was mainly provided to students and teachers. Additionally, we provided care to adults in hospitals, factories, primary care clinics, a mobile clinic in Gumri, and the Norwegian Hospital in Spitak. Once our clinics were ready for use, our therapists split their time between the schools and the clinics. The clinics were operational over two decades, providing mental health services for free to the population of Gumri, Spitak, and the adjacent villages. After the termination of the outreach program, the Gumri therapists continued providing mental health services in local clinics and schools. The Spitak clinic continued to function with the local government's support up to the time of writing this book.

# Diaspora Therapists Working in the Earthquake Zone

Armen Goenjian

## 2.1 Recruiting Therapists from the Diaspora

In February of 1989, after returning from Armenia to the United States, with the help of colleagues, we recruited sixty mental health workers from the United States and Europe to work in the earthquake zone. They were all volunteers. Prospective applicants were interviewed by two senior members of the Psychiatric Outreach Program to assess their qualifications. The applicants included psychologists, psychiatrists, social workers, and marriage and family counselors who spoke English and Armenian. Applicants with no clinical experience or those who wanted to do research were not recruited.

The majority of the volunteers stayed for an average of three weeks at a time. These rotations included six therapists, with one group leader who also worked with his/her colleagues in the field. The therapists were assigned to work at different locations, usually with a partner. At the end of the working day, they met for debriefing. These meetings were intended to provide emotional support to the teams and to learn from each other's experiences. The team leader had the additional assignment of assisting the team members with their emotional and organizational problems (e.g., transportation, housing) and facilitating services in the schools, hospitals, and the community. The group leaders kept notes of the therapists' positive and negative experiences and passed the information to the program director, who, in turn, shared that with prospective recruits. These experiences included treatment-related difficulties and successes, psychological reactions and problems of the therapists, shortage of food and difficult living conditions, and miscellaneous issues such as difficulties with foreign airlines. The therapists also had weekly respites. About half of the diaspora therapists went back for a second or more tours; some went yearly. Four clinicians continued working as consultant/supervisors, going back to Armenia once or twice a year for the next twenty years. Only two therapists were compensated for working in the earthquake zone, one for six months of work, and another for a year's work.

The candidate therapists from the diaspora were informed about the hardships of working in the earthquake zone; such as the shortages of food, lack of heat and electricity, and the inadequacy of working spaces and living quarters. They were informed about the difficulties of traveling within Armenia, including frequent delays, losing luggage, intrusive searches, and postponement of flights. We could only fly to Armenia via Moscow by Aeroflot.

Preparation of candidates included a revision in Armenian of the various post-traumatic clinical conditions, including, Posttraumatic Stress Disorder, depression, Separation Anxiety Disorder, Panic Disorder, grief reactions, and substance abuse. They were instructed in methods for conducting group therapy in the schools and, when indicated, individual therapy. They were informed about the psychological challenges, including vicarious traumatization and overidentification with the plight of the survivors. They were also told about their responsibilities, including working with principals, teachers, students, and parents. Finally, they were made aware of shysters (grifters) who may try to take advantage of them by mispresenting themselves or their family members as disabled victims to get financial assistance.

Preparation of the majority of candidates who were from Los Angeles included bi-monthly meetings with colleagues who had recently returned from Gumri or Spitak. Besides providing them with educational material on the commonly occurring psychological problems and effective treatment approaches, difficult clinical cases were discussed, and video footage was presented depicting the physical hardship of working and living in the earth-quake zone. In addition to providing necessary information to the therapists, these meetings enhanced camaraderie between them.

To be effective, it was important for therapists to be aware of their conflictual feelings about death, trauma, and injustice emanating from their past or present experiences. For some of the therapists, the earthquake-related deaths rekindled unresolved wounds of the 1915 Genocide of Armenians and engendered strong identification with the victims. This identification served as a motivating force for many. On the other hand, it proved detri-mental for those who over-identified with the victims and felt pity, fear, anger, and helplessness. Another problem that hindered the ability of a few therapists to work effec-tively was the strong need to be liked by their patients. They treated patients like friends without setting clear boundaries. Most problems of this nature were resolved after con-structive feedback was provided by their peers or group leaders. Pre-departure preparations, working with a partner in the trenches (e.g., schools, clinics, etc.), debriefings at the end of the working day with their colleagues and team leaders, and weekly respites helped reduce distress levels and prevent burnout.

During the first year after the earthquake, the therapists worked mostly in schools. Some also worked at hospitals, factories, and primary care clinics. They slept under tents, in mobile clinics, hospital wards, and homes of benevolent residents who could spare a room. Most therapists found their experience working in the field demanding but very gratifying. However, approximately 15% of the group proved to be ineffective in their work due to the stress they experienced. For example, one clinician became very distressed after two days of working in Gumri and claimed that working there was like working in a graveyard. She thought that by staying in Gumri, she was giving the wrong message to the people that it was all right to put up with the dreadful conditions. She decided to go to Yerevan and train local therapists instead of working with the survivors. Intervention by a senior experienced therapist did not reduce her anxiety. We agreed that the best solution was for her to teach graduate students at the University in Yerevan, which she did effectively.

Another highly qualified member who had worked with trauma survivors in the United States began experiencing gastrointestinal problems a few days after working in the field. He would get nauseated and vomit in the mornings, right before going to work. The team leader decided to give him a day off. That day he did not have nausea and did not vomit. The following morning the same symptoms recurred. When the group leader questioned the therapist about his well-being, he admitted that this whole experience with the survivors evoked past traumatic memories of relatives who were subjected to atrocities during the Armenian Genocide. And now, he could not bear hearing the sad stories of the survivors. He felt overwhelmed just as he used to when he heard about the suffering of his relatives. He was assigned to a less stressful task which he was able to perform without experiencing any more somatic problems.

In another instance, a clinician repeatedly minimized or failed to recognize blatant psychopathology, thereby denying patients the opportunity to receive help with their problems. For example, when a patient told him about her trauma-related symptoms, the therapist interrupted her with such statements as: "Your symptoms will go away or try to forget them." Intervention by one of the experienced therapists was successful. The therapist recognized the problem and was able to perform more effectively under supervision. In hindsight, the therapists who experienced difficulties were the ones who did not have a chance to participate in the initial preparatory group meetings. Those who were moderately anxious before departure had a harder time working with the victims.

## 2.2 Impact of the Relief Work on Therapists

During their tour in Armenia, most of the therapists had mild stress reactions appropriate to the circumstances. Even though they experienced a certain degree of sadness, anxiety, anger, frustration, and guilt, these reactions were manageable and did not interfere with their work. Only three out of sixty therapists had stronger reactions that interfered with their functioning, but these symptoms abated soon after intervention.

After returning home, the therapists had time to process their thoughts and feelings. The earthquake experience had a positive impact on the professional lives of many. The experience in Armenia motivated many to continue doing humanitarian work in Armenia and elsewhere. Over the next twenty years, they made significant contributions to the field of disaster psychiatry by training other professionals, lecturing on psychological sequelae of trauma and relief work, and writing scientific papers on trauma in journals and books to raise public awareness of the psychological sequelae of trauma. A few master's level therapists continued their education and got doctorate degrees in psychology. My experiences included sadness after my first visit in 1989. It lingered for a couple of months and then abated. I dealt with it by continuously working to implement the program. Support from my family, friends, and the relief organization allowed me to persevere with the work. Noteworthy were two dedicated team members who worked relentlessly to support the program for two decades. One was Dr. Louis Najarian, a prominent practicing child psychiatrist and clinical professor of psychiatry from Northshore Medical Center in New York, took a large salary cut in 1990, left his successful practice in New York, and worked for a year in the earthquake zone directing the teaching program and the clinics in Gumri and Spitak. Over the ensuing two decades, he went back to Armenia yearly to continue his mission to treat, teach, consult, and conduct research. The second member was Dr. Ida Karayan, an outstanding psychologist from Glendale, California, where she had her private practice and trained psychology interns from various campuses in Los Angeles. For two decades, beginning in 1989, she went to Armenia as a volunteer yearly to treat patients, train and supervise the staff of the Psychiatric Outreach Program (POP) clinics, and train therapists in Yerevan. The therapists trained by Dr. Karayan are currently treating displaced women and children who fled from Nagorno-Karabagh where they used to live and were relocated in border villages inside Armenia. See Figure 2.1 for a picture of a group of therapists from the Gumri clinic.

**Figure 2.1** A group of Psychiatric Outreach Program therapists in front of the Gumri clinic. On the far right (with bow tie) is Dr. Louis M. Najarian, and on the far left of the third row is Dr. Armen Goenjian. (A black- and- white version of this figure will appear in some formats. For the color version, please refer to the plate section.)

## 2.2.1 The Opportunists (Schemers)

Most people involved in disaster relief work in Armenia were there to help those who suffered. Unfortunately, disasters also appeal to scammers who find chaos after a major trauma an opportune time to exploit others. On one such occasion, there was a volunteer physician who offered help to the Armenian Relief Society with no compensation. After a brief period of working, he was hired to co-direct an eye clinic. The clinic assisted the poor with glasses imported from the diaspora. After working at the clinic for about a year, he fled to Russia with the organization's new car and a large cache of glasses. In another instance, a politically connected pedagogic institute supervisor wanted to be hired as a therapist without attending the required training classes. When she was rejected because of non-compliance, she filed a fabricated complaint with the Ministry of Education. After a brief investigation, the Deputy Education Minister apologized to us and reprimanded the supervisor. In another instance, a Project Hope employee from another country, who was working at a prosthesis clinic, was noted to be absent periodically. The supervisor investigated and found out that she and a colleague were going to Russia to pursue a political mission unrelated to the relief work. In another instance, a psychologist from Yerevan expressed a great desire to help the victims and pleaded to join our group. After working briefly, he made his intentions clear that he needed a visa and ticket to go to the United States. When his baseless demand was rejected, he abruptly stopped working.

## 2.3  The Headmasters of the Schools

During the first year, the objective of our program was to provide psychological assistance to the students and teachers. We found that the most effective way of working with children in their schools was to first meet with the headmasters of the schools before meeting with the teachers to explain our plan and obtain their approval to commence working with the teachers and students. Even though we had permission from the Minister of Education to work in the schools, we considered it appropriate to engage the headmaster and get his approval. First, we provided him with a brief description of the types of psychological sequelae that occur after disasters and the intervention we would be providing. Another reason for meeting with the headmasters was to give them an opportunity to bring up their earthquake-related personal problems, which otherwise they may not divulge in front of the teachers, and to provide them with constructive feedback about how to deal with their psychological problems. The third reason for the private meeting was to get their permission to meet with those teachers who may want to meet with us privately. Some teachers felt uncomfortable expressing their feelings and thoughts in the presence of an authority figure. They were reluctant to directly voice their complaints against their headmaster or the administrators overseeing the schools. Even though Armenia allowed more freedom of speech compared to numerous other Soviet Republics, there was still a pervasive fear of heads of institutions that were ultimately governed by Moscow. These fears were based on memories of persecutions dating back to the notorious Stalin era.

In one instance, by-passing the headmaster taught a valuable lesson. A few months after the earthquake, we arrived at a Spitak school around noon. Mr. Rustagyan, the headmaster, had left the school's premises to attend to a personal matter without telling the staff when he would be back. After waiting for a while, his assistant told us to start the meeting without Mr. Rustagyan. Soon after, Mr. Rustagyan returned and joined the meeting.

Meanwhile, a teacher was sharing a gut-wrenching story with the group. Mr. Rustagyan interrupted her by talking about an unrelated personal issue. I tried gingerly to shift the discussion back to the main theme. As the meeting continued, he kept interrupting others who were engaged in the discussions about their hardships. After a few interruptions, the principal was asked for feedback on the teachers' descriptions of their experiences and emotional pain. He was unable to relate to their plight. An hour had gone by, so we took a half-hour intermission. I invited the principal for a walk, and as soon as we found privacy, I asked him how he was doing. He opened up and said he wanted to talk about his problems but felt uncomfortable expressing his feeling in front of the teachers. He had to demonstrate to them that he was strong. He told me about the death of his wife and child during the earthquake and his loneliness and fears. He shared his feelings of guilt about liking a much younger woman and questioned whether it would be alright to pursue a relationship with her. In my private practice, I would have refrained from giving him advice, but I thought he was looking to me as an advisor, and I did not regard this as traditional therapy. I tried to be supportive and gave feedback to alleviate his guilt and anxiety. He expressed relief and thanked me. He asked for assurance that I would be available if he needed assistance. I assured him. When the group resumed, he no longer was disruptive. From then on, for many years, we worked harmoniously with the teachers and students in that school. He was always supportive and did not interfere with our work. About a year after our first meeting, he married the woman he had told me about. Two years later, they had a child. The lesson I learned was not to by-pass the headmaster before working with the rest of the staff.

## 2.4 The Teachers

After obtaining approval from the headmasters, we met with the teachers as a group and told them about the POP and its mission. Almost always, they were very receptive. They saw us as experts akin to their culture who were volunteering to help them. Being from the United States or Europe was never an issue. They were very eager to share their painful experiences, especially the women who felt more at ease in confiding their emotions. Men were more defensive and less expressive of personal feelings, focusing more on the problems of others or material hardships. The common themes that were brought up in those meetings included painful memories of the ill-fated day of the earthquake when they lost almost everything they had, along with hopes for the future. We listened, expressed empathy, and refrained from patronizing them or making threadbare and dismissive statements (e.g., "Don't think about it"; "Things will be okay"; "Have faith"; "Be brave"). They had already heard these "encouraging clichés" too many times from well-wishers. Such statements usually tuned them off. We shared information about the psychological sequelae of trauma, e.g., PTSD, depression, and grief reactions. We taught them relaxation techniques (e.g., deep breathing) and measures to cope with distortions in thinking, guilt feelings, and avoidant behavior. We stressed the importance of communicating with and providing emotional support to one another and avoiding alcohol and drugs to treat their symptoms. Examples were provided about children's reactions to trauma and other stresses. For example, being quiet or withdrawn may not be indicative that they were "okay;" that withdrawal may be related to PTSD or depression; how somatic complaints (e.g., headache or stomachache) may be indicative of emotional pain and should be explored; and how being inattentive in the classroom or not completing one's homework may be due to psychological difficulties or insomnia. We made suggestions about how to deal with such problems. The initial formal meeting with the teachers was followed by ongoing informal meetings to help them deal with their ongoing personal problems and the problems of the students. Figure 2.2 shows students in a makeshift classroom in Gumri.

## 2.5 Meeting with Students

During the first year after the earthquake, the therapists worked mostly in schools, usually in pairs. Conditions at the schools were chaotic. Schools were held under tents, makeshift structures, retrofitted buildings, or in the intact sections of school buildings. An expeditious way of carrying out the evaluation of students was to first meet with the entire class to discuss their traumatic experiences during the earthquake, their current psychological, social, and familial problems, and their views of their future. Meetings with the students covered informing them about psychological sequelae of trauma and loss and legitimizing post-traumatic stress reactions. Students recounted their earthquake-related traumatic experiences, including the most traumatic aspects, recurring memories, their explanations (and misconceptions) about the earthquake, and feelings of guilt for things they should or shouldn't have done. They were taught relaxation techniques to reduce the distress associated when recounting their traumatic memories of the earthquake and exposure to trauma and loss reminders. Distortions and misattributions were clarified and maladaptive

**Figure 2.2** Students in a makeshift classroom with their teacher in Gumri (Leninakan) in 1989. (A black- and- white version of this figure will appear in some formats. For the color version, please refer to the plate section.)

behaviors were addressed, e.g., avoidance, reckless behavior). They were encouraged to express their concerns and reach out for support from adults they trusted, socialize with peers, listen to music, and engage in sports if possible. Moderately severe to severe cases were referred for individual therapy. Children six to twelve years of age were involved in play therapy or drew pictures of the earthquake or their house and family. These pictures were platforms for further evaluation and discussion. Therapeutic booklets (described below) were also used to enhance these explorations. Teachers were also involved in the assessments. After the classroom session, therapists met with teachers to discuss their observations and planned how to deal with the children's problems in the classroom.

## 2.6  Therapeutic Booklets

Two therapeutic booklets in Armenian were prepared to help students and parents deal with psychological problems. The first was a children's coloring book of cartoon characters by Hanna-Barbera Productions (Figure 2.3). The booklet in Armenian entitled "Yogi Bear's Help After the Earthquake," provided explanations and recommendations by Yogi Bear regarding psychological problems after an earthquake. Permission to prepare the booklet was granted by Mr. Joe Barbera, head of Hanna-Barbera. He was touched by the relief work we were doing and pondered audibly, "If I ask the lawyers for permission to allow the publication in Armenian, this will be dragged out for a year." Then he turned to me and said, "Go ahead and prepare the book with Iraj (his artistic director)." So, we did go ahead and

**Figure 2.3** "Yogi Bear's Help After the Earthquake" (a Hanna-Barbera Production, 1989). (A black- and- white version of this figure will appear in some formats. For the color version, please refer to the plate section.)

write the original scripts in Armenian. The booklet facilitated children in expressing and communicating their thoughts and feelings during therapy. The second booklet, "The Emotional State of Children after a Quake and Ways to Help Them," was for parents. It explained the psychological sequelae of trauma and loss and provided suggestions for coping. Ms. Seta Manukian, an artist from Lebanon, volunteered to do the drawings for the booklet which depicted adolescents expressing different reactions (e.g., withdrawal, sadness) and parents engaging them in conversations or activities (Figure 2.4 shows a page from the booklet).

## 2.7 Summary

In conclusion, preparation for intervention required vetting therapists, informing those accepted to the program about the hardships and challenges of working in the earthquake

Նաև անգամներ վախի եւ տխրության հետեւանքով անչափահասները զանգվածային են մարմնական անհանգստություններից, ինչպես՝ փորի ցավից, գլխի ցավից, եւ այլն։ Պետք է խուսափել ձանձրանալ, կամ խստ յուրք վերաբերվել, երբ անչափահասը Նորից անդրադառնա իր ավելի վաղ հասակի սովորությունների, պահվածքին կամ վարվելակերպին։ Կարելիէ, որ ծնողները հասկանան Մման անհանգստությունների հիմնական պատճառները եւ ուշադրություն դարձնեն Նրանց աստճանին։ Թույլ տան, որ Նրանք արտահայտեն իրենց հոգեկան անհանգստությունները։ Նրանց բացատրեն, թարյերեն, հույս ներշնչեն եւ խուսափեն ծայրահեղ իրավիճակներից, ինչպես անտեսելը կամ յափազանց պահպանողական կեցվածք դրսեվորելը։ Անվստահության դեպքում պետք է անմիջապես բժշկի օգնության դիմել։

18

**Figure 2.4** A page from the booklet for parents, "The Emotional State of Children after a Quake and Ways to Help Them" (1989).

zone, and about the cultural, religious, and political nuances of Soviet Armenia. It also included reviewing commonly occurring post-trauma psychological sequelae and treatment modalities. Lastly, this chapter underscores the importance of working within the host country's educational hierarchy. The implementation of these steps was necessary for the success of the Psychiatric Outreach Program

# Treatment Outcome among Early Adolescents Two Decades Post-Earthquake

Armen Goenjian, Alan Steinberg, and Robert Pynoos

## 3.1 Introduction

The majority of treatment outcome studies after disasters among children and adolescents have been conducted within six to twelve months post-disaster (March et al., 1998; Chemtob et al., 2002; Kar 2009; Pityaratstian et al., 2015). Four studies have investigated longer treatment outcomes. Three were between two- to four-year follow-ups (Goenjian et al., 2005; Giannopoulou et al., 2006; Basoghlu et al., 2007), and one was a twenty-five-year post-disaster follow-up (Goenjian et al., 2020). Overall, these studies have shown a beneficial effect of a variety of post-disaster trauma-focused interventions in reducing the severity of PTSD symptoms. This chapter describes the post-disaster recovery program's intervention approach in Armenia and findings from three longitudinal treatment outcome studies. It also presents current practice guidelines for treating PTSD among children and adolescents and the results of meta-analyses comparing various types of treatments.

When 1.5 years had passed following the earthquake in Armenia, at a time when the chaotic conditions had subsided in Spitak and Gumri, and when people had settled in prefabricated or makeshift shanty homes and schools were operating more regularly, we assessed the psychological status of children and adolescents. We then implemented the school-based intervention program and conducted several studies over two decades. The school-based intervention program included students from schools located in the four main sections of Gumri and from the two main schools in the smaller city of Spitak. These schools were deemed to be representative of the schools in each city. Destruction, morbidity, and mortality were pervasive in both cities commensurate with the intensity of the earthquake. Within cities, mean Posttraumatic Stress Disorder – Reaction Index (PTSD-RI) scores for the same age groups at the different schools were consistently similar.

## 3.2 The Psychiatric Outreach Intervention Program

In 1980, the American Psychiatric Association (APA) added PTSD to the third edition of its *Diagnostic and Statistical Manual of Mental Disorders* (DSM-III) classification system. Although controversial when first introduced, the PTSD diagnosis filled an essential void in psychiatric practice. This important change stipulated that a traumatic life event served as the gateway to the diagnosis as a key causal precursor. Also, therapists began shifting the focus of therapy from dynamic psychotherapy toward behavioral therapies. Exposure therapy, which was an accepted method to decrease phobic symptoms, began to be employed to treat PTSD. Cognitive therapy was also being accepted as a formidable method for treating depression, and clinicians began using cognitive behavioral therapy to treat PTSD symptoms with favorable outcomes.

In 1989, the field of trauma psychiatry was still considered nascent. Two years earlier, the APA had redefined PTSD in the 1987 DSM-III R. Over the next two decades, the APA redefined the PTSD diagnosis two additional times. Treatment approaches were also going through modifications, again shifting away from dynamic psychotherapy toward cognitive behavioral therapies, and also included pharmacotherapy.

Our approach to treatment in the earthquake zone was a form of brief trauma- and grief-centered intervention focusing on the trauma and losses of the survivors and their current adversities and interpersonal issues rather than on past personal or family history (e.g., dynamics of the parent/child relationship). We also refrained as much as possible from the use of psychotropic medications with children and adolescents. The infrequent use of then available psychotropics included low dosages of tricyclic antidepressants, such as Imipramine and Norpramin.

By the end of the first year after the earthquake, we had gained a fair amount of knowledge about trauma-focused intervention. We learned from our mistakes and the feedback we received from the survivors. We realized the importance of incorporating the cultural, social, and religious nuances of the population in Northern Armenia into our approach to treatment. Even though the diaspora therapists were of the same ethnicity as the local population, spoke the same language, and shared many of their values, there were still many differences in political, religious, social, and cultural beliefs and practices. Understanding these differences and adjusting our approach during therapy helped form a stronger therapeutic alliance and better treatment retention.

The Psychiatric Outreach Program (POP) therapists worked in the schools during school hours (Figure 3.1). The work began after they were introduced to the students by the principal or teacher. Afterwards, the therapists made a brief statement to the students about the purpose of the school-based program. At 1.5 years after the earthquake, a group of students who were assessed for comorbid conditions, including PTSD, depression, and separation anxiety, received trauma-grief-focused psychotherapy. The treatment included four ninety-minute group therapy sessions, with each student receiving an average of two one-hour (range one to four) additional individual psychotherapy sessions. The number of sessions varied depending on the student's needs and the availability of therapists. For some students with severe symptoms, individual therapy extended up to six months. Parents were invited to participate in treatment based on the severity of their symptoms and family problems. A major goal of parental involvement was to enhance their support to the child.

Even though the therapists were knowledgeable about crisis intervention, interpersonal psychotherapy, and cognitive and exposure therapy techniques (Raphael, 1986; Saigh, 1987; Pynoos and Nader, 1988; Foa et al., 1989; Lyons and Keans, 1989), before beginning fieldwork, they were updated by the senior staff on psychoeducation, relaxation techniques, narrative-exposure therapy, cognitive behavioral therapy, and interpersonal therapy. Also, frequently manifested post-disaster clinical conditions were revisited, (e.g., PTSD, grief reactions, separation anxiety, panic attacks, and depressive disorder). Information about the experiences and recommendations of colleagues who had returned from the earthquake zone were shared with the new candidates. This information included challenges in dealing with shortages of resources, traveling in and out of the country, customs, housing, trans-portation, weather conditions, school personnel, and difficult patients. This information proved valuable, as new therapists were better prepared to deal with the daily challenges of their work.

**Figure 3.1** Students in a makeshift school classroom in Leninakan, 1990. (A black- and- white version of this figure will appear in some formats. For the color version, please refer to the plate section.)

Therapists were encouraged to be flexible in their approach, keeping focus on currently pressing problems. They were encouraged to adjust their interventions to the needs of the students as opposed to strictly adhering to a regimented protocol. For example, during a session where coping skills were being discussed, a student in distress brought up the topic of their mother's death. The therapist allowed the student to express her immediate concerns rather than interrupting her and insisting on continuing the discussion on coping skills. The acceptable alternatives the therapist had considered included either addressing the student's concern briefly, then continuing the earlier discussion on coping, and after the session, meeting with the student individually to deal in more depth with the mother's death. The other choice was to discuss the student's immediate problem by engaging the group members, some of whom had experienced similar losses, and postponing the discussion of coping skills. The therapist chose the latter approach.

## 3.3  Trauma-Grief-Focused Treatment Foci

There were seven therapeutic foci of our school-based treatment. These included:

1. *Post-Trauma Reactions:* To deal with their upsetting post-trauma reactions, students were taught relaxation techniques, such as diaphragmatic breathing and muscle relaxation. They were also instructed in positive visualization, thought stopping, and engagement in relaxing activities, such as listening to music.
2. *Trauma Narrative Exposure*: Students were asked to construct a trauma narrative covering events before, during, and after the earthquake and to identify their most

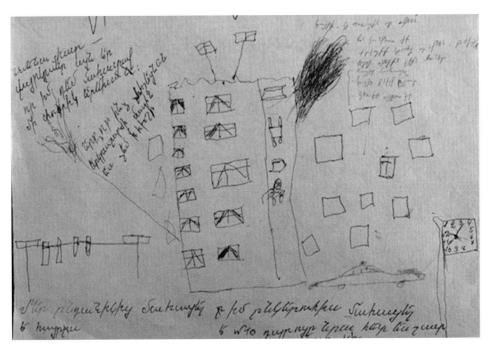

**Figure 3.2** Drawing by a sixth-grade student from Gumri who lost her father and classmates during the Spitak earthquake drawn at 1.5 years after the earthquake.
   N.B. The notation on the upper right corner was made by the therapist, and the one on the upper left corner was made by the teacher.

traumatic experience(s). For the younger age groups, the trauma-focused activity included drawing pictures of their earthquake experiences. Figure 3.2 is a drawing made by a sixth-grade student from Gumri whose father and best friend were killed in the earthquake. Her most traumatic memory was when she was standing outside their apartment, which was on fire. She witnessed a child (depicted in the drawing between the second and third floors) falling from one of the floors where there was a fire. The ambulance came (right lower corner of the picture). She thought that if the doctors had helped the people, they would not have perished. She wanted to become a doctor to prevent people from dying. On the far right is the clock representing the time of the earthquake at 11:41 a.m.

Up to the time of this drawing, this student had avoided talking about her earthquake experiences. After she drew the picture, she recounted her traumatic experiences during the earthquake, including the worst moment that she had avoided describing. As she became more engaged with the therapist, she began to express anger towards the doctors who could have saved the lives of the people who were begging for help.

In the *Trauma Narrative* component of the treatment, students were also asked to describe their emotions and thoughts related to these experiences, especially the feelings associated with the worst moments. In addition, students described any current avoidance, withdrawal, and aggressive or risk-taking behavior. They were assisted in dealing with their most traumatic memories during these sessions by recounting those memories coupled with relaxation techniques until they became more tolerable. In subsequent sessions, students refocused on the traumatic memories that were the most distressing and applied the relaxation techniques until the anxiety became manageable and avoidant behavior subsided. Also, therapists worked with them to clarify any distortions or misattributions of responsibility. For example, one student believed that because he ran to the left side of the building instead of to the right, his mother, who was following him, would not have been killed. Another student believed that the earthquake was caused by a thermonuclear explosion set off by Moscow.

3. *Trauma Reminders*: Students were asked to identify their most disturbing trauma reminders. They were assisted in identifying trauma reminders associated with symptoms (e.g., anxiety, moodiness) and were helped to increase tolerance for expected reactivity to reminders by using relaxation techniques when reminded. Also, they were encouraged to seek support from parents during and after exposure to reminders and avoid unnecessary exposure to painful reminders (e.g., destroyed buildings, frequent visits to the cemetery with family members).

4. *Grief Reactions*: Typically, working through the traumatic aspects of their earthquake experiences was followed by discussing issues of loss and grief reactions, accompanied by therapist efforts to increase group awareness of common aspects of grief. Students were assisted in coping with their grief reactions by reconstituting a non-traumatic mental representation of a deceased person to be able to engage in positive reminiscing. They were encouraged to talk about their grief and express their sadness with supportive family members and friends, to avoid self-pity and self-blame, to participate in activities that they previously enjoyed, and consider developing new relationships (e.g., with relatives or friends who may fill some of the void due to the loss).

5. *Post-earthquake Adversities*: Students were asked to identify post-disaster adversities (e.g., difficulties with their studies and disturbed relationships with friends due to current living conditions, lack of privacy). They received guidance to help them cope with changes and losses at home (e.g., ask parents for quiet time to study, change in room arrangements), and at school (stay late at school to finish homework). An important component of addressing post-earthquake adversities was to help students in problem-solving, including developing different ways of addressing the problem, selecting a strategy, and trying it out. We found that problem-solving for children often involved some assistance from adults.

6. *Coping Strategies*: Students were assisted in identifying and decreasing maladaptive coping behaviors, aggression, and avoidant behaviors (withdrawal from family and friends). They were again assisted in problem-solving regarding peer and family relationships and resuming constructive activities that countered their passivity and pessimism (e.g., sports, music, painting, volunteer work). The students were helped to identify and engage other individuals who could provide advice, counseling, or companionship. Subsequently, students were encouraged to engage in constructive thoughts, plan positive actions, and develop constructive plans for their future.

7. *Developmental Issues*: Students were helped to explore ways in which the earthquake and its aftermath had interfered with opportunities for their normal development, for example, not being able to have time for activities with their friends or engaging in

sports or hobbies. Some students described that they experienced an acceleration of their development by having greater responsibility in caring for younger siblings and being out on the street selling things to help with the family income. They were encouraged to problem-solve ways to address these issues and enlist parental support to get back on track with their development.

Overall, the interactions and discussions about their experiences during the sessions helped the group members. Students learned that they were not alone in experiencing post-trauma reactions (e.g., nightmares, fears of recurrence, avoidance, grief reactions) and how their peers were coping with their reactions. For example, a student ridiculed another for expressing her continued fears of a recurrence of the earthquake. Other students objected to the ridicule and were supportive of the girl for her admission of her fears. This opened opportunities for group discussion, and eventually, the ridiculing student admitted to having similar fears. At the end of the meetings, the therapists highlighted the important aspects of the session and recommended do's and don'ts (e.g., to express their fears and to seek assistance, not ridicule others, etc.).

Such do's and don'ts included utilizing relaxation techniques when experiencing trauma reminders, talking about their problems with their parents or teachers, avoiding isolation and withdrawal, avoiding drinking alcohol, exercising, refraining from blaming self or others, engaging in social activities and sports, and taking walks or listening to music when upset.

After meeting with the students, the therapists informed the teachers about their observations and made recommendations to the teachers about dealing with classroom problems. For example, a teacher was angry at a student for not paying attention in the classroom and not completing his homework. The therapist who had assessed the student earlier had found out that this student did not have a quiet place to study in the makeshift home and had not slept well. She then suggested to the teacher that the inattention may have been related to the student's insomnia. This explanation was helpful to the teacher who modified her attitude towards the student. In sum, we observed that the disaster affected the students differently depending on their objective and subjective earthquake-related experiences. For some, the terror felt during the earthquake was the most distressing aspect of the disaster; for others, losing an important person was the most troubling. Fears consumed some, others were overwhelmed by depression or both. Therapists who recognized these differences and adjusted treatment by addressing the most pressing current issues and concerns facing the students, rather than adhering to rigid therapy parameters, were more effective and better received. And their group members benefitted more. Likewise, those therapists who showed genuine compassion (not pity) were better received.

Our treatment studies were based on data collected by the most experienced therapists who had worked extensively with the survivors of the earthquake and were well-versed in conducting eclectic psychotherapy. The intervention studies conducted in the schools differed from intervention outcome research conducted under controlled conditions where the primary goal is to measure the effectiveness of specific treatment methods for a specific disorder. Subjects have to meet rigid inclusion and exclusion criteria, and treatment methods are strictly defined. For example, when evaluating the efficacy of a specific type of therapy for PTSD, children diagnosed with current comorbid major depression may be excluded based on the research protocol. The treatments are also

**Figure 3.3** Psychiatric Outreach Program therapists, Dr. Madeline Tashjian and Dr. Angela Boghosian, shown walking among the poorly insulated small makeshift homes in Gumri, 1990. (A black- and- white version of this figure will appear in some formats. For the color version, please refer to the plate section.)

specified (e.g., exposure therapy, pharmacotherapy). In the earthquake zone, the goal was to help as many children as possible with their earthquake reactions and current problems (e.g., PTSD, grief, depression, anxiety symptoms, current interpersonal problems, and adversities) during a limited time. To address these various pressing needs effectively, therapists had to be flexible in their treatment approach, choosing as appropriate among specific intervention strategies and practice elements. In addition, therapists promoted treatment engagement by establishing a strong therapeutic alliance with survivors, encouraging active participation in treatment, and maintaining sensitivity to cultural and religious traditions.

## 3.4  The 1.5 Year Comorbidity and the Three Treatment Outcome Studies

In 1990, 1.5 years after the Spitak earthquake, 218 school-aged adolescents from three cities at increasing distances from the epicenter of the earthquake (Spitak, Gumri, and Yerevan) were evaluated in their schools for PTSD, depression, and separation anxiety symptoms, and the contribution of exposure, gender, loss of family members, and loss of residence to these reactions (Goenjian et al., 1995). In Spitak, the city nearest to the epicenter of the earthquake, the destruction and mortality rate (16%) was the worst. In Gumri, 16.8 miles from the epicenter, there was also substantial destruction and death (7%), while in Yerevan, 47 miles from the epicenter, there was mild structural damage and very few casualties.

Instruments used for the 1.5-year comorbidity study included the UCLA Child Post-traumatic Stress Disorder Reaction Index (CPTSD-RI), the Depression Self-Rating Scale (DSRS) (Asarnow and Carlson 1985), and the section on Separation Anxiety Disorder (SAD) from the Diagnostic Interview for Children and Adolescents (Herjanic and Reich 1982). Psychometric properties of the PTSD-RI instrument have been reported by Steinberg et al., 2004. At twenty-five-year follow-up, we used the DSM III-R PTSD-RI and the DSM-5-based PTSD Checklist for DSM-5 (PCL-5). For depression, we used the Center for Epidemiological Studies Depression (CES-D) Scale (Demirchyan et al., 2011) because the DSRS did not have an adult version.

For the PTSD questionnaire, the index trauma was the Spitak earthquake. The frequency of symptom occurrence during the previous thirty days was rated on a five-point Likert scale: 0 = not at all to 4 = almost every day. Symptom scores of 2 (symptom occurring one to two times a week) to 4 (almost every day) were used to define symptom presence. In prior reports (Pynoos et al. 1993; Goenjian et al., 1995), a cut-off of $\geq 40$ on the PTSD-RI was used to detect a diagnosis of PTSD. For this study, the diagnosis of PTSD was based on more stringent criteria using a cut-off of 40 and a symptom cluster method (a minimum of 1B, 3C, and 2D category symptoms), as has been done in numerous prior studies on PTSD (McDonald and Calhoun, 2010) and in the twenty-five-year follow-up study in Armenia (Goenjian et al., 2020). As a result, the baseline rates are lower than the rates reported previously (Pynoos et al., 1993; Goenjian et al., 1995). For depression, a cut-off of 17 on the DSRS was used to determine the presence of a depressive disorder (major depression, dysthymic disorder, and adjustment disorder with depressed mood) (Asarnow et al., 1985). For CES-D, the recommended cut-off of 20 was used for estimation of clinical depression (Vilagut et al., 2016).

## Choice of Continuous and Binary Measures

Regarding the choice between continuous versus binary measures, many disaster articles had used PTSD diagnosis as an outcome measure, while others had used continuous scale scores. We used both continuous and binary measures. The continuous scale scores provided a more sensitive representation of the progression and course of symptoms compared to binary measures (i.e., rates meeting diagnostic criteria). In contrast, rates were deemed useful for cross-comparisons with other studies that used rates as a primary outcome measure. Minor, clinically irrelevant, changes on a continuous score from pre- to post-assessment above or below the cut-off score for the PTSD diagnosis can be clinically irrelevant yet be impactful and misleading by causing shifts in the diagnosis. For example, if the cut-off score for the diagnosis of PTSD is 40 on the PTSD-RI, then a change from 40 to 38 would not be a clinically meaningful change, yet altering the diagnosis may affect research outcome or one's eligibility to disability.

*Participants:* In 1990, 1.5 years after the Spitak earthquake, 164 early adolescents aged between twelve to fourteen years from Gumri (N = 94), Spitak (N = 70), and Yerevan (N = 61) were evaluated for PTSD, depression, and separation anxiety disorder. Information on these subjects has been reported previously (Goenjian et al., 1995). Within a few weeks after the assessment, school-based trauma-grief-focused brief psychotherapy was provided in some schools in Gumri and not others due to the shortage of qualified mental health workers. These schools were representative of the schools in the region. Destruction and mortality were widespread throughout the city such that the children across Gumri schools experienced similar levels of earthquake exposure. All students in the classrooms selected for the intervention participated. Data for the twenty-five-year follow-up study was collected in 2014.

In 1997, in the first outcome of psychotherapy study, published in the *American Journal of Psychiatry*, entitled "Outcome of Psychotherapy among Pre-adolescents after the 1988 Earthquake in Armenia" (Goenjian et al., 1997), a total of sixty-four students who were assessed for PTSD and depression symptoms at 1.5 years after the earthquake from four schools in Gumri were selected for inclusion in this study. Early adolescents were chosen because their cooperation with the research protocol and comprehension of the instruments would be better than those of younger children and because they would be available for longitudinal follow-up through their remaining school years as compared with older adolescents who would likely be lost to follow-up after graduation from school.

The treatment groups included students from two schools where they had received trauma-grief-focused therapy (N = 35, mean age = 11.7) shortly after the 1.5 year assessments. The control group included students from two other schools where treatment was not provided (N = 29, mean age = 11.8). At a three-year post-earthquake follow-up, they were reassessed for PTSD and depression symptoms using the same instruments, including the DSM III-R based PTSD Reaction Index and the Depression Self-Rating Scale (DSRS). The extent of damage to these schools and their neighborhoods was equivalent, and there was no socioeconomic difference between these groups.

In 2005, the second psychotherapy outcome paper, "A Prospective Study of Posttraumatic Stress and Depressive Reactions among Treated and Untreated Adolescents 5 Years After a Disaster," was published in the *American Journal of Psychiatry* (Goenjian et al., 2005), due to the multiplicity of hardships facing both the victims and the staff working in the earthquake zone and the lack of available mental health personnel, a power analysis was conducted to estimate group size necessary to obtain a significant result. The analysis indicated that twenty-one subjects per study group was the minimum number to get a significant result (power = 0.80, alpha = 0.01). Based on this analysis, we included every other untreated subject from the 1990 (original) cohort (Spitak not treated, N = 32; Gumri not treated, N = 27). However, for the treated group, we aimed to include all the subjects from the original group of thirty-eight students and retrieved thirty-six of them. Comparison of age, sex, loss of nuclear family members, PTSD-RI, and DSRS scores at 1.5 years for those students from the baseline group who did not participate in the five-year follow-up with the data for those who completed the five-year study yielded no significant differences.

Another follow-up study at twenty-five years post-earthquake titled "25-year Follow-up of Treated and Not-treated Adolescents after the Spitak Earthquake: Course and Predictors of PTSD and Depression," was published in *Psychological Medicine* (Goenjian et al., 2020). Seventy-six of the original ninety-four participants from Gumri were located, with only one refusing to participate. Three of the original group had died, and the remainder was lost to follow-up. Of these seventy-five participants, thirty-three were among the thirty-six students who were provided treatment at 1.5 years shortly after the baseline assessments and were followed-up at five years post-earthquake. The rest (N = 42) had not received mental health treatment up to the follow-up time. In Spitak, sixty-seven of the original seventy subjects were located and completed the study. None of these subjects had received mental health treatment since the earthquake. Two of the original group had died, and the third was lost to follow-up. The total number of participants in 2014 was 142 (87% of the original cohort). The high rate of capturing subjects at follow-up was due to the fact that many of the original participants had remained in the city they lived in at the time of the earthquake, were positive about participating, and were cooperative in helping to locate their peers from the original cohort.

## 3.4.1 The 1.5 Years Post-Earthquake Comorbidity Study Results

Figure 3.4 indicates that rates for PTSD, depressive disorder, and Separation Anxiety Disorder (SAD) followed a dose-of-exposure pattern. A similar dose of exposure pattern emerged for mean PTSD and depressive symptom severity scores and the mean number of SAD symptoms. These findings showed high rates of current PTSD and depressive disorder, with the Spitak group (the group that experienced the most destruction and mortality) showing the highest rates (55%) for PTSD and clinical depression (76%), followed by the pre-treatment combined Gumri group (PTSD = 35% and depression = 50%), and then the Yerevan group (PTSD = 11% and depression = 28%). The severity of PTSD symptoms across the three cities was significantly correlated with the severity levels of depression (r = 0.55, N = 218, p < .01).

The high PTSD rates at 1.5 years post-earthquake were attributable to the severity, multiplicity, and extent of disaster-related traumatic experiences during the earthquake and in the days after. These experiences included the direct threat of loss of life; witnessing destruction, mutilation, and death; the screams of people trapped under the rubble; and the smell of corpses. The absence of such horrifying disaster-related experiences in the Loma Prieta and Coalinga earthquakes in California, which were of similar magnitude to the Spitak earthquake, may explain the considerably lower reported frequency of PTSD rates among survivors of these two earthquakes (Bourque and Russell, 1993; Durkin, 1993).

Depressive symptoms were related to multiple types of losses and adverse conditions after the earthquake. These losses included deaths (e.g., relatives, classmates, friends, teachers); the departure of family members and friends (usually fathers to find work) to other countries; loss of homes; loss of social gatherings and social connectivity; loss of health

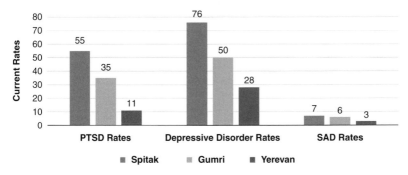

**Figure 3.4** Rates of PTSD, depressive disorder, and separation anxiety disorder (SAD) across three differentially exposed cities 1.5 years after the Spitak earthquake. (A black- and- white version of this figure will appear in some formats. For the color version, please refer to the plate section.)

(e.g., PTSD, physical disabilities due to earthquake-related injuries); and loss of valuable belongings. Other stresses included dysfunctionality within families related to PTSD, depression, alcohol abuse, unresolved grief, and financial problems.

Catastrophic disasters with widespread destruction, extreme horror and terror, and high mortality and morbidity rates are generally associated with high rates of PTSD. For example, in a study of children and adolescents after the 2004 Indian Ocean earthquake and tsunami, one of the worst natural disasters in decades, John et al., (2007) found the prevalence of acute PTSD to be 70.7%, and for delayed onset PTSD 10.9%. In a study among adolescents thirteen months after the Marmara earthquake in Turkey, Dogan (2011) found 76% of the adolescents had moderate to very severe levels of PTSD symptoms. One year after the 2009 Wenchuan earthquake, probable PTSD prevalence was 44.3% (Zhou et al., 2018). A year after the 2015 Nepal earthquake, the estimated prevalence of PTSD was 43.3%, and depression was 38.1% (Sharma and Kar, 2019) and a year after the Marmara earthquake, Basoglu et al., (2002) found the rate of PTSD and major depression to be respectively 43% and 31%.

Based on the results of our studies, we recognized the critical importance of documenting specific details of earthquake-related traumatic experiences, for example, being trapped, injured, being worried about a significant other, and seeing mutilating injuries and dead bodies. In addition to assessing a dose-response relation by geographic region, these exposure-related variables provided a more graded approach to characterizing exposure (e.g., mild, moderate, severe, and very severe). Also, we learned to inquire about which of the earthquake-related experiences was the most upsetting and then assessing PTSD symptoms in relation to the most traumatic earthquake experience. This provided an even more refined and graded approach for dose-response relation analyses. In subsequent studies, we continued to use this methodology to assess exposure to post-earthquake reactions. The first report using such an approach was among traumatized adults exposed to war, forced deportation, and/or earthquake (Goenjian et al., 1994).

## 3.4.2 The 1.5- and Three-Year Treatment Outcome Study

The 1.5-year treatment outcome study was the first published prospective study comparing treatment outcomes among treated and not treated early adolescents after a catastrophic natural disaster using pre- and post-intervention assessments of post-traumatic stress and depressive reactions (Goenjian et al., 1997). Figure 3.5 shows the severity of PTSD symptoms of the treated and not treated groups by time. The severity of PTSD symptoms (mean PTSD-RI scores) decreased significantly among the treated subjects (p < 0.01) between 1.5 and three years. In contrast, the severity of PTSD symptoms increased significantly among not treated participants (p < 0.01).

Concerning depressive symptoms (Figure 3.6), at 1.5 years, there was no significant difference between the mean DSRS scores of the two groups, but at three years, the mean score for the treated group was significantly lower than the score for the not treated group. Between 1.5 and three years, there was no change in the mean DSRS scores among the treated participants. However, among not treated participants, depressive symptoms worsened significantly over time (p < 0.01).

### Discussion

The severity of PTSD symptoms among not treated adolescents was associated with multiple ongoing and new adversities. In December 1991, the Soviet Union collapsed, and

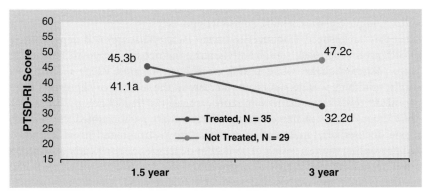

**Figure 3.5** PTSD-Reaction Index (PTSD-RI) scores at 1.5 and three years after the Spitak earthquake among treated and not treated early adolescents in Gumri. (A black- and- white version of this figure will appear in some formats. For the color version, please refer to the plate section.)
  Data from the *American Journal of Psychiatry* 1997; 154: 536–542.
  a ≈ b (p-value not significant)
  c > a (t = 3.12, df = 59, p < 0.01)
  d < b (t = -6.69, df = 59, p < 0.01)
  d < c (t = -7.64, df = 59, p <0.01)

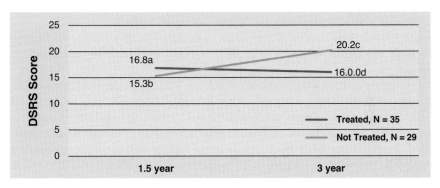

**Figure 3.6** Depression Self-Rating Scale (DSRS) scores at 1.5 and three years after the Spitak earthquake among treated and not treated early adolescents in Gumri. (A black- and- white version of this figure will appear in some formats. For the color version, please refer to the plate section.)
  Data from the *American Journal of Psychiatry* 1997; 154: 536–542.
  a ≈ b (p-value not significant)
  d < c (t = –4.09, df = 59, p < .01)
  c > b (t = 4.08, df = 59, p < .01)

with it came chaos. It resulted in a severe shortage of essential supplies, gas, heat, and electricity. In addition, the war with neighboring Azerbaijan escalated. People were still living in makeshift shoddy, poorly insulated structures or were homeless. The omnipresence of destroyed buildings served as constant reminders of the earthquake, as well as frequent memorials and visits to gravesites (a traditional ritual in Armenia). The reminders repeatedly triggered intrusive images and thoughts and, heightened psychological and physiological reactivity. Family lives were shattered as many family members (usually fathers) left the earthquake zone to find employment elsewhere or went to war. Social connectivity was disrupted. Unemployment was high, and so was poverty.

Against this backdrop, PTSD severity (mean PTSD-RI score) and depression severity (mean DSRS score) increased significantly among the not-treated youth between 1.5 and three years post-earthquake, while among treated participants, PTSD severity decreased significantly, and there was no significant increase in the severity of depression during the same period. At three years, depression scores among the treated group were significantly lower than those of the not treated group. These results demonstrated the benefit of the trauma-grief-focused brief intervention in alleviating Posttraumatic Stress Disorder symptoms and preventing the worsening of comorbid depression among early adolescents after a catastrophic natural disaster. It also demonstrated the cross-cultural applicability of Western therapeutic approaches and supported the general use of such school-based interventions after a major disaster.

## 3.4.3   The 1.5- and Five-Year Treatment Outcome Study

A second treatment outcome study was conducted five years after treatment that was provided at 1.5 years (Goenjian et al., 2005). At the time, it was one of the most extended prospective treatment outcome studies reported after a natural disaster that assessed the course of PTSD and depressive symptoms. It again evaluated the effectiveness of brief trauma- and grief-focused intervention in another group of treated and not treated adolescents from Gumri exposed to severe trauma. The results extended the findings of the previous three-year outcome study conducted among adolescents.

Figure 3.7 shows the results of this study, indicating that at 1.5 years post-earthquake, there was no significant difference in mean PTSD-RI scores between the treated and not treated groups.

Within-group by time analysis showed that mean PTSD-RI scores had decreased in both the treated ($p < 0.001$) and not treated groups ($p < 0.02$) (Figure 3.7, the two graphs on the left). The decrease in mean severity score (depicted by the blue bars in the figure) between 1.5 and five years was significantly greater among the treated youth, with the change in mean PTSD-RI severity score being three times greater among treated youth compared to not treated youth (16.3 vs. 5.4; $p < 0.001$).

Within-group by time (between 1.5 and five years) comparison of DSRS scores (Figure 3.7, the two graphs on the right) showed that the treated group scores tended to decrease ($p < 0.07$), while the not treated group scores increased ($p < 0.05$) as in the three-year follow-up study. The change in DSRS scores between 1.5 and five years among treated youth was significantly greater compared to the score of not treated youth ($p < 0.01$) (Figure 3.7).

By five years, the adversities described earlier for the three-year follow-up had continued. Still, there was a severe housing shortage, destroyed buildings were pervasive, and unemployment and poverty remained high. However, compared to previous years, there was more heat, electricity, and food available, although prices were soaring. Rebuilding and retrofitting of buildings continued, albeit at a slow pace. The war with Azerbaijan had ended.

Compared to baseline level, the severity of PTSD had decreased in both treated and not treated groups, although significantly more among the treated youth (Figure 3.7). In comparison, the severity of depression among the not treated youth at five years was higher

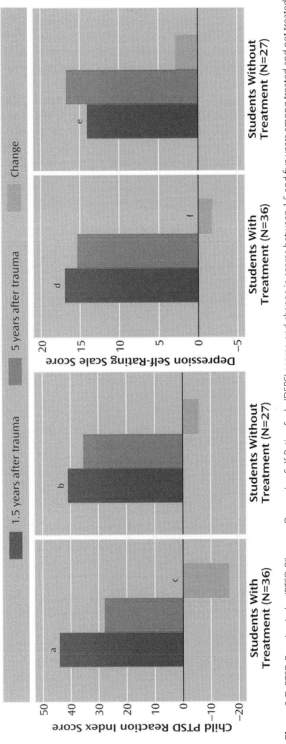

**Figure 3.7** PTSD-Reaction Index (PTSD-RI) scores, Depression Self-Rating Scale (DSRS) scores, and change in scores between 1.5 and five years among treated and not treated Gumri adolescents post-earthquake. (A black- and- white version of this figure will appear in some formats. For the color version, please refer to the plate section.) (Reprinted with permission from the *American Journal of Psychiatry* 2005; 162: 2302–2308.

than the baseline level and higher than the treated group at five years. There was a non-significant decrease in depression severity among the treated youth. The depression findings at three- and five-year follow-up were similar for both treated and not treated groups, i.e., higher than baseline among not treated and slightly lower than baseline for the treated group. However, the PTSD pattern was different: for the not treated group: at three years the mean PTSD-RI score was higher than the baseline level, but at five years, it was significantly lower than the baseline level, unlike depression, which was higher than baseline. Once again, these results indicated once that the treatment was effective in reducing PTSD severity and preventing an increase in depression.

## 3.4.4 The 1.5- and Twenty-Five-Year Treatment Outcome Study

The twenty-five-year follow-up study constituted the culmination of three decades of follow-up studies among children and adolescents extending to adulthood.

### PTSD Symptom Severity among Treated and Not Treated Groups at 1.5, Five, and Twenty-Five Years

Figure 3.8 shows the mean PTSD-RI scores in Gumri among the same treated and not treated participants at 1.5, five, and twenty-five years after the earthquake. At 1.5 years after the earthquake, before treatment was provided, there was no significant difference in PTSD severity scores between the two Gumri groups despite the treated group having slightly higher scores. At five years, symptoms had subsided in both groups, although more so among the treated youth. At twenty-five years, compared to the five-year follow-up, there was no further drop in the PTSD-RI scores in both groups; and as in the previous two follow-up periods, the treated participants had significantly lower PTSD-RI scores than the not treated ones.

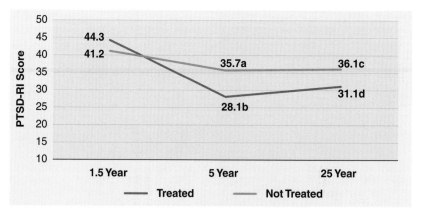

**Figure 3.8** The PTSD-Reaction Index (PTSD-RI) scores at 1.5, five, and twenty-five years after the 1988 Spitak earthquake for treated and not treated participants from Gumri. (A black- and- white version of this figure will appear in some formats. For the color version, please refer to the plate section.)
    At 1.5 years: no significant difference in the PTSD-RI scores between the two groups.
    At five years: mean PTSD-RI score: treated group (b) < not treated group (a) (p < 0.01).
    At twenty-five years: mean PTSD-RI score: treated group (d) < not treated group (c) (p < 0.05).
    Between five and twenty-five years: no significant change of mean PTSD-RI scores for either group.

### Severity and Rates of PTSD for Treated and Not Treated Groups at Twenty-Five-Years Post-Earthquake

The gains at five-year follow-up had persisted at twenty-five-year follow-up. The treated group showed a greater decrease in PTSD-RI scores between baseline and twenty-five years ($p < 0.03$) and had significantly lower mean PTSD-RI ($p < 0.02$) and PCL ($p < 0.02$) scores at twenty-five-years compared to the not treated group.

At twenty-five year follow-up, the estimated PTSD rates based on the PTSD-RI showed an approximate 60% decrease in both Gumri groups between 1.5 and twenty-five years. The PTSD rate of the Gumri treated group was 12%, and the not treated group was 14%. The rate based on the DSM-5 PCL scale was 9.1% for the Gumri treated group and 16.6% for Gumri not treated group.

### Comparison of PTSD B, C, and D Category Scores for the Treated and Not Treated Groups

Figure 3.9 shows the change in PTSD-RI subcategories B, C, and D scores between 1.5 and twenty-five years after the earthquake. The treated group had a significantly greater drop in mean B (Intrusion) and D (Arousal) category scores compared to the not treated group (B category: treated group = 0.72, not treated group = 0.29; D category treated group = 0.49, not treated group = 0.03). Within the treated group, the drop in B category scores was greater than for the C and D category scores, while within the not treated group, the drop in the C (Avoidance) category (0.48) was greater than the B category (0.29) and D category (0.03). The drop in the mean C category score was almost the same between the two groups (treated = 0.43; not treated = 0.48).

These findings indicate that treatment benefits were in B and D category symptoms, more so than for C category symptoms. Reduction in B category symptoms may have been due, in part, to the exposure component of therapy that included repeatedly going over the narrative of the earthquake trauma coupled with relaxation measures, helping students identify trauma reminders (that prompt intrusive phenomenon), and using relaxation techniques when reminded. Pro-active measures with parents and teachers to reduce unnecessary exposure to reminders may also have contributed to

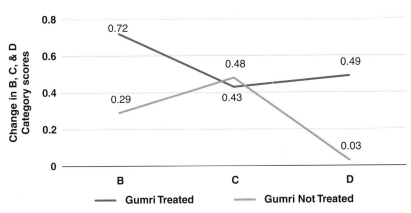

**Figure 3.9** Changes in mean B, C, and D category scores among treated and not treated subjects from Gumri between 1.5 and twenty-five years after the Spitak earthquake. (A black- and- white version of this figure will appear in some formats. For the color version, please refer to the plate section.)

a reduction in the severity of category B (Intrusion) symptoms. Helping them modify distorted thoughts and misattributions may also have helped in reducing B category symptoms.

Regarding C category symptoms, improvement occurred in both groups. One reason may be related to the ethos of the culture that promoted family bonding and community-member interactions. This lifestyle and the expectations exerted on people who tended to isolate after the earthquake may have reduced avoidant behavior.

As for the D category symptoms, such as angry outbursts and risky behavior, improvement among the treated group may have been related to the education component of therapy, informing students about anger management techniques (e.g., identifying problems that are sources for their anger, avoiding threatening confrontations, walking away from escalating situations, revisiting the issue when anger is diminished, and role-playing), and the consequences of impulsive and risky behaviors.

### Severity Scores and Rates of Depression for Treated and Not Treated Groups at Twenty-Five-Years Post-Earthquake

There was no significant difference in mean DSRS scores at 1.5 years after the earthquake between the Gumri treated and not treated groups. At the five-year follow-up, there was a divergence; depression for the treated group had subsided although not significantly, while for the not treated group, it increased (Figure 3.7). This trend continued, and at twenty-fve-year follow-up, there was a significant difference between the mean CES-D scores: the treated group = 12.7 vs. the not treated group = 20.7 t = -3.07; df = 72.9; $p < 0.01$).

Figure 3.10 shows the estimated rates of clinical depression at 1.5, five, and twenty-five years post-earthquake. It shows the rate increase among not-treated participants over time (31%, 44%, and 62%) and the concurrent decrease among the treated participants (45%, 30%, and 15%).

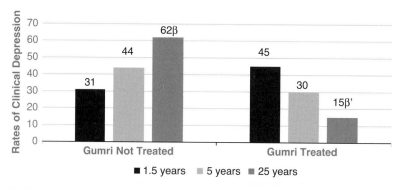

**Figure 3.10** Estimated rates of clinical depression among treated and not treated Gumri groups at 1.5, five, and twenty-five years post-earthquake. (A black- and- white version of this figure will appear in some formats. For the color version, please refer to the plate section.)
At 25 years the not treated group (β) > the treated group (β') ($X^2 = 7.41$; p = .006).

### Risk and Protective Factors for PTSD and Depressive Symptoms at Twenty-Five Years Post-Earthquake

Based on the backward multiple regression analysis, the best predictors of PTSD symptom severity at twenty-five years included:

*Risk and Protective factors*: Home destruction, baseline PTSD severity, post-earthquake adversities, chronic medical illnesses, and sex. Treatment and social support by family and friends.

Together these variables explained 36% of the variance in PTSR-RI severity scores.
The best predictors of depression at twenty-five years:

*Risk and Protective factors*: Home destruction, separation anxiety disorder symptoms, post-earthquake adversities, and chronic medical illnesses. Social support by family and friends.

Together these variables explained 40% of CES-D (depression) severity scores.

### Discussion: PTSD and Depression at Twenty-Five Years Post-Earthquake

There was no significant difference in both PTSD and depression scores at baseline between the treated and not treated groups in these studies. At the three-year follow-up, PTSD and depression scores were lower among the treated group compared to the not treated group. An important pattern emerged among not treated participants showing that mean PTSD and depression scores had increased at the three-year follow-up compared to those scores at 1.5 years. The five-year follow-up study showed that mean PTSD scores had subsided in both groups, significantly more among the treated group, while depression scores were higher in the non-treated group compared to their baseline scores and the five-year treatment group scores. Between five and twenty-five years, PTSD remained unchanged in both groups. Based on PCL-5 (DSM-5 criteria), 9% of treated participants and 16% of not treated participants met the criteria for PTSD diagnosis. As per the three-year and five-year follow-up assessments, depression severity (CES-D score) and rate at twenty-five years was significantly lower among the treated subjects (Figure 3.10).

The worsening of depression in the not treated group at five years compared to 1.5 years, during which period PTSD severity had subsided significantly, suggests that other factors, besides the earthquake experiences and PTSD symptoms, contributed to the persistence of depression. Likely reasons for the increase in PTSD and depressive symptoms during the early years after the earthquake included post-earthquake existential threats: lack of essentials such as food, medicines, construction material, extreme cold with no heating and electricity, and the ongoing war with Azerbaijan. Throughout the years, the persistence of depression was attributable to the adversities mentioned earlier, post-earthquake traumas, poverty, and unemployment (Statistical Committee of the Republic of Armenia, 2015). An increase of post-earthquake traumas after the earthquake was also found among adults in an epidemiologic study twenty-three years after the earthquake (Goenjian et al., 2018). These traumas included accidents and injuries due to recklessness, aggressive behaviors, and substance abuse. Treatment may have reduced aggressive and reckless behavior as it had specifically addressed the management of aggressive behavior and irritability during therapy.

Despite the decline in severity of PTSD symptoms up to the twenty-five-years follow-up, a sub-group of the participants in both cities continued experiencing substantial levels of

PTSD symptoms. In addition, they also were experiencing significant levels of depressive symptoms. This sub-group represented a public mental health problem for the region. In addressing chronic cases after major disasters, public mental health programs should include ongoing surveillance and treatment for PTSD, depression, and chronic illnesses. They should also include assessment of secondary stresses and adversities described above (e.g., housing shortage, unemployment), which could be relieved by assistance from government and non-governmental organizations.

In addition to treatment, social support by family and friends was significantly associated with lower severity of PTSD and depression scores, while post-disaster adversities, housing shortage, and chronic illness were associated with higher scores. McDermott et al., (2012) assessed the association of social connectedness and PTSD among youth three months after the 2006 category 5 Cyclone Larry in Queensland, Australia. The results showed that children with a lower number of social connections were almost four times more likely to experience severe to very severe PTSD. This finding suggested that prospectively identifying children with fewer social connections may present an opportunity for targeted resilience building in communities or regions at high risk for weather-related and other types of disasters.

In summary, these findings also suggest that in addition to psychotherapy, promoting social support and social connectivity and reducing the risk factors identified above may improve the outcome of PTSD and depression symptoms among survivors of disasters. The findings also indicate the feasibility of surveying students after a disaster and implementing large scale school intervention programs.

## 3.5 Recent Developments in Acute Post-Disaster Intervention

An early brief intervention that has been widely used after large-scale disasters is Psychological First Aid (PFA) (Watson et al., 2011). PFA is an evidence-informed skill-based approach to reduce acute post-disaster distress and promote adaptive functioning. A widely used PFA approach was developed by the National Child Traumatic Stress Network (NCTSN) and the National Center for PTSD (Brymer et al., 2006). PFA can be delivered by primary and emergency health care personnel, school crisis response teams, faith-based organizations, and disaster relief organizations. Based on the principles of fostering safety, calm, hope, connectedness, and self-efficacy, it includes eight core actions: (1) contact and engagement, (2) safety and comfort, (3) stabilization, (4) information gathering, (5) practical assistance, (6) connection with social supports, (7) information on coping, and (8) linking with collaborative services. Randomized controlled trials have yet to be conducted, although providers have rated PFA as appropriate.

Skills for Psychological Recovery (SPR) is another model also developed by the NCTSN and the National Center for PTSD (Berkowitz et al., 2010). SPR is designed to be implemented after PFA has been utilized or when more intensive intervention is needed. Like PFA, SPR was designed to be appropriate for all ages and can be delivered in a range of settings. SPR is not a formal mental health treatment but utilizes skills-building components from mental health treatment that have been found to be helpful in a variety of post-trauma situations. SPR includes a set of skill-building modules that include: (1) gathering information about current needs and concerns (psychological and non-psychological) and prioritizing assistance, (2) building problem-solving skills, (3) promoting positive activities, (4) managing reactions, (5) promoting helpful thinking, and (6) rebuilding healthy social connections. SPR also incorporates motivational enhancement principles, guidelines for prioritizing problems, and strategies for addressing skill implementation barriers. SPR is a promising evidence-informed intervention, although it awaits controlled studies to be considered fully evidence-based.

Disasters that affect entire communities and disrupt service systems limit their ability to meet community members' needs. Several interventions have been developed to address disasters with such wide-ranging effects. These programs often offer a range of services across levels of risk that include universal and targeted interventions. One example of this in the United States is the FEMA-funded Crisis Counseling Assistance and Training Program (CCP) (Norris and Bellamy, 2009). The CCP is designed to supplement community resources and build self- and community-efficacy. CCP services include public messaging and psychoeducation, assessment and referral, community outreach, brief supportive contact, and individual and group counseling using SPR. Rigorous controlled studies have not as yet been conducted on the CCP.

## 3.6 Reviews and Meta-Analyses of Treatments for PTSD, Depression, and Anxiety

### 3.6.1 Currently Recommended Psychotherapies for PTSD

The International Society for Traumatic Stress Studies guidelines (Foa et al., 2010) have recommended trauma-focused talking therapies as the first line of treatment for PTSD in youth. The Practice Parameters on disaster preparedness set by the American Academy of Child and Adolescent Psychiatry (AACAP) (Pfefferbaum et al., 2013) indicated that multimodal approaches using social support, psychoeducation, and cognitive-behavioral techniques have the strongest evidence and that psychopharmacologic intervention, even though not generally used, may be necessary as an adjunct to other interventions for children with severe reactions or coexisting psychiatric conditions. They have also indicated that these parameters were not intended to define the sole standards of care. As such, the parameters should not be deemed inclusive of all proper methods of care or exclusive of other methods of intervention.

In one of the most extensive meta-analyses for the treatment of PTSD among children and adolescents, Gutermann et al., (2016) found Cognitive Behavioral Therapy (CBT) yielded the largest effect size. CBT, especially when conducted as individual treatment with parents' inclusion, was a highly effective treatment for trauma symptoms. The review included survivors of various types of traumas. The results were very similar for all different kinds of traumatization, except for PTSD symptoms following a loss (usually of parents), resulting in a smaller effect size than the other groups.

In a review article on early mental health interventions among children and adolescents up to sixteen years, Pfefferbaum et al., (2017) reported that there was a dearth of treatment studies. Successful implementation of a range of early interventions included CBT, narrative exposure, meditation relaxation, debriefing, eye movement desensitization and reprocessing (EMDR), and novel approaches like massage and spiritual hypnosis. CBT, debriefing, massage, and spiritual hypnosis were superior to an inactive control group, and EMDR, combined with psychoeducation, was superior to a psychoeducation control group. The chaos of the post-disaster environment made it difficult to study interventions in the acute and early aftermath of disasters when security and physical concerns were priorities.

## Limitations of Approved Therapies

In a meta-analysis of psychotherapies for PTSD, Bradley et al., (2005) found that more than half of patients who completed treatment with various forms of cognitive behavioral therapy (CBT) or eye movement desensitization and reprocessing (EMDR) improved. However, the authors cautioned on applying these findings to patients treated in the community in that post-treatment, since the majority of patients continued to have substantial residual symptoms, and follow-up data beyond very brief intervals have been mostly absent. The exclusion criteria and failure to address polysymptomatic presentations in these studies rendered generalizability to the population of PTSD patients indeterminate. The authors recommended that future research intended to generalize to patients in practice should avoid exclusion criteria other than those a sensible clinician would impose in practice (e.g., schizophrenia), should avoid wait-list and other relatively inert control conditions, and should follow patients at least up to two years.

Another meta-analysis (Watts et al., 2013) concluded that it was not possible to identify a single "best" treatment and that selection between effective treatments is better guided by important real differences in the characteristics of the treatments, rather than selection based on small differences in the reported effectiveness. Ultimately, other factors, such as access, acceptability, and patient preference, should exert strong and appropriate influence over treatment choice.

Lastly, a review article of randomized clinical trials among veterans and military personnel found that 49% to 70% of participants receiving cognitive processing therapy (CPT) and prolonged exposure attained clinically meaningful symptom improvement (Steenkamp et al., 2015). However, mean post-treatment scores for CPT and prolonged exposure remained at or above clinical criteria for PTSD. Approximately two-thirds of patients receiving CPT or prolonged exposure retained their PTSD diagnosis after treatment (range, 60%–72%). CPT and prolonged exposure were minimally superior compared with non-trauma-focused psychotherapy comparison conditions. There are far fewer such informative treatment outcome studies conducted among children and adolescents. It is imperative to conduct more outcome studies among children and adolescents, including meta-analyses, to determine the long-term effectiveness of the various therapies for the treatment of PTSD and comorbid conditions.

## Treatment Drop-out

Over the past three decades, the field of child traumatic stress has witnessed a proliferation of trauma-focused, evidence-based treatments designed to effectively address the needs of children and families exposed to an array of traumatic events. However, these advances have not been coupled with advances in treatment engagement and retention strategies that facilitate adherence and completion of treatment (Ofonedu et al., 2017). Imel et al. (2013), in a meta-analysis of PTSD treatment studies, found the drop-out was lower in present-centered therapy (PCT), 22% compared to 36% for trauma-specific treatments.

In a meta-analysis (De Haan et al., 2013), reported rates of premature drop-out in child mental health services varied considerably, ranging from 28% to 75%. Treatment and therapist variables were overall stronger drop-out predictors than the pre-treatment child and family or parent variables. For instance, when the parent or child has experienced limited relevance of the treatment, the therapist could change some aspects of the therapy to make it more relevant and reduce the chances of drop out. Alternatively, therapists could be changed when the parent or child experiences a poor relationship with their current therapist.

### Inflated Results and Publication Bias

In a meta-analysis, Watts et al., (2013) found that there are many effective treatments for PTSD. Those with the largest amount of evidence include various types of CBT, eye movement desensitization and reprocessing, antidepressants (specifically Venlafaxine and SSRIs), Risperidone, and Topiramate. The results showed that the effect size for the psychotherapy treatments literature might be inflated to some degree, and that type of comparison strongly affected the effect size of psychotherapy studies, with wait-list control being associated "as expected" with larger effects. The authors noted that their findings suggested publication bias in the psychotherapy literature, with psychotherapy studies being more likely to be published when the results were positive.

## 3.6.2 Pharmacotherapy of PTSD

According to the AACAP guidelines (Pefferbaum et al., 2013), when used, medications should be considered an adjunct to psychotherapeutic interventions. They should focus on target symptoms, such as the acute onset of sleep disturbances, anxiety, depression, agitation, or aggressive behavior, that impair the child's capacity to meet the demands of everyday life. Selective serotonin uptake inhibitors (SSRIs) have a favorable risk-benefit profile and may effectively treat comorbid anxiety and depression. Although benzodiazepines are not usually recommended for use in children, on rare occasions, they may be helpful, e.g., decrease anxiety and improve sleep.

In 2018 the National Institute for Clinical Excellence (NICE) published its PTSD guidelines (available at: www.nice.org.uk/guidance/ng116) recommending against the use of medications to treat PTSD in children and adolescents because there was insufficient evidence on the use of drug treatments to prevent or treat PTSD in children and young people.

## 3.6.3 Psychotherapies for Depression among Children and Adolescents

In a recent review and meta-analysis of various treatments for depressive disorders among youth $\leq 18$ years old, Zhou et al., (2020) included sixteen placebo-controlled and head-to-head trials with antidepressants, seven psychotherapies, and five combinations of antidepressant and psychotherapy that are used for acute treatment. The results showed that fluoxetine plus cognitive behavioral therapy (CBT) was more effective than CBT alone and psychodynamic therapy, but not more effective than fluoxetine alone. Pharmacotherapy alone was more effective than psychotherapy alone. Only fluoxetine plus CBT and fluoxetine were significantly more effective than pill placebo or psychological controls. Only interpersonal therapy (IPT) was more effective than all psychological controls. According to the authors, the findings suggested that fluoxetine (alone or in combination with CBT) might be considered the best option to treat acute symptoms in children and adolescents with major depression.

## 3.6.4 Pharmacotherapies for Depression

Two types of selective serotonin reuptake inhibitors (SSRIs) have been approved by the United States Food and Drug Administration (FDA) to treat major depression among children and adolescents: fluoxetine for children ages eight or older and escitalopram for adolescents aged twelve to seventeen. Other SSRIs (e.g., citalopram, sertraline, fluvoxamine), SNRIs (e.g., venlafaxine, duloxetine), and tricyclic antidepressants (e.g., Norpramin) have also been used by physicians to treat depression in these age groups.

## 3.6.5  Treatments for Anxiety

### Meta-Analysis for Anxiety Disorder

In a review and meta-analysis study of sixty-nine randomized clinical trials comparing CBT and control conditions for anxiety-related disorders, Van Dis et al., (2020), suggested that CBT is associated with improved outcomes compared with control conditions until twelve months after treatment completion. After twelve months, effects were small to medium for generalized anxiety disorder and social anxiety disorder, large for PTSD, and not significant or not available for other disorders.

**Other Psychiatric Conditions** associated with disasters include substance abuse, panic attacks, manic or hypomanic episodes, psychotic symptoms, separation anxiety symptoms, obsessive-compulsive behavior, and insomnia.

# 3.7  Non-Psychiatric Problems after Disasters

After catastrophic disasters, victims face multiple pressing issues, including psychological, physical, financial, and housing difficulties. Serious physical injuries may take precedence over psychological needs, especially early on after the disaster, such as, incapacitating orthopedic and neurological problems (e.g., spinal cord injuries, cerebral hemorrhage), lacerated spleen or kidney failure due to massive muscle injury, etc. It is imperative to address the physical problems and severe psychiatric conditions first (e.g., acute psychosis, an imminent threat for suicide or violence). Other stressful situations that may take precedence and be related to substantial secondary stress including unsafe living conditions, (e.g., sleeping in parks or streets and being subjected to physical assault and animal attacks, exploitation by predators, freezing to death, and lack of food leading to starvation).

## 3.7.1  Discussion

After major disasters, clinicians' challenge is to prioritize the problems they encounter in therapy, especially during group therapy. Often there will be comorbid conditions directly related to the trauma (e.g., PTSD, depression, panic, separation anxiety, grief reactions) and/or relapse of pre-existing psychological problems (e.g., psychotic breakdown), which may be more problematic than PTSD or depressive symptoms.

Catastrophic disaster often results in the death of parents, siblings, relatives, friends, and teachers, resulting in strong grief reactions, which may also take precedence over other conditions. In the meta-analysis, Gutermann et al., (2016) found that treatment effects of various trauma-focused therapies for PTSD symptoms were similar across different kinds of traumas, except for symptoms following a loss (usually of a parent), which showed lower effect-size. The findings underscore the importance of addressing grief reactions in therapy.

Other significant long-lasting problems may arise due to changing family dynamics (e.g., father drinking heavily, not working, and other types of disruptions at home), poor living conditions (e.g., not having a place to live and having to move from one place to another), and medical illnesses without adequate treatment (e.g., head trauma causing encephalopathy, kidney disease related to trauma).

In our experience, trauma-grief-focused therapies were necessary to properly treat stress reactions (e.g., PTSD, depression, grief, and anxiety). However, these commonly occurring conditions may not be the priority when a child or adolescent is confronted with other types of serious problems such as physical safety, hunger, extreme poverty, and serious medical illnesses. These problems may be identified during the initial assessment or may arise during therapy.

The initial evaluation should be comprehensive. Besides evaluating for trauma exposure and PTSD symptoms, assessment should include other commonly co-occurring conditions (e.g., depression, panic, separation anxiety, grief reactions, substance use and abuse), past psychiatric problems, and other current problems, including medical, housing, nutritional, financial, and familial (e.g., separation of members).

Treatment should proceed according to the findings. When treatment comes to an impasse or the therapists feel helpless in dealing with their patients' overwhelming problems, consulting peers or more experienced therapists should be considered. The meta-analysis by de Haan et al., (2013) found that treatment and therapist variables were overall stronger drop-out predictors than pre-treatment child, family, or parent variables. These findings suggest that alternatives should be considered, including adjusting the treatment or changing therapists.

In addition to the traditional role of providing psychotherapy and pharmacotherapy, therapists can assist survivors by making appropriate referrals to agencies that can be of help (e.g., volunteer organizations, governmental and non-governmental organizations), and by being advocates for their patients (e.g., testifying, making recommendations to governing bodies).

## 3.8 Summary

### 3.8.1 School-Based Intervention and the Outcome of Longitudinal Studies

- There is a lack of controlled long-term post-disaster treatment follow-up studies among adolescents.
- The trauma-grief-focused intervention used after the Spitak earthquake included psychoeducation, relaxation methods, exposure component, cognitive restructuring of distortions and misattributions, problem-solving and coping skills to deal with trauma reminders, adversities, interpersonal conflicts, and grief reactions. None of the participants received pharmacotherapy.
- Providing treatment in the trenches may be difficult for some therapists. Before undertaking fieldwork, preparing potential candidates for the upcoming hardships and during their tour in the earthquake zone, regular meetings with peers and supervisors to address personal and patient-related problems can minimize problems, such as vicarious traumatization and burn-out.
- The results of the 1.5-year follow-up among differentially exposed early adolescents showed a dose-response relation for PTSD, depression, and separation anxiety

symptoms. The rates of PTSD and clinical depression were commensurate with the extent of morbidity, mortality, and destruction across cities.

- The results of the three- and five-year follow-ups were similar. Both groups demonstrated a significant treatment effect on PTSD symptoms. In both studies, PTSD symptoms subsided significantly, more among the treated youth, while depression increased among the not treated group and remained at baseline level among the treated group.

- At twenty-five-year follow-up, PTSD scores remained at the five-year level. The treated group scores were significantly lower than the scores of the not treated group.

- At twenty-five years, the severity of depression was significantly lower among the treated group compared to the not treated group.

- Except at baseline, at all follow-ups, depression scores were higher among the not treated group compared to the treated group.

- These studies demonstrated the beneficial long-term effects of trauma-grief-focused psychotherapy for the treatment of PTSD and depressive symptoms.

- The studies demonstrated the feasibility of screening and treating students in their classrooms after disasters.

- The increase of PTSD symptoms among not treated youth during the first three years after the earthquake was likely due to the ongoing trauma reminders (e.g., the omnipresence of destroyed buildings and memorials for the dead during their birthdays and anniversaries), war with neighboring Azerbaijan, other post-earthquake traumas (e.g., fights, accidents), and post-earthquake adversities.

- The increase of depression among the not treated youth was attributable to the unfavorable recovery environment with post-earthquake adversities and subsequent traumas. The adversities included shortages of housing, gas, medicines, food, transportation, jobs, and poverty.

- At twenty-five years, risk factors for PTSD and depression included home destruction, post-earthquake adversities, post-earthquake medical illnesses, female sex, PTSD and SAD severity at baseline.

- Protective factors for PTSD included trauma-grief-focused psychotherapy and social support.

- Despite the decline in PTSD scores, a sub-group of the population in both cities continued to experience substantial levels of PTSD and depressive symptoms. The rate of PTSD based on DSM-5 criteria for the Gumri treated group was 9.1%, and for the Gumri not treated group it was 16.6%. These rates represented an enduring public mental health problem for the region.

- In addressing chronic cases, mental health programs should include ongoing surveillance for PTSD and depression, post-earthquake adversities, and new onset of traumatic experiences.

- Treatment should be tailored, based on the results of the psychosocial assessment, including stress reactions, adversities, family dysfunction, educational challenges, financial hardship, and medical problems.

## 3.8.2 Recommended Treatments for PTSD

- Recommended therapies among adults based on shorter-term outcome studies indicate that trauma-focused treatments were superior to most other types of treatments. Despite the benefits, meta-analyses have shown that the effect size of the results was modest, indicating the need to develop treatment protocols and research further to establish their effectiveness and efficacy.
- It was not possible to identify a single "best" treatment for PTSD, and that selection between effective treatments is better guided by real significant differences in the characteristics of the treatments and the needs of the patients, rather than selection based on small differences in the reported effectiveness.
- A review of randomized clinical trials of the first-line trauma-focused interventions, CPT and PE, have shown clinically significant improvements for many patients with PTSD. However, non-response rates have been high, and trauma-focused interventions have shown "marginally superior" results compared with active control conditions.
- More than half of the patients who completed treatment with various forms of CBT or EMDR improved. However, the majority of patients continued to have substantial residual symptoms, and follow-up data beyond very brief intervals have been mostly absent.
- Some therapies may be better suited for one group of individuals but not others with the same diagnosis. More research on patient-tailored intervention is imperative.
- After a disaster, children and adolescents will have a variety of psychiatric disorders, not only PTSD (e.g., grief reaction, depression, anxiety). Thus, treatment should consider the child's clinical presentation and not focus solely on PTSD. Therapists should prioritize the needs of the patient and adjust therapy accordingly.
- Meta-analysis has shown that one of the most important reasons for high treatment drop-out was that patients' needs were not met by the treatment.
- Meta-analysis has also shown that treatment and therapist variables were overall stronger drop-out predictors than the pre-treatment child and family or parent variables.
- Post-treatment follow-up studies should extend beyond twelve months and should include the reasons, when available, for relapses and drop-outs.

## 3.8.3 Recommended Treatments for Depression and Anxiety

- Meta-analysis data suggested that CBT and IPT may be considered the best available psychotherapies for depression in children and adolescents. Of note, several alternative psychotherapies have been understudied in this age group.
- Sixty-nine randomized clinical trials comparing CBT and control conditions for anxiety-related disorders suggested that cognitive behavioral therapy is associated with improved outcomes compared with control conditions up to twelve months after treatment completion.

## 3.9 Conclusion

- After disasters, children and adolescents will have various psychiatric disorders, not only PTSD (e.g., depression, separation anxiety, grief reactions). Thus, treatment should take into consideration the clinical presentation of the child and not focus solely on PTSD.

- Most children exposed to mild to moderate severity levels of disasters will recover with social support, psychoeducation, and relaxation techniques.

- Because of the diverse post-traumatic trajectories, not every child will benefit from the same set of services. Of note, there is considerable overlap in treatment components of these various forms of therapies.

- In addition to treatment, additional factors that can potentially reduce PTSD and depression should be addressed, including promoting social support, addressing post-earthquake adversities, housing shortage, and chronic illness.

- Therapists should prioritize their patients' needs and adjust treatment accordingly and not insist on one treatment type. Recognition of early signs of treatment failure and adjustment of therapy may reduce the rate of early termination. When in doubt about the lack of progress, therapists should consider consulting peers and supervisors for a second opinion.

- Lastly, despite advances in the treatment of PTSD and depression, there is a need for improvement in existing treatments, delivery schedule (e.g., earlier intervention, more frequent follow-ups), and development and testing of therapies for comorbid conditions (e.g., depression, grief).

## References

Asarnow, J. R., & Carlson, G. A. (1985). Depression self-rating scale: Utility with child psychiatric inpatients. *Journal of Consulting and Clinical Psychology*, 53(4), 491–499. https://doi.org/10.1037/0022-006X.53.4.491.

Başoğlu, M., Salcioğlu, E., & Livanou, M. (2002).Traumatic stress responses in earthquake survivors in Turkey. *Journal of Traumatic Stress*, 15(4), 269–276. https://doi.org/10.1023/A:1016241826589.

Başoğlu, M., Salcioglu, E., & Livanou, M. (2007). A randomized controlled study of single-session behavioural treatment of earthquake-related posttraumatic stress disorder using an earthquake simulator. *Psychological Medicine*, 37, 203–213.

Berkowitz, S. Bryant, R. Brymer, M. Hamblen, J. Jacobs, A. Layne, C., & Watson, P. (2010). The National Center for PTSD & the National Child Traumatic Stress Network. Skills for psychological recovery: Field operations guide. Retrieved from http://www.ptsd.va.gov/profes sional/manuals/manual-pdf/SPR_Manual.pdf [last accessed July 15, 2021].

Bourque, L. B, & Russell, L. A. (1993). Experiences during and response to the Loma Prieta earthquake. Report to the Governor's Office of Emergency Services, State of California.

Bradley, R., Greene, J., Russ, E., Dutra., L. , & Western, D. (2005). A multidimensional meta-analysis of psychotherapy for PTSD. *American Journal of Psychiatry*, 162, 214–227. https://doi.org/10.1176/appi.ajp.162.2.214.

Brymer, M., Jacobs, A., Layne, C., Pynoos, R., Ruzek, J., Steinberg, A. . . . Watson, P. (2006). Psychological first aid: field operations guide. National Child Traumatic Stress Network, National Center for PTSD. Retrieved from: www.nctsn.org/resources/psychological-first-aid-pfa-field-operations-guide-2nd-edition

Chemtob, C. M., Nakashima, J. P., & Hamada, R. S. (2002). Psychosocial intervention for post-disaster trauma symptoms in elementary school children. *Archives of Pediatrics & Adolescent Medicine*,

156(3), 211. https://doi.org/10.1001/arch pedi.156.3.211.

De Haan, A. M., Boon, A. E., de Jong, J. T., Hoeve, M., & Vermeiren, R. R. (2013). A metaanalytic review on treatment dropout in child and adolescent outpatient mental health care. *Clinical Psychology Review*, 33(5), 698–711.

Demirchyan A., Petrosyan V., Thompson M. F. (2011). Psychometric value of the Center for Epidemiologic Studies Depression (CES-D) scale for screening of depressive symptoms in Armenian population. *Journal of Affective Disorders*, 133, 489–498.

Dogan, A. (2011). Adolescents' posttraumatic stress reactions and behavior problems following Marmara earthquake. *European Journal of Psychotraumatology*, 2, 10.3402/ejpt.v2i0.5825. https://doi.org/10.3402/ejpt.v2i0.5825.

Durkin, D. (1993). *Teaching Them to Read* (6th ed.). Boston: Allyn & Bacon.

Durkin, M. S., Khan, N., Davidson, L. L., Zaman, S. S., & Stein, Z. A. (1993). The effects of a natural disaster on child behavior: evidence for posttraumatic stress. *American Journal of Public Health*, 83(11), 1549–1553. https://doi.org/10.2105/ajph.83.11.1549.

Foa, E. B., Keane, T., Friedman, M., & Cohen, J. (2010). *Effective Treatments for PTSD. Practice Guidelines from the International Society for Traumatic Stress Studies.* New York: Guilford Press.

Foa, E. B., Steketee, G., Olasov, B. (1989). Behavioral/cognitive conceptualizations of posttraumatic stress disorder. *Behavior Therapy*, 20, 155–176.

Giannopoulou, I., Dikaiakou, A., & Yule, W. (2006). Cognitive-behavioural group intervention for PTSD symptoms in children following the Athens 1999 earthquake: a pilot study. *Clinical Child Psychology and Psychiatry*, 11, 543–553.

Goenjian, A. K., Najarian, L. M., Pynoos, R. S., Steinberg, A. M., Petrosian, P., Setrakyan, S., & Fairbanks, L. A. (1994). Posttraumatic stress reactions after single and double trauma. *Acta Psychiatrica Scandinavica*, 90, 214–221. https://doi:10.1111/j.1600-0447.1994.tb01580.x.

Goenjian, A. K., Pynoos, R. S., Steinberg, A. M., Najarian, L. M., Asarnow, J. R., Karayan, I., ... Fairbanks, L. A. (1995). Psychiatric comorbidity in children after the 1988 earthquake in Armenia. *Journal of the American Academy of Child and Adolescent Psychiatry*, 34(9), 1174–1184. https://doi.org/10.1097/00004583-199509000-00015.

Goenjian, A. K., Karayan, I., Pynoos, R. S., Minassian, D., Najarian, L. M., Steinberg, A. M., & Fairbanks, L. A. (1997). Outcome of psychotherapy among early adolescents after trauma. *The American Journal of Psychiatry*, 154(4), 536–542. https://doi.org/10.1176/ajp.154.4.536.

Goenjian, A. K., Walling, D., Steinberg, A. M., Karayan, I., Najarian, L. M., & Pynoos, R. (2005). A prospective study of posttraumatic stress and depressive reactions among treated and untreated adolescents 5 years after a catastrophic disaster. *American Journal of Psychiatry*, 162(12), 2302–2308. https://doi.org/10.1176/appi.ajp.162.12.2302.

Goenjian, A. K., Khachadourian, V., Armenian, H., Demirchyan, A., & Steinberg, A. M. (2018). Posttraumatic stress disorder 23 years after the 1988 Spitak earthquake in Armenia. *Journal of Traumatic Stress*, 31, 47–56. https://doi:10.1002/jts.22260.

Goenjian, A. K., Steinberg, A. M., Walling, D., Bishop, S., Karayan, I., & Pynoos, R. (2020). 25-year follow-up of treated and not-treated adolescents after the Spitak earthquake: course and predictors of PTSD and depression. *Psychological Medicine*, 1–13. Advance online publication. https://doi.org/10.1017/S0033291719003891.

Gutermann, J., Schreiber, F., Matulis, S., Schwartzkopff, L., Deppe, J., & Steil, R. (2016). Psychological treatments for symptoms of posttraumatic stress disorder in children, adolescents, and young adults: a meta-analysis. *Clinical Child and Family Psychology Review*, 19, 77–93.

Herjanic B., Reich W. (1982). Development of a structured psychiatric interview for children: agreement between child and parent on individual symptoms. *Journal of Abnormal Child Psychology*, 10, 307–324.

Imel, Z. E., Laska, K., Jakupcak, M., & Simpson, T. L. 2013. A meta-analysis of dropouts during treatment for posttraumatic stress disorder. *Journal of Consulting and Clinical Psychology*, 81, 394–404. https://doi: 10.1037/a0031474.

John, P. B., Russell, S., & Russell, P. S. (2007). The prevalence of posttraumatic stress disorder among children and adolescents affected by tsunami disaster in Tamil Nadu. *Disaster Management & Response*, 5(1), 3–7. https://doi.org/10.1016/j.dmr.2006.11.001.

Kar N. (2009). Psychological impact of disasters on children: review of assessment and interventions. *World Journal of Pediatrics*, 5 (1), 5–11. https://doi.org/10.1007/s12519-009-0001-x.

Lyons. J. A., & Keans, T. M. (1989). Implosive therapy in the treatment of combat-related PTSD. *Journal of Traumatic Stress*, 2, 137–152.

March, J. S., Amaya-Jackson, L., Murray, M. C., & Schulte, A. (1998). Cognitive-behavioral psychotherapy for children and adolescents with posttraumatic stress disorder after a single-incident stressor. *Journal of American Academy of Child and Adolescent Psychiatry*, 37(6), 585–593.

McDermott, B., Berry, H., & Cobham, V. (2012). Social connectedness: a potential aetiological factor in the development of child post-traumatic stress disorder. *Australian and New Zealand Journal of Psychiatry*, 46, 109–117.

McDonald, S. D., & Calhoun, P. S. (2010). The diagnostic accuracy of the PTSD checklist: a critical review. *Clinical Psychology Review*, 30(8), 976–987. https://doi.org/10.1016/j.cpr.2010.06.012.

Norris, F. H., & Bellamy, N. D. (2009). Evaluation of a national effort to reach Hurricane Katrina survivors and evacuees: The Crisis Counseling Assistance and Training Program. *Administration and Policy in Mental Health and Mental Health Services Research*, 36(3), 165–175. https://doi.org/10.1007/s10488-009-0217z

National Institute for Clinical Excellence (NICE) (2018). *Post-traumatic stress disorder NICE guidelines (update): guideline consultation*. London: NICE. Available at: www.nice.org.uk/guidance/NG116. Published December 5, 2018.

Ofonedu, M. E., Belcher, H. E., Budhathoki, C., & Gross, D. A. (2017). Understanding barriers to initial treatment engagement among underserved families seeking mental health services. *Journal of Child and Family Studies*, 26(3), 863–876.

Pfefferbaum, B., Shaw, J. A., & the American Academy of Child and Adolescent Psychiatry Committee on Quality issues. (2013). Practice parameters on disaster preparedness. *Journal of the American Academy of Child and Adolescent Psychiatry*, 52(11), 1224–1238.

Pfefferbaum, B., Nitie, P., Tucker, P., & Newman, E. (2017). Early child disaster mental health interventions: a review of the empirical evidence. *Child & Youth Care Forum*, 46, 621–642. https://doi.org/10.1007/s10566-017-9397-y.

Pityaratstian, N., Piyasil, V., Ketumarn, P., Sitdhiraksa, N., Ularntinon, S., & Pariwatcharakul, P. (2015). Randomized controlled trial of group cognitive behavioral therapy for posttraumatic stress disorder in children and adolescents exposed to tsunami in Thailand. *Behavioral and Cognitive Psychotherapy*, 43, 549–561.

Pynoos, R. S., & Nader, K. (1988). Psychological first aid and treatment approach to children exposed to community violence: research implications. *Journal of Traumatic Stress*, 1, 445–473.

Pynoos, R. S., Goenjian, A., Tashjian, M., Karakashian, M., Manjikian, R., Manoukian R., ... Rairbanks, L. A. (1993). Posttraumatic stress reactions in children after the 1988 Armenian earthquake. *British Journal of Psychiatry*, 163, 239–247.

Raphael, B. (1986). *When Disaster Strikes: How Individuals and Communities Cope with Catastrophe*. New York: Basic Books.

Saigh, P. A. (1987). In vitro flooding of an adolescent's posttraumatic stress disorder. *Journal of Clinical Child Psychology*, 16, 147–150.

Sharma, A., & Kar, N. (2019). Posttraumatic stress, depression, and coping following the 2015 Nepal Earthquake: a study on adolescents. *Disaster Medicine and Public Health Preparedness*, 13(2), 236–242. https://doi.org/10.1017/dmp.2018.37

Steenkamp, M. M., Litz, B. T., Hoge, C. W., & Marmar, C. R. (2015). Psychotherapy for military-related PTSD: a review of randomized clinical trials. *Journal of the American Medical Association* 314(5), 489–500. https://doi.org/10.1001/jama.2015.8370.

Steinberg, A. M., Brymer, M. J., Decker, K. B., Pynoos, R. S. (2004). The University of California at Los Angeles Posttraumatic Stress Disorder Reaction Index. *Current Psychiatry Reports*, 6, 96–100.

Van Dis, E. A. M, van Veen, S. C., Hagenaars, M. A., Batelaan, N. M., Bockting, C. L. H., van den Heuvel, R. M. . . . Engelhard, I. M. (2020). Long-term outcomes of cognitive behavioral therapy for anxiety-related disorders: a systematic review and meta-analysis. *Journal of the American Medical Association of Psychiatry*, 77(3), 265–273. https://doi.org/10.1001/jamapsychiatry.2019.3986.

Vilagut, G., Forero, C. G., Barbaglia, G., & Alonso, J. (2016). Screening for depression in the general population with the Center for Epidemiologic Studies Depression (CES-D): a systematic review with meta-analysis. *PLoS One*, 11(5), e0155431. https://doi.org/10.1371/journal.pone.0155431.

Watson, P. J., Brymer, M. J., & Bonanno, G. A. (2011). Postdisaster psychological intervention since 9/11. *American Psychologist*, 66(6), 482–494. https://doi.org/10.1037/a0024806.

Watts, B. V., Schnurr, P. P., Mayo, L., Young-Xu, Y., Weeks, W. B., & Friedman, M. J. (2013). Meta-analysis of the efficacy of treatments for posttraumatic stress disorder. *Journal of Clinical Psychiatry*, 74 (6): e541-550. https://doi.org/10.4088/JCP.12r08225.

Yasinskia, C., Hayesa, A. M., Alperta, E., McCauley, T., Ready, C. B., Webb, C., & Deblinger, E. (2018). Treatment processes and demographic variables as predictors of dropout from trauma-focused cognitive behavioral therapy (TF-CBT) for youth. *Journal of Behavioral Research and Therapy*, 107, 10–18.

Zhou, X., Wu, X., Zhen, R. (2018). Patterns of posttraumatic stress disorder and posttraumatic growth among adolescents after the Wenchuan Earthquake in China: a latent profile analysis. *Journal of Traumatic Stress*, 31, 57–63.

Zhou, X., Teng, T., Zhang, Y., Del Giovane, C. D., Furukawa, T. A., Weisz, J. R., . . . Peng Xie, M. D. (2020). Comparative efficacy and acceptability of antidepressants, psychotherapies, and their combination for acute treatment of children and adolescents with depressive disorder: a systematic review and network meta-analysis. *Lancet Psychiatry*, 7, 581–601.

# Course and Predictors of PTSD and Depression among Not Treated Children and Adolescents over Two Decades

Armen Goenjian, Alan Steinberg, and Robert Pynoos

## 4.1 Background

Catastrophic disasters with widespread destruction and high mortality/morbidity rates are generally associated with high rates of PTSD. For example, in a study of children and adolescents after the 2004 Indian Ocean earthquake and tsunami, one of the worst natural disasters in decades, John et al. (2007) found the prevalence of acute PTSD to be 70.7%, and for delayed onset PTSD, another 10.9%. In a study among adolescents thirteen months after the Marmara earthquake in Turkey, Dogan (2011) found 76% of the adolescents had moderate to very severe levels of PTSD symptoms. One year after the 2009 Wenchuan earthquake, the prevalence of probable PTSD among youth was 44.3% (Zhou et al., 2018), and a year after the 2015 Nepal earthquake, the estimated prevalence of PTSD was 43.3% and depression 38.1% (Sharma and Kar, 2019). Six months after the Category 5 Hurricane Mitch, the mean PTSD-RI score among adolescents from the most affected city of Posoltega was severe (58.6), while the mean DSRS (depression) score was above the cut-off for clinical depression (22.6) (Goenjian et al., 2001).

As indicated above, the prevalence of PTSD among children and adolescent survivors of disasters has varied widely. Wang et al. (2013), in a review of sixty cross-sectional and twenty-five longitudinal studies, found that the prevalence of PTSD after disasters ranged between 1% to 95%. These studies included earthquakes (2.5% to 95%); tsunamis (6.0% to 70.7 %); hurricanes and tornadoes (1.0% to 90%); and ship disaster (50% to 89.5%).

In a review article on the epidemiology of PTSD after disasters, Galea et al. (2005) noted that information gained from intermediate and long-term studies can help to shape public health policies and minimize the long-term psychological consequences of disasters, which may impose a much greater societal burden than the short-term transient burden of early-onset PTSD.

There is a distinct lack of long-term prospective disaster studies of the psychological sequelae among disaster survivors. The majority of studies conducted among children and adolescents do not extend longer than twelve months post-disaster (Wang et al., 2013; Terasaka et al., 2015). Only about 10% of these studies have extended beyond three years. Consequently, there is a lack of information on the natural course as well as risk and protective factors of psychological sequelae past three years.

The 2008 Wenchuan earthquake in China was one of the deadliest disasters in the past five decades. In a ten-year review, Liang et al. (2019) identified fifty-eight articles on PTSD among survivors of the Wenchuan earthquake, forty-five of which reported prevalence rates and risk factors. Of these, eighteen were conducted among children and adolescents. Only five were longitudinal studies; one was among adults, and four were among children and adolescents. The longest of the four studies was a two-year follow-up.

There are only a few follow-up reports on PTSD among children and adolescents exposed to natural disasters which look beyond a decade (Green et al., 1994; Morgan et al., 2003; McFarlane and Van Hoof, 2009; Najarian et al., 2011; Thordardotir et al., 2016; Goenjian et al., 2020). At seventeen-year follow-up of children who were initially assessed at two years after the Buffalo Creek Dam collapse, the estimated flood-related rate of PTSD had subsided from 32% to 7% (Green et al., 1994). Thirty-three years after the Aberfan disaster in Wales, 46% had experienced PTSD at some point since the disaster, while the current rate was 29% (Morgan et al., 2003). At a two-year follow-up after the Spitak earthquake, the rate of PTSD among pre-adolescents and adolescents was 32% (Najarian et al., 1996), and at twenty-year follow-up, the rate was 21% (Najarian et al., 2011). Sixteen years after an avalanche in Iceland, the current rate of PTSD among adults, who were children and adolescents at the time of the avalanche, was 16% (Thordardotir et al., 2016).

As for depression, thirty-seven years after the Tangshan earthquake, in a cross-sectional study among a mixed group of exposed adolescents and adults, a significant association was found between earthquake exposure and depression among women (Gao et al., 2019). However, this study did not report on PTSD. For the most part, depression studies have assessed current and lifetime stress reactions retrospectively at follow-up except for the twenty-five-year follow-up study by Goenjian et al. (2020), which was done prospectively.

The twenty-five-year follow-up study after the Spitak earthquake presented in this chapter is the longest prospective study of PTSD and depression among exposed adolescents. These adolescents were evaluated previously at 1.5 and five years after the earthquake. This chapter presents three longitudinal studies and several cross-sectional studies among not treated adolescents exposed to the Spitak earthquake. It describes the course of PTSD and depression, as well as the predictors associated with PTSD and depressive symptoms. Of note, most of these studies were conducted under less-than-ideal conditions in the earthquake-ravaged cities. We owe the completion of these studies to the tireless efforts of the dedicated mental health workers of the Psychiatric Outreach Program of the Armenian Relief Society and the cooperation of the young people, their teachers, and headmasters.

## 4.2 Methods

### 4.2.1 Instruments

To assess the course of PTSD symptoms at follow-up, we used the UCLA PTSD-Reaction Index (PTSD-RI) (based on DSM III-R diagnostic criteria), which we had used at 1.5 years after the Spitak earthquake. We used the same instrument at the follow-up periods to minimize potential confounds by using another instrument for comparison with baseline measures. For instance, the revised edition of the instrument based on DSM-5 introduces new symptoms and a new category to the diagnostic criteria. We also included for the follow-up the Armenian version of the PTSD Check List (PCL) based on DSM-5 criteria (Demirchyan et al., 2015) to estimate the current rate of PTSD. For the PTSD questionnaires, the index trauma was the Spitak earthquake. Psychometric properties of the PTSD-RI have been reported elsewhere (Steinberg et al., 2004; Steinberg et al., 2013).

Of importance, continuous and binary measures for PTSD were used for different reasons. The continuous scale scores provided a more sensitive representation of the progression of symptoms compared to binary measures, i.e., rates meeting diagnostic criteria. Assessment of rates was deemed useful for cross-comparisons with other studies that used rates as a primary outcome measure.

The rates reported in this chapter and elsewhere in the book were based on more strict guidelines than previously reported (Pynoos et al., 1993; Goenjian et al., 1995), which were based on a PTSD-RI cut-off score of 40. The criteria for the diagnosis of PTSD in the presentations below are based on a symptom cluster method (a minimum of 1B, 3 C, and 2D category symptoms), and a minimum score of 40 as has been done in numerous prior studies on PTSD (McDonald and Calhoun, 2010). As a result, the baseline rates reported are lower than the rates reported previously. For the PCL scale, the diagnosis of PTSD was derived by ascertaining the presence of at least 1B, 1 C, 2D, 2E, and category G criteria. About half of published child and adolescent disaster studies after a disaster have assessed PTSD by using the PTSD-RI scale.

Depression at 1.5 years was evaluated by using the twenty-one-item Depression Self-Rating Scale (DSRS) designed for use with children and adolescents (Asarnow et al., 1985). Mean total scores were used for the analysis. A cut-off score of $\geq 17$ was used to diagnose clinical depression (e.g., major depression, dysthymic disorder, and adjustment disorder with depressed mood) (Asarnow and Carlson, 1985).

At the twenty-five-years follow-up, instead of using the DSRS scale (which had not been validated among adults), depression was assessed by using the modified validated Armenian version of the Center for Epidemiological Studies Depression Scale (CES-D) (Demirchyan et al., 2011). Mean total scores were used for the analyses. A cut-off score of $\geq 20$ points was used to diagnose clinical depression (Vilagut et al., 2016).

## 4.2.2  Participants

In 1990, 1.5 years after the Spitak earthquake, 164 early adolescents aged between twelve to fourteen years from Gumri (N = 94) and Spitak (N = 70) were evaluated for PTSD, depression, and Separation Anxiety Disorder (SAD). Information on these subjects has been reported previously in Goenjian et al., (1995) and in Chapter 3 of this book. For the five-year follow-up (Goenjian et al., 2005), due to the multiplicity of hardships facing both the victims and the staff working in the earthquake zone and the lack of available mental health personnel, a power analysis was conducted to estimate the group size necessary to obtain a significant result. The analysis indicated that twenty-one subjects per study group were the minimum necessary to get a significant result (power = 0.80, alpha = 0.01). Based on this analysis, we included every other untreated subject from the original study (Spitak: N = 32, Gumri: N = 27). Comparison of age, sex, loss of nuclear family members, and the PTSD-RI and DSRS scores at 1.5 years for those who did not participate in the five-year follow-up with those who completed the five-year study, yielded no significant differences.

For the twenty-five-year post-earthquake study (Goenjian et al., 2020), seventy-six of the original ninety-four participants from Gumri were located, with only one refusing to participate. Three of the original group had died, and the rest were lost to follow-up. Of these seventy-five participants, thirty-three were among the thirty-six students who were provided with treatment at 1.5 years, shortly after the baseline assessments. The rest (N = 42) had not received mental health treatment up to the follow-up time. In Spitak, sixty-seven of the original seventy subjects were located and completed the study. None of these subjects had received mental health treatment since the earthquake. Overall, 87% of the original group was retrieved for the follow-up.

## 4.3 PTSD and Depression among Differentially Exposed Groups at 1.5 and Five Years Post-Earthquake

### 4.3.1 PTSD Severity and Rates

Figure 4.1 shows the severity of PTSD symptoms (PTSD-RI scores) among not treated adolescents (aged twelve to fourteen) from the differentially exposed cities Spitak, Gumri, and Yerevan, at 1.5 and five years after the earthquake. The most severely affected city was Spitak, with extensive destruction and a high mortality rate, followed by Gumri, the less severely affected city, and Yerevan, where there was minimal destruction and death.

**Dose-Response Relation**

As anticipated, at 1.5 years after the earthquake, the severity of PTSD symptoms (PTSD-RI scores) was commensurate by city with the intensity of the earthquake, destruction, mortality, and morbidity (Figure 4.1). The group from Spitak with the most severe earthquake exposure had the highest mean PTSD-RI score (53.0 severe) followed by the group from Gumri (41.1) and then Yerevan with the lowest score (34.7 moderate severity). As an example, a score of 53 translates to experiencing all the PTSD symptoms listed on

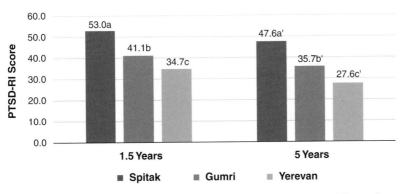

**Figure 4.1** Mean PTSD-RI scores at 1.5 and five years after the Spitak earthquake among differentially exposed not treated adolescents. Data from the *American Journal of Psychiatry*, 2005. (A black- and- white version of this figure will appear in some formats. For the color version, please refer to the plate section.)
At 1.5 years, between-city comparisons: a > b > c ($P < 0.001$).
At five years, between-city comparisons: a' > b' > c' ($P < 0.001$).
Within-city comparisons (between 1.5 and five years): a > a', b > b', c > c' (all ps < 0.05).

the PTSD-RI scale two to three times a week. A score of 41 translates to PTSD symptoms occurring one to two times a week.

### The Course of PTSD Symptoms and Rates of PTSD

At five-year follow-up, mean PTSD-RI scores had decreased in all three cites (Figure 4.1), again showing a dose–response relation. Within-city comparison between 1.5 and five years shows a significant decrease in all the cities (Figure 4.1). The Spitak group score at five years was low-severe (47.6), the Gumri group score was moderate (35.7), and the Yerevan group score was mild (27.6). PTSD rates at 1.5 and five years were as follows: Spitak 55% and 46% (respectively); Gumri 35% and 11%.

## 4.3.2  Depression Severity and Rates

Figure 4.2 shows the severity of depressive symptoms (DSRS scores) of the not treated groups in Spitak, Gumri, and Yerevan (aged twelve to fourteen) at 1.5 and five years after the earthquake.

### Dose–Response Relation

The results at 1.5 years also show a dose–response relation, with the Spitak group showing the highest mean DSRS score followed by the Gumri and Yerevan groups (Figure 4.2). The Spitak group mean DSRS score was 19, above the cut-off score of 17 for clinical depression. Next was the Gumri group score (15.2), followed by the Yerevan group score (12.9). There was a similar dose–response relationship at five years follow-up.

### The Course of Depressive Symptoms and Rates of Clinical Depression

Within-city comparisons between 1.5 and five years, the pattern of mean DSRS scores differed from that of PTSD scores. At five years, there was a significant increase in the mean DSRS score of the Gumri group (Figure 4.2) while the mean PTSD score had subsided significantly. Also, at five years, there was a non-significant increase in mean

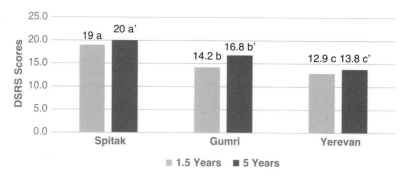

**Figure 4.2** Mean DSRS scores at 1.5 and five years post-earthquake among differentially exposed not treated adolescents. (A black- and- white version of this figure will appear in some formats. For the color version, please refer to the plate section.)

At 1.5 years, between-city comparisons of DSRS scores: a > b > c ($P < 0.001$).

At five years, between-city comparisons of DSRS scores: a' > c' ($P < 0.001$).

Within-city by time comparison of DSRS scores: b' > b ($P < 0.05$).

DSRS scores of the Spitak and Yerevan groups compared to their baseline scores, while PTSD scores had dropped significantly in the three cities (Figure 4.1). The mean DSRS score in Spitak at five years was 20, above the cut-off for clinical depression of 17, while the score for Gumri was 16.8, just below the cut-off. The rates of clinical depression (e.g., major depression, dysthymic disorder, and adjustment disorder) at 1.5 and five years were as follows: Spitak 76% and 68% (respectively); Gumri 31% and 44% (Figure 4.6).

In mild disasters, those who have PTSD are generally the more vulnerable individuals, (e.g., individuals with pre-existing psychological problems, low education, family history of anxiety, loss of family members, female gender, genetically vulnerable, etc.). However, when the trauma is very severe, a larger proportion of the population will succumb regardless of the presence of known pre-existing vulnerability. The more traumatized population of Spitak had the highest rate of PTSD and the highest mean PTSD-RI scores compared to the lesser traumatized groups of Gumri, followed by the Yerevan group.

These studies showed that mean PTSD-RI scores followed a dose-response relation at 1.5 and five years even though PTSD symptoms had subsided in the three cities at five years. At 1.5 and five years, depression also followed a dose–response relation; however, at five years the pattern had changed. There was a significant increase in depression in the Gumri group, while there were non-significant increases in the other two groups. The cause for early depression may have been multifactorial, directly related to the earthquake trauma, losses (human and material), severe injuries, loss of social connectivity, the break-up of families, housing shortages, and PTSD symptoms. The increase of depression at five years cannot be attributed to PTSD symptoms which had subsided in the three cities at five years. The most significant increase of depression was in Gumri, where the adverse conditions were more dismal than in Spitak and Yerevan.

## 4.4  PTSD and Depression at Twenty-Five-Year Follow-Up

## 4.4.1  PTSD at 1.5, Five, and Twenty-Five Years Post-Earthquake

Figure 4.3 shows the mean PTSD-RI scores at 1.5, five, and twenty-five year follow-ups. There was a significant decrease in PTSD-RI scores in the Spitak group at both follow-up periods. In Gumri, there was a significant decrease at the five-year follow-up. However, at twenty-five years, there was no significant difference between the five-year and twenty-five-year follow-up scores (35.7 vs. 36.1). Between-group comparisons showed that the Spitak group scores were significantly higher than the Gumri group scores at 1.5 and five years. But at twenty-five years, there was no significant difference between the two groups even though the Spitak scores were slightly higher (Gumri = 36.1; Spitak = 39.3). These latter scores translate into experiencing PTSD symptoms one to two times a week. Also, at twenty-five years, there was no significant difference between the mean PCL-5 scores of Spitak and Gumri not treated groups (Gumri = 33.2 vs. Spitak = 31.5).

### Discussion

As with the PTSD-RI scores, the mean PCL-5 scores at twenty-five years did not significantly differ between the Spitak and Gumri not treated groups (Gumri = 33.2 vs. Spitak = 31.5).

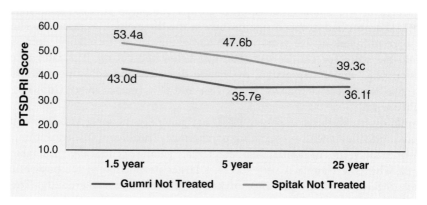

**Figure 4.3** PTSD-RI scores at 1.5, five, and twenty-five years post-earthquake among not treated subjects from Gumri and Spitak. (A black- and- white version of this figure will appear in some formats. For the color version, please refer to the plate section.)

Within-group comparisons of PTSD-RI scores: a > b ($P = 0.01$); b > c ($P = 0.01$); d > e ($P = 0.005$); e ≈ f (n.s.); a > c ($P < 0.001$); d > f ($P = 0.002$).
Between-group comparisons of PTSD-RI scores: a > d ($P < 0.001$); b > e ($P < 0.001$); c ≈ f (n.s.).

At both follow-up periods, the scores for both groups showed that symptoms continued throughout early adolescence into adulthood, suggesting that interventions were indicated at multiple intervals post-disaster.

Figure 4.4 shows the convergence of the plotlines of the PTSD rates (based on PTSD-RI) for the two groups between five and twenty-five years, similar to the convergence of the plotlines of PTSD-RI scores in Figure 4.3. At 1.5 years, the estimated rate of PTSD in Spitak (55%) was higher than the rate of the Gumri group (35%) commensurate with the severity of the peritraumatic events, including the intensity of the earthquake and multiple powerful

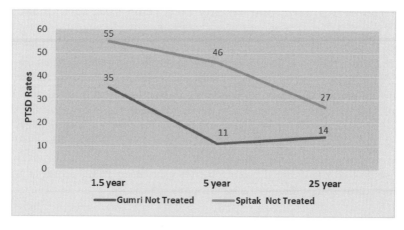

**Figure 4.4** Estimated PTSD rates, based on PTSD-RI, among not treated groups from Gumri and Spitak at 1.5, five, and twenty-five years post-earthquake. (A black- and- white version of this figure will appear in some formats. For the color version, please refer to the plate section.)

aftershocks, pervasive destruction, and high mortality rate. At five-year and twenty-five-year follow-ups, PTSD rates of the Spitak group decreased, while the PTSD rates in Gumri showed a significant decrease at five years, and at twenty-five years, there was a non-significant increase. At twenty-five years, the rates between Gumri and Spitak did not differ significantly, even though Spitak was somewhat higher. This no significant difference between the two groups at twenty-five years was consistent with the severity scores based on the PTSD-RI (Figure 4.3) and PCL-5. For the combined Spitak and Gumri groups, the PTSD rates dropped from an initial 48% to 22% between 1.5 and twenty-five years.

Despite the decrease in the PTSD rates between 1.5 and twenty-five years, a substantial portion of the participants in both cities met the criteria for PTSD. These rates indicate a residual burden on the survivors, their families, and society. These rates are comparable to the rate (29%) among students who survived the Aberfan disaster thirty-three years later (Morgan et al., 2003); an avalanche in Iceland (16%) sixteen years later (Thordardotir et al., 2016); and Vietnam war veterans fifteen or more years after the war: 13.7% among Whites, 20.6% among African Americans, and 27.9% among Hispanics (Schlenger et al., 1992).

These studies show that severe traumas, regardless of the type of trauma, may result in severe psychological sequelae. As we indicated earlier, we relied on continuous scores as a better way to monitor change in the clinical status of the survivors. We have also measured rates for cross-comparisons with other studies after disasters that have reported only rates.

In our studies, the dose–response relation did not persist at twenty-five-year follow-up when the severity of PTSD symptoms did not differ significantly between the two groups. The decline of severity scores and rates in the Spitak group between five and twenty-five years (Figures 4.3 and 4.4), and the plateauing of severity scores and rates in Gumri during the same period was associated with relatively more favorable conditions in Spitak. At the twenty-five-year follow-up, participants from Spitak reported experiencing significantly fewer post-earthquake stresses and adversities (e.g., lack of heating, electricity, living space, transportation) (Spitak 73.1% vs. Gumri 90.5%; $P < 0.03$) and fewer post-earthquake traumas compared to the Gumri group (Spitak 38.8% vs. Gumri 54.8%) (Goenjian et al., 2020). The findings in the regression analysis (Table 4.1) indicated that lack of housing and adversities were risk factors for PTSD at twenty-five years, while social support was a protective factor.

The faster removal of destroyed structures (i.e., trauma reminders), and the building of new apartments, a social center, a park, a theater, and a church were meaningful for a small city like Spitak. These changes helped reduce reactions to trauma reminders, reduced the housing shortage, enhanced social gatherings and activities, and improved people's morale. The then-new mayor of Spitak, who had succeeded an ineffective one, was credited for the better management of public affairs, including the rebuilding of the city. He held government workers accountable and was lauded with reducing corruption. Compared to Gumri, city-wide, there was less unemployment and poverty in Spitak (Statistical Committee of the Republic of Armenia, 2015).

The present results among adolescents extend prior shorter-term findings among adults. For example, after the 2008 Hurricane Ike, (Cerda et al. 2013) assessed adult survivors three times over an eighteen-month period. Ongoing post-hurricane daily stresses were associated with PTSD symptoms and functional impairment at the second (three to seven months after the first interview) and third interview (seven to twelve months after the second interview), but not the initial interview (two to five months after the hurricane). Norris et al. (1999), in a study among adults six and thirty months after the 1993 Hurricane Andrew, found that the initial measures of background characteristics, stresses, and resources were relatively good predictors of symptom severity but relatively poor predictors of clinical change. Whether an individual's symptoms remained stable, improved, or worsened had more to do with subsequent stresses and resource levels than with earlier stresses and resources.

## 4.4.2 Change in Mean B, C, and D Category Scores between 1.5 and Twenty-Five Years after the Earthquake

To better understand the course of PTSD symptoms, we investigated the change in mean PTSD-RI-derived B, C, and D category scores. Figure 4.5 shows the mean change in B, C, and D category scores, between 1.5 and twenty-five years, among not treated subjects from Gumri and Spitak. The Spitak group scores showed a greater drop in all three categories. The drops across the three categories in Spitak were similar (B = 0.49, C = 0.55, D = 0.52). The Gumri group showed a drop of B and C category scores and only a minuscule drop in the D category scores. The between-group comparisons showed that the C category change in Gumri was similar to the Spitak group, but the B category was less so.

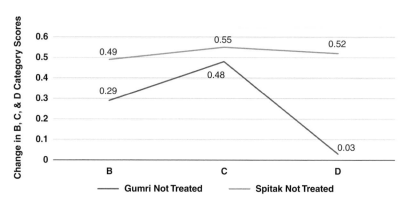

**Figure 4.5** Change in mean B, C, and D category scores between 1.5 and twenty-five years post-earthquake among not treated participants from Spitak and Gumri. (A black- and- white version of this figure will appear in some formats. For the color version, please refer to the plate section.)

**Discussion**

Figure 4.5 shows the changes in mean B, C, and D category scores between 1.5 and twenty-five years after the Spitak earthquake. The changes in B and D category scores were significantly greater for the Spitak group. There was no significant difference in the change of C category scores. The faster removal of trauma reminders (destroyed homes, schools, workplaces) in Spitak may explain the greater drop in B category scores. In contrast, up to the twenty-five-year study, throughout Gumri, the destroyed structures, dilapidated make-shift homes, and abandoned wagons used as residences were constant distressing reminders of the earthquake (Figure 4.7).

As described above, the construction of social centers, a church, apartments in the center of the city, and reconstruction of an open recreational area in Spitak, made a meaningful impact in this small city. It enhanced constructive social gatherings (e.g., playing sports) and promoted mutual support. These pro-social settings promoted positive interactions among the youth and likely contributed to the greater drop of D category symptoms, such as reckless behavior and inappropriate expression of anger.

Regarding C category symptoms, improvement occurred in both groups. One reason may have been the ethos of the culture that encourages frequent gatherings (e.g., celebrations) of friends and family members. This lifestyle may have exerted collective pressure on individuals to refrain from isolation.

## 4.4.3   Age and PTSD

### Children Six to Seven Years Old versus Nine to Ten Years Old at the Time of the Earthquake

In a study on moral development among adolescents 6.5 years post-earthquake, the mean PTSD-RI score among sixteen-year-old students from Spitak (the high earthquake exposure group) was 40.9, while among the thirteen-year-old students, the score was lower (35.9) (Goenjian et al., 1999). Among students from Yerevan (the control group with mild exposure), the mean score for the sixteen-year-old group was 30.6, and for the thirteen-year-old group, it was also lower (22.8).

This pattern of lower scores among thirteen-year-old students vs. the sixteen-year-olds suggests that as six- and seven-year-old children (at the time of the earthquake), these thirteen-year-old students may have been less affected by the trauma of the earthquake and/or post-earthquake adversities than the sixteen-year-old students who were nine to ten years old during the earthquake.

In a ten-year review article of eighteen studies among children and adolescents exposed to the catastrophic Wenchuan earthquake, Liang et al. (2019) found "older age or senior grade" survivors to be at higher risk for PTSD. The younger children may have been less vulnerable to the earthquake or subsequent adversities than older children due to psychological or neurobiological factors or due to parents being more nurturing and protective of the younger children. As a result, they may have been less affected by post-disaster adversities and recovered faster. Longitudinal studies are necessary to disentangle whether younger children are less vulnerable or equally vulnerable as older children but recover faster.

### Comparison of PTSD Symptoms Two Decades after the Earthquake among Those Who Were Early Adolescents and Those Who Were Adults during the Earthquake

The long-term differential effect of trauma on adults vs. children and adolescents is an important area that has not been investigated adequately. The consensus has been that children are more vulnerable to trauma than adults. The present findings extend shorter-term findings. Comparison of the mean PCL-5 scores, from a prior twenty-three-year follow-up study of survivors from Gumri and Spitak who were adults at the time of the earthquake (Goenjian et al., 2018), with the PCL-5 scores of the not-treated adolescents at the twenty-five-year follow-up, showed a differential effect of age at the time of exposure. Those who were early adolescents at the time of exposure showed significantly higher mean PCL scores at follow-up (Spitak M = 31.5; Gumri M = 33.2) compared to those who were adults at the time of exposure (Spitak M = 25.3; Gumri M = 19.7) ($P < 0.01$ for both cites). The results suggest that, compared to adults exposed to the earthquake, early adolescents exposed to the earthquake were at higher risk for PTSD. The increased vulnerability of these adolescents may be due to neurobiological (De Bellis and Zisk, 2014) and/or psychological factors, e.g., due to a lack of experience with facing and overcoming hardships and a comparatively smaller coping repertoire.

## 4.4.4 Depression Severity Scores and Rates 1.5, Five, and Twenty-Five Years Post-Earthquake

### Severity Scores for Depression

At 1.5 and five years, the DSRS (a child and adolescent instrument) was used to measure the severity of depression (Figure 4.2), while at twenty-five-year follow-up, the CES-D (an adult instrument) was used in place of the DSRS scale which had not been validated among adults. At 1.5 years, the mean DSRS score for the Spitak group was significantly higher than the Gumri group (Spitak 19 vs. Gumri 14.2; $P < 0.01$). At five years, the mean DSRS scores had gone up for both groups (Spitak 20; Gumri 16.8). The increase was significant for the Gumri group ($P < 0.05$). At twenty-fiveyears, the Spitak group mean CES-D score had reversed direction. It was significantly lower than the Gumri group score (Spitak 13.6 vs. Gumri 20.7; $P < 0.01$).

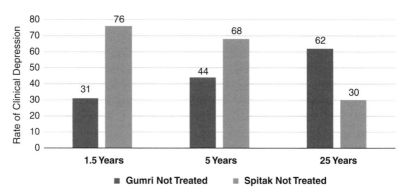

**Figure 4.6** Estimated rates of clinical depression among not treated groups from Gumri and Spitak at 1.5, five, and twenty-five years post-earthquake. (A black- and- white version of this figure will appear in some formats. For the color version, please refer to the plate section.)

### Rates of Clinical Depression

The estimated rates for clinical depression at 1.5 and five years post-earthquake were higher for the Spitak not treated group (Figure 4.6). However, at twenty-five years, the rate for the Spitak group was lower than the rate for the Gumri not treated group (Spitak 30% vs. Gumri 62%). The higher rates in Gumri at twenty-five years were attributed mainly to more adversities and post-earthquake traumas compared to the Spitak group.

### Discussion

The majority of studies after natural disasters among children and adolescents have focused on PTSD. Few have assessed depression, and even fewer monitored its course. In a comprehensive review article among children and adolescents, Lai et al. (2014) found only twenty-seven studies (38% of the seventy-two studies examined) reported prevalence rates of depression in their sample. The prevalence rates ranged from 2% to 69%. Regarding risk factors, no single risk factor profile emerged for developing depressive symptoms. Possible risk factors explored included female gender, exposure variables, and severity of PTSD symptoms.

In one of the few longer-term studies, Green et al. (1994) found the rate of major depression was 33%, two years after the Buffalo Creek disaster. At a seventeen-year follow-up, the rate was 13%. Liu et al. (2011) assessed children (grades 3 to 5) six and twelve months after the powerful Sichuan earthquake. The prevalence rates for depression at the two time-points were 14.5% and 16.1%. In another study after the Wenchuan earthquake, Zhang et al. (2012) found the rates of moderate depression among adolescents were 39.4%, 36.9%, and 29.4% at six, twelve, and eighteen months after the earthquake. Three months after the Pranitha earthquake using the DSRS (same instruments as used in Armenia), Roussos et al. (2005) found the rate of clinical depression was 3.9%, and at thirty-two-month follow-up it was 3.6% (Goenjian et al., 2011).

As with PTSD-RI scores, the DSRS scores at 1.5 years after the earthquake followed a dose–response relation (Figure 4.2). The Spitak group had the highest mean DSRS score, followed by the Gumri group and then the Yerevan group. The mean score for Spitak (18.7) was above the cut-off for clinical depression ($\geq 17$), while in Gumri, it was below the cut-off, followed by Yerevan. However, unlike PTSD severity scores, which had subsided at five years, the mean DSRS score in Gumri, had increased significantly (Figure 4.2). And at twenty-five years, the pattern had reversed; the mean CES-D scores and the rates of depression (Figure 4.6) were higher in the Gumri group compared to the Spitak group which were higher at 1.5 and five years. Dose–response relation of the earthquake trauma (death and destruction) had dissipated at twenty-five years (rates: Spitak 30% vs. Gumri 62%; mean CES-D scores: Spitak 13.6 vs. Gumri 20.7 ($P < 0.01$)).

A disparate recovery environment between the two cities best explained the divergence of the rates in Figure 4.6, which shows an increase in depression rates in Gumri and a decrease in depression rates in Spitak between five and twenty-five years. The increase of depression in Gumri is unlikely due to earthquake-related PTSD severity, which had plateaued by five years after the earthquake while depression was increasing. The Spitak group had experienced fewer adversities and post-earthquake traumas, as noted earlier (Goenjian et al., 2018). In short, city-wide conditions had improved at a faster pace in Spitak. The reconstruction proceeded at a faster pace. Housing shortages decreased, pro-social activities increased, and unemployment and poverty were less (Statistical Committee of the Republic of Armenia, 2015). These favorable changes were reflected in the lower CES-D scores at twenty-five years. Meanwhile, the negative conditions in Gumri continued and impeded recovery and contributed to the persistence or increase of depression.

The significant increase of depressive symptoms in Gumri and their persistence in Spitak was problematic for an already burdened community with high unemployment, poverty, and lack of resources for subsistence. These findings two decades after the earthquake indicate the importance of monitoring depression early on after disasters, in addition to monitoring PTSD symptoms. Such findings constitute a public mental health problem that requires intervention for both moderate or severe PTSD and depressive symptoms. Both conditions can significantly interfere with functioning (e.g., interpersonal, social, academic, and work) and increase the risk of substance abuse, aggressive behavior, and suicide.

Our findings confirm and extend prior shorter-term findings among adults. Between three and four years after the 2009 Black Saturday fires in Australia, Bryant et al. (2018) found that post-disaster stresses contributed to worsening PTSD and depression. The relative impact of ongoing stress may increase as time passes by the creation of a vicious cycle (e.g., disability due to depression and PTSD may alienate support systems, compound financial losses, lead to break-up of relations, and create problems in the workplace that can further exacerbate depression and impede recovery from PTSD).

A review of the literature on depression after disasters among youth by Lai et al. (2014) suggests that depression may arise secondary to PTSD symptoms. The authors raised the yet unsettled question of whether depression occurs as a symptom secondary to PTSD or whether depression develops independently of PTSD symptoms. Cheng et al., 2018 analyzed the course of depression vis-à-vis PTSD and identified two stages. The model showed a mutual effect between PTSD and depressive symptoms during the early period (up to 2.5 years), whereas the depressogenic model was supported during the later period (up to four years). The results showed that the stability of depressive symptoms tended to increase over time, while the stability of PTSD symptoms tended to subside.

Our findings extend the findings of Lai et al. (2014) and Cheng et al. (2018). Initially, PTSD symptoms were primarily associated with the extensive traumatic experiences (e.g., destruction, traumatic deaths) and depression associated with both traumatic experiences and the multiple types of losses (e.g., deaths, material, freedom, prospects, the break-up of families). At twenty-five years, PTSD and depressive symptoms in Spitak had decreased significantly, while in Gumri, PTSD symptoms plateaued after five years, while depression increased. Even though chronic PTSD may contribute to the persistence of depressive symptoms, these findings indicated that with time, variables other than PTSD symptoms (which had plateaued) contributed to the increase of depressive symptoms such as post-earthquake adversities, chronic medical illnesses, and post-earthquake traumas that may have exacerbated depressive symptoms. It is also noteworthy that the post-earthquake adversities had a greater impact on depressive symptoms than on PTSD symptoms. Future prospective studies should consider including contemporaneous measurements of potential risk factors for both PTSD and depression. Such data can be helpful in understanding the interplay of these risk factors and their causal role in the course of PTSD and depression.

## 4.5 The Best Predictors of PTSD Symptoms at Twenty-Five-Year Follow-Up

Table 4.1 shows the best predictors of PTSD symptoms at twenty-five years. Seven variables that predicted 36% of the variance for PTSD-RI at twenty-five years included: home destruction at the time of the earthquake; PTSD-RI severity at 1.5 years post-earthquake; treatment at 1.5 years; post-earthquake adversities; post-earthquake chronic illnesses; social support by family and friends; and female gender. Four variables predicted 33% of PCL-5 scores at twenty-five years. These included treatment, post-earthquake adversities, chronic illnesses, and social support.

**Table 4.1** Best predictors of PTSD-RI and PCL-5 scores in the final model of the regression analysis at twenty-five years post-earthquake
Reprinted from *Psychological Medicine*, January 2020.

| Best predictors in the final model | B | β | P |
|---|---|---|---|
| **PTSD-RI at 25 years** | F(6,127) = 9.98, P < .001, R² = .36 | | |
| 1. Home destruction | −3.826 | −.146 | .055 |
| 2. PTSD-RI at 1.5 years | .263 | .212 | .005 |
| 3. Treatment | 4.898 | .250 | .032 |
| 4. Post-EQ adversities | −8.128 | −.250 | .001 |
| 5. Post-EQ chronic illnesses | 1.877 | .224 | .003 |
| 6. Social support | −.415 | −.265 | < .001 |
| 7. Sex | 3.606 | .138 | .059 |
| 8. Nuclear family deaths | | | |
| 9. Severe injuries due to EQ | | | |
| 10. Post-EQ trauma | | | |
| 11. DSRS at 1.5 years | | | |
| 12. SAD at 1.5 years | | | |
| 13. Education | | | |
| **PCL score at 25 years** | F(4,127) = 15.78, P < .001, R² = .33 | | |
| 1. Home destruction | | | |
| 2. PTSD-RI at 1.5 years | | | |
| 3. Treatment | 6.542 | .192 | .009 |
| 4. Post-EQ adversities | −5.186 | −.140 | .053 |
| 5. Post-EQ chronic illnesses | 3.396 | .354 | < .001 |
| 6. Social support | −.526 | −.294 | < .001 |
| 7. Sex | | | |
| 8. Nuclear family deaths | | | |
| 9. Severe injuries due to EQ | | | |
| 10. Post-EQ trauma | | | |
| 11. DSRS at 1.5 years | | | |

CES-D = Center for Epidemiologic Studies – Depression; EQ = earthquake; PCL = PTSD checklist; PTSD-RI = post-traumatic stress disorder-reaction index; SAD = separation anxiety disorder.
Reference groups for the regression analyses included: no home destruction, treatment group, no adversities, no death, no injury. For continuous variables such as chronic medical illnesses, social support +/- values should be interpreted in the same manner as +/- values in correlations.

## 4.6  Best Predictors of Depressive Symptoms at Twenty-Five-Year Follow-Up

Table 4.2 shows the best predictors for depression (CES-D scores) at twenty-five years. These variables predicted 40% of the variance of CES-D. The predictors included home destruction, post-earthquake adversities, post-earthquake chronic illnesses, post-earthquake trauma, separation anxiety disorder severity, and social support by family and friends.

Multiple studies conducted among children and adolescents have identified various predictors of PTSD, e.g., sex, race, education, pre-existing psychiatric conditions, prior history of trauma, family history of psychopathology, level of education, trauma-related injury, death toll, personal losses, and social support (Furr et al., 2010; Terasaka et al., 2015). In a review article of studies among youth and adults, Galea et al. (2005) reported that the most consistently documented determinant of risk for PTSD across studies was the magnitude of the exposure to the event. In a study among youth in Nicaragua six months after Hurricane Mitch, we found the strongest predictor of PTSD-RI score was the severity of the hurricane's impact, accounting for 47% of the variance (Goenjian et al., 2001). Similarly, in our 1.5-year study, the level of exposure to the earthquake was the strongest predictor of the severity of PTSD symptoms (Goenjian et al., 1995). The highest severity of PTSD was in Spitak (53.1), the most severely impacted city, followed by Gumri (41.1) and then Yerevan

**Table 4.2** The best predictors of CES-D scores in the final model of the regression analysis at twenty-five years post-earthquake

| Best predictors in the final model CES-D score at 25 years | B | β | p |
|---|---|---|---|
| | $F(6,128) = 14.08, P < .001, R^2 = .40$ | | |
| 1. Home destruction | −3.160 | −.131 | .065 |
| 2. PTSD-RI at 1.5 years | | | |
| 3. Treatment | | | |
| 4. Post-EQ adversities | −6.785 | −.226 | .002 |
| 5. Post-EQ chronic illnesses | 2.798 | .362 | < .001 |
| 6. Social support | −.420 | −.290 | < .001 |
| 7. Sex | | | |
| 8. Nuclear family deaths | | | |
| 9. Severe injuries due to EQ | | | |
| 10. Post-EQ trauma | .880 | .120 | .093 |
| 11. DSRS at 1.5 years | | | |
| 12. SAD at 1.5 years | .791 | .155 | .026 |
| 13. Education | | | |

Reprinted from *Psychological Medicine*, January 2020.
CES-D = Center for Epidemiologic Studies – Depression; EQ = earthquake; PCL = PTSD checklist; PTSD-RI = post-traumatic stress disorder-reaction index; SAD = separation anxiety disorder.Reference groups for the regression analysis included: no home destruction, treatment group, no adversities, no death, no injury.

(34.7), the least severely impacted city. At twenty-five years, there was no significant difference in both PTSD-RI and PCL scores between the Gumri and Spitak groups.

The above regression analysis indicates that post-earthquake adversities had a greater impact on the twenty-five-year PTSD-RI severity score than did baseline PTSD-RI scores, which were congruous with the severity of earthquake trauma. With time, post-earthquake risk factors such as adversities, post-earthquake traumas, and lack of social support had become more important determinants of PTSD symptom severity than the initial exposure. The regression analysis also shows that loss of home was a risk factor for both PTSD and depression. This finding is consistent with our twenty-three-year follow-up study among those who were adults at the time of the earthquake. In comparing two groups that had lost their homes, the group that received housing assistance did significantly better than the group that did not receive assistance by 6 points on the PCL-5 scale (Goenjian et al., 2018). As reported previously in numerous studies, female gender appeared to be a risk factor for both PTSD and depression; however, the question remains as to whether this finding is due to females being simply more willing to express their symptoms.

Higher levels of current social support were inversely related to PTSD-RI and CES-D scores at twenty-five years. The association of PTSD symptoms and social support extends prior findings among adults in this population (Goenjian et al., 2018) and children after other disasters (Udwin et al., 2000; Mcdermott et al., 2012; Thordarottir et al., 2016). The association of PTSD and social support may be bi-directional (Kaniasty and Norris, 2008; Platt et al., 2016), where ongoing social support may contribute to the resolution of PTSD symptoms, while ongoing severity of PTSD symptoms may alienate sources of social support. The bi-directionality of social support may also apply to depression. Future prospective

**Figure 4.7** Gumri 1997, a destroyed building, one of many, next to makeshift homes. (A black- and- white version of this figure will appear in some formats. For the color version, please refer to the plate section.)

studies assessing the relation of various types and extent of social support with PTSD and depression may provide helpful information for the treatment of PTSD and depression.

McDermott et al. (2012) assessed the association of social connectedness and PTSD among youth three months after the 2006 category-5 Cyclone Larry in Queensland, Australia. The results showed that low-connected children were almost four times more likely to experience severe to very severe PTSD. This finding suggests that identifying poorly connected children with low social support may present an opportunity for targeted intervention.

## 4.7 The Best Predictors of Post-Earthquake Chronic Medical Illness

The variables included in the regression analysis for the best predictors of chronic medical illness since the earthquake included the following independent variables: sex, education, severe injury sustained at the time of the earthquake, adversities since the earthquake, baseline PTSD-RI and DSRS severity scores, social support, post-earthquake trauma, and PCL-5 score at twenty-five years. Overall, the severity of PTSD symptoms at twenty-five-year follow-up and education were the best predictors of chronic medical illness, contributing to 26% of the variance. With few exceptions, such as childhood asthma, almost all of the illnesses endorsed by the participants were manifested during adulthood. This finding is consistent with the twenty-three-year follow-up study among those who were adults at the time of the earthquake. Chronic medical illness was a predictor of PCL severity (Goenjian et al., 2018). In a four-year follow-up study among adult survivors of the Spitak earthquake, Armenian et al. (1998) found an increase in heart disease, newly reported hypertension, diabetes, and arthritis among survivors.

With respect to these findings, chronic PTSD may have caused physiologic changes (e.g., in the limbic-hypothalamic-pituitary-adrenal axis (LHPA), sympathetic-adrenal-medullary (SAM), and immune systems), and increased the risk for chronic illnesses such as immunological and cardiovascular disorders (Boscarino 2005; DeBellis 2014). Alternatively, chronic medical problems may have interfered with remission of PTSD symptoms (e.g., causing irritability, insomnia, problems with concentration and attention), difficulties in working and participating in social activities. The finding of long-term health problems underscores the importance of monitoring survivors of disasters with moderate or severe PTSD and depressive symptoms for chronic medical illnesses in addition to psychological sequelae. Early treatment for PTSD and depression may avert or minimize the onset or progression of chronic medical illnesses.

The association of higher levels of education with a lower likelihood of experiencing chronic illness may have been due to subjects being more knowledgeable about health issues, increased detection of signs of disease early on, the timely use of medical services, and, in general, living a healthier lifestyle. Further research is needed to investigate the relationship between physiologic changes related to PTSD and the onset and exacerbation of chronic medical illnesses.

## 4.8 Loss of One or Both Parents and Depression

Six-and-a-half years after the Spitak earthquake, parentally bereaved adolescents and a comparison group with no parental loss from the city of Gumri were evaluated (Goenjian et al., 2009). Orphans scored significantly higher on the depression scale than those who lost

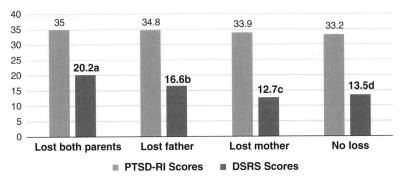

**Figure 4.8** Mean PTSD-RI and DSRS scores for not treated early adolescents who lost one or both parents during the earthquake and the control group without parental loss 6.5 years after the Spitak earthquake. Data from the *Journal of Affective Disorders*, 2008. (A black- and- white version of this figure will appear in some formats. For the color version, please refer to the plate section.)
Bonferroni post-hoc test results: *a* > *b*, *c*, and *d* scores (all Ps < 0.001); *b* > *c* and *d* scores (P < 0.002).

a father, who in turn scored significantly higher than those who lost a mother (Mean DSRS scores: orphans 20.2 > loss of father 16.6 > loss of mother 12.7) (Figure 4.8). Depression scores for orphans fell above the cut-off for clinical depression of 17. PTSD scores within each group fell in the moderate range of severity, with no significant difference between the groups.

## 4.8.1 Loss of Parents, PTSD, and Depression

In the 1.5-year follow-up study among early adolescents (Goenjian et al., 1995), there was a significant correlation between the extent of loss of nuclear family members and DSRS scores (r = 0.38, P < 0.05) and a weaker correlation with PTSD-RI scores (r = 0.22, P < 0.05). At 6.5-year follow-up, bereaved orphans, and to a lesser degree, those who had lost a father, were at risk for clinical depression. However, PTSD severity did not differ between the three bereaved groups and the control group who had the same level of trauma exposure. This finding suggests that the primary determinant for PTSD severity was the severity of exposure to the earthquake, which was similar for these adolescents and had subsided in intensity over the ensuing six years. The loss of parents may have had a lesser effect on PTSD during the first few years after the earthquake, which may have subsided with time, but the effect on depression persisted. Liu et al. (2019), at five years after the Yushu earthquake, found a significant association between PTSD and bereavement. The severity of exposure to trauma for the bereaved groups and controls was not factored in the analysis. The bereaved group may have been exposed to more severe traumatic experiences that caused the deaths of family members. Teasing the effect of exposure in such analysis would be helpful in distinguishing whether bereavement independently contributed to PTSD severity.

The mean DSRS score for orphans in Gumri (20.2) fell above the cut-off for clinical depression (≥ 17). Such levels of depressive symptoms carry increased risk for major impairments in adolescence, e.g., a decline in academic performance (Van Eerdewegh et al., 1982; Harris 1991, Liu et al., 2019), disrupted interpersonal functioning (Harris

1991), and in adulthood, e.g., maladjustment, major depressive disorder, dysthymia, and problem drinking (Lewinson et al., 1999; Aalto-Setala et al., 2002).

The finding of a higher level of depression among those who lost a father compared to those who lost a mother may be related to the greater security and economic losses associated with the loss of a father. In the case of a mother's death, fathers in Armenia usually re-marry, or extended family members (aunts and grandmothers) take on the surrogate mother role. These factors may make the transition easier for those who lost a mother. In the case of a father's death, mothers re-marry less frequently than widowed fathers. The child may be deprived of a father figure, and the mother ends up with the burden of caring for the family (emotionally and financially). She may develop depressive symptoms, which in turn can have an additional negative impact on the child.

## 4.9 Separation Anxiety

The prevalence rate of Separation Anxiety Disorder (SAD) among early adolescents during the 1.5 years after the earthquake across the three cities also exhibited a dose–response relation (Spitak, 49%; Gumri, 39%; Yerevan, 23%; (Chi-Square = 9.32, df = 2, $P < 0.01$). At 1.5 years, diagnosis of current SAD was 7% in Spitak, 6% in Gumri, and 3% in Yerevan. Symptoms included worrying about something bad happening to their parents or them; refusing to go to school because they were afraid something bad would happen to their parents or loved ones; being upset to be left alone in a room; when leaving home experiencing stomachache, headache, nausea or vomiting; and missing school for two weeks because they did not want to leave their parent or leave the house.

Separation anxiety disorder symptoms at baseline predicted depression at twenty-five years. Many of the early adolescents in the aftermath of the earthquake were fearful of something bad happening to them again or to their caregivers and, as a result, avoided separation from them by refusing to go to school (Goenjian et al., 1995). Genetic vulnerabilities may also play a partial explanatory role. A multigenerational family study from Gumri after the earthquake found a significant genetic correlation between anxiety symptoms and depression ($r_g$ 0.54), indicating pleiotropy (shared genetic vulnerability) (Goenjian et al., 2008). This shared genetic vulnerability may have contributed to the predictive value of SAD in predicting depression. Future studies should assess SAD symptoms longitudinally to determine whether SAD symptoms manifest during adulthood as other forms of anxiety or depression and how much the baseline SAD affects daily functioning, such as social, familial, and academic, over time.

## 4.10 Quality of Life

In addition to measuring pathological conditions such as PTSD and depression, it is important to also assess the general well-being of survivors using available instruments. In the past two decades, there has been a shift in mental health services from an emphasis on treatment focused on reducing symptoms, based on a narrow conception of health and disease, to a more holistic approach that considers both well-being and the functioning of an individual. Quality of Life (QOL) instruments have been used to measure the overall well-being, recovery, social functioning, and life satisfaction of an individual. They provide another perspective on the sequelae after natural disasters.

Three months after the 1999, 6.0-magnitude Parnitha earthquake (also known as The Athens and Ano Liosia earthquake) struck Greece, in collaboration with the Ministry of

Health and Social Welfare of Greece and Attiki Child Psychiatric Hospital, we conducted a school-wide survey of 1,685 students from the city of Ano Liosia, the epicenter of the earthquake, and 252 students from a less affected city of Daffni located 10 km from the epicenter (Roussos et al., 2005). Thirty-two months after the earthquake, we conducted a follow-up study among 549 students from the original group from Ano Liosia who were still in school (Goenjian et al., 2011). In addition to PTSD and depression, we investigated quality of life (QOL).

The Quality of Life Questionnaire (QOLQ) included twenty-four items related to family relations, social interactions, anxiety/somatic complaints, alcohol-/drug-related academic problems, and risk-taking behavior. The total QOLQ score and its five domain scores were significantly correlated with PTSD-RI and DSRS scores ($P < 0.01$). The independent variables that best predicted total QOLQ score at thirty-two months included the DSRS scores at three months accounting for 16% of the variance, followed by loss of employment by a family member or financial problems in the family (5%), followed by the level of education (3%), and having been seriously injured or ill since the earthquake (3%). Together the variables accounted for 27% of the total variance. These findings indicate that the QOL measures can provide important information regarding the post-disaster psychosocial lives of adolescents, complementing the symptom measures for PTSD and depression, and serve as a useful tool to monitor the course of recovery.

## 4.11 Summary

Some key findings and lessons learned from the work described in this chapter include:

- During the first five years after the earthquake, the severity of earthquake-related exposure was the best predictor of PTSD symptoms, exemplified by a dose–response relation at 1.5 and five years follow-up (Spitak > Gumri > Yerevan).
- At twenty-five-year follow-up, the dose–response relation of depression and PTSD observed at 1.5 years had abated. At 1.5 years, the mean depression and PTSD severity scores were higher for the Spitak group, but at twenty-five years the depression severity score for the Gumri group was higher, and there was no significant difference in the PTSD severity scores between the two groups.
- The use of a dose-of-exposure design in collecting data on the mental health impact across age and exposure groups can be vital during the early years after a disaster in guiding planners to identify at-risk groups and allocating resources accordingly, especially in areas where resources may be scarce.
- Substantial levels of PTSD and clinical depression found in subgroups of the participants at twenty-five years post-earthquake represents an important public mental health problem. In addressing chronic cases, mental health recovery programs should include ongoing surveillance for the post-earthquake onset of traumatic experiences, prolonged grief reactions, and chronic medical illnesses. Recovery programs need to monitor these clinical conditions over multiple time points, accompanied by intervention strategies.
- The findings also strongly indicate that public mental health recovery programs should strive to mitigate ongoing post-disaster adversities. In so doing, governmental and non-governmental agencies may play a key role in the mental health recovery of survivors. Improvements in the social ecology can foster social interaction (e.g., visits to relatives, participation in community activities).

- The best predictors of twenty-five-year PTSD and depression severity included post-earthquake adversities (e.g., lack of heat, electricity, food, transportation, and congested living conditions), earthquake-related loss of home, PTSD-RI at baseline (for predicting PTSD severity), post-earthquake traumas, chronic medical illnesses, separation anxiety disorder symptoms at baseline (for predicting depression severity), and social support of family and friends (a protective factor for both traits).
- The post-earthquake intervening adversities (stresses) better predicted twenty-five-year follow-up PTSD and depression severity than the baseline PTSD and depression severity.
- The relatively faster improvement of PTSD and depressive symptoms in the Spitak group was attributable to fewer adversities, such as lack of heat, electricity, housing, destroyed buildings (trauma reminders), and post-earthquake traumatic experiences. These favorable conditions were commensurate to the faster rebuilding city-wide, decreased poverty and unemployment.
- These studies indicated that continuous scale scores (e.g., PTSD-RI, PCL, and DSRS scores) provide more sensitive measurements than rates of disorder for monitoring the course of post-disaster reactions. Rates were reported in our studies as they were helpful for cross-comparisons with other studies that have only reported rates.
- Comparison of our findings with those after human-perpetrated traumas indicate that exposure to a catastrophic natural disaster can result in high levels of psychiatric morbidity and that the severity of the mental health impact after a disaster (e.g., earthquake, hurricane, flood, tsunami, typhoon, tornado, etc.) is best described by characterizing specific objective features of exposure (e.g., destruction, morbidity, mortality, witnessing injury and death, being trapped) and subjective features (e.g., fear, helplessness, horror).
- Findings indicated that orphans were at high risk for clinical depression. Recovery programs should identify high-risk bereaved groups who have lost nuclear family members and require special attention for prolonged grief and depressive reactions.
- Six- to seven-year-old children were at lower risk for PTSD compared to nine- to ten-year-old children. Further studies are needed to replicate these results and investigate potential mechanisms by which age may constitute a protective or vulnerability factor.
- The association of chronic PTSD symptoms and the post-earthquake onset of chronic illnesses may be due to the untoward physiological impact of chronic PTSD on health (e.g., alterations in the LHPA-axis, SMA-axis, and immune system) and to the interference of chronic health conditions with the resolution of PTSD symptoms.
- The finding of the interrelation of long-term health problems, PTSD, and depression underscores the importance of monitoring survivors of disasters for both PTSD, depression, and medical illnesses, and suggests that intervention of these domains may have a positive reciprocal effect. Moreover, early treatment for PTSD and depression may avert or minimize the onset or progression of chronic medical illnesses.

## 4.12 Key Recommendations for Disaster Mental Health for Youth

- Schools constitute the most effective and efficient venue for post-disaster screening to ascertain the nature and severity of the impact on children and adolescents and to plan for needed interventions.

- Students should be screened in selected schools sampled from across earthquake exposure levels to better understand features of objective and subjective exposure, along with levels of PTSD, depression, anxiety, and grief reactions. It is advisable to initially screen a small representative sample rather than conduct large-scale school-wide assessments. Only after the physical well-being and safety of survivors have been addressed, should school-wide surveys be implemented to identify those who need assistance.
- Schools also constitute a key venue for delivering post-disaster mental health intervention for affected children, adolescents, their families and school personnel. It is essential to work closely with school principals, teachers, and the school community to facilitate the implementation of both school-based screening and treatment.
- In addressing earthquake-related mental health issues for children and adolescents, recovery programs should include ongoing surveillance that includes assessing current levels of adversities, new onset of traumatic experiences and losses, physical health, quality of life, and school and family functioning.
- Primary care and pediatric settings offer another venue for identifying youth at risk and a referral to a recovery mental health program.
- Mental health recovery programs should find ways to promote social interaction and constructive activities for youth. Enlisting public and private organizations and religious groups to allocate resources for establishing social activity centers for youth and families can be critical to maintaining social connections after a disaster. Public health and housing programs should be encouraged to mitigate ongoing post-disaster adversities (e.g., food, lighting, gas, electricity, transportation) and address housing shortages. Improvements in these areas can also foster social interaction (e.g., visits to relatives, participation in community activities).

# References

Aalto-Setala, T., Marttunen, M., Tuulio-Henriksson, A., Poikolainen, K., & Lonnqvist, J. (2002). Depressive symptoms in adolescence as predictors of early adulthood depressive disorders and maladjustment. *American Journal of Psychiatry*, 159, 1253–1257.

Armenian, H. K., Melkonian, A. K., & Hovanesian, A. P. (1998). Long term mortality and morbidity related to degree of damage following the 1988 earthquake in Armenia. *American Journal of Epidemiology*, 148, 1077–1084. https://doi.org/10.1093/oxfordjournals.aje.a009585.

Asarnow, J. R., & Carlson, G. A. (1985). Depression Self-Rating Scale: Utility with child psychiatric inpatients. *Journal of Consulting and Clinical Psycholgy*, 53, 491–499.

Boscarino, J. A. (2005). Post-traumatic stress disorder and physical illness results from clinical and epidemiologic studies. *Annals of the New York Academy of Sciences*, 1032, 141–153. https://doi.org/10.1196/annals.1314.011" https://doi.org/10.1196/annals.1314.011.

Bryant, R. A., Gibbs L., Gallagher, H. C., Pattison, P., Lusher, D., MacDougall, C., ... Forbes, D. (2018). Longitudinal study of changing psychological outcomes following the Victorian Black Saturday bushfires. *Australian & New Zealand Journal of Psychiatry*, 52(6), 542–551. https://doi.org/10.1177/0004867417714337.

Cheng, J., Liang Y. M., Fua, L., & Liua, Z. K. (2018). Post-traumatic stress and depressive symptoms in children after the Wenchuan Earthquake. *European Journal of Psychotraumatology*, 9, 1472992. https://doi.org/10.1080/20008198.2018.

Cerda, M., Bordelois, P. M., Galea, S., Norris, F., Tracy, M., & Koenen, K. C. (2013). The course of post-traumatic stress symptoms and functional impairment following a disaster: what is the lasting influence of acute vs. ongoing traumatic events and stressors? *Social Psychiatry and Psychiatric Epidemiology*, 48, 385–395.

De Bellis, M. D., & Zisk, A. (2014). The biological effects of childhood trauma. *Child and Adolescent Psychiatric Clinics of North America*, 23(2): 185–222. https://doi.org10.1 016/j.chc.2014.01.002.

Demirchyan, A., Petrosyan, V., & Thompson, M. F. (2011). Psychometric value of the Center for Epidemiologic Studies Depression (CES-D) scale for screening of depressive symptoms in Armenian population. *Journal of Affective Disorders*, 133, 489–498.

Demirchyan, A, Goenjian, A. K., & Khachadourian, V. (2015). Factor structure and psychometric properties of the Posttraumatic Stress Disorder (PTSD) Checklist and DSM-5 PTSD symptom set in a long-term post-earthquake cohort in Armenia. *Assessment*, 22, 594–606.

Dogan, A. (2011) Adolescents' post-traumatic stress reactions and behavior problems following Marmara earthquake. *European Journal of Psychotraumatology*, 2, 10.3402/ ejpt.v2i0.5825. https://doi:10.3402/ejpt.v2i0. 5825.

Furr, J. M., Corner, J. S., Edmunds, J. M., & Kendall, P. C. (2010) Disasters and youth: a meta-analytic examination of post-traumatic stress. *Journal of Consulting and Clinical Psychology*, 78, 765–780.

Galea. S., Nandi, A., & Vlahov, D. (2005). The epidemiology of post-traumatic stress disorder after disasters. *Epidemiologic Reviews*, 27, 78–91.

Gao, X., Leng, Y., Guo, Y., Yang, J., Cui, Q., Geng, B., . . . Zhou Y. (2019). Association between earthquake experience and depression 37 years after the Tangshan earthquake: a cross-sectional study. *BMJ Open*, 9(8), e026110. https://doi.org/10.1136/ bmjopen-2018-026110.

Goenjian, A. K., Pynoos, R. S., Steinberg, A. M., Najarian, L. M., Asarnow, J. R., Karayan, I. . . . Fairbanks, L. A. (1995). Psychiatric co-morbidity in children after the 1988 earthquake in Armenia. *Journal of the*

*American Academy of Child and Adolescent Psychiatry*, 34, 1174–1184.

Goenjian, A. K., Stilwell, B. M., Steinberg, A. M., Fairbanks, L. A., Galvin, M. R., Karayan, I., & Pynoos, R. S. (1999). Moral development and psychopathological interference with conscience functioning after trauma. *Journal of the American Academy of Child and Adolescent Psychiatry*, 38, 376–384.

Goenjian, A. K., Molina, L., Steinberg, A. M., Fairbanks, L. A., Alvarez, M. L., Goenjian, H. A., & Pynoos R. S. (2001). Post-traumatic stress and depressive reactions among Nicaraguan adolescents after Hurricane Mitch. *American Journal of Psychiatry*, 158, 788–794.

Goenjian, A. K., Walling, D., Steinberg, A. M., Karayan, I., Najarian, L. M., & Pynoos, R. S. (2005). A prospective study of post-traumatic stress and depressive reactions among treated and untreated adolescents 5 years after a catastrophic disaster. *American Journal of Psychiatry*, 162, 2302–2308.

Goenjian, A. K., Noble, E. P., Walling, D. P., Goenjian, H. A., Karayan, I., Ritchie, T., & Bailey, J. N. (2008). Heritabilities of symptoms of post-traumatic stress disorder, anxiety, and depression in earthquake-exposed Armenian families. *Psychiatric Genetics*, 18, 261–266.

Goenjian, A. K., Walling, D., Steinberg, A. M., Roussos, A., Goenjian, H. A., & Pynoos, R. S. (2009). Depression and PTSD symptoms among bereaved adolescents 6.5 years after the 1988 Spitak earthquake. *Journal of Affective Disorders*, 112, 81–84.

Goenjian, A. K., Roussos, A., Steinberg, A. M., Sotiropoulou, C., Walling, D., Kakaki, M., & Karagianni, S. (2011). Longitudinal nc study of PTSD, depression and quality of life among adolescents after the Parnitha earthquake. *Journal of Affective Disorders*, 133(3), 509–515.

Goenjian, A., Khachadourian, V., Armenian, H., Demirchyan, A., & Steinberg, A. M. (2018). Post-traumatic stress disorder 23 years after the 1988 Spitak earthquake in Armenia. *Journal of Traumatic Stress*, 31, 47–56.

Goenjian, A., Steinberg, A., Walling, D., Bishop, S., Karayan, I., & Pynoos, R. S. (2020). 25-year follow-up of treated and not-treated adolescents after the Spitak earthquake: course and predictors of PTSD and depression. *Psychological Medicine*, 14, 1–13. Advance online publication. https://doi.org/10.1017/S0033291719003891.

Green, B. L., Grace, M. C., Vary, M. G., Kramer, T. L., Gleser, G. C., & Leonard, A. C. (1994). Children of disaster in the second decade: a 17-year follow-up of Buffalo Creek survivors. *Journal of the American Academy of Child and Adolescent Psychiatry*, 33, 71–79.

Harris, E. S. (1991). Adolescent bereavement following the death of a parent: an exploratory study. *Child Psychiatry and Human Development*, 21(4), 267–281.

John, P. B., Russell, S., & Russell, P. S. (2007) The prevalence of post-traumatic stress disorder among children and adolescents affected by tsunami disaster in Tamil Nadu. *Disaster Management & Response*, 5(1), 3–7.

Kaniasty, K., & Norris, F. H. (2008). Longitudinal linkages between perceived social support and post-traumatic stress symptoms: sequential roles of social causation and social selection. *Journal of Traumatic Stress*, 21, 274–281.

Lai, B. S., Auslander, B. A., Fitzpatrick, S. L., & Podkowirow, V. (2014). Disasters and depressive symptoms in children: a review. *Child & Youth Care Forum*, 43(4), 489–504. https://doi.org/10.1007/s10566-014-9249-y.

Lewinson, P. M., Rohde, P., Klein, D. N., & Seeley, J. R., (1999). Natural course of adolescent major depressive disorder: I. Continuity into young adulthood. *Journal of the American Academy of Child and Adolescent Psychiatry*, 38(1), 56–63.

Liang, Y, Cheng, J, Ruzek, J. I., & Liuc Z. (2018) Posttraumatic stress disorder following the 2008 Wenchuan earthquake: a 10-year systematic review among highly exposed populations in China. *Journal of Affective Disorders*, 243, 327–339. https://doi.org/10.1016/j.jad.2018.09.047.

Liu, M., Wang, L., Shi, Z., Zhang, Z., Zhang, K., & Shen, J. (2011). Mental health problems among children one-year after Sichuan earthquake in China: a follow-up study. *PLoS One*, 6(2), e14706.

Liu, S., Lu, L., Bai, Z., Su, M., Qi, Z., Zhang, S., . . . Lii, K. (2019). Post-traumatic stress and school adaptation in adolescent survivors five years after the 2010 Yushu earthquake in China. *International Journal of Environmental Research and Public Health*, 16(21), 4167. https://doi.org/10.3390/ijerph16214167" https://doi.org/10.3390/ijerph16214167.

McDermott, B., Berry, H., & Cobham, V. (2012). Social connectedness: a potential aetiological factor in the development of child post-traumatic stress disorder. *Australian and New Zealand Journal of Psychiatry*, 46, 109–117.

McDonald, S. D., & Calhoun, P. S. (2010). The diagnostic accuracy of the PTSD checklist: a critical review. *Clinical Psychology Review*, 30, 976–987.

McFarlane, A. C., & Van Hooff, M. (2009). Impact of childhood exposure to a natural disaster on adult mental health: 20-year longitudinal follow-up study. *British Journal of Psychiatry*, 195, 142–148.

Morgan, L., Scourfield, J., Williams, D., Jasper, A., & Lewis, G. (2003). The Aberfan disaster: 33-year follow-up of survivors. *British Journal of Psychiatry*, 182, 532–536.

Najarian, L. M., Goenjian, A. K., Pelcovitz, D., Mandel, F., & Najarian, B. (1996). Relocation after a disaster: post-traumatic stress disorder in Armenia after the earthquake. *Journal of the American Academy of Child & Adolescent Psychiatry*, 35(3), 374–383. https://doi.org/10.1097/00004583-199603000-00020.

Najarian, L. M., Sunday, S., Labruna, V., & Barry, I. (2011). Twenty-year follow-up of adults traumatized during childhood in Armenia. *Journal of Affective Disorder*, 135, 51–55.

Norris, F. H., Perilla, J. L., Riad, J. K., Kaniasty, K., & Lavizzo, E. A. (1999). Stability and change in stress, resources, and psychological distress following natural disaster: findings from Hurricane Andrew. *Anxiety, Stress, and Coping*, 12, 363–396. https://doi.org/10.1080/10615809908249317

Platt, J. M., Lowe, S. R., Galea, S., Norris, F. H, & Koenen, K. C. (2016). A longitudinal study of the bidirectional relationship between social support and post-traumatic stress following a natural disaster. *Journal of Traumatic Stress,* 29, 205–213.

Pynoos, R. S., Goenjian, A., Tashjian, M., Karakashian, M., Manjikian, R., Manoukian, G., . . . Fairbanks, L. A. (1993). Post-traumatic stress reactions in children after the 1988 Armenian earthquake. *British Journal of Psychiatry,* 163, 239–247.

Roussos, A., Goenjian, A. K., Steinberg, A. M., Sotiropoulou, C., Kakaki, M., Kabakos, C., Manouras, V. (2005). Post-traumatic stress and depressive reactions among children and adolescents after the 1999 earthquake in Ano Liosia, Greece. *American Journal of Psychiatry,* 162, 530–537.

Schlenger, W. E., Kulka, R. A., Fairbank, J. A., Hough, R. L., Jordan, B. K., Marmar, C. R., & Weiss, D. S. (1992). The prevalence of post-traumatic stress disorder in the Vietnam generation: a multimethod, multisource assessment of psychiatric disorder. *Journal of Traumatic Stress,* 5, 333–363.

Sharma, A., & Kar, N. (2019). Post-traumatic stress, depression, and coping following the 2015 Nepal earthquake: a study on adolescents. *Disaster Medicine and Public Health Preparedness,* 13, 236–242.

Statistical Committee of the Republic of Armenia: Part 1 – Armenia: Poverty profile in 2008–2015; retrieved from: www.armstat.am/file/article/poverty_2016_eng_2.pdf [last accessed July 16, 2021].

Steinberg, A. M., Brymer, M. J., Decker, K. B., & Pynoos, R. S. (2004). The University of California at Los Angeles Posttraumatic Stress Disorder Reaction Index. *Current Psychiatry Reports,* 6, 96–100.

Steinberg, A. M., Brymer, M. J., Kim, S., Ghosh, C., Ostrowski, S. A., Gulley, K., Briggs, E. C., & Pynoos, R. S. (2013). Psychometric properties of the UCLA PTSD Reaction Index: *Part 1, Journal of Traumatic Stress,* 26, 1–9.

Terasaka, A., Tachibana, Y., Okuyama, M., & Igarashi, T. (2015). Post-traumatic stress disorder in children following natural disasters: a systematic review of the long-term follow-up studies. *International Journal of Child, Youth and Family Studies,* 6, 111–133.

Thordardottir, E. B., Valdimarsdottir, U. A., Hansdottir, I., Hauksdóttir, A., Dyregrov, A., Shipherd, J. C. . . . Gudmundsdottir, B. (2016). Sixteen-year follow-up of childhood avalanche survivors. *European Journal of Psychotraumatology,* 7, 30995. https://doi.org/10.3402/ejpt.v7.30995.

Udwin, O., Boyle, S., Yule, W., Bolton, D., & O'Ryan, D. (2000). Risk factors for long-term psychological effects of a disaster experienced in adolescence: predictors of post-traumatic stress disorder. *Journal of Child Psychology and Psychiatry,* 41, 969–979.

Van Eerdewegh, M. M., Bieri, M. D., Parrilla, R. H., & Clayton, P. J. (1982). The bereaved child. *British Journal of Psychiatry,* 140, 23–29.

Vilagut, G., Forero, C. G., Barbaglia, G., & Alonso, J. (2016). Screening for depression in the general population with the Center for Epidemiologic Studies Depression (CES-D): a systematic review with meta-analysis. *PLoS One,* 11(5), e0155431. https://doi.org/10.1371/journal.pone.0155431.

Wang, C. W., Chan, C. L. W., & Ho, R. T. H. (2013). Prevalence and trajectory of psychopathology among child and adolescent survivors of disasters: a systematic review of epidemiological studies across 1987–2011. *Social Psychiatry and Psychiatric Epidemiology,* 48, 1697–1720.

Zhang, Z., Ran, M. S., Li, Y. H., Ou, G. J., Gong, R. R., Li, R. H., . . . Fang, D. Z. (2012) Prevalence of post-traumatic stress disorder among adolescents after the Wenchuan earthquake in China. *Psychological Medicine,* 42 (8), 1687–1693. https://doi.org/10.1017/S003329 1711002844" https://doi.org/10.1017/S0033291711002844.

Zhou, X., Wu, X., & Zhen, R. (2018). Patterns of post-traumatic stress disorder and post-traumatic growth among adolescents after the Wenchuan earthquake in China: a latent profile analysis. *Journal of Traumatic Stress,* 31, 57–63. https://doi.org/10.1002/jts.22246.

# Conscience, Moral Injury, and Psychopathology

Barbara Stilwell and Matthew Galvin

## 5.1 Conscience Development

We begin this chapter with an abbreviated tour through our empirical findings regarding the development of conscience in children and adolescents. If the reader would like to examine this material at a more leisurely pace, we recommend the book, *Right vs Wrong; Raising a Child with a Conscience* (Stilwell et al., 2000).

### 5.1.1 Conceptualization: The Anchor Domain

The formation of conscience is an intrinsic part of moral development. As values are formed within the dynamics of attachment experiences, and emotions and willpower are organized on behalf of carrying out those values, the processes coalesce into the mental construct of conscience, the moral heart of the personality. Empirical studies with normal youth between the ages of five and seventeen, using a semi-structured instrument, the Stilwell Conscience Interview (SCI) (Stilwell, 2002a), demonstrated a five-stage hierarchical progression in how this sample of youth defined and understood their personal conscience (Stilwell et al., 1991). The instrument consists of fifteen open-ended questions to which the youth responded with great interest. A sample question is as follows: "When you have done something that displeases your conscience, what happens on the inside of you? How does it show on the outside."

In a nutshell, the hierarchical progression within this age range moves from an *external stage*, during which young children believe *right or wrong* to be what adults tell them to do or not do; to a *brain/heart stage* during which children (ages seven to eleven), begin to incorporate moral rules to be carried out in literal fashion; to a *personified stage* (ages twelve to thirteen) during which the conscience becomes an internal entity with whom one can process moralized feelings, values, and behavior; to a *confused stage* (ages fourteen to fifteen) during which the mid-adolescent struggles with multiple sources of moral authority; to an *integrated stage* (ages sixteen to seventeen) during which the older adolescent is able to recognize good within evil, evil within good, and begins to independently process moral responsibility for his or her future self. Beyond this age range, continuing brain development and moralizing experiences undoubtedly lead to further hierarchical organization of the conscience.

### 5.1.2 Supporting Domains of Conscience

Conceptualization of conscience, the anchor domain of this empirical research, correlated well with progression in four supporting domains (Stilwell et al., 1994, 1996, 1997, 1998).

1. *Moralization of attachment*, in which attachment experiences with caretakers engender the *who* of conscience. The *who* of conscience develops in accordance with how

caretakers first nurture it. Warm, supportive relationships between child and caretaker(s) build empathic understanding and a desire to please and conform. Repeated moral learning experiences consolidate into a *security-empathy-oughtness* bond of mutual regard and moral expectation. As development progresses, moralizing experiences with other caring adults (e.g., extended family, teachers, coaches, religious leaders) expand the desire to emulate and incorporate characteristics of those admired.

2. *Moral valuation,* in which choosing and thinking through authority-derived, peer-derived, and self-derived rules for living form the *what and why* of conscience. *Authority-derived values* emerge from moralizing experiences that build respect for people in authority, institutions, or deity. *Peer-derived values* emerge from moralizing experiences that build respect for equality, justice, and the common good. *Self-derived values* emerge from moralizing experiences that build respect for self and responsibility for one's future. It is within the valuation domain that moral frustrations and dilemmas are debated with one's conscience. Moral challenges may either deepen or reshape values and beliefs.

3. *Moral–emotional responsiveness,* in which shifts in arousal and mood in anticipation of or following wrongdoing OR rightdoing activate restraint or virtuous striving and, in the case of wrongdoing, are followed by efforts at reparation and healing in order to return to an *am good/ready to do good* sense of self. As one young teenager said, "I just stayed in my room until I could figure out how to make it right with . . . [name left out]."

4. *Moral volition,* in which self-evaluation and chosen moral actions form the *how and when* of conscience, leading to prosocial or inhibitory actions on behalf of moral values. Moral volition requires mental and physical energy for action or restraint. Quoting a child from our study, "When I finally stopped being mean to . . ., I liked myself better." It is within this domain that procrastination and fear balance courage and determination.

To provide a sample from a typical interview, we present one from a seventeen-year-old girl describing how her thinking about cheating changed during her senior year in high school. Her discussion demonstrates how a moralizing experience can lead to a more comprehensive view of responsibility, both toward self and others. Her conclusions are representative of older adolescents functioning at the Integrated Stage of conscience development (Stilwell et al., 2000, p. 167).

INTERVIEWER: What are your best reasons for not cheating?

OLDER ADOLESCENT: The reason I don't think I'd do it again is that one time, my friend—she cheated on a real big history test in a class where we have the hardest teacher in the school. And she got an "A" on it, and I got a "C" on it, and I studied the night before so hard. I was so mad. And she just sat over by this girl that's like really, really smart. And she just cheated off of her. I wanted to tell on her so bad 'cause when we got our report card, she got a better grade than I did. She did that on two tests. When you're studying, that's just not right. So that kind of taught me a lesson about how I felt when she did that—*like the rest of the class [was wronged]*. So, I mean, I've never done it on a big test. If I cheated on a big test now, I'd tell the teacher. A year ago, I wouldn't have.

The authors are grateful to the 122 young people who, having few disadvantages in their lives, provided us with a baseline understanding from which to compare and contrast the ways in which conscience formation and functioning work in youth who have not been so blessed. It should also be noted that, even with excellent rearing in the most advantageous circumstances, a conscience never functions like a smooth-running machine; human fallibility, temptation, deprivation, coercion, confusion, indecision, competing values, and procrastination are always complicating the best of moral intentions. The older one gets, the greater the challenges.

## 5.2 From Wrongdoing to Moral Injury

### 5.2.1 Moral Injury

Incidents of wrongdoing are part of ordinary growing up, and growing up is never completely finished. With the assistance of prodding parents, teachers, principals, coaches, religious educators, peers, and self-appraisal, wrongdoing introduces a youngster to the moral emotions – mainly shame and guilt; to defense mechanisms – mainly denial and blame; to confessions – partial or complete, spontaneous or induced; to reparation – spontaneous or required; and finally, to forgiveness – sincere or not. Within everyone's memory are forceful admonitions like: "I can't believe you did that!" "Don't ever do that again!" "Stay in your room until . . . ." "You're grounded!" "You will return that [stolen item] and apologize!"

Moral injury is wrongdoing at a far deeper level than described above. Moral injury is a devastating and reverberating blow to the foundation of how we believe life should be lived, what we have come to expect from an authority, ourselves and others, what holds our world together. The causes of moral injury to our conscience may come from outside ourselves – from compelling situations that force us to compromise our own moral mandates – or from inside ourselves – from intolerable actions of our own doing. To build an understanding of the incremental, insidious pathway to deeper and deeper moral injury, we would like to describe how we have come to use the descriptors *moralizing, demoralizing, and re-moralizing* in studying the formation and functioning of conscience. The following discussion will show how these three types of moral experiences can flow from one to another and then circle back.

### 5.2.2 Moralization, Demoralization, Re-moralization

**Moralizing Experiences**

*Moralizing experiences* are ones that create an ever-maturing sense of moral responsiveness and responsibility. Throughout the lifespan, both children and adults may have mind-changing experiences – even to the point of reaching an epiphany – that render former thinking and behavior *wrong.* A smile-producing childhood example is that of a ten-year-old disadvantaged boy who was accustomed to stealing whatever he needed or wanted. Then he entered a foster home with strict rules, rewards, and punishments. After testing the system thoroughly, it finally dawned on him one day that "you can get about anything you want around here *if you ask.*"

A more profound moralizing experience comes from the life story of John Newton, who changed from being a foul-mouthed, swashbuckling, authority-defying sailor and slave trader to become a repentant and empathic clergyman (Ailkin, 2013). Today he is remembered as the lyricist of the hymn, *Amazing Grace.*

Amazing grace! How sweet the sound
That saved a wretch like me.
I once was lost, but now am found,
Was blind but now I see.

## Demoralizing Experiences

We use the descriptor, *demoralizing*, not in the dictionary sense of losing hope, confidence, or becoming dispirited (*New Oxford American Dictionary*, 2010), but to describe the impact of experiences that wound already established domains of conscience. Sometimes, demoralization is a step in the process of developing new insight. During that process, there may indeed be a temporary "loss of spirit" or even depression. Here is one childhood example: Think of a young child living in what he has considered to be a secure and happy home. Suddenly his parents tell him that they are getting a divorce, arousing fears of abandonment in him. This announcement comes to him as a shock. He immediately wonders: What did I do wrong to make it happen? What can I do to bring my parents back together?

With his world as he knew it shattered, his need for security and emotional well-being requires that he restructure his sense of *family* by accepting an altered base of security: both parents love him, even though they can't get along well enough to live together. While the child may adapt to his new reality with seeming ease, the moral residue of his experience may be long-lasting, affecting his future beliefs about trust, love, commitment, and the institution of marriage. The reframing experience may broaden his young world view (e.g., lots of kids in my class have gone through this, too) or, perhaps, have a gloomy, destructive effect (e.g., holidays will never be the same again).

Another example is that of a sophomore college student who, having been reared in a religious faith that taught a creationist view of the age of the earth, had that religious viewpoint confronted every time her geology professor required that the students write the geologic time scale on a test. This happened every six weeks and it was worth 20% of the her grade. The demoralization came not from the expansion of her scientific knowledge but from disillusionment with the admired religious leaders who had taught her creationist viewpoint as a matter of fact and faith. Idolization and idealization took a sophomoric blow.

## Re-Moralization

*Re-moralization* is the long and arduous process of re-establishing a moral foundation after a previous one has been shattered. It follows demoralization of the severest kind when the foundations upon which one's conscience have been built – trust, harmony, rules for living, and moral agency – are shattered. This is *moral injury*. The range of moral injuries include ones that occur during development (e.g., abuse and neglect); adult human-to-human injustice (e.g., rape, fraud, spread of disease, killing); or group-to-group injustice (e.g., oppression, war, genocide). Moral injury can also come from realizing the harm we are doing to the earth that supports life (e.g., climate change, depletion of natural resources) or from coping with earth-changing events such as natural disasters.

The psychological/psychiatric sequelae most observable and definable in the aftermath of traumatic experiences are symptoms of post-traumatic stress disorder and depression, even to the point of suicide. While these symptoms may be relieved through self-healing or professional help, the suffering person may also need to work through the arduous mental task of finding ways to integrate moral injury in newly made meaning fitted to living in a world turned upside down – in order to deal with moral injury. Expectations that "time will heal" are inadequate. Acceptance, forgiveness of self or others, and re-moralization may be required. An example of the arduousness of the process comes from the life of Eva Kor, who after years of suffering, not only forgave Dr. Mengele for the medical experiments he had performed on her and her twin sister during the Holocaust, but went on to become a morally inspiring speaker and leader of tours to Auschwitz (Kor and Buccieri, 2009). During a gripping commencement address to a group of college graduates, she reminded them to hug their parents because she never had the chance to do that.

## 5.2.3 Context of Moral Injury

Moral injuries occur in many contexts, each one of which is destructive to human dignity and well-being. Among the many contexts of moral injury are: abusive developmental experiences; interpersonal violence; and government oppression, racial disparity, genocide, war, pandemics, drought, manmade disasters, and natural disasters. In any of these contexts, a person may experience crushing, demoralizing events that completely undermine the foundations of his or her conscience; may create distrust of all authority, including faith in God; and may unleash revengeful desires to abuse someone else.

We will focus on three contexts in which moral injury is prominent:

1. Moral injury experienced by combat veterans – because this is the context in which the first scientific definitions of moral injury were formulated, including instrument design and research within this particular population.
2. Cumulative adverse childhood and adolescent experiences in psychiatrically hospitalized youth – because this is the context in which we began to understand: (a) impaired conscience development; (b) psychopathological interference to conscience functioning; and (c) in retrospect, how that understanding anticipated the current concept of moral injury.
3. Natural disaster, specifically the Armenian earthquake of 1988 – because this is the context in which we designed an instrument to measure both moral development and psychopathological interference to conscience functioning in adolescents affected by a natural disaster.

### Moral Injury in Combat Veterans

Anticipating recent research, Verkamp studied moral injury in war from medieval to modern times, noting that, in addition to trauma-related stress, soldiers might also experience moral pain, deserving of our healing effort (Verkamp, 1993).

Pressure from Việt Nam veterans themselves was effective in bringing about the inclusion of post-traumatic stress disorder (PTSD) into the psychiatric diagnostic system (Stein and Rothbaum, 2018). However, it became apparent that many soldiers suffered from something more than reliving the trauma of the war. Something else bothered them, at the core of their being. Many spoke of their "loss of soul" when previously held moral and religious beliefs were turned upside down as they were conscripted into a war over which the nation that was conscripting them was wrought with ambivalence. Emotionally, many were caught between the patriotism of their World War II veteran fathers and increasing anti-war sentiment. Some were disturbed by the failure of religious leaders to take a stand on the justification of this war in light of the commandment, "thou shalt not kill."

Among the demoralized were those who concluded that the killing had been meaningless; winning was impossible; the propaganda that denigrated the culture of the land they were in had been untrue; that they had participated in poisoning the land they were trespassing (and sometimes themselves); and that the lack of public support when they returned home reinforced their demoralization (Hattan, 2018). However, the most seriously demoralized – or better put, *anti-moralized* – were those soldiers who, undoubtedly with prior deficiencies in conscience, became *callous and unemotional* in executing their orders, even finding satisfaction in the killing, burning, and raping (Burns and Novick, 2017).

The scientific study of moral injury seeks to understand the human response to life threats; how personal identity is damaged; how it correlates with or is separate from PTSD. Currier designed a military version of a scale for measuring self-directed and other-directed moral injury (Currier et al., 2019). Theoretically, the scale resonates well with the conscience domains of moral-emotional responsiveness and moral valuation. As defined by him:

> Self-directed moral injury occurs when the person feels directly responsible for perpetrating transgressive acts on others. Self-directed moral injury is characterized by painful feelings of pervasive shame and guilt; beliefs/attitudes about being unlovable, unforgivable, or incapable of moral decision-making.

In cases of betrayal or bearing witness to others' acts of moral wrongdoing for which an individual does not feel personally responsible, other-directed moral injury produces feelings of anger, moral disgust, and vengeance towards the responsible person(s).

These investigators studied whether moral injury and PTSD are separate entities, related to each other in a time-lag fashion, or are reciprocal entities. Their mixture of findings is prescient to discussion later in this chapter.

## Developmental Moral Injury

Investigators of moral injury in combat veterans appeared to be working with individuals in whom conscience had already become more or less established. However, investigation in developmental moral injury must take into account that in younger persons, conscience is still very much a work in progress.

When a young child grows up with adversities – poverty, abuse, neglect, parental addiction, abandonment, poor schooling, inadequate nutrition or medical care, a violent neighborhood, a war zone, a refugee camp, a pandemic – he or she does not register those experiences as moral injuries. *What is, simply is.* For example, when a child's alcoholic father beats him or the child finds that Dad *just isn't there* when inebriated, the child may think: "This is just the way it is; sometimes my dad is nice to me; I must have been *born bad* to get all those beatings." When a child's emerging identity is built from experiences that cause him to denigrate himself and feel responsible for adult behavior that he cannot possibly control, a punitive and rejecting conscience is in the making to which he may later react with hateful, destructive behavior toward himself and others.

This same child in whom maltreatment has engendered a negative foundation for conscience formation is also likely to have deficits in neurobiological connectivity, expressed as lags in cognitive development, impaired emotional regulation, impulsive thinking and behavior, lack of future-oriented motivation, or inadequate capacity to relate to others (van der Kolk, 2014; Sapolsky, 2017). These deficits, in turn, further compromise healthy conscience development and functioning.

However, even the child who believes he was "born bad" has a rudimentary sense of goodness and rightfulness somewhere in the universe. Seeking love and fairness in life is believed by some to be universal. The building blocks that lead to a well-functioning conscience – trust, emotional harmony, meaningful rules for living, and energy channeled toward moral choice and action – develop in aberrant ways when growing up is full of chaos, rejection, hatred, and unconscionable treatment by adults. The *who, what, why, how, and when* of conscience come together in fragmented form, full of paucities, inconsistencies, revengeful emotional tones, or denial. As one conduct-disordered twelve-year-old put it, "I know what a conscience is, but I ain't got one." This boy knew that morality existed, but he denied that it had anything to do with his life experiences.

## Sequelae of Developmental Moral Injury

People who enter adolescence or adulthood feeling deficient in moral worth may function with a conscience that has limited or negative motivational force. Instead of seeking the *right* thing to do, they may look at life only in terms of what they *rightfully* deserve. For others, adverse childhood experiences may actually promote moral growth and dedication to not repeat abusive behavior. Life tragedies or challenges may engender a moral awakening allowing them to turn negative into positive, as in the case of John Newton (previously described). For others, life may be endured with pessimistic resignation – always expecting the worst and ready to take a pragmatic survivalist approach to whatever comes along; the voice of conscience is irrelevant. A quote from a fifteen-year-old boy in juvenile detention is given here: "Done my crime; doin' my time." In the worst sequela, conscience turns in on itself with sociopathic consequences.

## Moral Injury in Natural Disaster

When devastating events occur that are beyond human control, moral injury cannot be attributed to the physical forces that caused them. We cannot blame the earthquake, the volcanic eruption, or the tsunami for causing moral harm. However, our intense desire to know "why?" may plunge us deeply into superstitious, philosophical, or religious searching. Did a higher power in the universe purposely make this disaster happen? Are human moral deficiencies the cause? Is God punishing us? What can we do to appease that force?

In the "Developmental Moral Injury" section above, the boy who concluded that he was born bad due to the beatings of his alcoholic father, may well have received many compensatory affirmations that ameliorated the developmental moral injury done by his father. However, when the bowels of the earth open up, leaving thousands of people dead, trapped in the rubble, injured, and screaming with pain, philosophical or religious *what-did-we-do-wrong* moral questioning crescendo.

At these times, children, as well as adults, may grapple with deeply held moral or religious beliefs. For example, after Nicaragua's 1988 Hurricane Mitch, an adolescent boy was greatly offended by a song that blamed God for the ravages of the hurricane. Although he may have harbored those feelings himself, he was deeply troubled because his religious training had taught him that it was a sacrilege to feel this way. He had been taught that God was beneficent, not punitive (A. Goenjian, personal communication).

While we adults may have the advantage of scientifically understanding weather patterns or the movement of tectonic plates, we have no better answers than children to the philosophical or irrational questions that swell up during a natural disaster. During the Armenian earthquake of 1988, a young boy ran one way while his mother ran another way trying to escape from a collapsing building. The mother was killed. The boy blamed himself for running the wrong way, superstitiously or irrationally, thinking that he could have saved his mother if he had run the other way (A. Goenjian, personal communication).

Philosophical pondering aside, disaster forces victims to focus on the pragmatics of moral responsiveness and responsibility. How did we fail to prepare for this disaster? What do we have to do now? What should we do to prevent harm in the future? These are the conjoined demands of survival and conscience. For example, after the Armenian earthquake of 1988, a certain engineer felt pangs of guilt over having followed the direction of a supervisor to use less steel and cement than the building code required in the construction of an apartment building. The building fell during the earthquake, resulting in the death of many residents. The engineer felt he had contributed to the collapse and later committed suicide.

## 5.3 Seeking the Moral Domain in the Psychiatric Diagnostic System

Where does moral pain fit in the psychiatric diagnostic system? In this section we invite the reader to follow our rationale in examining relationships between: (1) moral development and conscience (previously described); (2) the lack of a moral component in current psychiatric nosology; and (3) findings supporting the concept of psychopathological interference to conscience functioning. Our goal is to find a conceptual home for moral injury within the psychiatric diagnostic system.

### 5.3.1 Psychopathological Syndromes

Psychopathological syndromes are defined as "significant disturbances in cognition, emotional regulation, or behavior that impair an individual's functioning in social, occupational, or other important *areas of functioning*" (American Psychiatric Association, 2013). None of the syndromes nor the important areas of functioning include the moral domain. That is not to say that psychiatry does not have moral concern for its patients. Historically, the field took a big leap forward in developing *moral treatment* after Philippe Pinel unchained the "insane" in mental hospitals in 1791 (Pinel, 1806). Psychiatric patients were then deemed neither *bad* nor under demonic possession, but rather *sick* and in need of humane treatment.

In spite of being a profession with a moral commitment to treat patients and their needs ethically, its diagnostic system has avoided focusing on the relationship between moral pain, psychopathology, and conscience. Perhaps this omission is due to an unspoken professional mandate to avoid being judgmental. If moral pain or conscience were included in the diagnostic system, it might be seen as blurring the separation between *sickness* and *badness*.

It cannot be denied that the conscience is a motivational force within human life. When delays, arrests, deviancies – or even accelerations – in moral functioning are left out of psychiatry's diagnostic system, acknowledgment of the full extent of mental suffering (or thriving) is lacking. At a minimum, psychiatric nosology would capture mental suffering more completely if the moral domain were included in the "areas of functioning" that are required to be impaired to validate a diagnosis.

An even more meaningful goal would be to directly include disturbances in conscience functioning as (a) sequelae of psychopathology, (b) co-occurrences, or (c) integral criteria within specific syndromes. This approach resonates with the question raised above by Currier regarding moral injury in combat veterans: are moral injury and PTSD separate entities, related to each other in a time-lag fashion, or reciprocal entities? We will explore parallels to this conundrum more fully below.

Even though impairments in conscience functioning are not addressed *directly* in psychiatric diagnoses, *indirect evidence* is present in some syndromes. We present two examples below.

## Conduct Disorder

Conduct Disorder (CD) is described as a "pattern of behavior in which the basic rights of others or major age-appropriate societal norms or rules are violated" (DSM-5, pp. 221–223). Even with the specificity of the symptom clusters of aggressiveness, destructiveness, deceitfulness, and rule violation, the syndrome offers an incomplete picture of the motivational forces governing a particular youth's misbehavior. Why is he having so much trouble living in society? Is his conscience totally dysfunctional or are there fragments in some conscience domains that careful inquiry could detect?

If the assessment were to delve into the heart of his or her personality with a conscience-centered interview, focused on each domain – the *who, what, why, how, and when* of conscience – motivational forces within this youth might be uncovered, some pro-socially oriented, some not. The search might enhance understanding of the links between developmental moral injuries, conduct-disordered symptoms, and conscience functioning. Treatment planning could then focus on strengthening whatever partially developed domains of conscience are present.

Here is a case in point: A twelve-year-old boy was placed in a long-term psychiatric residential facility because of severely aggressive behavior directed toward his mother, siblings, school peers, and school staff. He had suffered at least five adverse childhood events growing up, including, at the age of three, knowing about (if not witnessing) his father dousing his mother and a sibling with gasoline, intent on burning them, when thankfully a grandparent intervened. His own antisocial behaviors included setting a stolen mattress on fire and attempting to strangle his sister.

A previous psychiatric evaluation had concluded: "Operational judgement poor due to poor impulse control. Insight zero."

However, during a conscience-sensitive interview done by one of the authors, this boy had no hesitation in describing his dichotomized good and bad conscience, normally characteristic of a seven- to eleven-year-old. His "bad conscience" promoted such behaviors as "hitting, yelling, aggravating, antagonizing" while his "good conscience" promoted such things as "being happy, sharing and giving and being thankful, showing manners, and stuff like that." He drew a picture of his conscience as being on a railroad track that diverged, with his good conscience going down one track, his bad conscience going full speed down the other track. He elaborated that he often needed to flip a switch to get back to the good track.

Ongoing conscience-sensitive interviewing by the treatment team regarding *any* moralized attachment experiences, *any* functioning moral-emotions, *any* moral reasoning ability, or *any* attempts to control his "bad" conscience would point the way to helping him lead a less conduct-disordered life. Rudiments of moral motivation were there.

### Post-Traumatic Stress Disorder

Although post-traumatic stress disorder (PTSD) criteria are also indirect in addressing the moral domains, the diagnostic clusters come very close to linking together moral injury, conscience functioning, and psychopathology (DSM-5, pp. 143–149). Cluster A criteria, "exposure to actual or threatened death, serious injury, or sexual violence," is synchronous with moral wounding. Cluster A also provides context for the symptoms that follow it, creating a *wholeness* to the syndrome. The clusters dealing with intrusive, avoidant, cognitively distorted, and hyper-aroused emotions are compatible with disruptions in all domains of conscience . . . and moral injury.

A case in point is given here: A fifteen-year-old girl, who had been sexually molested by her father, had such intense PTSD symptomatology that therapist after therapist, inpatient program after inpatient program, failed to help her resolve or even lessen her psychic pain. Periods of fairly normal functioning would suddenly be interrupted with outbreaks so disturbing that she required a padded "quiet" room where she screamed and hit the padded walls for hours. Her psychiatrist (one of the authors) recalled how, even in a period of calm after one of these outbreaks, the patient threatened to kill her if she made her talk about "anything." The patient had so much moral pain that she couldn't even talk about it.

## 5.4 Psychopathological Interference to Conscience Functioning: Concept Development

### 5.4.1 Psychiatrically Hospitalized Boys

At the 1993 annual meeting of the *American Academy of Child and Adolescent Psychiatry*, the authors presented a workshop entitled *Conscience Delays and Deficiencies in Psychopathology* (Stilwell and Galvin, 1993). From the analysis of both clinical records and Stilwell Conscience Interviews (SCIs) of psychiatrically hospitalized boys who had experienced abuse and neglect, we developed five-point scoring formats for measuring both developmental *sufficiency* and psychopathological *deficiency* in each of the five domains of conscience. The sufficiency scores followed the pathway of normal conscience development as described in research papers cited at the beginning of this chapter as well as the book *Right vs Wrong, Raising a Child with a Conscience* (Stilwell et al., 2000). Deficiency scores were derived from analysis of patient SCI interviews, clinical records, therapy sessions, and day-to-day management of the boys' behavior on the ward, in the hospital school, and in recreational settings.

The more we delved into examining the conscience of these boys, the more we were intrigued by how psychopathology was related to its malformation or malfunctioning. In line with the field of developmental psychopathology in which development and psychopathology are seen as each having their own trajectory, yet continuously interacting with each other (Cicchetti, 2016), the more inclusive term, *psychopathological interference to conscience functioning* (PI), was chosen. We then began to record SCI interviews with a larger group of hospitalized youth, both boys and girls, children and adolescents. The interviews with adolescents with PTSD particularly interested us in the way in which the severity of their symptoms intuitively correlated with moral suffering.

## 5.4.2 Children Suffering from Natural Disaster

At the invitation of Dr. Armen Goenjian who, along with a team of other mental health professionals and members of the Psychiatric Outreach Program for Armenia (Goenjian, 1993), studied the psychological/psychiatric effects of natural disaster with the goal of designing and evaluating treatment programs, we accepted the challenge to develop a structured instrument that would measure both moral development and PI in adolescents who had suffered from a natural disaster.

The development of the structured instrument was derived from the following experiences: (1) the previously mentioned SCI findings from advantaged youth, from which we laid out five stages of conscience formation in five domains; (2) the previously mentioned SCI findings and clinical experience with boys with Conduct Disorder who were being treated in a university-associated program for at least a six to nine months stay. From that experience, we laid out preliminary criteria for PI, followed by (3) SCI findings and clinical experience with some 100 other hospitalized children and adolescents in the same university-associated treatment program. Special attention was paid to interviews and clinical experiences with adolescents suffering from PTSD. Cumulative developmental moral injuries were profound. The investigators were highly involved in their multifaceted treatment program (e.g., going to camp with patients; directly attending to them during flashbacks). They really *knew* these young people: their skills, their symptomatology, and their deficiencies in conscience!

## 5.4.3 The Structured Stilwell Conscience Interview

The Structured Stilwell Conscience Interview (SSCI) consists of twenty-four items, each of which has five gradations (Stilwell, 2002b). The gradation in items assessing moral development progresses through five increasingly comprehensive levels of understanding personal moral functioning. The gradations in the items assessing PI reflect five increasing levels of interference to conscience functioning in the domains of conceptualization, valuation, and moral-emotional responsiveness. The subjects are not limited to one choice for each item; they can check any response that reflects their experience. However, the items checked that indicate the most advanced level of moral development and the most impaired level of PI are the ones selected for scoring.

The first four items ask the subjects to assess belief in their own personal goodness or badness, how that belief came to be, and what factors limit that belief. Sample responses include: "I was born with goodness in me." "I believe I had a good side that got ruined in growing up." "I do not believe I am basically bad, but I have had to do bad things to survive (e.g., steal)." "I believe I am basically a bad person."

The next four items ask the subjects to define how they conceptualize their conscience. Sample responses include: "My conscience is a little person (e.g., voice) inside me that helps me make good decisions about right and wrong." "My conscience is divided into a good and bad conscience; they fight with each other." "After (a certain event) I no longer cared about right and wrong."

The next eight items deal with moral-emotional responsiveness. The subjects are asked to assess how they feel when they have done something good or bad – something their conscience approves or disapproves – and how it shows on the outside of them. Sample responses to acts of goodness include: "I feel energetic and want to do more good things." "I feel more connected to my spiritual self or my beliefs." "I turn around and do something bad; I might pick a fight."

Reactions to self-acknowledged bad behavior in the eyes of conscience include such responses as: "I am very busy or fidgety." "I am really irritable and mean to everyone." "I feel guilty and can't get it off my mind until I do something about it." "I am constantly on the lookout for people who are against me."

With regard to reparation and healing after wrongdoing, the subjects chose such responses as: "I admit to what I did wrong when questioned." "I stay by myself for a while." "I drink alcohol or use drugs."

The next four items have to do with the incorporation of values into the conscience. Subjects are asked to list the main "do's and don'ts" in their conscience and to justify their reasons and justifications for following or not following them. Sample justifications for "dos" include: "Doing these things pleases other people and makes me feel proud" and "Doing these things makes the world work a little bit better." Sample justifications for "don'ts" include: "I will get in big trouble." "It will ruin my future as a trustworthy person."

The last two items have to do with moral volition. Items describing adequate moral willpower include "My religious beliefs give me strength," "I always keep the future in mind," and "I believe my decisions affect my relationships with my family, myself, and my surroundings." Items describing deficiencies in moral will power include: "I get depressed." "I get confused." "The world around me is basically evil."

## 5.5 Lessons from Youth Traumatized by a Natural Disaster

### 5.5.1 The Armenian Earthquake of 1988

The devastating Armenian Earthquake of 1988 was the impetus for using the SSCI to study moral development and psychopathological interference to conscience functioning (PI) effects on children suffering from this catastrophic event (Goenjian et al., 1999). The participating group were six- to nine-year-olds when the earthquake struck and were now thirteen to sixteen. Although the PI section of the SSCI was developed from experience with youth who were *disadvantaged* by having been exposed to multiple childhood adversities, we hoped that the instrument would also be helpful in discerning PI in more *advantaged, but severely* traumatized, teenagers.

In the Goenjian study reported in 1999, the objectives were to "compare moral development and PI among adolescents exposed to different degrees of earthquake-related trauma and to investigate the relationship of moral development and PI to exposure to trauma, severity of PTSD symptoms, post-earthquake adversities, and extent of loss of nuclear family members." The findings of the study showed more PTSD symptomatology, greater amounts of PI, and yet (surprisingly) more advanced levels of moral development than those who resided in a city more removed from the earthquake zone. The study was repeated to confirm these findings.

This hypothesis-seeking correlational study suggests that psychopathology emerging from trauma leads to impairments in conscience functioning, the foundation of one's moral being. Although this investigation predates the increasingly prevalent studies of moral injury in both military and civilian populations, psychopathological interference to conscience functioning may be yet another way of addressing moral injury, using a different approach and different language.

### 5.5.2 Advanced Moral Development in Youth After Trauma

A major, and somewhat surprising finding that the SSCI revealed in the Goenjian study was that the adolescents living at the epicenter of the earthquake, Spitak, showed greater advances in moral development than did their peers living in the marginally affected capital, Yerevan. They affirmed responses indicating: "that their conscience does not always know the right answer and that they have to make their own decisions about right and wrong (stage 5); that they learned how to be good from their own mistakes (stage 4); and that they learned how to be good by thinking about how good and bad are tied together (stage 5)" (Goenjian et al., 1999, p. 382). The article goes on to describe that, during and after the earthquake, children had to take on many survival-oriented responsibilities such as "having to take care of siblings and other dependent, disabled, and elderly family members, having to find wood to burn for cooking and heat, and having to sell things on the street to earn extra money for the family."

The conundrum of the more traumatized Spitak adolescents showing both more advanced moral development, while at the same time greater PI than the less-traumatized Yerevan group, is open to speculation. In the authors' opinion, a reasonable explanation begins with remembering what our sample of "advantaged" youth taught us about their transition in conceptualizing conscience as they moved from the Confused stage of mid-adolescence to the Integrated stage of later adolescence (Stilwell et al., 1991). Mid-teens at the Confused stage were skeptical of what their elders had taught them, were overly dependent on peer opinion and example, and were willing to experiment with a variety of behaviors. By the time they had transitioned to the Integrated stage, their tone and thinking were more settled. They spoke about the person they wanted to be in the future, how they should be responsible to a larger group than just themselves and their friends, and how there is sometimes good within evil and evil within good.

Therefore, while conscience functioning among the more traumatized Spitak teens could have been compromised by hardship, uncertainty, fear, loss, grief, depression, and periodic loss of impulse control, the responsibility that the earthquake and its aftermath thrust upon them may have accelerated their awakening to understanding the pragmatics of survival, the greater needs of family and community, and responsibility for their own future.

Advanced moral development – self-reliantly responding to what has to be done for self and others – is undoubtedly the life story of many survivors, many of whom go on to make future moral commitments related to their traumatizing experiences. For example: Ari, a fourteen-year-old boy at the time of the earthquake in Gyumri, the second most devastated city, shared his reflections to a reporter for Eurasianet on December 7, 2018, the thirty-year anniversary of the earthquake (Lurye, 2018). Among his comments were: "Everyone's destiny was changed in forty-five seconds. What I went through made me stronger. Made me more driven to do what I did." The memories of this former national judo athlete included the entrapment of him and his mother under apartment-building rubble for days with a block of cement serendipitously serving as a tourniquet for his bleeding leg; memories of others screaming and crying until death quieted them; the amputation of both of his legs; and multiple reconstructive surgeries, which brought him to the United States. He now works for a utility company where one of the projects he's most proud of involves making gas pipes more resilient in case of a natural disaster.

## 5.5.3 Climate Change: Human-Created Natural Disaster

A sense of moral injury may come from the realization of what civilization is doing to itself and the world. For example, many young people have moral concerns about the threat of climate change. Many feel angry that the adult world is robbing them of their future by failing to radically address this issue. Such a person is fifteen-year-old Greta Thunberg from Sweden (Thunberg et al., 2018). She has transcended personal neuro-developmental problems to become an active person of conscience.

With the continuous support of a very nurturant family, Greta has grown up suffering from several psychiatric disorders, including anorexia nervosa, obsessive-compulsive disorder, and Asperger's syndrome. It appears that the latter syndrome helped solidify her moral volition.

Greta considers Asperger's syndrome to be a gift because it allows her to address the catastrophic problem of climate change in "black- and- white" terms, while being totally resistant to criticism. With parents following her moral commitment rather than leading her to it, she refuses to fly, maintains a vegan diet, and buys only necessities. Well-read in scientific studies on climate change as well as the opposing arguments, she uses her voice of conscience to address national and international powers about the radical changes that need to be made to avert robbing her and every other child of their future.

## 5.5.4 Structured Stilwell Conscience Interview Analysis: Conscience Domains, PTSD, and Psychopathological Interference

We will now take a deeper look at what the youth in the Armenian study taught us in this exploratory study about the relationships between moral development, PTSD symptomatology, and psychopathological interference to conscience functioning. We will organize the discussion in this manner:

1. The five domains of conscience will be topic headings, followed by;
2. The DSM-5 PTSD clusters relevant to each domain, followed by;
3. Comparisons, contrasts, and speculations regarding the three groups: (a) the less traumatized Yerevan group; (b) the more traumatized Spitak group; and (c) the non-traumatized group from normative Stilwell studies. The strengths and weaknesses of the investigation will be discussed along the way.

### Conceptualization of Conscience

Post-traumatic stress disorder diagnostic criteria contain no language addressing the concept of conscience itself. However, the effects of severe trauma on conscience functioning may be implied when depersonalization or derealization has been "specified." Depersonalization and derealization are symptoms of *dissociative identity disorders,* describing disturbances in identity or personality (DSM-5, pp. 155, 157). Since conscience is the "heart of the personality," PI could result in feeling distant from one's own conscience. Indeed, several youth in the Spitak sample endorsed the statement: "After a certain event, I stopped caring about right or wrong."

It is common for non-traumatized adolescents to say that their conscience "forgot to work" when they are rationalizing some misbehavior. In a parallel way, the less traumatized Yerevan group was more likely to indicate this kind of forgetting. In contrast, the Spitak group was more likely to indicate that their conscience was at war with itself, divided into good and bad parts.

Although non-traumatized seven- to eleven-year-olds may also maintain a division between good and bad when describing their conscience, they do not say that the parts are at war with each other. The warring component is reminiscent of the twelve-year-old boy described above in the "Conduct Disorder" section in whom multiple aggressive developmental adversities paralleled multiple aggressive actions of his own. In him, his "bad" conscience repeatedly outraced his "good conscience." Having far less developmental adversities, the consciences of some Spitak youth may have been experiencing a war between internal mandates to be more adult-like in carrying out responsibilities (good conscience) vs. wanting to just be teenagers, who are ubiquitously prone to engaging in occasional misbehavior (bad conscience).

## Moralization of Attachment

The bedrock value of this domain is *trust*. Trust is developed within the security-empathy-oughtness bond with primary caretakers. A child's moralizing experiences in family relationships engender mutual understanding, respect, and a desire to please and conform. PTSD criteria (Cluster D) that relate to trust are:

> . . . no one can be trusted . . . the world is completely dangerous . . . feelings of detachment or estrangement from others.

Unfortunately, the SSCI does not include items directly addressing moralization of attachment. In contrast, the unstructured SCI queries, administered to both non-traumatized youth and youth with developmental moral injuries, ask questions such as: "What is the first thing that you can remember doing that was called "'good or right?'" " . . . that was called "'bad or wrong?'" "Other than yourself, who is most pleased when you have done something good or right? . . . bad or wrong?" The interviewer then notes who the youth lists as "authors" of his or her list of "do's and don'ts." The point of these inquiries is to determine how *foundational* attachment experiences with family members have been in the establishment of the child's conscience.

Considering that the children in this study were six- to ten-years-old at the time of the earthquake, foundational moralizing experiences with attachment figures would already have been solidly in place. Even though physical and mental well-being would have been disarmed by the disaster, basic trust and respect for family, community, and culture would probably have been preserved or even strengthened. Without data, we can only speculate.

## Moral Valuation

Moral valuation is the process of thinking through one's best reasons or justifications for following or *not* following self-identified "do's and don'ts" – rules for living derived from moralizing experiences with authority, peers, or self. Moral valuation provides the logic of conscience. A traumatic injury can impact mental processing by creating distortions in perception, memory, or consequential thinking. Distortions can broaden into negative thinking about not only self but the community, government, deity, or universe. Items from PTSD Clusters D and E indirectly suggest a connection between the traumatic injury and the cognitive processing necessary for moral valuation:

> . . . problems with concentration; inability to remember an important aspect of the traumatic event(s) (dissociative amnesia); negative beliefs (I am bad . . . my whole nervous system is permanently ruined); persistent distorted cognitions about the cause or consequence of the traumatic event(s) that lead the individual to blame himself/herself or others.

The SSCI was not as sensitive as it could have been in detecting ways in which disturbances in cognitive functioning might have interfered with the processing required for moral valuation. The extent of moral injury and pragmatic responsibilities in parents' lives may not have allowed much time to help the teenagers "think things through." This is suggested by the response: "I learned how to be good from my own mistakes," endorsed more frequently by the Spitak group.

With PTSD symptoms present in both groups, but more prevalent in the Spitak group, it is probable that invasive traumatic memories and worries about family and survival would have interfered with concentration and learning. This interference may have been particularly disturbing if there was a "rule" in their conscience about being a good student or making good grades. Furthermore, more adolescents from Spitak seemed to be prone to negative thinking as they more frequently endorsed the item, "the world around me is basically evil." Negative thinking could have depleted their energy and been used as a justification for not pursuing required tasks in a responsible way.

## Moral-Emotional Responsiveness

Moral-emotional homeostasis is a state in which one has a baseline feeling of personal goodness and a readiness to do the right thing. An emotion is experienced as morally induced when it is consistently associated with a sense of oughtness. Positive emotions that are morally recruited include excitement, pride, or elation. Negative emotions include fear, guilt, anxiety, contempt, and shame. In the study of advantaged youth, those without developmental adversities, reactions to wrongdoing separated into two factors: (1) anxiety and mood disturbances and (2) physiological responsiveness, reparation, and healing.

PTSD criteria indirectly suggesting impairment in moral-emotional responsiveness resulting from traumatic injury are included in Clusters B, D, and E:

> . . . marked physiological reactions to internal or external cues that symbolize . . . traumatic event(s); . . . hyper-vigilance; exaggerated startle response; sleep difficulties; persistent negative emotional state (e.g., fear, horror, anger, guilt, shame) . . . persistent inability to express positive emotions . . . . . . intrusive distressing memories . . . distressing dreams . . . dissociative reactions (flashbacks).

No criteria address reparation or healing processes after wrongdoing or having been wronged.

Although the SSCI includes eight items related to moral-emotional responsiveness, only one item is included in the Goenjian report: external response to having done something wrong. The responses most frequently checked were "I look ashamed or guilty to any observer. I want to talk to someone about how to make it right"(stage 4) and "I turn inward to myself to figure out what to do" (stage 5). Both of these items indicate developmental sufficiency. We don't know if they also selected items indicative of PI, such as: "Sometimes I am too depressed to follow my conscience." "My bad mood makes me do bad things" or "I have done unforgivable things." Also not reported were responses, healthy or not, to items about the processes of reparation and healing.

## Moral Volition

Moral volition involves one's sense of agency. It addresses self-evaluation and commitment to carrying out self-chosen actions, positive or negative (e.g., retribution or revenge).

Impairment may involve inaction, irrational action, or immoral action. PTSD criteria indirectly related to dysfunction in the domain of moral volition come from Clusters C and E. Relevant descriptors include:

> ... persistent avoidance of stimuli associated with the traumatic event(s) in the form of distressing memories or external reminders; markedly diminished interest or participation in significant activities; irritable behavior and angry outbursts; reckless or self-destructive behavior.

Both the less traumatized Yerevan and the more traumatized Spitak groups selected items reflecting a loss of moral willpower due to confusion. The Spitak group was more likely to attribute the loss of moral willpower to "The world around me is basically evil."

### Commentary

The SSCI was specifically designed to compare moral development and PI in contrasting groups of adolescents who had experienced different levels of trauma from a natural disaster. However, the experiential base for developing the instrument came from youth suffering from a far different kind of trauma – multiple developmental traumas. Would we find a commonality in the effects of different kinds of trauma? Furthermore, would the meaning of the queries change when the instrument was administered in a classroom setting to youth speaking another language, growing up in a different culture under a different form of government? Although the SSCI needs some fine-tuning, it did support a universality in the relationships between trauma, psychopathology, and conscience malfunctioning. With time-unlimited, semi-structured interviews, these adolescents could have taught us even more about the effects of natural disasters on moralization, demoralization, and re-moralization.

## 5.6 Expansions in Conscience-Sensitive Assessment

The best way to understand human suffering (or thriving) is to *listen*. In psychiatric research, dimensional or dichotomous methods of categorizing human suffering are essential in determining diagnostic validity, seeking biological correlates, and evaluating treatment effectiveness. For clinicians, perusing checklist items is also useful in focusing or expanding the range of listening.

However, when the suffering to be *heard* is beyond the established range of the *Diagnostic and Statistical Reference Manual*, the psychiatrist and other mental health professionals must learn to listen outside of the DSM box. A new focus and range of listening are required for suffering related to moral injury and conscience malfunctioning. In pursuing additional ways of listening to moral suffering beyond the open-ended questions of the SCI or structured items checked on the SSCI, Galvin and the Indiana University Conscience Project have expanded conscience-sensitive assessments in several ways (Galvin, 2014;Galvin et al., 2006, 2019).

### 5.6.1 Conscience-Relevant Referral Materials

When a child or adolescent is admitted to a psychiatric residential center, he usually comes with a stack of referral materials (e.g., previous evaluations from psychiatrists, psychologists, social workers, teachers, juvenile case managers), all reviewing adverse child events and highlighting despicable behaviors at home, at school, or in the community. Since reports that highlight the negative are more conducive to securing admission, the conscience-sensitive psychiatrist will have to be diligent in looking for the slightest evidence of moral adequacy. Is there even the slightest evidence of meaningful attachment experiences; empathic emotional responsiveness; respect for authority, peers, or self; or conscionable actions? Any clues at all will guide the psychiatrist and the treatment staff to listen for fragments of conscience upon which to build a moralizing or re-moralizing treatment plan.

## 5.6.2 Conscience-Sensitive Evaluation

Time constraints imposed by practicality and third-party payers demand that a psychiatric evaluation be efficiently directed toward establishing DSM diagnoses. At best, only one hour is allowed. In addition to establishing the diagnosis(es), the second usual expectation is assessment of the patient's psychopharmacological history for necessary medication continuations or adjustments. These goals, although necessary, limit the psychiatrist's ability to really get to *know* the patient.

Although checklists are useful, the personal interview is the most meaningful part of the examination. Galvin has developed *conscience-sensitive methods* for making inquiries into domains of conscience while doing an initial DSM manual-oriented evaluation (Galvin et al., 2006, 2019). An example follows, using the customary psychiatric examination format. Actual quotes from an identity-concealed patient are followed by ALERT messages, indicating which moral domains need to be explored further in the initial evaluation and in subsequent therapy sessions. Pertinent questions from the SCI should be included.

*Chief concern*: "I make bad mistakes: doing drugs, smoking – which I still want to do – having sex at a young age. Just choices and decisions." ALERT: moral valuation and volition.

*History of present illness*: The patient indicated there were times in her life that she had been subject to low self-esteem and suicidal thinking (including a threatened attempt with a knife while she was under the influence of alcohol and drugs but which was foiled by her brother) but denied the latter in the present. ALERT: moral attachment, self-affirming values.

*Personal history*: Examiner continues a discussion of drug use: "You've told me about recreational drugs you would use like marijuana and some you would not use like heroin. What are some of the "because" reasons for these choices?" ALERT: reasoning and justification in the valuation domain.

*Review of systems*: Examiner: "You've told me that you first became sexually active at age (X) years and that you've had sexual partners and that you usually practice safe sex by using condoms. Are there some "do's and don'ts" you think are important about your sex life? ALERT: valuation and volition domains.

## 5.6.3 Conscience-Sensitive Inquiries and Tasks

After the initial psychiatric diagnostic assessment, a trained conscience-sensitive therapist can follow up on the ALERTs in the initial evaluation and proceed with *conscience-sensitive inquiries and tasks*. Three such tasks are: (1) the moralized genogram; (2) the value matrix; and (3) the suicide walk. These tasks can be both diagnostic and therapeutic. Although these tasks are suitable for a variety of traumatized patients with various psychiatric diagnoses, the case of a particular suicidal adolescent will be used for illustration.

## 5.6.4 Treatment of a Suicidal Adolescent

The value that a person places on life is a matter of conscience – who or what are you willing to live for and why. When an adolescent is psychiatrically hospitalized after a persistent period of talking and writing about suicide, and then, on admission, takes a miraculous *flight into health* hoping for a quick discharge, the clinician is left with difficult assessment and treatment planning tasks. Galvin advocates approaching this conundrum with three exercises delving into the conscience domains of attachment, valuation, and volition (Galvin et al., 2006).

### The Moralized Genogram

The moralized genogram (or triple pass genogram) is designed to assess the strength of *moral attachment* in an individual. First, the adolescent (with the help of a family member) was assisted in drawing a genogram, identifying family relationships and psychiatric disorders. On the second *passthrough* of the same diagram, she identified family members with whom she experienced the most emotional warmth and those with whom she experienced the most emotional conflict. On the third *passthrough,* she identified the family members who care the most about her moral worth (her goodness) and those who care the least. This exercise helped identify *who* in the family provided the strongest security-empathy-oughtness connection with her. Whom might she be willing to live for? In this case, it was the adolescent's mother.

### The Value Matrix

The value matrix is designed to assess the strength in a patient's *valuation domain* of conscience. It helps a person go as deeply as possible in examining his or her reasons and justifications for following or not following self-defined moral mandates. In this case, the main mandate to be processed was the value of living or dying. The patient was assisted in constructing a two-by-two table with the positive and negative forms of the mandate at the top. She was then asked to write or tell the "becauses" she would choose for each one. Then she was asked to *block* the first "because" and choose other ones ... and then other ones. In other words, "if the first 'because' could be removed, what would your reason be then?" The goal was to help her proceed from more superficial to deeper motivations. At first, reasons might be irrational, unrealistic fantasies, or excessively emotional statements (e.g., revenge fantasies). Effort is made to *pull out* the most sound reasons for honoring responsibility to self or others. In this case, reasoning ability was limited, but she settled on "I would hurt Mommy" as her best reason not to die.

### The Suicide Walk

The suicide walk is designed to assess the *volition domain* of a suicidal patient's conscience. It uses fantasy to achieve this goal. The patient was asked to write an essay pretending that she had already committed suicide, including what led up to the event, what went on at the funeral, what were the reactions of the important people in her life, and how did her death affect them after she was gone. The patient was then asked to read the essay aloud to her therapist, peer therapy group, or family, followed by her own and others' comments and reactions. The goal was to help the patient act in ways that replace fantasied thoughts and relationships with real ones. In this case, the patient concluded that her suicide would break her family's heart "and destroy them."

These three conscience-sensitive tasks suggested that decreasing the risk of suicide in this patient would best be served by working to strengthen the security-empathy-oughtness bond between her and her mother – the conscience domain of moral attachment.

### Summary

When a person, in this case an adolescent girl, is thinking about or planning suicide, the moral meaning of attachment experiences, value formation, emotions, and actions is broken. The power of conscience has been depleted of energy. Any remaining psychic energy is being directed toward becoming non-existent or at least not being "here." When the trauma of hospitalization for this adolescent led her to magically negate what she had been considering for weeks, the therapist's moral discovery work revealed at least a fragment of *security-empathy-oughtness* bonding to her mother. This meant that the adolescent's conscience could possibly be further *moralized or re-moralized* to value not only that relationship but also self-worth and other values in living.

## 5.6.5  Integrating Moral Injury, PI, and DSM-5

Most psychiatric treatment interventions require listening with an ear tuned to DSM-5 symptoms and clusters. The overall goal of DSM-5-oriented treatment is to help patients thrive within the reality of their culture by reducing symptomatology and fostering adaptation. Cognitions *ought to* become reality-oriented; emotions *ought* to become well regulated; behavior ought to become productive, creative, and society-conforming; relationships *ought* to become functional and fulfilling.

We hoped that the reader noticed the "oughts" in the last sentence. These are the oughts for psychiatry itself, its own professional moral mandate to utilize the scientific method to find the best possible biological treatments, the best forms of psychotherapy, and the best environmental supports for enhancing human adaptation. What about the oughts in patients' lives, the moral mandates that govern what they expect from themselves and others? What about their conscience? How well is their conscience dealing with the reality in which they are living?

Thanks to the professionals who listened to combat veterans, who came to realize that they were suffering from something more than PTSD, that they had *moral injuries* (Shay, 1995; Litz et al., 2009). The relatively new field of moral injury has accomplished much in (a) comprehensively defining moral injury (in our language, wounds to conscience); (b) applying the concept in both military and civilian contexts; and (c) developing clinical interventions and research approaches with great specificity. For example, in the area of cognition, Farnsworth draws a careful distinction between interventions that address distorted descriptive cognitions, which can be logically challenged, and prescriptive cognitions that require interventions that honor deeply held values and beliefs without logically challenging them (Farnsworth, 2019). This distinction is very important in determining which PTSD symptoms can be ameliorated through cognitive processing therapy and which ones are resistant to that approach.

The scientific studies of moral injury and PI dovetail in that they both require thinking outside the conceptual boundaries of DSM-5. Both approaches to human suffering honor the moral realm. Interventions suggested or employed by Farnsworth and Galvin have some similarities. For example, in the domain of moral valuation, Farnsworth's suggested interventions for exploring moral values, including balancing descriptive and prescriptive cognitions, are similar to the value matrix described above. In the moral-emotional domain, interventions promoting acceptance of past wrongs as well as compassion for self and others resonate with the reparation and healing component of that domain. In the conceptualization and moral volition domains, interventions that promote psychological distancing from the past and moving forward in life with values-consistent behavior resonate with the insightful changes that occur as youth transition from one stage of conceptualization to a more comprehensive one and actually change their behavior in the light of more comprehensive moral thinking.

A final anecdote about dealing with moral injury:

> Parents of an adolescent boy were concerned about their son's oppositional behavior. They said he had an "attitude." They wanted him to see a psychiatrist. He opposed that idea but reluctantly came for one family interview. He refused to come back. Then, one day, he told his parents that he wanted to start coming ... on his own. He had just gotten his driver's license. They were pleasantly surprised.

With obvious emotional distress, he told the psychiatrist about having stolen a gun from a department store some time back. He had no intentions of killing himself or anyone else. He just did it for the thrill of getting away with it. He hid the gun for a long time. Then, one day, he borrowed the family car, took the gun to a bridge over a reservoir, and dropped it in the water. He didn't want his parents to know, but he wanted someone to know. He needed a moral connection with someone, even though he only came for one appointment. Behaviors described by parents in that one family interview pointed toward a tentative diagnosis of oppositional defiant disorder or maybe conduct disorder. In contrast, the adolescent's concern was in the moral realm and he resolved it the best way he knew how.

## 5.7 The Conscience Journey: Review and Final Thoughts

### 5.7.1 Review

Seeking the moral meaning of suffering and thriving is a long journey. The authors have sought to discover the moral meaning that children and adolescents make out of their lives in normal circumstances and under extreme stress. It began accidentally when we learned that psychiatric patients over the age of six could readily talk about their conscience or its rudiments. We also discovered that the concept of conscience did not readily fit into psychiatry's diagnostic system.

Since our training was oriented toward psychopathology, we naturally wanted to know how conscience malfunctioning could fit into psychiatry's diagnostic system. However, this goal required the study of normal conscience development as a precedent. We developed a time-unlimited, semi-structured interview, the SCI, for children and adolescents who were free of bio-psychosocial impairment – known as the *advantaged* group. Deliberate analysis of their interviews resulted in the five-stage, five-domain construct of conscience, described in the first part of this chapter.

Youth with moderate-to-serious mental illness were then interviewed with the same time-unlimited, semi-structured interview. The content of the interviews, particularly those from psychiatrically hospitalized, conduct-disordered boys, was far different from those from the advantaged group. This group came to be known as the *disadvantaged* group. Following the thinking of the field of developmental psychopathology, we developed scales of deficiency and sufficiency in moral functioning. With additional interviews, particularly of adolescents suffering from PTSD, the deficiency scale transformed into *psychopathological interference to conscience functioning, PI.*

The next opportunity came from a request to structure the SCI into an instrument that could examine differential effects of trauma on adolescents suffering, not from multiple developmental adversities, but from the trauma of a natural disaster. That instrument became known as the Structured Stilwell Conscience Interview (SSCI). The study demonstrated that natural disasters could have differential effects on both moral development, PTSD symptomatology, and psychopathological interference to conscience functioning, according to the severity of the trauma and its aftermath.

An ongoing task is to integrate thinking about moral development, PI, and moral injury. The conundrums are familiar: Where does the conscience fit into the psychiatric diagnostic system? Where does moral injury fit into the same system, particularly with reference to PTSD? Do different kinds of moral injury have a differential impact on the psyche?

The authors approached these conundrums first with a description of moralization, demoralization, and re-moralization. We then examined three different contexts of moral injury: combat veterans, developmental adversities, and natural disaster.

Finally, we present a formulation that integrates our current thinking about conscience, psychopathology, and moral injury:

1. Trauma of varying types and sources can lead to
2. human suffering, expressed as psychopathology, which can be accompanied by
3. demoralization within the person's emerging or fully formed conscience.
4. When a person's conscience is morally injured, the loss of moral meaning, expressed as despair, confusion, and disillusionment, requires
5. re-moralization to relieve the suffering.

This formulation would be easier to present, or perhaps not needed, if the malfunctioning of the conscience was integrated into the psychiatric diagnostic system either as one of the required domains of functioning, a component of specific diagnoses, or as a diagnostic category in its own right.

## 5.7.2 Final Thoughts

Humans require an internal moral guide to make sense out of the complexities of living on earth. The mental construct of conscience comes into being as we progress through the lifespan, making moral sense out of our baseline needs for attachment and nurturance, emotional harmony within self and with others, values of fairness and responsibility, and our desire to behave and our expectations for others to behave in line with those values.

Along the way, unconscionable human behavior, including our own, or events beyond our control may disrupt the formation or functioning of conscience. When life events are morally overwhelming, when life is not what we believe it *should be,* moral distress may be experienced as moral injury.

In turn, a moral injury may precipitate or intensify psychiatric symptoms, particularly PTSD. In contrast, a moral injury may prompt the finding of new moral meaning, restructuring the conscience to deal with life's disappointments, complexities, or wrongs. Thus, moral development and conscience, moral injury, and psychopathology are integral parts of the dynamic human process of keeping life going and making moral sense of it.

Continued clinical experience, creative assessment tools, and research will help further this human story.

# References

Ailkin, J. (2013). *John Newton: From Grace to Amazing* Grace. Wheaton, IL: Crossway.

American Psychiatric Association (2013). *Diagnostic and Statistical Manual of Mental Disorders* (*Desk Reference*, 5th ed.). Arlington, VA: American Psychiatric Publishing.

Burns, K., and Novick, L. (2017). The Vietnam War. Public Broadcasting Series. Available at: https://kenburns.com/films/vietnam/.

Cicchetti, D. (2016). Understanding developmental pathways from adversity to maladaptation, psychopathology, or resilience. *Bulletin of the American Academy of Arts & Sciences*, Spring, 27–28.

Currier, J. M., McDermott, R. C., Farnsworth, J. K., Borges, L. M. (2019). Temporal associations between moral injury and posttraumatic stress disorder symptom clusters in military veterans. *Journal of Traumatic Stress*, 32, 382–392.

Farnsworth, J., (2019). Is and ought: descriptive and prescriptive cognitions in military-related moral injury. *Journal of Traumatic Stress*, 32, 373–381.

Galvin, M. (2014). Psychiatric diagnostic (DSM-5) contexts of psychopathological interference in conscience formation and functioning across the youth-span: a guideline. *Conscience Works: Theory, Research and Clinical Applications*, 4, 1–40. Retrieved from https://scholarworks.iupui.edu/handle/1805/6583.

Galvin, M., Fletcher, J., & Stilwell, B. (2006). Assessing meaning of suicidal risk behavior in adolescents: three exercises for clinicians. *Journal of the American Academy of Child and Adolescent Psychiatry*, 45, 745–748.

Galvin, M., Hulvershorn, L, Gaffney, M. (2019). Conscience relevance and sensitivity in psychiatric evaluations in the youth-span. *Adolescent Psychiatry*, 9, 167–184.

Goenjian, A. K. (1993). A mental health relief program in Armenia after the 1988 earthquake: implementation and clinical observations. *British Journal of Psychiatry*, 169, 230–239.

Goenjian, A., Stilwell, B., Fairbanks, L., Galvin, M., Karaya, I., & Pynoos, R. (1999). Moral development and psychopathological interference in conscience functioning among adolescents after trauma. *Journal of the American Academy of Child and Adolescent Psychiatry*, 38, 376–384.

Hattan D., (2018). *Invisible Scars of War: A Veteran's Struggle with Moral Injury*. Woodstock, IL: Woodstock Square Press.

Kor, E., & Buccieri, L. (2009). *Surviving the Angel of Death: The Story of a Mengele Twin in Auschwitz*. Terre Haute, IN: Tanglewood Publishing Company.

Litz, B. T., Stein, N., Delaney, E., Leibowitz, L., Nash, W. P., Silva, C., & Maguen, S. (2009). Moral injury and moral repair in war veterans: a preliminary model and intervention strategy. *Clinical Psychology Review*, 29, 695–706. https://doi.org/10.1016/j.cpr.2009.07.003.

Lurye, S. (2018). Thirty years after the Armenian earthquake, a New Yorker remembers his rescue. December 7, 2018. http://t.me/eurasianetnews.

*New Oxford American Dictionary*, 3rd ed. (2010). New York, NY: Oxford University Press.

Pinel, P. (1806). *A Treatise on Insanity*. Messers Cadell & Davies, Strand. https://doi.org/10.1037/10550-000.

Sapolsky, R. M. (2017). *Behave: The Biology of Humans at our Best and Worst*. New York, NY: Penguin.

Shay, J. (1995). *Achilles in Vietnam: Combat Trauma and the Undoing of Character*. New York, NY: Touchstone.

Stein, M. and Rothbaum, B. (2018). 175 years of progress in PTSD therapeutics: learning from the past. *American Journal of Psychiatry*, 175, 508–516.

Stilwell, B. (2002a). Trauma, moral development, and conscience functioning. *Conscience Works, Theory, Research and Clinical Applications*, 2(1), 1–4. Appendix A: The Stilwell Conscience Interview, English and Spanish versions (original work published November 5, 1994). Retrieved from http://scholarworks.iupui.edu/handle/1805/15746 [last accessed July 19, 2021].

Stilwell, B. (2002b). Trauma, moral development, and conscience functioning. *Conscience Works, Theory, Research and Clinical Applications*, 2(1), 1–4. Appendix B: The Stilwell Structured Conscience Interview. English and Armenian versions (original work published February 11, 1999). Retrieved from http://hdl.handle.net/1805/15743[last accessed July 19, 2021].

Stilwell, B., Galvin, M. (1993). Clinical assessment of the conscience delays and deficiencies in psychopathology. Workshop. Annual Meeting of AACAP, San Antonio, TX. *Scientific Proceedings of the Annual Meeting of the American Academy of Child and Adolescent Psychiatry*, 9, 16.

Stilwell, B., Galvin, M., & Kopta, M. (1991). Conceptualization of conscience in normal children and adolescents ages 5 to 17. *Journal of the American Academy of Child and Adolescent Psychiatry*, 30, 16–21.

Stilwell, B, Galvin, M., & Kopta, M. (2000). *Right vs. Wrong: Raising a Child with a Conscience*. Bloomington, IN: Indiana University Press.

Stilwell, B., Galvin, M., Kopta, M., & Norton, J. (1994). Moral-emotional responsiveness: a two-factor domain of conscience functioning. *Journal of the American Academy of Child and Adolescent Psychiatry*, 33, 130–139.

Stilwell, B., Galvin, M., Kopta, M., & Padgett, R. (1996). Moral valuation: a third domain of conscience functioning. *Journal of the American Academy of Child and Adolescent Psychiatry*, 35, 230–239.

Stilwell, B., Galvin, M., Kopta, M., & Padgett, R. (1998). Moral volition: the fifth and final domain leading to an integrated theory of conscience understanding. *Journal of the American Academy of Child and Adolescent Psychiatry*, 37, 202–210.

Stilwell, B., Galvin, M., Kopta, M., Padgett, R., & Holt, J. (1997). Moralization of attachment: a fourth domain of conscience functioning. *Journal of the American Academy of Child and Adolescent Psychiatry*, 36, 1140–1147.

Thunberg G., Thunberg S., Ernman M., Ernman B. (2018). *Our House Is on Fire: Scenes of a Family and a Planet in Crisis*. London: Penguin Books.

van der Kolk, B. A. (2014). *The Body Keeps the Score*. New York, NY: Penguin Press.

Verkamp, B. (1993). *Moral Treatment of Returning Warriors in Early Medieval and Modern Times*. Chicago, IL: University Chicago Press.

# Natural Disasters and Relocation

## 6

Louis M. Najarian and David Pelcovitz

## 6.1 Introduction

The initial response to a natural disaster is determined by a number of factors which depend on the unique nature of the disaster, including intensity, loss of life, and pre-disaster community cohesiveness. Empirical studies conducted over the last several decades have documented the importance of crucial factors such as the safety of survivors, medical/health needs, shelter, and the immediate resumption of normal daily activities such as work and school for children.

Often a natural disaster is so severe that relocation from the damaged area is necessary. The focus of this chapter is a systematic review of studies that have assessed the impact of relocation on survivors. One way to examine the effect of relocation is by examining the natural disaster through the lens of an individual seeking psychological help from a mental health professional. We can ask the disaster survivor what their symptoms are, as well as their intensity and the duration of any discomfort, and what makes it better? Specific questions that are asked include: what is the intensity and extent of damage to their homes and the extent of destruction in the city? Where did the victims go? How far, and how long were they away? Did they relocate permanently, or did they return to the reconstructed home, or to a different community?

This current literature review of the last ten years addressed all these questions to survivors regarding their experiences of disasters. Their answers always led to more questions. Every individual requesting psychological help for non-disaster-related issues presents with their own individual differences regarding personality, history, intensity of symptoms, and cultural issues. So do natural disasters. Earthquakes are sudden with no warning and last one to four minutes, with the length of aftershocks ranging from seconds to weeks, even months after the initial event. The extent of the destruction requiring relocation for safety and living differs according to the environmental and cultural preparedness of a specific region (e.g., Armenia, Iran, Taiwan, Puerto Rico, Japan, Turkey, New Zealand, and the United States).

A powerful example of this is evident when we compare the environmental preparedness in San Francisco during the 1989 earthquake with the 1988 Armenian earthquake. Although both earthquakes were of similar intensity, San Francisco's earthquake caused sixty-three deaths (Pointer et al., 1992) compared to at least 25,000 deaths in Armenia (Noji et al., 1990). In Armenia, more than 500,000 individuals were displaced compared to 12,035 from the epicenter of the San Francisco earthquake. There was only a small amount of damage to San Francisco requiring limited relocation, while, due to far less rigorous enforcement of building codes, Armenia experienced a greater loss of life and property damage.

Hurricanes and floods present with different "temperaments" in the nature of disaster (e.g., Katrina, Sandy). Warning by meteorologists may allow for cultural "preparedness" but one never truly knows the temperament of the hurricane or flood. The damaging effect of a flood may continue for days, with exposure to destruction until the waters recede. The temperament of the hurricane may present with warning signs and then unleash its fury while an anxious population waits to see its destruction as it passes in a few hours. Tsunamis and tornados are similar to hurricanes but give little or no warning, and then the onslaught comes, leaving victims traumatized. Fires occur suddenly, without warning, and their characteristic is determined by the environment, either in a city or wilderness, with or without damage to homes.

The general consensus from studies on the effect of relocation after a natural disaster is that relocated individuals have more psychological symptoms of stress, PTSD, and depression compared to those who stayed, regardless of the type of natural disaster.

We summarize studies of various natural disasters that have extensively examined the effect of relocation on affected populations in Armenia, New Orleans, eastern New York, Japan, Iran, Taiwan, New Zealand, Puerto Rico, and Turkey.

## 6.2 Armenia

### 6.2.1 The Spitak Earthquake

The devastating earthquake in Spitak, Armenia, on December 7, 1988, killed more than 25,000 people and necessitated the relocation of thousands of families to safer areas. Many individuals relocated to hotels in Yerevan, the capital of Armenia, located 110 kilometers from the epicenter, where there was little damage and minimal deaths.

Teams of mental health professionals from the United States provided crisis intervention to victims of direct exposure relocated to Yerevan and those who remained in Gyumri, the largest city damaged by the earthquake. According to clinicians working with the relocated survivors, those individuals living in a hotel within an intact city with such commodities as heat, electricity, and running water, with their children attending school in intact buildings, maintaining some semblance of normal life, appeared to adapt better to the disaster than those individuals living in trailers or tents in the earthquake zone without everyday conveniences.

A study on relocation by Najarian et al. (1996), conducted 2.5 years after the earthquake, included three groups of children aged eleven to thirteen and their mothers: an exposed group from Gyumri that relocated to Yerevan, a group with similar exposure that remained in Gyumri, and a comparison group with mild exposure in Yerevan (Najarian et al., 1996; 2001). The two similarly exposed Gyumri groups had equal rates of PTSD and depression, but the children who remained in Gyumri had fewer behavior problems and socialization issues. The mothers in both exposed groups had similar rates of PTSD, while the relocated mothers had significantly higher depression scores. The pervasive unrepaired, damaged structures, 2.5 years after the event (when the study took place), served as daily reminders of the disaster in Gyumri. The mothers and their children who remained in Gyumri benefited from the "tie to the community" despite the adversities (e.g., lack of heat, electricity, transportation, etc.) and the pervasive traumatic reminders. They functioned better than the relocated group. Although both relocated and not relocated groups had equally high rates of PTSD, the mother–child pairs who remained in the earthquake city functioned better (Najarian et al., 2001).

The Armenian experience suggests that remaining in the affected city after a disaster promoted better adaptation to the adversities of the trauma in spite of years of delay in reconstruction and return to normal services. Armenia is a homogeneous country, and the areas affected by the earthquake included families with several generations living and working in the area. The exposed families, who remained in the devastated area and demonstrated greater improvement, support Dr. Kai Erikson's findings after the Buffalo Creek disaster (Erikson, 1976). He stressed the importance of the "tie to the community" as a cornerstone of the process of improving recovery by enhancing social support provided by extended family, neighbors, and the Church.

Another study in Armenia, conducted twenty years after the earthquake, compared subjects who had similar exposure to the earthquake (Najarian et al., 2017). One group stayed in Vanadzor, the affected city, another group relocated to Yerevan but later returned to Vanadzor, and a third group left permanently. The results were contrary to most findings of relocated individuals, but the demographics may explain the differences. Relocated subjects who returned reported significantly higher rates of PTSD and SCL-90 scores compared to those who stayed in Vanadzor but the permanently relocated to Russia and eastern Europe had significantly lower scores on all instruments compared to the other two exposed groups. The permanently relocated group, who happened to be visiting family during the summer when the study was conducted, were younger, more educated, and not married. They moved to Armenian communities in the diaspora, where they maintained their culture in Russia and eastern Europe and established successful careers and families. These results are similar to the theme in the book *Outliers: The Story of Success* (Malcolm Gladwell, 2008), which states that fortuitous timing (dissolution of the Soviet Union) coupled with a number of other variables associated with recovery – including younger age, being single, and higher levels of education – all were associated with individuals willing to take a chance together with the unleashed creativity afforded by the opportunity to begin a new life in a different environment.

## 6.3  The United States

### 6.3.1  Hurricane Katrina

In August 2005, Hurricane Katrina slammed into southeastern Louisiana, killing 1,800 people, requiring 35,000 to be rescued, and 1.7 million to be relocated (Hansel et al., 2013). Four years after the hurricane, the National Child Traumatic Stress Network conducted a needs assessment of 795 children with an average age of 14.8, who were relocated to Baton Rouge, located eighty miles from New Orleans. The students were divided into three groups: 34% were relocated permanently to Baton Rouge, 44% had returned to their original zip code, and 22% had returned to a different zip code. The permanently relocated group reported more symptoms of depression and PTSD compared to both returned groups. No mention was made regarding how long the returned groups remained in Baton Rouge. Although not stated, the return to a different zip code may have reflected severe damage and the inability to live in the prior zip code.

The different stress reaction trajectories of children and adolescents in response to the relocation is an important contribution of the study. The adolescents did better when returned to their familiar home environment, whereas the younger children required more time to adapt to their surroundings. This difference may be explained by "place attachment"; the struggle with identity, independence, and separation was conflictual in the relocated city for adolescents but not for younger children. When returning home, the adolescents felt more comfortable in a familiar environment, while younger children experienced more anxiety in adapting. All groups indicated that the primary stresses were parental unemployment, guests living in their home, prior trauma, and separation from parents. In conclusion, the study would have been stronger if more information was available about where the relocated subjects resided in Baton Rouge and if they returned to their original repaired homes or other residences due to the extent of damage to their primary home.

In another study, two years after Katrina, 612 students took part, of which sixty-six were displaced twenty-four hours before Katrina struck, in order to provide safety (Blaze et al., 2009). The displaced group reported higher levels of psychological distress and post-traumatic symptoms. The displaced students were unable to return to their destroyed homes. The greater the distance from home and the longer the time away contributed to higher stress rates in the adolescent permanently relocated group. The location and circumstances of their displacement were not included in the study. Having more knowledge about their hurricane exposure compared to the other students and the post-hurricane period would have clarified which aspect contributed to their symptoms; the initial trauma, absence of decent housing, and/or separation from the community or their families.

A valuable study of relocation after hurricane Katrina was conducted among 392 mothers adopting Hobfoll's Conservation of Resources (COR) theory to understand the effect of relocation and other determinants of individual responses to the disaster (Fussell et al., 2014). Hobfoll posits that individuals seek to conserve resources such as valued objects, familiar surroundings and conditions, personal routines, and energy (Hobfoll, 2001). All the subjects were forced to relocate because of the damage to their homes. Twenty-four percent returned to their pre-disaster homes after a few moves to nearby locations. Forty-eight percent relocated to a new state after a few moves before permanent relocation. Twenty-six percent experienced multiple moves over a prolonged period of time at a great distance from their pre-disaster home and eventually returned to New Orleans. The mothers relocated to a different state, and the mothers with extended periods of movement at a greater distance from New Orleans experienced significantly higher psychological distress than the first relocated group who were displaced for a briefer period of time and shorter distance from home. The geographic location, multiple moves, and housing types in some relocated groups contributed to the high recorded stress levels. Among some, the displacement weakened the survivor's capacity to conserve resources. The most important risk factors included loss of social support, unemployment, financial loss, and child psychopathology. This study highlights the importance of various aspects involved with relocation that can impact survivors' stress reactions. It is possible that survivors with fewer moves and a shorter time away were exposed to less severe traumatic experiences, based on the fact they returned to their homes quickly (possibly because there was less damage to them). They had less severe PTSD symptoms, possibly due to less severe exposure and not necessarily due to the relocation effect. Across-group comparisons of exposure would have been helpful to separate the effect of relocation and exposure on PTSD and depressive symptoms.

Tucker et al., (2018) evaluated thirty-four adult survivors from Katrina relocated to Oklahoma twenty months post-Katrina and matched them with thirty-four Oklahoma residents exposed to a lower level of trauma. Katrina survivors had higher PTSD and depression symptoms and higher autonomic measures, reflecting higher baseline blood pressure and heart rate, and higher interleukin-2 reflecting cell-related immunity. This study demonstrated that relocated victims are subject to increased psychological symptoms, cardiovascular risks, and immunologic alterations. This is relevant in light of the increased rate of myocardial infarcts after Katrina.

In summary, hurricane Katrina has been described as the worst natural disaster in US history, causing devastating destruction and loss. Even in a major developed city such as New Orleans, the recovery took years, forcing the relocation of people to other parts of Louisiana, Arkansas, Oklahoma, Texas, and Florida. Relocation to other areas was a risk factor for PTSD and depression. The relocated individuals suffered more losses: family members, homes, jobs, financial security, and social networks.

## 6.3.2 Hurricane Sandy

On October 29, 2012, Hurricane Sandy devastated areas of New York City and eastern Long Island, destroying more than 300,000 homes and killing sixty citizens (Schwartz et al., 2018). A sample of 1,615 adults with similar exposure and complete loss of residence were studied four years after Sandy, comparing perceived stress, depression, anxiety, and PTSD between displaced and non-displaced subjects. Subjects living in shelters had a 48% greater chance of having PTSD compared to those living with friends or relatives.

Another study, in which two communities devastated by Hurricane Sandy were offered money by the State of New York either to move to another location or use the money to remain in their repaired homes, was conducted by Binder and colleagues (2015). This study offers important information for governmental policies. The home buyout program was intended to facilitate permanent relocation of residents away from areas at risk of future hazards. Oakwood Beach is a residential community on the eastern shore of Staten Island, and Rockaway Park is located on the Rockaway Peninsula in Queens. Both communities had similar socioeconomic status; they were blue-collar workers with governmental jobs who had lived in their respective one-dwelling homes for two or more generations. They both felt a sense of community, "an oasis" in New York City, a "connection to community," "a piece of the American Dream," with the opportunity to walk on the beach and "get sand in your shoes." Pfefferbaum's Resilience Survey (2013), indicated that both communities scored highly. Both communities had deep personal, family, and intergenerational ties to the area which contributed to a strong "sense *of place.*" Both communities demonstrated two characteristics of disaster resilience by *adapting to an event* (Rockaway Park) and *change* (Oakwood Beach). Oakwood Beach accepted the buyout, and residents moved to another location because they had experienced several hurricanes in the past and the community was also beginning to change, with developers building high-rise apartments. The Rockaway Park community stayed because Sandy was their first major natural disaster, and they felt it was an anomaly and they would rebuild. Both decisions must be understood in the local historical, cultural context and the "connection to place" or Erikson's "tie to the community" (Erikson, 1976). A follow-up of outcome measures in both communities would have enhanced decisions by government policymakers regarding future buyouts when the destruction is severe.

## 6.3.3 Hurricane Maria

Hurricane Maria ravaged Puerto Rico in 2018, displacing several hundred residents to Florida (Sesin, 2017). Several years prior to the hurricane, a study of mental illness in the

Puerto Rican community indicated the baseline prevalence of depression was 19.4%, generalized anxiety was 7.3%, and PTSD was 6.8% (Scaramutti et al., 2019). Following the hurricane, two groups of similarly exposed subjects (relocated and remained) experienced high rates of depressive symptoms, anxiety symptoms, and PTSD compared to pre-hurricane status. However, subjects displaced to Florida experienced clinical levels of depression (46.5%), anxiety (25%), and PTSD (65.7%), significantly more than those subjects remaining in Puerto Rico (depression 32.7%; anxiety 27%; PTSD 43.6%).

Individuals who left Puerto Rico suffered greater personal and property loss, which must be considered a risk factor for higher symptoms in addition to the effect of relocation. These findings are important because of the availability of baseline prevalence rates of mental illness. The study showed a significant increase in PTSD and depression among those who were relocated.

## 6.4 Turkey

Studies of two earthquakes in Turkey have slightly different results based on the design of the studies but in general, support the view that relocation from a natural disaster causes more psychological stress.

In August and November 1999, two seismic events occurred 200 miles from Ankara, the capital of Turkey, which is considered to be an area safe from earthquakes. Approximately 20,000 people were killed (Kilic et al., 2006). In October and November 2011, two earthquakes in Van caused the collapse and severe damage to 49,000 buildings and 644 people were killed (Sezgin et al., 2016). Van, located in southeastern Turkey, sits on a seismic fault and is prone to earthquakes and tremors.

### 6.4.1 The Van Earthquake

This study was conducted a year after the Van earthquake, among relocated and remaining groups of women between the ages of fifteen to sixty-seven with similar socioeconomic backgrounds. The study highlights the difficulty in assessing the effect of relocation (Sezgin et al., 2016). Both groups experienced similar exposure, but the relocated women had not only experienced the loss of their homes but also received less social/financial assistance when they moved to nearby villages or Istanbul. When the relocated group returned one year after the earthquake (when the study was conducted), they demonstrated high levels of intrusive symptoms, somatization, hostility, and socialization problems compared to the group that had not relocated. The relocated group experienced more mental health problems and PTSD symptoms compared to the group that had stayed. Although all subjects had a similar level of exposure, the group that remained had not lost their homes. The loss of homes in the relocated group may have had an additive effect to that of relocation on severity of PTSD and depression.

A second study in Van examined 541 men and women selected from a sample and divided them into three groups: those who had relocated to Istanbul permanently; those who had relocated to Istanbul and then returned to Van; and those who never left Van but relocated internally to safer residences such as tents or containers in the city of Van (Salcioglu et al., 2018). All three groups suffered severe damage and loss to their homes. Both groups that left had friends, family, or financial resources to relocate to Istanbul. The prevalence of PTSD was 21.6% and depression 17.4% for all subjects combined. The rate of PTSD and depression was higher in the group that stayed in Van, having relocated within the city for safer residences, compared to the two groups who relocated permanently to Istanbul and those who returned from Istanbul. However, there was no statistical significance between rates of PTSD and depression between the three groups. Relocation of survivors within the city to tents and trailers was a significant predictor for PTSD symptoms for those survivors who remained. The remaining group continued to experience aftershocks, anticipatory fear of future earthquakes, and lack of a sense of control, all predictors of stress reactions.

Both relocated groups had stayed with friends or family and maintained cohesiveness within their families that may have served as protective factors. Strengths of this study included data that the relocated subjects left within a mean of fifteen days following the earthquake, and reasons for leaving were fear of earthquakes, difficult living conditions in tents, and property and financial losses. The relocated group that had returned stayed in Istanbul for a mean of 155 days. They returned because of social and emotional problems, were granted government housing, and had decreased fear of earthquakes. A follow-up psychological assessment among the permanently relocated survivors in Istanbul would have provided important information on the long-term effect of relocation.

## 6.4.2 The Marmara Earthquakes

Kilic et al. (2006) studied 526 survivors of the Marmara earthquakes four years after the two events (one in August and another in November 1999) that killed about 20,000 people. The study divided the subjects into two groups, including those subjects who lived permanently in the earthquake zone, were exposed to the earthquake, and subsequently relocated to Ankara, where they stayed with relatives. The non-relocated subjects, who were residents of Ankara with a summer home in the earthquake area and had been visiting the area for a holiday, were equally exposed and returned immediately to their permanent residences in Ankara. Both groups left for Ankara soon after the earthquake, having witnessed horrible scenes, including, rescue efforts of loved ones. They were fearful of future earthquakes because the area was not known for seismic activity, job losses, and interrupted education for their children. Relocation predicted depression but not post-traumatic stress symptom severity four years post-earthquake. The fact that depression predominated and not PTSD is consistent with another study which showed that untreated PTSD symptoms subsided while depression increased five years after the Spitak earthquake (Goenjian et al., 2005). This study exemplifies the difficulty of evaluating the effect of relocation as an independent factor when the subjects experienced such extensive damage to property, loss of family and ties to their community, necessitating displacement and establishing a new life elsewhere.

Kilic et al. (2011) examined the effect of parental psychopathology among 104 children (forty-three boys and sixty-one girls), aged between eight to fifteen, exposed to the same Marmara earthquake previously mentioned, and the effect of relocation on the children. Studies often investigate a mother's impact on children during trauma (Laor et al., 1997; Najarian et al., 2001), but the authors examined both mothers' and fathers' reactions to trauma and relocation away from the earthquake area. As in the prior Ankara study, it is difficult to distinguish whether severe damage/loss or displacement as independent factors contributed to the outcomes. Although the relocated fathers' stress scores (primarily irritability) were significantly higher than the non-relocated fathers' stress scores, there was no significant difference in the stress scores of both groups of children. The relocation did not appear to have a significant effect on the children's psychopathology. This may be explained partly by the fact that relocated families remained intact with both parents, and although relocation may have had an effect, the presence of stable adaptation with resilience on the part of the fathers' functioning and the cultural role of the father as a strong leader mitigated possible negative effects of relocation on the children.

## 6.5 Iran

### 6.5.1 Manjil–Rudbar Earthquake

On June 21, 1990, an earthquake of 7.5 on the Richter scale devastated 700 primarily agricultural villages in Manjil, Iran, killing 40,000 people. Eleven years later, the government initiated a program of forced resettlement in post-disaster Iran (Badri et al., 2006). The article describes a list of nine best practices, such as providing social support, supporting economic development together with the adoption of appropriate compensation policies, and engaging stakeholders in the recovery process. The goals were well formulated and logical, but unfortunately, they were not implemented.

Essentially the victims were relocated to another area where a larger village was created next to a provincial capital. The victims were farmers and required shelter, land for farming, and social support. The main economic activity was farming and livestock. The forced relocation did not provide sufficient land, equipment, and economic assistance for the farmers to start again. Competition emerged with the host city as women in the host city were given more favorable governmental jobs and relocated women continued doing agricultural work. Many positive aspects may have emerged from the involuntary resettlement if more sustainable development goals were enforced by governmental agencies. Lessons learned from this project would be helpful for implementing a more successful resettlement program in rural agricultural areas in case of future catastrophic disasters. The basic goal of sustainable development was not achieved, the relocated survivors lost access to natural resources, and there was a decline in their ability to cope with the post-disaster situation.

## 6.6 New Zealand

### 6.6.1 Christchurch Earthquake

The study on relocation by Hogg et al., (2016) after the February 22, 2011, Christchurch magnitude 6.3 earthquake in New Zealand was unique because it included subjects seeking treatment for mood and anxiety symptoms one year prior to the earthquake. The study compared mood and anxiety symptoms of subjects seeking treatment in the community one- and two-years post-earthquake to the one-year pre-earthquake data of subjects seeking treatment. The samples were divided into four groups: subjects who stayed in Christchurch with little or no damage to homes; subjects who relocated to other zip codes within the city because of significant damage; subjects who moved out of Christchurch and returned within one year to their original zip code; and subjects who relocated permanently out of the city because of severe damage to their homes.

The group that was relocated within the city and the group that had left the city and then eventually returned, were significantly more likely to seek treatment for mood and anxiety symptoms compared to those who did not relocate. The permanently relocated subjects sought treatment more than those that remained, but not significantly more than the two groups (one moving within the city and the other moving out of the city, both eventually returning to Christchurch).

The study included the socioeconomic status of the survivors relative to the degree of damage. The returnees who had moved out of the city and those moving within the city were the poorest and sustained the greatest damage to their homes. As a result of the damage, the returnees moved out of the city to temporary housing, eventually to return to their original homes; the in-city group relocated permanently to new residences within the city immediately after the earthquake. The second-year follow-up study indicated that the permanently relocated subjects were especially vulnerable and seeking treatment for anxiety and mood disorders significantly more than the other three groups.

The study represents a significant addition to our knowledge of the impact of relocation after a natural disaster because it used pre- and post-national register data for individuals seeking treatment. A limitation of this study was the absence of instruments to measure PTSD, anxiety, or depression. Nevertheless, it adds to the literature that relocation after a disaster is a risk factor for emotional disturbance in all victims, especially the elderly and those with pre-existing mental illness.

## 6.7 Taiwan

### 6.7.1 Chi-Chi Earthquake

On September 21, 1999, an earthquake in Taiwan measuring 7.3 on the Richter scale, killed 2,471 individuals. The study examined subjects over the age of fifty-five. One group remained in their homes (N = 48), and another group was relocated (N = 56) because of the damage to their homes (Watanabe et al., 2004). Depression was the only condition studied at both six- and twelve-months post-earthquake. The displaced individuals experienced significantly higher levels of depression than those who remained. The study did not ascertain whether the higher depression among the relocated was due to the severity of the exposure at the time of the earthquake and loss of their homes or relocation. However, it identified factors that lessened depressive symptoms after twelve months, which included support from extended family and neighbors, and establishing neighborhood associations, religious groups, and social clubs.

## 6.8 Japan

### 6.8.1 Tōhoku Earthquake and Tsunami (The Great Japan Earthquake and Tsunami)

On March 11, 2011, a magnitude 9.0 earthquake in the northern part of the main island of Japan was followed by a tsunami in the coastal areas (Yokoyama et al., 2014). There were 15,984 confirmed deaths and 2,553 people missing. Together with the extensive property damage, this natural disaster is considered to be the most devastating in Japan's history. A number of well-designed prospective studies systematically documented the psychological, social, and health impact of relocation with a unique focus on elderly survivors. Data from a nationwide study in 2010 that examined prospective predictors of healthy aging was used as baseline data for several post-earthquake studies (Saito, 2014).

In a particularly well designed natural study, Hikichi et al. (2017) had baseline data for older adults gathered before the disaster, who lived close to the epicenter of the earthquake. Two and a half years after the disaster, they found that those who were relocated had more social participation and informal socializing than those who moved on their own. Prior to the disaster, the culture of the provinces studied included periodic disaster preparedness drills and organization of fire brigades. The researchers hypothesized that group relocation allowed those survivors to preserve and strengthen those social bonds.

Another unique cross-sectional study conducted after the earthquake and tsunami also included data gathered before the disaster as part of the Japan gerontological evaluation study that analyzed the mental health of survivors two and a half years before the earthquake and tsunami (Sasaki et al., 2018). The focus of that study was to investigate whether the type of residential housing predicted levels of depression in survivors. Participants who moved into new housing were one and a half times more likely to self-report symptoms of depression than those who stayed in their community. The type of accommodation associated with higher levels of depression included prefabricated housing. The association of depression with the type of housing was, presumably, the lack of privacy, high level of noise because of thin walls, and lack of community cohesion in a housing situation that did not promote interaction and support. A recent study after the Great Japan earthquake suggests an increase in alcohol consumption (Hikichi et al., 2019) and a decline in physical health (Yzermans et al., 2005) among relocated survivors.

An important component to keep in mind in understanding the unique presentation after a tsunami is cultural differences in approaches to mental health in Asian communities. A Western model did not necessarily transfer well in working with Buddhist physicians after the tsunami in Sri Lanka. Using a "train the trainer model," which included one of the authors (DP) as a trainer of "best practices" regarding PTSD, there was little interest on the part of the local physicians to utilize the information provided. They showed far more interest in anger management and teaching girls and women self-defense.

In another study showing the impact of differing cultural norms on psychological sequelae, Fernando (2008) found that compared to Christian children who had survived war and violence, Buddhist and Hindu children had lower rates of PTSD despite greater exposure. The lower PTSD rate may be the result of a cultural tradition that promotes active acceptance of pain and suffering coupled with a belief in reincarnation. Sri Lankans were reported by Dr. Fernando as far more likely to experience physical symptoms after trauma. They reacted to disaster as if they had experienced a physical blow to the body. Rather than present with traditional PTSD symptoms, their focus was on the damage that the tsunami did to social relationships. Those isolated from their social network after the disaster who were not able to fulfil their role in their kinship group fared much more poorly. They conceived of the damage done by the tsunami as occurring not inside their mind but outside their self, in the social environment (Watters, 2011). As Watters writes regarding Western advice for self-care guided by the recommendation to "put on your oxygen mask first before helping your child": "For a Sri Lankan, the very expression of mental health might be embodied in the act of helping others. Putting the oxygen mask over the mouth of the child in the next seat would be the very thing that would allow (the adult) to breathe" (Watters 2011, p. 96).

# 6.9  Conclusion

After an extensive review of the literature for the last ten years on natural disasters and the effect of relocation, the majority of the research suggests that relocating away from the disaster area is a risk factor for developing PTSD, depression, and anxiety.

Several trends emerge in the literature. People with lower socioeconomic status are generally the ones who move more often. They do not have the resources to remain in a damaged, unsafe area and end up living in camps with tents or container dwellings for years. The elderly are at higher risk because of isolation and lack of social support. Pre-existing emotional conditions are always a greater risk for exacerbation when confronted with a new stressful life circumstance such as relocation. Studies examining children and adolescents surprisingly demonstrate more adaptive functioning than expected. Although many studies indicate the child's reaction depends on the mother's coping with the stress of the trauma, surprisingly, the father's adaptation and employment have emerged as a uniquely protective factor in children's reactions.

Complicating factors in studying relocation as an isolated determinant affecting the mental health of victims' reactions to disasters are confounding factors, such as the extent of damage, loss, and safety, making relocation necessary. The difficulty is in teasing out the effect of the destruction and losses from the effect of relocation on the stress reactions, e.g., PTSD and depression. Teasing out the effects of these variables is difficult, as seen in many of the aforementioned studies. It requires careful assessment of the extent of damage, loss, death, unemployment, adversities, and the extent of social support available in the displaced area and controlling for the contribution of each variable to the outcome.

The consistent ingredient of resilience and recovery in the mitigation of emotional disturbance documented in all of the studies reviewed here is emotional and material support. This included financial, residential, employment, medical, and psychosocial. With regard to the Armenian experience, the main benefit to the victims in Gyumri and Spitak may have been the presence by the diaspora-supported Psychiatric Outreach Program, which provided continued assistance. It enabled the mental health team, all fluent in the Armenian language, to remain present on a continuous basis for twenty-five years. The team leaders from the United States continued to go back and forth to Armenia regularly, which stands in contrast to typical practice which provides short-term mental health support – usually followed by the mental health team's return to their countries.

# 6.10  Recommendations

1. In determining the hierarchy of priorities guiding treatment planning in survivors of natural disasters, an analogy is often given of a pebble thrown into a pond forming concentric circles, the circle (subjects) closest to the point of impact (disaster) require the most attention. Accordingly, in order of priority, we should direct our efforts to:

   (a)  Addressing physical injury and general health
   (b)  Rebuilding homes and infrastructure as soon as possible
   (c)  Economic/employment support
   (d)  Resumption of schools

2. The research suggests that a pivotal role played by communities was fostering a sense of cohesiveness and belonging. Disaster survivors who recover with the support of their

community show better mental health outcomes, especially when, prior to the event, the community was provided with disaster preparedness that brought the community together.

3. When Western-trained professionals offer assistance to countries with Eastern cultures and differing value systems, cultural sensitivity on the part of the mental health clinicians is crucial.

4. As demonstrated in this review, research designs that investigate relocation as an independent variable are extremely difficult. A confounding variable that is seen in many studies is that displaced individuals compared to non-displaced individuals often have had more severe traumatic experiences and more losses (material and death), and as a result, they are expected to experience more distress compared to others who were relocated but had less severe traumatic experiences and losses. The availability of pre-disaster data on the population, as in Puerta Rico, New Zealand, and Japan, provides an excellent opportunity to study relocation. Ideally, research on the impact of relocation would require a control group with the same degree of exposure and losses as the relocated group. Also, information on prior mental illness, severity of exposure to the trauma, the extent of destruction of residence, loss of family members, and details about the relocation would be helpful to tease out the contribution of relocation, losses, and exposure to the outcome variables. An ideal design would also include longitudinal assessments over time to determine what improved and why in both those who stayed and those who relocated.

# References

Badri, S. A., Asgary, A., Eftekhari, A. R., & Levy, J. (2006). Post-disaster resettlement, development, and change: a case study of the 1990 Manjil earthquake in Iran. *Disasters*, 30, 451–468.

Binder, S. K., Baker, C. K., & Barile, J. P. (2015). Build or relocate? Resilience and post disaster decision-making after Hurricane Sandy. *American Journal of Community Psychology*, 56, 180–196.

Blaze, J. T., Shwalb, D. W. (2009). Resource loss and relocation: a follow-up study of adolescents two years after Hurricane Katrina. *Psychological Trauma Theory, Research, Practice and Policy*, 1, 312–322.

Erikson, K. T. (1976). *Everything in Its Path: Destruction of Community in the Buffalo Creek Flood*. New York, NY: Simon & Schuster.

Fernando, G. A. (2008). Assessing mental health and psychosocial status in communities exposed to traumatic events: Sri Lanka as an example. *American Journal of Orthopsychiatry*, 2, 229–239.

Fussell, E., Lowe, S. R. (2014). The impact of housing displacement on mental health of low-income parents after Hurricane Katrina. *Social Science and Medicine*, 113, 137–144.

Gaithri, A. F. (2008). Assessing mental health and psychosocial status in communities exposed to traumatic events: Sri Lanka as an example. *American Journal Orthopsychiatry*, 78, 229–239.

Gladwell, M. (2008). *Outliers: The Story of Success*. New York, NY: Little Brown and Company.

Goenjian, A. K., Walling, D., Steinberg, A. M., Karayan, I., Najarian, L. M., & Pynoos, R. S. (2005). Five years post-disaster: a prospective study of posttraumatic stress and depressive symptoms among treated and untreated adolescents. *American Journal of Psychiatry*, 162, 1–7.

Hansel, T. C., Osofsky, J. D., Osofsky, H. J., Friedrich, P. (2013). The effect of long-term relocation on child and adolescent survivors of Hurricane Katrina. *Journal of Traumatic Stress*, 26, 613–620.

Hikichi, H., Sawada, Y., Tsuboya, T., Aida, J., Kondo, K., Koyama, S., & Kawachi, I. (2017). Residential relocation and change in social capital: a natural experiment from the 2011

Great East Japan Earthquake and Tsunami. *Science Advances*, 3, e1700246.

Hikichi, H., Aida, J., Kondo, K., Tsuboya, T., Kawachi, I. (2019). Residential relocation and obesity after a natural disaster: a natural experiment from the 2011 Japan earthquake and tsunami. *Scientific Reports*, 9, 374. https://doi.org/10.1038/s41598-018-36906-y.

Hobfoll, S. E. (2001). The influence of culture, community, and the nested-self in the stress process: advancing conservation of resources theory. *Applied Psychological International Review*, 50, 337–421.

Hogg, D., Kingham, S., Wilson, T. M., Ardagh, M. (2016). The effect of relocation and level of affectedness on mood and anxiety symptom treatments after the 2011 Christchurch earthquake. *Social Science and Medicine*, 152, 18–26.

Kilic, C., Aydin, I., Taskintuna, N., Ozcurumez, G., Kurt, G., Eren, E., Lale,T., Ozel, S., & Zileli, L. (2006). Predictors of psychological distress in survivors of the 1999 earthquakes in Turkey: effects of relocation after the disaster. *Acta Psychiatra Scandanavia*, 114, 194–202.

Kilic, C., Kilic, E. M., & Aydin, I.O. (2011). Effect of relocation and parental psychopathology on earthquake survivor-children's mental health. *Journal of Nervous and Mental Disease*, 199, 335–341.

Laor, N., Mayers, L., Golomb, A., Silverberg, D. S., Weizman, R., & Cohen, D. (1997). Israeli preschool children under scuds: a 30-month follow-up. *Journal of the American Academy of Child and Adolescent Psychiatry*, 36, 349–356.

Najarian, L. M., Goenjian, A. K., Pelcovitz, D., Mandel, F., & Najarian, B. (1996). Relocation after a disaster: posttraumatic stress disorder in Armenia after the earthquake. *Journal of the American Academy of Child and Adolescent Psychiatry*, 35, 374–383.

Najarian, L. M., Goenjian, A. K., Pelcovitz, D., Mandel, F., & Najarian, B. (2001). The effect of relocation after a natural disaster. *Journal of Traumatic Stress*, 14, 511–526.

Najarian, L. M., Majeed, M. H., Gasparyan, K. (2017). Effect of relocation after a natural disaster: 20-year follow-up. *Asian Journal of Psychiatry*, 29, 8–12.

Noji, E. K., Kelan, G. D., & Armenia, H. K. (1990). The 1988 earthquake in Soviet Armenia: a case study. *Annals of Emergency Medicine*, 16, 891–897.

Pfefferbaum, R. L., Pfefferbaum, B., Van Horn, R. L., Klomp, R. W., Norris, F. W., & Reissman, D. B. (2013). The communities advancing tool kit (CART): an intervention to build community resilience to disasters. *Journal of Public Health Management and Practice*, 19, 250–258.

Pointer, J. E., Michaelis, J., Saunders, C., Martchenke, J., Barton, C., Palefox, J., Kleinrock, M., & Calabro, J. J. (1992). The 1989 Loma Pieta earthquake: impact on hospital patient care. *Annals of Emergency Medicine*, 21, 1228–1233.

Saito, M., Kondo, K., Kondo, A., Abe, A., Ojima, T., & Suzuki, K. (2014). JAGES group, relative deprivation, poverty and subjective health: Jages cross-sectional study. *PLOS ONE*, 9, e111169.

Salcioglu, E., Ozden, S., & Furkan, A. (2018). The role of location patterns and psychosocial stressors in posttraumtic stress disorder and depression among earthquake survivors. *Journal of Nervous and Mental Disease*, 206, 19–26.

Sasaki, Y., Aida, J., Tsuji, T., Miyaguni, Y., Tani, Y., Koyama, S., Matsuyama, Y., Sato, Y., Tsuboya, T., Nagamine,Y., Kameda, Y., Saito, T., Kakimoto, K., Kondo, K., & Kawachi, I. (2018). Does type of residential housing matter for depressive symptoms in the aftermath of a disaster? Insights from the Great East Japan earthquake and tsunami. *American Journal of Epidemiology*, 187, 455–464.

Scaramutti, C., Salas-Wright, C. P., Vos, S. R., Schwartz, S. J. (2019). The mental health impact of Hurricane Maria on Puerto Ricans in Puerto Rico and Florida. *Disaster Medicine and Public Health Preparedness*, 13, 24–27.

Schwartz, R. M., Rasul, R., Kerath, S. M., Watson, A. R., Lieberman-Cribin, W., Liu, B., Taioli, E. (2018). Displacement during Hurricane Sandy: the impact on mental health. *Journal of Emergency Medicine*, 16, 17–27.

Sesin, C. (2017) Over 200,000 Puerto Ricans have arrived in Florida since Hurricane Maria. www.nbcnews.com/news/latino/over-200,000-puerto-ricans-have-arrived-florida-hurricane-maria-n825111 [last accessed August 1, 2021].

Sezgin, U., Punamaki, R-L. (2016). Women's disaster-related mental health: the decision to leave or to stay after an earthquake. *Traumatology*, 22, 40–47.

Tucker, P., Pfefferbaum, B., Zhao, Y. D., Johnson, S., Mistry, A., & Khan, S. Q. (2018). Association of biological markers in hurricane survivors: heart rate variability interleukon-2 and interleukon-6 in depression and PTSD. *American Journal of Disaster Medicine*, 13, 267–278.

Watanabe, C., Okumura, J., Chiu, T., & Wakal, S. (2004). Social support and depressive symptoms among displaced older adults following the 1999 Taiwan earthquake. *Journal of Traumatic* Stress, 17, 63–67.

Watters, E. (2011). *Crazy Like Us: The Globalization of the American Psyche.* New York, NY: Simon and Schuster.

Yokoyama, Y., Otsuka, K., Kawakami, N., Kobayashi, S., Ogawa, A., Tannno, K., Onoda, T., Yaegashi, Y., Sakata, K. (2014). Mental health and related factors after the Great East Japan earthquake and tsunami. *PLOS One*, 9, e102497.

Yzermans, C. J., Donker, G. A., Kerssens, J. J., Dirkzwager, A. J. E., Soeteman, R. J. H., ten Veen, P. M. H. (2005). Health problems of victims before and after disaster: a longitudinal study in general practice. *International Journal of Epidemiology*, 34(4), 820–828.

# Long-Term Course of PTSD and Depression Among Adults, Mediating and Moderating Factors in Recovery, and Current Trends for Treatment

Armen Goenjian, Alan Steinberg, and Robert Pynoos

## 7.1 Cross-Sectional and Longitudinal Studies after the Spitak Earthquake and Human-Perpetrated Trauma

### 7.1.1 PTSD Severity Among Elderly and Younger Adults 1.5 Years after the Spitak Earthquake

One and a half years after the Spitak earthquake, 179 adult survivors, including differentially exposed older and younger adults, were evaluated with the UCLA PTSD-Reaction Index (PTSD-RI) (Goenjian et al., 1994a). Figure 7.1 presents the mean PTSD-RI scores of the four groups. The findings showed a clear dose–response relation. The elderly from Spitak, a city with very severe earthquake exposure, had the highest mean PTSD-RI scores, followed by the scores of younger and older Gumri adults with severe exposure; last was the least-exposed Yerevan group.

PTSD-RI scores for the elderly subjects from Gumri were higher compared to younger adults, although the difference did not reach significance. However, there was a significant difference in symptom profiles. Elderly subjects in Gumri scored lower on intrusive (recurrent intrusive phenomena, reactivity to reminders) and higher on hyperarousal symptoms (e.g., hypervigilance, exaggerated startle reaction, irritability, insomnia) than did younger adults. A possible explanation for the lower severity of intrusive symptoms is that elderly subjects were less exposed to earthquake-related trauma. Also, they may have participated less in rescue efforts in the aftermath. As a result, they may have been less likely to be re-exposed to horror and grotesque sights of injury and death. Further, lower levels of intrusive symptoms may have been due to age-related memory impairments interfering with the formation and recall of traumatic imagery. The higher hyperarousal symptoms among the elderly may have been related to increased vulnerability to dysregulation in this group because of age-related changes in brainstem inhibitory mechanisms that modulate startle reactions and/or inhibitory processes regulating autonomic arousal. Also, some arousal symptoms, such as sleep disturbances, may be independently associated with aging.

These differences indicate the need to adjust PTSD treatment for the elderly by assessing and targeting interventions focusing on hyperarousal symptoms using anxiety management techniques (relaxation training, controlled breathing, cognitive restructuring, and psychotropic medications if necessary).

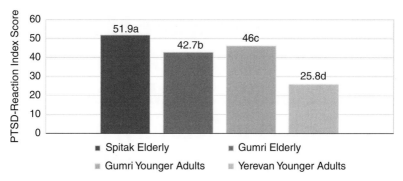

**Figure 7.1** Mean PTSD-Reaction Index scores 1.5 years after the 1988 Spitak earthquake among elderly and younger adults from differentially exposed groups. Data from Goenjian et al., *American Journal of Psychiatry*, 1994a. (A black- and- white version of this figure will appear in some formats. For the color version, please refer to the plate section.)
a > b ~ c > d (F = 53.8, df = 3, 175, P <0.001)

A positive correlation was found between the loss of family members and severity of post-traumatic stress reactions. Higher PTSD scores may have been related to the traumatic death of a nuclear family member, including a continued preoccupation with horrifying imagery regarding the manner of the family member's death and the degree of their suffering. Addition, higher PTSD scores may also have been due to the detrimental effect of disturbances in functioning of the family, thereby compromising the recovery environment and impeding the resolution of PTSD symptoms.

These findings, combined with previous findings of a comparable severity of post-traumatic stress reactions among school-age children in the earthquake zone, suggest that the Spitak earthquake resulted in a multigenerational psychiatric calamity for the survivors. The repercussions of this event, superimposed on the psychic scars left by the 1914–1915 Armenian Genocide and intensified by the post-earthquake political and economic threats, may have altered the individual and social character of the people in this region.

## 7.1.2 Single and Double Trauma (Spitak Earthquake and Political Violence)

The general trauma literature in the early nineties suggested that the severity of PTSD symptoms was worse among survivors of human-perpetrated traumas than natural disasters. Our clinical experience among the survivors of the Spitak earthquake did not support that contention.

The Spitak earthquake occurred on December 7, 1988. Earlier that year, in February 1988, pogroms were perpetrated against Armenians in Azerbaijan. The two most terrorized cities in Azerbaijan were Sumgait and Kirovabad, where for weeks, the Armenian quarters were under siege. There was widespread persecution, murder, beatings, burning of people, destruction of property, and looting. The majority of survivors fled to Armenia. Some settled in the earthquake zone. Others settled in Byureghavan, a town near Yerevan, located about fifty miles from the epicenter. As in Yerevan, it sustained mild damage due to the earthquake.

Armenia's tragic circumstances allowed for the assessment of the severity and symptom profile of the post-traumatic stress reactions to a catastrophic natural disaster and political violence. We were also able to evaluate the contribution of recent prior exposure to violence to the post-traumatic stress reactions of those who were subsequently exposed to the earthquake (the double trauma group). The study included 202 adults exposed to the earthquake, violence in Azerbaijan, or both (Goenjian et al., 1994b). We explored in detail the types of traumatic experiences that survivors had experienced and rated the groups' exposure as 0 = none, 1 = mild, 2 = moderate, 3 = severe, and 4 = very severe. Subjects who had been in Azerbaijan who were rated as very severe reported experiencing or witnessing mutilation or torture. Many witnessed the stabbing, burning, or murder of a nuclear family member or close friend. For example, 65% of the survivors from Sumgait, who had experienced very severe exposure to violence, lost at least one nuclear family member due to the violence; 26% lost more than one nuclear family member.

High rates of severe post-traumatic stress reactions were found among the most severely exposed groups irrespective of the type of trauma, i.e., violence or earthquake (Figure 7.2). There was no difference in symptom profile for subjects exposed to earthquake vs. violence. These similarities in severity and symptom profile may be attributable to common features of the exposures, which included experiencing directly threats to life and witnessing injury, mutilation, and death. Furthermore, recent prior exposure to violence contributed to the severity of the reaction to the earthquake.

Figure 7.2 shows PTSD-RI scores for three groups. The level of trauma exposure, regardless to the type of trauma, was directly associated with the severity of post-traumatic stress reactions.

The Sumgait group (exposed to violence only) with very severe exposure (3.7 out of 4) and the Spitak group, also with very severe exposure to earthquake, had the highest PTSD-RI

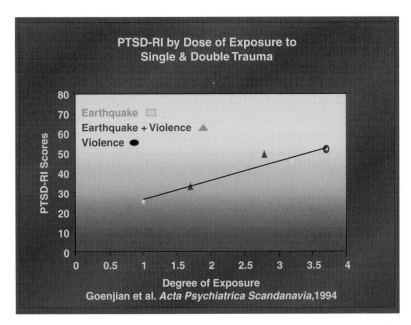

**Figure 7.2** Mean PTSD-Reaction score by degree of exposure to earthquake, violence, or both. (A black- and- white version of this figure will appear in some formats. For the color version, please refer to the plate section.)

scores (Sumgait group mean PTSD-RI = 51.6; Spitak group = 52.3). The double-trauma group with moderate-severe exposure to violence and subsequent earthquake (severity 2.9), had a significantly higher level of PTSD-RI scores (47.9) compared to the single-trauma Gumri group exposed to severe trauma (severity 3.3) PTSD-RI = 46. The double-trauma groups' scores were higher than the moreseverely exposed single trauma Gumri group scores, suggesting an additive effect of prior trauma to the reaction of a subsequent trauma. The graph indicates that the mean scores on the PTSD-RI across exposure groups conformed to a dose–response relation pattern.

In recent years, numerous rigorous studies after major disasters have found severe psychological sequelae. For example, in a multistage sampling study of adults after the catastrophic Bam earthquake that killed 26,000 people in Iran, Divsalar and Dehesh (2020) found that the mean PTSD Checklist (PCL) score among adults was above the cut-off for severe PTSD. Among adult survivors of the Wenchuan earthquake, Wang et al. (2011) found the rate of PTSD was 62.8% more than a month after the disaster, while Zhang and Ho (2011), using the Impact of Event Scale-Revised (IES-R), found high severity (mean = 43) and high rates of PTSD (82.6%, using cut-off score of 33) one to two months after the Wenchuan earthquake. In a study among adults one to three years after Hurricane Sandy, Ruskin et al. (2018) found the PTSD rate was 70.5%. The depression rate was 44.2% among those who lacked access to medical care.

The severity and chronicity among the earthquake victims in Armenia were attributable not only to the intensity of the earthquake but to earthquake-related widespread destruction and mortality, prolonged post-earthquake stressful conditions (e.g., lack of heat, electricity, gas, housing, transportation), and the slow recovery and rebuilding of the city. Compounding this misery was the war with Azerbaijan and the associated blockade that barred the transport of essential supplies for subsistence to the country.

All subjects had responded to the PTSD-RI questions listing the earthquake as the index trauma except for the Sumgait group, which listed the violence as the index trauma (as they were not exposed to the earthquake). A stepwise regression analysis was performed among those who were exposed to the earthquake and earthquake/violence to determine whether prior exposure to violence added to the severity of post-traumatic reactions to the earthquake. The PTSD-RI scores corresponded strongly with the level of exposure ($r = 0.65$, $P < 0.01$). After the effect of the earthquake exposure was removed, the level of prior exposure to violence made a smaller but significant contribution to predicting the severity of post-traumatic stress reactions (partial $r = 0.22$, $P < 0.01$). The combination of the two exposure ratings explained 45% of the variance in PTSD-RI score ($R^2 = 0.45$).

The double-trauma Sumgait/Kirovabad group, which had less severe exposure to the earthquake (they were farther from the epicenter than those in Gumri) than the single-trauma Gumri group (Figure 7.2), had higher PTSD-RI scores compared to the Gumri group (Sumgait/Kirovabad = 47.4; Gumri = 46.0). These results supported the additive effect hypothesis, i.e., the severity of PTSD symptoms related to the earthquake was higher than expected for the double-trauma group.

This finding indicated that recent prior exposure to humanperpetrated trauma constituted a risk factor for the severity of subsequent earthquake-related post-traumatic stress reactions. One mechanism for the additive effect may be that a previous trauma results in physiological vulnerability to arousal symptoms that is manifested upon exposure to a subsequent trauma (Pitman et al., 1990). Another is that a previous trauma may result in psychological vulnerability. For example, current exposure may mobilize and exacerbate latent negative self-images developed from a prior exposure (Horowitz et al., 1980). Future studies should include obtaining a history of prior trauma and attempts to assess the mechanism(s) by which such an additive effect occurs.

These adverse mental health consequences may seriously jeopardize the psychological resilience and adaptational capacity of a population confronted with the arduous task of rebuilding their nation doubly challenged by war and disaster. The finding of the additive effect of previous trauma to the effect of a subsequent trauma on PTSD symptom severity was extended further in subsequent studies listed under cumulative traumas below.

## 7.1.3  Earthquake and Political Violence: Course of PTSD, Depression, and Anxiety Symptoms at 1.5 and 4.5 years Follow-Up

A follow-up of the single- and double-trauma study was conducted 4.5 years post-earthquake (Goenjian et al., 2000). This study included three groups from the 1.5 year study, including the Sumgait and Gumri groups exposed to severe trauma and the Yerevan group with mild-moderate earthquake exposure. The purpose of this study was to measure the course of PTSD, depression, and anxiety symptoms. The Yerevan group served as a control group. We used the PTSD-RI and self-report versions of the Hamilton Depression and Anxiety scales. In a previous report, we had estimated the rates of PTSD based on a cut-off of 40 on the PTSD-RI (Goenjian et al., 1994a). The current estimate for a PTSD diagnosis was revised based on more stringent guidelines. In addition to using the cut-off score of 40, we used the symptom cluster method (a minimum of 1B, 3C, and 2D category symptoms with moderate or higher symptom severity) as has been previously recommended and used in numerous prior PTSD studies (McDonald and Calhoun, 2010). As a result, the baseline rates reported are lower than the rates reported previously.

Table 7.1 shows the PTSD-RI scores for the subjects from Gumri (exposed to severe earthquake trauma) and Sumgait (exposed to severe violence). The mean PTSD-RI scores for both groups were rated as severe at 1.5 and 4.5 years and did not differ significantly from one another. These scores were considerably higher than the scores of the Yerevan group at both times (all p values < 0.05). Similarly, the depression and anxiety scores of the Gumri and Sumgait groups did not differ significantly from one another and were significantly higher than the scores of the Yerevan group at both times (all p values < 0.05). Overall, the depression scores improved significantly over time, with no significant difference in the pattern of improvement between groups. The anxiety scores of the Sumgait and Yerevan groups subsided, but the Gumri group scores remained the same.

Post-traumatic stress, anxiety, and depressive reactions were highly inter-correlated within and across both time intervals (r values ranged between 0.64 and 0.79). In short, there were no significant differences in PTSD severity, symptom profile, or course between those exposed to severe earthquake trauma vs. those exposed to severe violence.

The estimated PTSD rates (based on B, C, and D symptom cluster and cut-off of 40 method) were high in both severely exposed groups: at 1.5 years: Sumgait = 47% and Gumri = 40%; at 4.5 years: Sumgait = 31% and Gumri = 37%. None of the subjects from the Yerevan group met criteria for a PTSD diagnosis at both times.

The comparable severity of PTSD symptoms and rates among Gumri residents exposed to severe earthquake trauma and Sumgait residents exposed to severe violence was attributable to the extreme nature of their traumatic experiences. Nearly every adult in both groups experienced a significant direct threat to their lives and witnessed horrifying sights for many

**Table 7.1** Post-traumatic stress, anxiety, and depressive reactions among seventy-eight Armenian subjects exposed to severe or mild earthquake trauma or severe violence after 1.5 and 4.5 years

| Reaction measure and assessment point | Score | | | | | | Effect | | | | | | | | |
| --- | --- | --- | --- | --- | --- | --- | --- | --- | --- | --- | --- | --- | --- | --- | --- |
| | Gumri residents exposed to severe earthquake trauma | | Sumgait residents exposed to severe violence | | Yerevan residents exposed to mild earthquake trauma | | Group | | | Time | | | Interaction of group and time | | |
| | Mean | SD | Mean | SD | Mean | SD | F | df | p | F | df | p | F | df | p |
| PTSD Reaction Index | | | | | | | 68.70 | 2, 75 | < 0.001 | 2.33 | 1, 75 | n.s. | 0.60 | 2, 75 | n.s. |
| After 1.5 years | 49.7 | 8.5 | 50.8 | 12.6 | 28.5 | 10.3 | | | | | | | | | |
| After 4.5 years | 47.2 | 12.6 | 50.8 | 7.6 | 24.8 | 9.8 | | | | | | | | | |
| Modified Hamilton depression scale | | | | | | | 33.67 | 2, 73 | < 0.001 | 18.53 | 1, 73 | < 0.001 | 1.62 | 2, 73 | n.s. |
| After 1.5 years | 27.6 | 10.6 | 30.6 | 11.8 | 13.4 | 7.6 | | | | | | | | | |
| After 4.5 years | 24.3 | 9.1 | 21.6 | 9.8 | 9.2 | 7.3 | | | | | | | | | |
| Modified Hamilton anxiety scale | | | | | | | 39.06 | 2, 74 | < 0.001 | 8.56 | 1, 74 | < 0.01 | 3.20 | 2, 74 | < 0.05 |
| After 1.5 years | 26.1 | 11.7 | 28.9 | 12.0 | 9.8 | 6.9 | | | | | | | | | |
| After 4.5 years | 26.2 | 10.8 | 22.8 | 7.8 | 7.2 | 6.0 | | | | | | | | | |

(Reprinted from the *American Journal of Psychiatry*, 2000)

days. The high rates and persistence of PTSD symptoms in these groups are consistent with findings from other studies among severely traumatized individuals, e.g., among World War II POWs, the PTSD rate was 70% (Sutker et al., 1993). Among Cambodian refugees, the rate was 86% (Carlson and Rosser-Hogan, 1991).

The persistence of PTSD symptoms among adults in Gumri and Sumgait also appeared to be related to the unremitting severity of multiple stresses experienced after both the earthquake and violence. Both groups lost their homes, jobs, and social connectivity and were living impoverished lives. The ongoing war with Azerbaijan was another potential threat to their lives. They also were contending with ongoing trauma reminders that continuously reactivated symptoms, e.g., the omnipresence of destroyed buildings in Gumri, the ongoing news of the war, the presence of disabled veterans of the war and the earthquake victims, and the homeless refugees. Continued PTSD symptoms contributed to secondary problems, such as marital discord and disturbances in occupational and social functioning that compromised their ability to cope with PTSD symptoms.

The severity of depression scores among the Sumgait and Gumri groups was commensurate with the losses (deaths and material losses, such as homes, valuables), disruption of family and social life, unemployment, and poverty. Additionally, the forced deportation of the Sumgait group was another factor contributing to depression. Comorbid PTSD and anxiety may have also contributed to their depression.

In the longest cross-sectional study after a natural disaster, thirty-seven years after the 1976 Tangshan earthquake in China where 400,000 people died, Gao et al. (2019) assessed depression using the Center for Epidemiologic Studies Depression (CES-D) scale among exposed subjects. The results extended findings from prior studies confirming the chronicity of depression. Survivors who had lost relatives during the earthquake were nearly three times as likely to have depression as those who had not experienced the earthquake, while those who had not lost relatives during the earthquake were 1.69 times as likely. Level of earthquake exposure was significantly associated with depression in women with or without bereavement, but not among men. These findings underscore the importance of monitoring and treating depression after disasters, especially among vulnerable women.

Kessler et al. (1995) found the presence of multiple psychiatric disorders in individuals with PTSD. For example, affective disorders were two to three times more likely to occur in those with PTSD, while anxiety disorders were two to four times more likely. The chronic symptoms of depression and anxiety in this study, as in other post-disaster studies, indicate the importance of comprehensive assessment and ongoing monitoring of PTSD, depression, anxiety, and prolonged grief symptoms and adjusting treatment accordingly. This combination of conditions can be extremely disabling. Additionally, many individuals with these symptoms resort to drug and alcohol use, often leading to addiction. In the National Comorbidity Study, individuals with PTSD were two to three times more likely to also have a comorbid substance use disorder.

In a review of suicide rates after natural disasters in 377 counties in the United States, Krug et al. (1999) assessed change in suicide rates during the thirty-six months before and forty-eight months after disasters and aligned the data around the month of the disaster. Suicide rates increased in the four years after floods by 13.8% ($P < 0.001$); in the two years after hurricanes by 31.0% ($P < 0.001$); and in the first year after earthquakes by 62.9% ($P < 0.001$). Suicide rates did not change significantly after tornadoes or severe storms.

In another review, Jafari et al. (2020) reported risk factors associated with suicide after natural disasters, most of which were earthquakes from East Asian countries. Risk factors included gender (female), age (adolescents and elderly), history of serious mental disorders, depression, PTSD, loss of family members, low economic status, low social support, and injury to the individual and to family members.

In summary, these findings indicate that clinical evaluation of individuals exposed to earthquake or violence should include evaluation of PTSD, anxiety, depressive reactions, prolonged grief, substance abuse, and risk for suicide. Intervention strategies should address these co-existing symptoms. The findings suggest that early mental health intervention may prevent the chronicity of stress reactions among victims of extreme traumas and reduce the risk of suicide.

### 7.1.4  Epidemiologic Study of Differentially Exposed Groups at Two- and Twenty-Three-Year Follow-Up

To our knowledge, this study was the first population-based prospective study of PTSD extending past two decades after a natural disaster (Goenjian et al., 2018). The study examined the prevalence and predictors of PTSD among 725 differentially exposed survivors at two to three years and twenty-three years after the Spitak earthquake. The assessment for PTSD in 1991 was based on the Diagnostic Interview Schedule (DIS) (Robins, Helzer, Croughan, and Ratcliff, 1981), then a widely used structured diagnostic instrument. The follow-up evaluations included assessment for PTSD using the Armenian version of the PTSD Check List-5 (PCL-5) based on DSM-5 criteria (Demirchyan et al., 2015).

For the whole sample, the rate of PTSD attributed to the earthquake decreased from 48.7% in 1991 to 11.6% in 2012 ($P < 0.001$) (Figure 7.3). At 1.5 years, there was a dose–response relation: the higher the exposure to the earthquake, the higher the rate of PTSD. However, at twenty-three-year follow-up, there was no significant difference between the

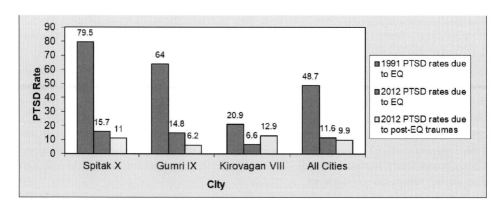

**Figure 7.3** Earthquake-related rates of post-traumatic stress disorder (PTSD) in 1991, and rates of PTSD due to the earthquake and post-earthquake traumas in 2012. Reprinted from the *Journal of Traumatic Stress* (2018). (A black-and-white version of this figure will appear in some formats. For the color version, please refer to the plate section.) Intensities of the earthquake on the Medvedev-Sponheuer-Karnik-64 scale are indicated by roman numerals next to the names of the cities. The rates were calculated among participants with valid responses to all variables presented in the figure (N = 717).
EQ = earthquake.

rates for the Spitak and Gumri groups. The Spitak group, which was facing fewer adversities, had improved more than the Gumri group.

At twenty-three-year follow-up, 15.7% of participants who were in Spitak (the highest exposure group) and 6.6% of participants who were in Kirovagan (the lowest exposure group) met criteria for PTSD. Additionally, at twenty-three-year follow-up, another 9.9% of all the participants met PTSD criteria due to post-earthquake traumas identified as the current most bothersome traumatic experience. Post-earthquake traumatic experiences among these adults had increased five-fold compared to the pre-earthquake traumatic experiences ($P < 0.001$). Reasons for this increase were related to increases in aggressive behavior (e.g., fights, stabbings), accidents due to reckless driving, physical and sexual abuse, and increased substance abuse since the earthquake. Anecdotal reports by the head physician in the main emergency room of Gumri indicated that before the earthquake, violent acts (e.g., stabbings) occurred a few times a year, but since then, they occurred more frequently,"almost a few times a month."

Multiple regression analysis showed the following risk factors positively associated with PTSD: *earthquake-related job loss, exposure to post-earthquake traumas, depression at baseline,* and *chronic illness* since the earthquake. Protective factors included *housing assistance* within two years after the earthquake, *support of family and/or friends,* and to a lesser degree, *higher education* and *high living standard*. These findings indicate that even though PTSD rates subside significantly after a catastrophic disaster, earthquake-related PTSD can persist among a subgroup of exposed individuals in the region (11.6%). This rate constitutes a continuing public mental health problem, especially given that another 9.9% of the follow-up group also met the criteria for PTSD due to exposure to other types of traumas after the earthquake that resulted in a combined PTSD rate of 21.5% at follow-up.

Predictors of PTSD identified in this study may guide planning of acute and longer-term post-disaster public mental health recovery programs. Job losses were due to the pervasive destruction of workplaces and lack of funds to continue operations. Conversely, PTSD symptoms may have contributed to the inability to work, and job loss as a feature of the recovery environment may have contributed to the persistence of PTSD symptoms. Intervention by the central government and non-governmental organizations to rebuild and create work opportunities may enhance the course of recovery for a large proportion of the affected population.

A higher standard of living subsequent to the earthquake was associated with less-severe PTSD symptoms. Better living conditions created a less stressful environment, which may have enhanced recovery from PTSD. In contrast, the added distress due to poor living conditions and impoverishment may have interfered with the resolution of PTSD symptoms.

Regarding loss of housing, those who received housing assistance during the ensuing two years after the earthquake scored 6.2 points lower on the PCL scale at the twenty-three-year follow-up compared with those who had loss of housing but no assistance. The finding strongly suggests that post-disaster recovery programs should include assistance with housing. The present findings extend earlier findings in this population, where cumulative material losses (e.g., house, car, furniture, money, etc.) were the best predictor of PTSD after the earthquake (Armenian et al., 2000). Similar findings related to financial losses have been reported in a short-term follow-up after Hurricane Katrina (Galea et al., 2008).

The relation of chronic illness to PTSD severity in the present study is consistent with similar findings among adults who were adolescents two decades earlier at the time of the earthquake (Goenjian et al., 2020). These results extend prior findings related to the association of physical illness and PTSD after exposure to combat (Schnurr et al., 2000; Boscarino, 2004) and earthquake (Armenian et al., 1998). For example, seventeen years after combat, an association was found between chronic PTSD and autoimmune illnesses (Boscarino, 2004). A four-year follow-up among survivors of the Spitak earthquake found an increase in heart disease and newly reported hypertension, diabetes, and arthritis (Armenian et al., 1998). Chronic illness may be a moderating factor for PTSD. Alternatively, it is possible that those with PTSD are more vulnerable to chronic illness, as the study among Armenian children at twenty-five-year follow-up suggested (Goenjian et al., 2020). The finding of long-term health problems underscores the importance of monitoring survivors of disasters with moderate or severe PTSD and depressive symptoms for chronic medical illnesses. In addition, early treatment for PTSD and depression may avert or curtail the onset or progression of chronic medical illnesses.

There was an inverse association between perceived support of family and friends and PTSD symptoms (i.e., the more the perceived support, the less severe the PTSD symptoms). The association between support of family and friends and PTSD may be bi-directional. Ongoing social support may have contributed to the resolution of PTSD symptoms, while the ongoing severity of PTSD symptoms may have negatively affected the acquisition and maintenance of social support. Regardless of the direction of causation, the present findings suggest the importance of assessing the availability and utilization of family and friends for support after disasters, along with interventions to bolster social support.

The majority of natural disaster studies have been followed up for one to two years. As noted above, many studies of PTSD after natural disasters have suggested that symptoms may be less severe compared to human-perpetrated traumas (Steinglass and Gerrity, 1990; Acierno et al., 2007) and decrease within a few years after exposure. Generally, these are disasters where the mortality, destruction, and post-disaster secondary stresses are not severe and are not long-lasting. However, numerous studies have shown that sequelae of natural disasters can be severe and chronic, as has been documented in the 4.5- and twenty-three-year post-earthquake follow-up studies above.

The few long-term (over a decade) studies after natural disasters have also documented the severity and chronicity of PTSD symptoms. Among cross-sectional studies, thirty-six years after the Vajont Dam collapse and flooding in Northern Italy, Favaro et al. (2004) found that the PTSD rate was 42% among highly exposed individuals, and thirty-three years after the Aberfan coal slag heap collapsed on a school in Wales, Morgan et al. (2003) reported that the rate of PTSD among survivors was 29%. Twelve years after the catastrophic Bam earthquake in Iran, Divsalar and Dehesh (2020) found prevalence rates of PTSD and depression to be 38.7% and 40.1%, respectively. Nine years after the powerful 2008 Sichuan earthquake, Cao et al. (2018) found that the rate of PTSD was 16%. Ten years after the Piper Alpha oil platform disaster, Hull et al. (2002) found the current rate of PTSD to be 21%. Two of these long-term studies were longitudinal. In a fourteen-year follow-up study after the Buffalo Creek dam collapse, Green et al. (1990) found the rate of PTSD was down from 44% at two years to 28%. Twenty years after the Spitak earthquake, the PTSD rate among survivors was 21%, down from 32% at 2.5 years when the survivors were early adolescents (Najarian et al., 2011). The aforementioned PTSD rates varied between 16% to 42%, with a median of 28%. The rate of PTSD (21.5%) in the earthquake cities at twenty-three-year follow-up was comparable with the above high rates.

## 7.2 Variations of Trauma Reactions

Two determinants of PTSD severity are the vulnerability of the individual exposed to trauma and the severity of the traumatic event (e.g., death, destruction, injuries, being buried). Vulnerabilities include genetic and other non-genetic vulnerabilities such as pre-existing psychiatric problems, family history of psychiatric problems, low socioeconomic status, low education level, past history of trauma, childhood abuse, and female gender. Post-disaster factors include post-disaster traumas, comorbid conditions, post-trauma adversities, and chronic medical illnesses.

The next section presents findings since the Spitak earthquake on the cumulative effect and delayed manifestation of post-trauma reactions. The single and double trauma study among victims of the earthquake and human-perpetrated violence was one of the earliest studies where trauma exposure was measured on a severity scale (Figure 7.2). The study results showed that past trauma had an additive effect on PTSD symptoms related to earthquake trauma exposure subsequently.

## 7.2.1 Cumulative Effect of Trauma

Harville et al. (2018) evaluated southern Louisiana women, most of whom had experienced multiple hurricanes as well as the Gulf oil spill. Findings showed that exposure to multiple disasters was associated with increased severity of PTSD and depression. Habituation, where people are posited to become accustomed to another disaster after experiencing one, was not observed; however, there was limited evidence for sensitization, i.e., people who have experienced previous disasters react more strongly to new disasters than would be expected.

Suliman et al. (2009) assessed PTSD and anxiety among South African adolescents exposed to single vs. multiple discrete life-threatening traumas. Controlling for sex, stressful life experiences in the past year, and childhood adversity, the researchers found a cumulative trauma exposure effect on PTSD and depression symptoms. An increase in the number of traumas was linearly associated with an increase in symptoms of PTSD and depression. There was no cumulative effect on anxiety.

Geng et al. (2018) assessed the effects of two earthquakes among adolescents five years apart: initially 3.5 years after the 2008 Wenchuan earthquake (1.5 years before the Ya'an earthquake) and subsequently one week after the 2013 Ya'an earthquake. Wenchuan earthquake-related PTSD and depression positively predicted mental health problems following the Ya'an earthquake, including acute stress and PTSD symptoms. The results demonstrated that repeated experiences of disasters have adverse additive effects on adolescent mental health. The findings also provided empirical support for stress sensitization effects with regard to acute stress disorder and PTSD.

Schumm and colleagues (2006) assessed how child abuse, adult rape, and social support impact inner-city women. The results showed that the effects of interpersonal trauma had a cumulative effect such that women who experienced either child abuse or adult rape were six times more likely to have probable PTSD. In contrast, women who experienced both child abuse and rape were seventeen times more likely to have probable PTSD.

After the 2010 Chile earthquake of magnitude 8.8, Fernandez et al. (2017) studied a large sample of adults who had undergone a structured psychiatric diagnostic interview before being exposed to the earthquake. They found that individuals with pre-disaster PTSD had the highest odds of developing post-disaster PTSD relative to individuals with no pre-disaster diagnosis: pre-disaster dysthymia predicted the development of disaster-related PTSD.

## 7.2.2 Delayed Onset PTSD

In a review article on "delayed-onset" PTSD (onset greater than six months after a traumatic event), Andrews et al. (2007) found that studies consistently showed that delayed-onset PTSD in the absence of any prior symptoms was rare, whereas delayed onset that represented exacerbations or reactivations of prior symptoms accounted on average for 38.2% and 15.3%, respectively, of military and civilian cases of PTSD.

In a recent meta-analysis of delayed-onset PTSD, Utzon-Frank et al. (2014) reported that across thirty-nine prospective studies, the occurrence of delayed-onset PTSD as ascertained by interview or questionnaire, most often if not always, was preceded by subthreshold PTSD symptoms. The authors also noted that contextual factors and biased recall may inflate the reporting of PTSD and recommended a cautious interpretation of prevalence rates.

Bryant et al. (2018) conducted a two-wave study among survivors after the 2009 Black Saturday fires in Australia. Wave one was at three to four years after the fires, and wave two was at five years. At follow-up, property loss in the fires and other life stresses predicted late-onset fire-related and general PTSD and depression. The authors suggested that the late-onset may have been due to worsening or delayed expression of symptoms as time elapsed. The extent to which people suffered property loss resulted in ongoing difficulties in resuming prior levels of occupational or domestic functioning and subsequently compounding their stress reactions, e.g., due to financial stress arising from legal proceedings, rebuilding costs, and loss of income.

# 7.3 Mortality and Morbidity Associated with Traumas

## 7.3.1 The Spitak Earthquake

At a four-year follow-up of adult survivors of the Spitak earthquake, Armenian et al. (1998) found that the highest number of deaths from all causes and from heart disease were observed within the first six months after the earthquake. Comparison of newly reported heart disease and matched non-heart-disease controls showed that losses (of possessions and family members) were positively related to an increase in heart disease (odds ratios for "loss scores" of 1, 2, and 3 were 1.3, 1.8, and 2.6, respectively). There were similar findings with regard to losses of possessions and family members and newly reported hypertension, diabetes mellitus, and arthritis. These findings suggested that survivors who sustain such losses are at risk for heart and other chronic diseases and should be closely monitored for long-term physical morbidity.

## 7.3.2 The Great Japan Earthquake

Li et al. (2019) assessed the association of exposure to the Great East Japan earthquake and tsunami and depression, PTSD, and mortality among older survivors. In this prospective study, baseline data were collected seven months before the disaster as part of a national survey. At 2.5 years follow-up after the disaster, they found 32.8% of the participants had post-disaster depression and 25.2% PTSD. Mortality data collected up to 3.3 years after the disaster survey showed that depression was significantly associated with an elevated risk of death, while PTSD was not. Participants with comorbid depression and PTSD had no greater risk of death than those with depression only.

### 7.3.3  Hurricane Katrina

Edmondson et al. (2013) assessed the association of psychiatric symptoms in the year after Hurricane Katrina and subsequent hospitalization and mortality among end-stage renal disease patients. In terms of psychological burden, 24% of participants met criteria for PTSD based on DSM-IV criteria, with 46% reporting symptoms consistent with a diagnosis of depression. Depressive symptoms, but not chronic PTSD symptoms, were related to an increased risk of both all-cause and cardiovascular-related hospitalizations and mortality. As with the Li et al. (2019) study, comorbid PTSD and depressive symptoms did not appear to increase the risk of adverse outcomes associated with depressive symptoms alone.

### 7.3.4  War Veterans

In a prospective study among veterans, Boscarino (2008) found that PTSD was associated with heart disease mortality among veterans who were free of heart disease at baseline. This study suggested that early-age heart disease may be an outcome after military service among PTSD-positive veterans. Controlling for lifetime depression only slightly altered the results.

### 7.3.5  Coronary Artery By-Pass Surgeries

Dao et al. (2010) examined the effect of clinical depression, PTSD, and comorbid depression and PTSD on in-hospital mortality after a coronary artery bypass grafting surgery. The results showed that depression, PTSD, and comorbid depression and PTSD were prevalent in patients undergoing coronary artery bypass grafting procedures (25.9%, 14.7%, and 9% respectively). All three conditions increased the risk of death by magnitudes comparable with well established physical health risk factors after such surgery. After adjusting for potential confounding factors, there was an increased likelihood of in-hospital mortality among those who had depression, PTSD, or both compared with that seen in patients who remained alive. The odds ratios were as follows: for depression 1.24; PTSD 2.09; and comorbid depression and PTSD 4.66.

## 7.4  Current Trends in Post-Disaster Interventions for PTSD, Moral Injury, Depression, and Prolonged Grief

### 7.4.1  Recommended Treatments for PTSD

In an article examining various practice guidelines for the treatment of PTSD and related conditions, Forbes et al. (2010) reported that consensus strongly supported the use of trauma-focused psychological treatment for PTSD among adults. The guidelines recognized some benefits of pharmacotherapy for the treatment of PTSD. The guidelines cautioned against the routine use of psychological debriefing as an early preventive intervention for populations exposed to trauma.

In 2017, the American Psychological Association and the U.S. Veterans Health Administration, Department of Defense strongly recommended prolonged exposure (PE), cognitive behavioral therapy (CBT), and cognitive processing therapy (CPT) (Watkins et al., 2018). These treatments are all trauma-focused and directly address memories of the traumatic event or thoughts and feelings related to the traumatic event. Other recommended therapies included: brief eclectic psychotherapy (BET); narrative exposure therapy (NET); stress inoculation training (SIT); present-centered therapy (PCT); and interpersonal psychotherapy (IPT). In a meta-analysis comparing PE, CPT, and trauma-focused CBT, findings did not show that one treatment outperformed the others (Powers et al., 2010; Cusack et al., 2016).

Prolonged exposure is a specific type of cognitive-behavioral therapy that teaches individuals to gradually approach trauma-related memories, feelings, and situations. By facing what has been avoided, an individual gradually learns that the trauma-related memories and cues are not dangerous and do not need to be avoided.

Cognitive behavioral therapy focuses on the relation between thoughts, feelings, and behaviors; targets current problems and symptoms; and focuses on changing patterns of behaviors, thoughts, and feelings that lead to difficulties in functioning. Cognitive processing therapy is a specific type of cognitive behavioral therapy that helps patients learn how to modify and challenge unhelpful beliefs related to trauma.

## 7.4.2  Limitations of Approved Therapies for PTSD and Drop-Outs

In a review article of randomized clinical trials for military-related PTSD, Steenkamp et al., (2015) found that 49% to 70% of participants receiving cognitive processing therapy and prolonged exposure attained clinically meaningful symptom improvement (defined as a 10- to 12-point decrease in interviewer-assessed or self-reported symptoms). However, mean post-treatment scores for CPT and PE remained at or above clinical criteria for PTSD, and approximately two-thirds of patients receiving CPT or PE retained their PTSD diagnosis after treatment (range, 60% to 72%). Based on these findings, the authors concluded that there was a need for improvement in existing PTSD treatments

In a meta-analysis of psychotherapy for PTSD, Bradley et al. (2005) found that more than half of patients who completed treatment with various forms of cognitive behavior therapy or eye movement desensitization and reprocessing (EMDR) improved. However, the authors cautioned about applying these findings to patients treated in the community in that post-treatment, the majority of patients continued to have substantial residual symptoms, and follow-up data beyond very brief intervals have been largely absent. The exclusion criteria and failure to address polysymptomatic presentations in these studies rendered generalizability to the broad population of PTSD patients undetermined. The authors recommended that future research intended to generalize to patients in practice should avoid exclusion criteria other than those a reasonable clinician would impose in practice (e.g., schizophrenia), should avoid wait-list and other relatively inert control conditions, and should follow patients at least up to two years.

In a meta-analysis of PTSD treatment studies, Imel et al. (2013), found the aggregate proportion of drop-outs across all treatments was 18.3%. The drop-out rate was lower in present centered therapy (PCT), 22%, compared to 36% for trauma-specific treatments.

## 7.4.3  Inflated Results and Publication Bias

In a meta-analysis, Watts et al. (2013) found that there are a large number of effective treatments for PTSD. Those with the largest amount of evidence include various types of CBT, EMDR, antidepressants (specifically venlafaxine and SSRIs), risperidone, and topiramate. The authors indicated that the effect sizes reported in the psychotherapy treatment literature might be inflated to some degree, and that type of comparison strongly affected the effect size of psychotherapy studies, with wait-list control being associated "as expected" with larger effects. The authors also noted that their findings suggest the possibility of publication bias in the psychotherapy literature, with psychotherapy studies being more likely to be published when the results were positive. Watts et al. (2013) concluded that it was not possible to identify a single "best" treatment and that selection between effective treatments is better guided by important real differences in the characteristic of the treatments, rather than selection based on small differences in the reported effectiveness. Ultimately, factors such as access, acceptability, and patient preference, should exert strong and appropriate influence over the choice of treatment.

## 7.4.4 Pharmacotherapy for PTSD

According to the American Psychological Association Guidelines (Courtois et al., 2017), four medications have received a conditional recommendation for use in treating PTSD: sertraline, paroxetine, fluoxetine, and venlafaxine. The current evidence base for PTSD psychopharmacology is strongest for the selective serotonin reuptake inhibitors (SSRIs): sertraline, paroxetine, and fluoxetine, as well as the selective serotonin-norepinephrine reuptake inhibitor (SNRI) venlafaxine. Medications that help decrease physical symptoms associated with PTSD include prazosin (Minipress), clonidine (Catapres), guanfacine (Tenex), and propranolol. Other medications like duloxetine (Cymbalta), bupropion (Wellbutrin), and desvenlafaxine (Pristiq) have also been used to treat PTSD. All of the antidepressants described above are also effective in treating comorbid major depressive disorder (MDD). Other less directly effective, but nevertheless potentially helpful medications for managing PTSD include traditional mood stabilizers, as well as mood stabilizers that are also antipsychotics. Antipsychotic medicines seem to be most useful in the treatment of PTSD in those who suffer from agitation, dissociation, and hypervigilance.

## 7.4.5 Treatment of PTSD and Moral Injury

Moral injury is defined as transgressive harms and outcomes of those experiences with lasting psychological, biological, spiritual, behavioral, and social impact of perpetrating, failing to prevent, or bearing witness to acts that transgress deeply held moral beliefs and expectations (Litz et al., 2009). Moral injury has been explored primarily among military personnel but also can occur after disasters when a survivor makes a morally objectionable decision under duress. As a result of their action, others may have been harmed. Studies have shown that war zone service can entail morally troubling events that threaten or violate veterans' deeply held values and beliefs. In such cases, veterans may struggle with PTSD symptoms along with cognitive, emotional, behavioral, and spiritual expressions of suffering that align with conceptual definitions of moral injury (Currier et al., 2019).

Similarly, morally objectionable acts related to disasters may cause moral injury. For example, an engineer in Armenia was commissioned to build an apartment at a location where he thought it would be unsafe to build because of the soil's hazardous composition and the inadequacy of the necessary materials. The engineer proceeded with the building of the apartment. During the Spitak earthquake, the building collapsed, and children died. The engineer had PTSD symptoms and strong guilt feelings regarding his decision to proceed with the construction. Subsequently, he attempted suicide.

Farnsworth (2019) argued that moral injury and PTSD could be differentiated, at least in part, by distinguishing between cognitions that describe what is and cognitions that prescribe what ought to be. For the treatment of moral injury, he contended that the use of PE or CPT might not be adequate to correct beliefs about themselves or others concerning moral injuries involving acts of moral transgressions or morally ambiguous situations. The author recommended further research to improve current treatments for moral injury.

## 7.4.6   Psychotherapies for Depression

In an extensive meta-analysis of therapies for depression among adults, Cuijpers et al. (2020) assessed fifteen types of psychotherapies. These included: acceptance and commitment therapy; mindfulness-based cognitive behavior therapy (CBT); guided self-help using a self-help book from David Burns; Beck's CBT; the "Coping with Depression" course; two subtypes of behavioral activation; extended and brief problem-solving therapy; self-examination therapy; brief psychodynamic, non-directive counseling; full and brief interpersonal psychotherapy; and life review therapy. All fifteen types of psychotherapy, generic and specific, showed significant moderate to large effects. Psychodynamic therapy, the "Coping with Depression" course, and a specific version of PST (self-examination therapy) had effect sizes smaller than g = 0.5. All the other therapies had effect sizes ranging from g = 0.57 for full interpersonal psychotherapy to g = 1.07 for extended problem-solving therapy. However, the evidence was not conclusive because of high levels of heterogeneity, publication bias, and the risk of bias in the majority of studies.

## 7.4.7   Treatment of Prolonged (Complicated) Grief

Prolonged grief appears to be the most common form of complicated grief in adults. It is different from normal grief in that the immediate grief reactions persist over time with more or less undiminished strength, causing a considerable loss of everyday functioning. Lundorff et al. (2017), in a first systematic review and meta-analysis of the prevalence of prolonged grief, found that one out of ten bereaved adults was at risk. Higher mean age was associated with a higher prevalence of prolonged grief.

In a review article on randomized controlled trials (RCTs), Wittouck et al. (2011) evaluated grief intervention to prevent or treat complicated grief in adults who suffered the death of a loved one. Fourteen RCTs were included (n = 1,655 participants): nine preventive interventions and five treatment interventions. The interventions for prevention were targeted at high-risk groups such as spouses and those who had lost a loved one due to suicide, while treatment interventions were targeted at a broader range of people. Group and individual therapy sessions were used, ranging from one to twelve sessions for preventive interventions and ten to sixteen sessions for treatment interventions. Preventive interventions did not show a significant difference between preventive grief interventions and controls at post-intervention and follow-up. Treatment interventions showed significant benefit of complicated grief treatments compared to controls at post-intervention and at follow-up.

In a recent systematic review and meta-analysis of RCTs of psychological interventions for grief in adults, Johannsen et al. (2019) evaluated thirty-two studies that included passive control (control, wait-list), active control (attentional control, non-specific therapeutic components, e.g., active listening) and competing for control (treatment programs with specific therapeutic components, e.g., interpersonal therapy and CBT). Overall, the results showed a statistically significant and positive effect of psychological interventions at post-intervention, corresponding to a small effect size (Hedges' g: 0.41, p > .001). At follow-up (length not specified), the effect of psychological interventions for grief continued to be statistically significant. The results suggest that psychological interventions for grief reactions may be most efficacious if offered to bereaved individuals who are a minimum of six months post-loss. Due to a scarcity of high-quality RCTs, heterogeneity of subjects, and publication bias, the authors of the meta-analyses have been cautious in their interpretations and have recommended further research to improve understanding of the effectiveness of therapeutic approaches. In summary, the studies indicate that psychotherapy addressing grief issues has a modest effect.

## 7.5 Potential Protective Factors

### 7.5.1 Social Support

Social support is thought to help survivors cope with disaster-related stresses and protect against adverse mental health outcomes such as PTSD and depression. Lack of social support has been associated with higher levels of PTSD symptoms; conversely, social support has been associated with lower levels of PTSD symptoms. Recent studies have addressed the cause–effect relation of PTSD and social support.

In a longitudinal study among Gulf war veterans, King et al. (2006) conducted a cross-lagged analysis of the relation between social support and PTSD symptom severity. Social support was assessed using a ten-item scale adapted from the National Vietnam Veterans Readjustment Study at Time 1 (one to two years after the war) and at Time 2, (five years after Time 1) with another instrument, the six-item version of RAND Medical Outcome Questionnaire. The results showed a strong negative relation between PTSD at Time 1 and social support at Time 2, while social support at Time 1 did not predict PTSD at Time 2. The findings suggest that, over time, interpersonal problems associated with PTSD may have a detrimental influence on the quality and quantity of available social support resources.

In another study after the 1999 tropical storm in the Gulf of Campeche, Mexico, Kaniasty and Norris (2008) conducted a longitudinal study among adults consisting of four waves from six to twenty-four months after the disaster. Perceived social support from family was measured using eight items from the twenty-two-item *Provisions of Social Relations Scale,* which assesses feelings of closeness, willingness to take time to talk, reassurance of worth, ability to relax when together, confidence that the source would be there if needed, and the belief that the support provider has confidence in the respondent. The questions were focused exclusively on family social support. The results indicated that *social causation* (more social support leading to less PTSD) explained the support-to-distress relation in the earlier post-disaster phase, six to twelve months after the impact. Both *social causation* and *social selection* (more PTSD leading to less social support) mechanisms emerged as significant paths in the midpoint of the study (twelve and eighteen months). Only *social selection* accounted for the support-to-distress relationship at eighteen to twenty-four months after the event. The authors opined that interpersonal and social dynamics of disasters may explain why these two contrasting causal mechanisms emerged over time and that further studies are needed to identify the key features of different stresses that influence the order of social causation and social selection mechanisms.

In a study of social factors after disasters, Bryant et al. (2017) studied the association of social networks and PTSD among adults three to four years after the 2009 bushfires in the state of Victoria, Australia. Social networks were assessed by asking participants to nominate people with whom they felt personally close. These nominations were used to construct a social network map that showed each participant's ties to other participants they nominated and also to other participants who had nominated them. This map was then analyzed for prevailing patterns of mental health outcomes. The risk for depression was higher among participants who reported fewer social connections, were connected to other depressed people, or were connected to people who had left their community. The risk for PTSD was higher if fewer people reported being connected with the participant, if those who felt close to the participant had higher levels of property loss, or if the participant was linked to others who were themselves not interconnected. The findings indicate the need for further studies to understand better how social structures after disasters moderate mental health trajectories. Such knowledge can lead to more effective social interventions.

The above studies point to the importance of social support after disasters to prevent or ameliorate stress reactions. Social support may be provided by family members, friends, community, and religious organizations. Further longitudinal studies assessing various aspects of social support, including social connectedness among various age and ethnic groups, are recommended.

## 7.5.2 Religion

Researchers have identified a range of protective factors and coping strategies, including personal faith and involvement in religious communities, that may help attenuate the psychological impact of natural disasters (Smith et al., 2000; Chan and Rhodes, 2013).

Smith et al. (2000) studied the relationship between religious coping by church members and psychological and religious outcomes at six weeks and six months following the 1993 Midwest flood. Findings showed that religious attributions and coping activities predicted improved psychological and religious outcomes at both six weeks and six months after controlling for flood exposure and demographics. The results also suggested that positive religious coping may moderate the relation between religious dispositions and psychological and religious outcomes. Religion may be an important part of the coping process for events that confront people with limitations of human power and control. The findings suggest that interventions that empower religious individuals and communities may enable them to recover and find meaning in the midst of tragic events. Future research can further elucidate the role of religion in coping after crises.

A meta-analysis of forty-nine studies with a total of 105 effect sizes was conducted by Ano and Vasconcelles (2005) to quantitatively examine the relation between religious coping and psychological adjustment to stress. Positive and negative forms of religious coping were related to positive and negative psychological adjustment. The results indicated a moderate positive relationship between positive religious coping strategies and positive outcomes. Individuals who used religious coping strategies such as benevolent religious reappraisals, collaborative religious coping, and seeking spiritual support typically experienced more stress-related growth, spiritual growth, positive affect, and had higher self-esteem.

High negative religious coping strategies (e.g., felt punished by God, attributed their situation to the work of the devil) were positively associated with negative psychological adjustment to stress. That is, individuals who reported using negative forms of religious coping experienced more depression, anxiety, and distress. One possible explanation for this finding is that negative religious coping represents a burden for people undergoing stressful situations. The results of this meta-analysis have implications for the treatment of psychological disorders. Since religion provides a variety of resources and burdens for people dealing with stressful situations, sensitivity towards religious issues may be helpful (and crucial) for building the therapeutic alliance and promoting healing and growth for certain clients, particularly because religion is an important influence in many people's lives (Bergin and Jensen, 1990). In addition, because positive religious coping was associated with better psychological adjustment in the current study, understanding positive forms of religious coping may help practitioners to better assist their clients with accessing valuable spiritual resources.

In another study, four years after Hurricane Katrina, Chan and Rhodes (2013) examined positive and negative religious coping strategies and their relation with post-traumatic stress (PTS), psychological distress, and post-traumatic growth (PTG) among exposed adult women. Positive religious coping was associated with PTG. Negative religious coping was associated with psychological distress, but not PTS. The findings indicate that relief workers and mental health care providers should take note of the protective role of religion in the lives of survivors and make efforts to restore faith-based organizations (e.g., to provide a place for and means to worship and practice one's faith) and be aware of the potential risk that negative religious coping might pose for long-term symptomatology.

## 7.6 Summary and Recommendations

### 7.6.1 Spitak Earthquake Findings

- There was a dose–response relation of exposure to the severity of earthquake trauma and PTSD symptom severity at 1.5 years among the three cities, but not at 4.5 years post-disaster.
- At 1.5 years after the earthquake, the severity of PTSD symptoms was slightly (not significantly) higher among elderly compared to younger adults. But in contrast to younger adults, intrusive symptoms were significantly less pronounced, and hyperarousal symptoms were more pronounced. These differences indicate the need to adjust treatment for the elderly by focusing more on hyperarousal symptoms, potentially using anxiety management techniques.
- Post-traumatic stress disorder severity scores among adults with severe earthquake exposure and those exposed to severe political violence were similar.
- In the double trauma study, the use of graded severity of exposure demonstrated an additive effect of prior exposure to violence to the effect of subsequent earthquake exposure on PTSD symptom severity.
- Among a substantial portion of the earthquake and political violence survivors, PTSD and depression were chronic and co-occurred at 1.5- and 4.5-year follow-up.
- Chronicity of symptoms of PTSD and depression were associated with multiple persistent stresses, including lack of housing, electricity, heat, gas, transportation, essential supplies (medicines, building material), pervasive trauma reminders (destroyed buildings, frequent memorials, disabled people; in the case of refugees the ongoing war, deaths, injuries), unemployment, break-up of families, and poverty.
- At twenty-three-year follow-up, PTSD rates related to the earthquake had subsided from 48.6% at two to three years to 11.6% at twenty-three years. Post-earthquake traumas (e.g., stemming from aggressive and reckless behaviors, accidents) had increased five-fold

compared to the pre-earthquake period, and 9.9% of the participants had PTSD related to post-earthquake traumas.

- Risk factors at twenty-three-year follow-up included earthquake-related job loss, exposure to post-earthquake traumas, depression at baseline, and chronic illness since the earthquake. Protective factors associated with PTSD included housing assistance within two years after the earthquake, support of family and/or friends, and to a lesser degree, higher education and high living standard.

## 7.6.2 Lessons Learned from Disasters since the Spitak Earthquake

### Cumulative Trauma

- The number of exposures to traumatic events was positively associated with increased severity of PTSD and depression (additive effect).
- There is limited evidence for sensitization, i.e., people who have experienced previous disasters react more strongly to new disasters than expected.

### Delayed-Onset PTSD

- Delayed-onset PTSD in the absence of any prior PTSD symptoms was rare. More commonly, delayed onset represented exacerbations or reactivations of prior symptoms.
- Delayed-onset PTSD is most often, if not always, preceded by sub-threshold PTSD symptoms.
- The greater number of stressful life events better explain delayed-onset PTSD.

### Mortality and Morbidity Associated with Trauma

- After the Spitak earthquake, the highest number of deaths from all causes was observed within the first six months.
- The risk for newly reported heart disease, hypertension, diabetes mellitus, and arthritis was associated with increasing levels of loss of possessions and deaths of family members.
- After the Great East Japan earthquake and tsunami, mortality up to three years after the disaster showed that depression was significantly associated with an elevated risk of death, while PTSD was not.
- After Hurricane Katrina, depressive symptoms, but not chronic PTSD symptoms, were related to an increased risk of both all-cause and cardiovascular-related hospitalizations and mortality among end-stage renal failure patients.
- Early-age heart disease may be an outcome after military service among PTSD-positive veterans.

## 7.6.3 Treatments for PTSD and Depression

- Practice guidelines for the treatment of PTSD and related conditions strongly support the use of trauma-focused psychological treatments for PTSD among adults.
- The American Psychological Association in 2017 strongly recommended prolonged exposure (PE); cognitive behavioral therapy (CBT); and cognitive processing therapy (CPT) as treatments.
- In a meta-analysis comparing PE, CPT, and trauma-focused CBT, results have not shown that one treatment outperformed the other.

- In another meta-analysis, more than half of patients who completed treatment with various forms of cognitive behavior therapy (CBT) or eye movement desensitization and reprocessing (EMDR) improved. In applying these findings to patients treated in the community, post-treatment, the majority of patients continued to have substantial residual symptoms, and follow-up data beyond very brief intervals have been largely absent.
- In another meta-analysis, the aggregate proportion of drop-outs in PTSD across all active treatments was 18.3%. The drop-out was lower in present centered therapy (PCT), at 22%, compared to 36% for trauma-specific treatments.
- Another meta-analysis reported that it was not possible to identify a single "best" treatment. Selection between effective treatments may be better guided by important real differences in the characteristics of the treatments rather than selection based on small differences in the reported effectiveness. Factors such as access, acceptability, and patient preference should exert strong and appropriate influence over the choice of treatment.
- The current evidence base for PTSD psychopharmacology is strongest for the SSRIs sertraline, paroxetine and fluoxetine, and the SNRI venlafaxine.
- For the treatment of moral injury and PTSD, the use of PE or CPT may not be adequate to correct beliefs about themselves or others with regard to moral injuries involving acts of moral transgressions or morally ambiguous situations.
- For prolonged grief, there was no significant difference between preventive grief interventions and controls. However, treatment interventions showed significant benefit of complicated grief treatments at post-intervention and follow-up.
- Further research is needed to improve our understanding of risk and protective factors and the effectiveness of therapeutic approaches for bereavement.

## 7.6.4 Potential Protective Factors

### Social Support
- Many studies have found a positive relation between social support and decrease of PTSD symptoms. The relation may be bi-directional, i.e., more social support leading to less PTSD and more PTSD leading to less social support.
- Treatment for PTSD and enhancing social support (by family, friends, and the community) enhance recovery by preventing a vicious cycle (PTSD ↔ social support) that can lead to chronicity and despair.

### Religion
- The findings suggest that interventions that empower religious individuals and communities may enable them to recover and find meaning amid tragic events.
- Individuals who used religious coping strategies such as benevolent religious reappraisals, collaborative religious coping, seeking spiritual support, etc., typically experienced more stress-related growth, spiritual growth, positive affect, and had higher self-esteem. Individuals who reported using negative forms of religious coping experienced more depression, anxiety, and distress.
- Since religion provides a variety of resources and burdens for people dealing with stressful situations, the sensitivity of therapists towards religious issues may be helpful for building the therapeutic alliance and promoting healing and growth for religious individuals.

- The findings indicate that relief organizations and mental health workers should be cognizant of the protective role of religion in the lives of survivors and make efforts to restore faith-based organizations (e.g., provide a place to practice one's faith).

# References

Acierno, R., Ruggiero, K. J., Galea, S., Resnick, H. S., Koenen, K., Roitzsch, J., . . . & Kilpatrick, D. G. (2007). Psychological sequelae resulting from the 2004 Florida hurricanes: implications for post-disaster intervention. *American Journal of Public Health*, 97, S103–S108. https://doi.org/10.2105/AJHP.2006.087007

Andrews, B., Brewin, C. R., Philpott, R., & Stewart, L. (2007). Delayed-onset post-traumatic stress disorder: a systematic review of the evidence. *American Journal of Psychiatry*, 164, 1319–1326.

Armenian, H. K., Melkonian, A. K., & Hovanesian, A. P. (1998). Long-term mortality and morbidity related to degree of damage following the 1988 earthquake in Armenia. *American Journal of Epidemiology*, 148, 1077–1084.

Armenian, H. K., Morikawa, M., Melkonian, A. K., Hovanesian, A. P., Haroutunian, N., Saigh, P. A., . . . & Akiskal, H. S. (2000). Loss as a determinant of PTSD in a cohort of adult survivors of the 1988 earthquake in Armenia: implications for policy. *Acta Psychiatrica Scandinavica*, 102(1), 58–64. https://doi.org/10.1034/j.1600-0447.2000.102001058.x/pdf

Ano, G. G., & Vasconcelles, E. B. (2005). Religious coping and psychological adjustment to stress: a meta-analysis. *Journal of Clinical Psychology*, 61, 461–480. https://doi.org/10.1002/jclp.20049

Bradley, R., Greene, J., Russ, E., Dutra., L., & Western, D. (2005). A multidimensional meta-analysis of psychotherapy for PTSD. *American Journal of Psychiatry*, 162, 214–227. https://doi.org/10.1176/appi.ajp.162.2.214

Bergin, A. E., & Jensen, J. P. (1990). Religiosity of psychotherapists: a national survey. *Psychotherapy*, 27, 3–7.

Boscarino, J. A. (2004). Post-traumatic stress disorder and physical illness: results from clinical and epidemiologic studies. *Annals of the New York Academy of Sciences*, 1032, 141–153. https://doi.org/10.1196/annals.1314011

Boscarino, J. A. (2008). Prospective study of PTSD and early-age heart disease mortality among Vietnam veterans: implications for surveillance and prevention. *Psychosomatic Medicine*, 70(6), 668–676. https://doi.org/10.1097/PSY.0b013e31817bccaf

Bryant, R. A., Gallagher, H. C., Gibbs, L., Pattison, P., MacDougall, C., Harms, L., . . . & Lusher, D. (2017). Mental health and social networks after disaster. *American Journal of Psychiatry*, 174(3), 277–285. https://doi.org/10.1176/appi.ajp.2016.15111403

Bryant, R. A., Gibbs, L., Gallagher, H. C., Pattison, P., Lusher, D., MacDougall, C., . . . & Forbes, D. (2018). Longitudinal study of changing psychological outcomes following the Victorian Black Saturday bushfires. *Australian & New Zealand Journal of Psychiatry*, 52(6), 542–551. https://doi.org/10.1177/0004867417714337

Cao, C., Wang, L., Wu, J., Li, G., Fang, R., Cao, X., . . . Elhai, J. (2018). Patterns of post-traumatic stress disorder symptoms and post-traumatic growth in an epidemiological sample of Chinese earthquake survivors. *Frontiers in Psychology*, 9, 1549. https://doi.org/10.3389/fpsyg.2018.01549

Carlson, E. B., & Rosser-Hogan, R. (1991). Trauma experiences, post-traumatic stress, dissociation, and depression in Cambodian refugees. *American Journal of Psychiatry*, 148, 1548–1551.

Cerda, M., Bordelois, P. M., Galea, S., Norris, F., Tracy, M., & Koenen, K. C. (2013). The course of post-traumatic stress symptoms and functional impairment following a disaster: what is the lasting influence of acute vs. ongoing traumatic events and stressors? *Social Psychiatry and Psychiatric Epidemiology*, 48, 385–395.

Chan, C. S., & Rhodes, J. E. (2013). Religious coping, post-traumatic stress, psychological distress, and post-traumatic growth among female survivors four years after Hurricane Katrina. *Journal of Traumatic Stress*, 26(2), 257–265.

Courtois, C. A., Sonis, J., Brown, L. S., Cook, J., Fairbank, J. A., Friedman, M., Schultz, P. (2017). American Psychological Association Clinical Practice Guideline for the Treatment of Posttraumatic Stress Disorder (PTSD) in Adults. Adopted as APA Policy February 24, 2017.

Cuijpers, P., Karyotaki, E., De Wit, L., Eber, D. D. (2020). The effects of fifteen evidence-supported therapies for adult depression: a meta-analytic review. *Psychotherapy Research*, 30(3), 279–293. https://doi.org/10.1080/10503307.2019.1649732.

Currier, J. M., McDermott, R. C., Farnsworth, J. K., & Borges, L. M. (2019). Temporal associations between moral injury and post-traumatic stress disorder symptom clusters in military veterans. *Journal of Traumatic Stress*, 32, 382–392.

Cusack, K., Jonas, D. E., Forneris, C. A., Wines, C., Sonis, J., Middleton, J. C., ... & Gaynes, B. N. (2016). Psychological treatments for adults with post-traumatic stress disorder: a systematic review and meta-analysis. *Clinical Psychology Review*, 43, 128–141. https://doi.org/10.1016/j.cpr.2015.10.003.

Dao, T. K., Chu, D., Springer, J., Gopaldas, R. R., Menefee, D. S., Anderson, T., ... & Nguyen, Q. (2010). Clinical depression, post-traumatic stress disorder, and comorbid depression and post-traumatic stress disorder as risk factors for in-hospital mortality after coronary artery bypass grafting surgery. *Journal of Thoracic and Cardiovascular Surgery*, 140, 606–610.

Demirchyan, A., Goenjian, A. K., & Khachadourian, V. (2015). Factor structure and psychometric properties of the Posttraumatic Stress Disorder (PTSD) Checklist and DSM-5 PTSD symptom set in a long-term post-earthquake cohort in Armenia. *Assessment*, 22(5), 594–606. https://doi.org/10.1177/1073191114555523.

Divsalar, P., & Dehesh, T. (2020). Prevalence and predictors of post-traumatic stress disorder and depression among survivors over 12 years after the Bam Earthquake.

*Neuropsychiatric Disease and Treatment*, 16, 1207–1216.

Edmondson, D., Gamboa, C., Cohen, A., Anderson, A. H., Kutner, N., Kronish, I., ... & Muntner P. (2013). Association of post-traumatic stress disorder and depression with all-cause and cardiovascular disease mortality and hospitalization among Hurricane Katrina survivors with end-stage renal disease. *American Journal of Public Health*, 103, e130–e137. https://doi.org/10.2105/AJPH.2012.301146.

Farnsworth, J. K. (2019). Is and ought: descriptive and prescriptive cognitions in military-related moral injury. *Journal of Traumatic Stress*, 32, 373–381.

Favaro, A., Zaetta, C., Colombo, G., & Santonastaso, P. (2004). Surviving the Vajont disaster: psychiatric consequences 36 years later. *Journal of Nervous and Mental Disorders*, 192, 227–231.

Fernandez, C. A., Vicente, B., Marshall, B. D. L., Koenen, K. C., Arheart, K. L., Kohn, R., ... & Buka, S. L. (2017). Longitudinal course of disaster-related PTSD among a prospective sample of adult Chilean natural disaster survivors. *International Journal of Epidemiology*, 46(2), 440–452. https://doi.org/10.1093/ije/dyw094.

Forbes, D., Creamer, M., Bisson, J. I., Cohen, J. A., Crow, B. E., Foa, E. B., ... & Ursano, R. J. (2010). A guide to guidelines for the treatment of PTSD and related conditions. *Journal of Traumatic Stress*, 23 (5), 537–552. https://doi.org/10.1002/jts.20565.

Galea, S., Tracy, M., Norris, F., & Coffey, S. F. (2008). Financial and social circumstances and the incidence and course of PTSD in Mississippi during the first two years after Hurricane Katrina. *Journal of Traumatic Stress*, 21, 357–368. https://doi.org/10.1002/jts.20355.

Gao, X., Leng, Y., Guo, Y., Yang, J., Cui, Q., Geng, B., ... Zhou, Y. (2019). Association between earthquake experience and depression 37 years after the Tangshan earthquake: a cross-sectional study. *BMJ Open*, 9, e026110. https://doi.org/10.1136/bmjopen-2018-026110.

Geng, F, Zhou, Y, Liang, Y, & Fan, F. (2018). A longitudinal study of recurrent experience of earthquake and mental health problems among Chinese adolescents. *Frontiers in Psychology*, 9, 1259. https://doi.org/10.3389/fpsyg.2018.01259.

Goenjian, A., Najarian, M., Pynoos, R. S., Steinberg, A. M., Manoukian, G., Tavosian, A., & Fairbanks, L. (1994a). Post-traumatic stress disorder in adults and elderly after the 1988 earthquake in Armenia. *American Journal of Psychiatry*, 151, 895–901.

Goenjian, A., Najarian, L. M., Pynoos, R. S., Steinberg, A. M., Petrosian, P., Setrakyan, S., & Fairbanks, L. A. (1994b). Post-traumatic stress reactions after single and double trauma. *Acta Psychiatrica Scandanavia*, 90, 214–221.

Goenjian, A. K, Najarian, L. M., Steinberg, A. M., Fairbanks, L. A., Tashjian, M., & Pynoos, R. S. (2000). A prospective study of post-traumatic stress, anxiety, and depressive reactions after earthquake and violence. *American Journal of Psychiatry*, 157, 911–916.

Goenjian, A. K., Khatchadourian, V., Armenian, H., Demirchyan, A., & Steinberg, A. M. (2018). Post-traumatic stress disorder 23 years after the 1988 Spitak earthquake in Armenia. *Journal of Traumatic Stress*, 31, 47–56.

Goenjian, A. K., Steinberg, A. M., Walling, D., Bishop, S., Karayan, I., & Pynoos, R. (2020). 25-year follow-up of treated and not-treated adolescents after the Spitak earthquake: course and predictors of PTSD and depression. *Psychological Medicine*, 1–13. Advance online publication: https://doi.org/10.1017/S0033291719003891.

Green, B. L., Lindy, J. D., Grace, M. C., Gleser, G. C., Leonard, A. C., Korol, M., & Winget, C. (1990). Buffalo Creek survivors in the second decade: stability of stress symptoms. *American Journal of Orthopsychiatry*, 60, 43–54. https://doi.org/10.1037/h0079168.

Harville, E. W., Shankar, A., Dunkel Schetter, C., & Lichtveld, M. (2018). Cumulative effects of the Gulf oil spill and other disasters on mental health among reproductive-aged women: The Gulf Resilience on Women's Health Study. *Psychological Trauma: Theory, Research, Practice, and Policy*, 10(5), 533–541. https://doi.org/10.1037/tra0000345.

Horowitz, M. J., Wilner, N., Marmar, C., & Krupnick, J. (1980). Pathological grief and the activation of latent self-images. *American Journal of Psychiatry*, 137(10), 1157–1162. https://doi.org/10.1176/ajp.137.10.1157.

Hull, A. M., Alexander, D. A., & Klein, S. (2002). Survivors of the Piper Alpha oil platform disaster: long-term follow-up. *British Journal of Psychiatry*, 181, 433–438. https://doi.org/10.1192/bjp.181.5.433.

Imel, Z. E., Laska, K., Jakupcak, M., & Simpson, T. L. (2013). Meta-analysis of dropouts during treatment for post-traumatic stress disorder. *Journal of Consulting and Clinical Psychology*, 81, 394–404. https://doi.org/10.1037/a0031474.

Jafari, H., Heidari, M., Heidari, S., & Sayfouri, N. (2020). Risk factors for suicide behaviours after natural disasters: a systematic review. *Malaysian Journal of Medical Sciences*, 27(3), 20–33. https://doi.org/10.21315/mjms2020.27.3.3.

Johannsen, M., Damholdt, M. F., Zachariae, R., Lundorff, M., Farver-Vestergaard, I., & O'Connor, M. (2019). Psychological interventions for grief in adults: a systematic review and meta-analysis of randomized controlled trials. *Journal of Affective Disorders*, 253, 69–86. https://doi.org/10.1016/j.jad.2019.04.065.

Kaniasty, K., & Norris, F. H. (2008). Longitudinal linkages between perceived social support and post-traumatic stress symptoms: sequential roles of social causation and social selection. *Journal of Traumatic Stress*, 21, 274–281. https://doi.org/10.1002/jts.20334.

Kessler, R. C., Sonnega, A., Bromet, E., Hughes, M., & Nelson, C. B. (1995). Post-traumatic stress disorder in the National Comorbidity Survey. *Archives of General Psychiatry*, 52, 1048–1060.

King, D. W., Taft, C., King, L. A., Hammond, C., & Stone, E. R. (2006). Directionality of the association between social support and post-traumatic stress disorder: a longitudinal investigation. *Journal of Applied Social*

*Psychology*, 36(12), 2980–2992. https://doi. org/10,1111/j.0021–9029.2006.00138.x.

Krug, E. G., Kresnow, M. J., Peddicord, J. P., Dahlberg, L. L., Powell, K. E., Crosby, A. E., & Annest, J. L. (1999). Suicide after natural disasters. *New England Journal of Medicine*, 340(2), 148.

Li, X., Jun Aida, J., Hikichi, H., Kondo, P., & Kawachi, I. (2019). Association of post-disaster depression and post-traumatic stress disorder with mortality among older disaster survivors of the 2011 Great East Japan *earthquake* and *tsunami*. *JAMA Network Open*, 2(12), e1917550. https://doi.org/10.10 01/jamanetworkopen.2019.17550.

Liang, Y., Cheng, J., Ruzek, J., & Liu, Z. (2019). Post-traumatic stress disorder following the 2008 Wenchuan earthquake: a 10-year systematic review among highly exposed populations in China. *Journal of Affective Disorders*, 243, 327–339.

Litz, B. T., Stein, N., Delaney, E., Lebowitz, L., Nash, W. P., Silva, C., & Maguen, S. (2009). Moral injury and moral repair in war veterans: a preliminary model and intervention strategy. *Clinical Psychology Review*, 29, 695–706. https://doi.org/10.1016/ j.cpr.2009.07.003.

Lundorff, M., Holmgren, H., Zachariae, R., Farver-Vestergaard, I., & O'Connor, M. (2017). Prevalence of prolonged grief disorder in adult bereavement: a systematic review and meta-analysis. *Journal of Affective Disorders*, 212, 138–149. https://doi.org/10. 1016/j.jad.2017.01.030.

McDonald, S. D., & Calhoun, P. S. (2010). The diagnostic accuracy of PTSD checklist: a critical review. *Clinical Psychology Review*, 30, 976–987.

McFarlane, A. C. (1988). The longitudinal course of post-traumatic morbidity. The range of outcomes and their predictors. *Journal of Nervous and Mental Disease*, 176, 30–39.

Morgan, L., Scourfield, J., Williams, D., Jasper., A., & Lewis, G. (2003). The Aberfan disaster: 33-year follow-up of survivors. *British Journal of Psychiatry*, 182, 532–536. https://doi.org/10.1192/bjp.182.6.532.

Najarian, L. M., Sunday, S., Labruna, V., & Barry, I. (2011). Twenty year follow-up of adults traumatized during childhood in Armenia. *Journal of Affective Disorders*, 135, 51–55. https://doi.org/10.1016/j.jad.2011.06. 038.

Norris, F. H., Perilla, J. L., Riad, J. K., Kaniasty, K., & Lavizzo, E. A. (1999). Stability and change in stress, resources, and psychological distress following natural disaster: findings from Hurricane Andrew. *Anxiety Stress & Coping*, 12, 363–396.

Pitman, R. K., van der Kolk, B. A., Orr, S. P., & Greenberg, M. S. (1990). Naloxone-reversible analgesic response to combat-related stimuli in post-traumatic stress disorder: a pilot study. *Archives of General Psychiatry*, 47(6), 541–544. https://doi.org/10.1001/archpsyc. 1990.01810180041007.

Powers, M. B., Halpern, J. M., Ferenschak, M. P., Gillihan, S. J., & Foa, E. B. (2010). A meta-analytic review of prolonged exposure for post-traumatic stress disorder. *Clinical Psychology Review*, 30, 635–641. https://doi. org/10.1016/j.cpr.2010.04.007.

Robins, L. N., Helzer, J. E., Croughan, J., & Ratcliff, K. S. (1981). National Institute of Mental Health Diagnostic Interview Schedule. Its history, characteristics, and validity. *Archives of General Psychiatry*, 38(4), 381–389. https:doi.org/10.1001/archpsyc. 1981.01780290015001.

Ruskin, J., Rasul, R., Schneider, S., Bevilacqua, K., Taioli, E., & Schwartz, R. M. (2018). Lack of access to medical care during hurricane Sandy and mental health symptoms. *Preventive Medicine Reports*, 10, 363–369. https://doi.org/10.1016/j.pmedr.20 18.04.014.

Schnurr, P. P., Spiro, A., & Paris, A.H. (2000). Physician-diagnosed medical disorders in relation to PTSD symptoms in older male military veterans. *Health Psychology*, 19(1), 91–97. https://doi.org/10.1037//0278-6133. 19.1.91.

Schumm, J. A., Briggs-Phillips, M., & Hobfoll, S. E. (2006). Cumulative interpersonal traumas and social support as risk and resiliency factors in predicting PTSD and depression among inner-city women.

*Journal of Traumatic Stress*, 19, 825–836. https://doi.org/10.1002/jts.20159.

Smith, B., Pargament, K., Brant, C., & Oliver, J. (2000). Noah revisited: religious coping by church members and the impact of the 1993 Midwest flood. *Journal of Community Psychology*, 28, 169–186. https://doi.org/10.1002/(SICI)1520-6629(200003)28:23. 0.CO;2-I.

Steenkamp, M. M., Litz, B. T., Hoge, C. W., & Marmar, C. R. (2015). Psychotherapy for military-related PTSD: a review of randomized clinical trials. *JAMA*, 314(5), 489–500. https://doi.org/10.1001/jama. 2015.8370.

Steinglass, P., & Gerrity, E. (1990). Natural disasters and post-traumatic stress disorder: short-term vs. long-term recovery in two disaster affected communities. *Journal of Applied Social Psychology*, 20, 1746–1765. https://doi.org/10.1111/j.1559-1816. 1990.tb01509.x.

Suliman, S., Mkabile, S. G., Fincham, D. S., Ahmed, R., Stein, D. J., & Seedat, S. (2009). Cumulative effect of multiple traumas on symptoms of post-traumatic stress disorder, anxiety, and depression in adolescents. *Comprehensive Psychiatry*, 50(2), 121–127. https://doi.org/10.1016/j.comppsych.2008.0 6.006.

Sutker, P. B., Allain, A. N. Jr., Winstead, D. K. (1993). Psychopathology and psychiatric diagnoses of World War II Pacific theater prisoner of war survivors and combat veterans. *American Journal of Psychiatry*, 150, 240–245.

Utzon-Frank, N., Breinegaard, N., Bertelsen, M., Borritz, M., Eller, N. H., Nordentoft M, . . . & Bonde, J. P. (2014). Occurrence of delayed-onset post-traumatic stress disorder: a systematic review and meta-analysis of prospective studies. *Scandinavian Journal of Work, Environment & Health*, 40(3), 215–229. https://doi.org/10.5271/sjweh.3420.

Wang, B., Ni, C., Chen, J., Liu, X., Wang, A., Shao, Z., . . . & Yan, Y. (2011). Post-traumatic stress disorder 1 month after the 2008 earthquake in China: Wenchuan earthquake survey. *Psychiatry Research*, 187(3), 392–396.

Watkins, L. E., Sprang, K. R, & Rothbaum, B. O. (2018). Treating PTSD: a review of evidence-based psychotherapy interventions. *Frontiers in Behavioral Neuroscience*, 12, 258. https://doi.org/10.3389/fnbeh.2018.00258.

Watts, B. V., Schnurr, P. P., Mayo, L., Young-Xu, Y., Weeks, W. B., & Friedman, M. J. (2013). Meta-analysis of the efficacy of treatments for post-traumatic stress disorder. *Journal of Clinical Psychiatry*, 74(6), e541–e550. https://doi.org/10.4088/JCP.12r08225.

Wittouck, C., Van Autreve, S., De Jaegere, E., Portzky, G., & van Heeringen, K. (2011). The prevention and treatment of complicated grief: a meta-analysis. *Clinical Psychology Review*, 31(1), 69–78. https://doi.org/10.1016/j.cpr.2010.09.005.

Zhang, Y., & Ho, S. M. (2011). Risk factors of post-traumatic stress disorder among survivors after the 512 Wenchuan earthquake in China. *PLoS One*, 6(7), e22371. https://doi.org/10.1371/journal.pone. 0022371.

# How the Spitak Earthquake Contributed to our Understanding of the Genetics of PTSD and Associated Disorders

Julia Bailey and Armen Goenjian

## 8.1 Introduction

The Spitak earthquake in Armenia offered a unique opportunity to study the genetics of post-traumatic stress disorder (PTSD) and related conditions like depression. PTSD has been a difficult disorder to study with traditional genetic study designs because exposure to a traumatic event is required, which rarely happens to genetically related individuals. Research has shown that factors such as type, intensity, and frequency of trauma influence PTSD symptoms, as do gender and age (Goenjian et al., 1995; Goenjian et al., 2020). The earthquake was a natural disaster that affected the entire region of northern Armenia. All family members were exposed to the same horrific trauma at the same time, minimizing, but not eliminating, variability of exposure factors that may confound PTSD symptom profile.

The families that participated in the Spitak Earthquake Genetic Study (SEGS) were ascertained from Gumri, a city close to the epicenter where 50% of the buildings were damaged beyond repair or completely destroyed, and 7% of the population died. All the inhabitants were exposed to the catastrophe, and almost all exhibited symptoms of PTSD (Goenjian et al., 1994a, 2000). Twelve multigenerational families (three to five generations) comprised of 202 individuals were enrolled in the study and assessed for PTSD as well as depression and anxiety symptoms (see Figure 8.1). Detailed assessment was made of the trauma associated with the earthquake, including prior traumatic experiences, along with other information that might affect the expression of the disorder. All participants witnessed destruction; 90% witnessed dead bodies left lying in the streets; 92% saw severely injured people. Regarding *subjective experiences* of *fear* during the earthquake, 89% responded "a whole lot" and the remaining 11% responded "a lot." All subjects easily met the diagnostic Category A exposure criterion for PTSD.

This was a unique cohort in that these families came from one of the oldest genetically isolated ethnic groups, had similar socio-economic status (as did most Armenians in Soviet Armenia), similar family sizes (large), and were from the same religion. Since PTSD symptoms were present in almost all inhabitants of Spitak, families were randomly ascertained from the population. This is unlike case-control studies, which are based on a probands disease-seeking status, which limits the phenotypes (traits) under study. Families were recruited without prior knowledge of their psychiatric status, such as PTSD or depression. As a result, genetics of other traits (e.g., depression) could also be studied without bias. This unique family-study cohort was appropriate to assess the heritability of PTSD and associated disorders, as well as localize genetic causes (i.e., genes). This study was able to advance the field of PTSD genetics by demonstrating the heritability of vulnerability

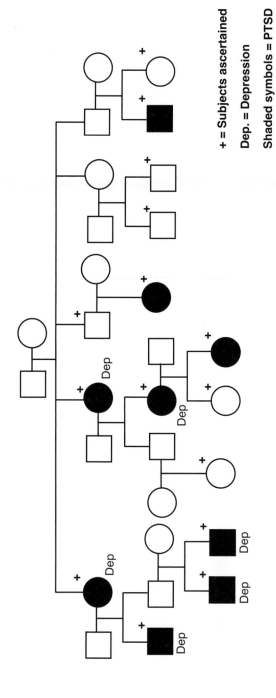

**Figure 8.1** One of the twelve pedigrees ascertained for the SEGS. '+' indicates the individuals ascertained in the study; the filled-in status shows those affected with PTSD, while 'Dep' indicates individuals affected by depression.

of PTSD in multi-generational families that was previously only shown in twins, as well as demonstrating pleiotropy of PTSD, depression, and anxiety. This study also identified specific genes that were associated with PTSD in this cohort.

## 8.2 Non-Genetic Risk Factors for PTSD

Before studying the genetics of PTSD, we assessed the contribution of environmental confounders as well as age and sex, to assess more accurately the heritability of PTSD. To assess these confounders, an earthquake-related profile was obtained for each participant on objective experiences during the earthquake, including the destruction of residence, deaths of relatives, seeing dead bodies, being seriously hurt, and seeing someone else injured. Additionally, subjects were questioned on pre-earthquake and post-earthquake traumatic experiences. Participants were also questioned on three items evaluating subjective experiences of exposure: fear of the earthquake, fear of getting badly hurt or dying, and fear that someone else would be badly injured or die. The earthquake profile was incorporated into the variance component analyses, and it was shown that measured covariates explained ~20% of the variance of the trait. Covariates that were significantly associated with PTSD symptoms included the sex of the individual (females had higher scores), witnessing a death during the earthquake, and exposure to trauma before the earthquake. The effect of sex has been documented in this Armenian population (Goenjian et al., 1997) and among Nicaraguans exposed to hurricane Mitch, who had high levels of PTSD symptoms (Goenjian et al., 2001). The effects of prior trauma have also been documented (Goenjian et al., 1994b). The ability to assess these variables and incorporate them into analyses minimized confounders and made these genetic studies more powerful. In contrast, controlling confounding variables in case-control or population-based studies with variable exposures may not be feasible.

## 8.3 Importance of Genetics of PTSD

Genetics is important not only to understand the cause of a disease but also to recognize how individuals respond to particular therapies. Drug metabolism is under genetic control, and genetic predispositions govern susceptibility to side effects in some cases. At least nine gene therapies have been approved for certain kinds of cancer, some viral infections, and a few inherited disorders. A related drug type interferes with faulty genes by using stretches of DNA or RNA to hinder their workings (Daley, 2019). Another potential benefit of knowing vulnerability genes for PTSD is being able to identify individuals at risk of PTSD and reduce their exposure to tasks that involve subjection to other potentially highly traumatic events, such as war theater.

## 8.4 Heritability of PTSD

The genetics of PTSD is still nascent. Few studies have documented the heritability of vulnerability for PTSD. Heritability is a metric used in genetics that estimates the proportion of phenotypic variance of a trait that is due to genetic causes (genes) in that population. It reveals if a trait has a genetic predisposition, which means genes can be found. Heritability can be measured using twin and multi-generational family studies.

### 8.4.1 Twin Studies

Heritability is measured in twin studies by comparing the disease susceptibility between twins who share 100% of their DNA (monozygotic or identical twins) with twins who share

50% of their DNA (dizygotic or fraternal twins). Genetic diseases will show more concordance/correlation with monozygotic twins. Significant heritability of PTSD has been found in both veteran (Lyons et al., 1993; True et al., 1993) and non-veteran populations (Stein et al., 2002), with estimates ranging from $h^2 = 0.20$–$0.38$). The heritability estimates are similar in different studies despite significant differences in cohorts. The veteran study was comprised of only male twin pairs who had undergone combat duty, while the non-veteran cohort was population-based, not treatment-seeking, and consisted of both male and female twin pairs. This implies that genetic mechanisms may be similar in military vs. non-military PTSD populations. A limitation of the twin study method is that it cannot easily incorporate covariates or control for confounders that might influence the expression of PTSD. To study the effects of covariates, ad hoc analyses must be performed by stratifying the sample over the variable of interest. For example, to study the effect of gender on heritability estimates, the twin study cohort needs to be stratified into same-sex twin pairs of males and females, thereby limiting sample size and severely reducing the power. Multi-generational family studies can incorporate confounding variables into heritability estimates.

## 8.4.2 Family Study in Armenia

Family studies can be used to assess heritability by comparing the correlations of the observed phenotype (trait) to the expected theoretical correlations based on genetic relationships. Using variance component quantitative statistical methods allows for estimation of heritability with the incorporation of environmental and biological covariates/confounders in the analyses. After adjusting for sex, age, and multiple environmental risk factors such as pre- and post-earthquake traumatic experiences, earthquake-related home destruction, severe injury and death of a family member, the heritability of PTSD-RI (the quantitative measure) in the SEGS sample was $h^2 = 0.41$ (p = 0.001), (Figure 8.2) which means that 41% of the variation seen in PTSD symptom severity can be explained by genetics (Goenjian et al., 2008). This estimate is slightly higher than that seen in the twin studies due to the incorporation of covariates, thereby providing a more valid estimate. The estimate is not far-off from the other estimates and could also be explained by methodological differences, including estimations of PTSD severity.

## 8.4.3 Heritability of PTSD Based on DSM IV and 5

One of the difficulties of studying PTSD is the highly changeable diagnostic criteria over time by the American Psychiatric Association. PTSD was initially labeled as "shell shock." It went through various diagnostic refinements, including a large change between the DSM-IV and DSM-5 versions of the *Diagnostic and Statistical Manual* (DSM). The major differences between DSM-IV and DSM-5 includes the deletion of the A2 criteria (the person's feeling of intense fear), splitting category C (avoidance and numbing) symptoms to C (avoidance) and D (negative alterations in mood and cognition), and the addition of new items to category D and one new item to category E, which was formerly category D.

Post-traumatic stress disorder, by definition, is a dichotomous disorder classified as Yes/No. One can also use psychometric instruments to measure PTSD symptoms quantitatively by using instruments such as the PTSD-Reaction Index (Steinberg et al., 2013), from which one can derive diagnosis for PTSD based on DSM diagnostic criteria.

In our multi-generational study, the heritability ($h^2$) of vulnerability to PTSD symptoms based on DSM-IV and DSM-5 criteria after adjusting for covariates was respectively 0.41

(p < 0.001) (Fig. 8.2) and 0.60 (p < $10^{-4}$) (Goenjian et al., 2015). The two scores were highly correlated (r = 0.96, p < 0.0001). The heritability of vulnerability to DSM-5 category B (re-experiencing) severity score was 0.75 (p < 0.0001); category C (avoidance/numbing) was 0.64 (p < 0.001); D category (negative alterations of cognition and mood) 0.58 (p < 0.001), while category E symptoms (arousal symptoms), formerly categorized as DSM-IV category D symptoms, were not significantly heritable ($h^2$ = 0.19). The differences in $h^2$ based on the different DSM classifications imply that comparing results from different studies that have used different DSM criteria may not be pragmatic and could be why some studies have failed to replicate results of gene findings. It is also possible that non-replications were due to differences in gene expression in different populations.

With regard to using dichotomous or continuous measures as an outcome variable for PTSD, we think continuous measures are more stable over time, and better reflect the fluctuations of the clinical status of the participants. They are less affected by the changing diagnostic criteria for the disorder and can be recoded as needed. Continuous (quantitative) analyses are also more powerful than dichotomous analyses (Bailey and Almasy, 1995).

### 8.4.4 Heritability of Depression and Anxiety in the Armenian Family Study

Depression and anxiety were measured in the family study using the Beck Depression and Anxiety Inventories, which also provide a quantitative measure. Since families were not ascertained by any phenotype, we were also able to perform analyses like the PTSD analyses on the other two phenotypes (Goenjian et al., 2008). After adjusting for covariates, heritability of depression measured quantitatively had significant, high genetic heritability, $h^2$ = 0.66 (p < 0.001), (Figure 8.2) higher than the rates found in the literature (26% to 39%) (Wurtman et al., 2005); anxiety was also heritable, $h^2$ = 0.61% (p < 0.001). Both depression and anxiety were significantly associated with sex (female) and age (older individuals). Additionally, depression was associated with the death of a family member, while anxiety was associated with witnessing death during the earthquake.

## 8.5 The Genetic Relation of PTSD with Depression and Anxiety

Comorbidity of PTSD and other psychiatric disorders, like depression, anxiety, has been documented in numerous psychiatric epidemiological studies where more than one condition is found in the same individual (Ruskin et al., 2018; Sharma and Kar, 2019). Longitudinal studies after the Spitak earthquake have shown significant comorbidity of PTSD, depression, and anxiety among survivors (Goenjian et al., 1995; Goenjian et al., 2000). Results of family studies have suggested that PTSD and depression may share a genetic link (i.e., share susceptibility genes) (Davidson et al., 1985, 1989; Dierker and Merikangas, 2001; Koenen et al., 2003).

The expression of the same gene as different traits (e.g., PTSD and depression) is labeled pleiotropy and is statistically described by genetic correlations ranging from 0 (no genes in common) to 1 (sharing all genes). In a study among 6,744 male Vietnam veterans (the Vietnam Veterans Study), Koenen et al. (2008) found a high depression–PTSD genetic correlation ($\rho_g$ = 0.77; 95% CI, 0.50–1.00) and a modest individual-specific environmental correlation ($\rho_g$ = 0.34; 95% CI, 0.19–0.48). Common genetic liability explained 62.5% of depression–PTSD comorbidity. Additive genetic influences common to depression account for 58% of the genetic variance in PTSD. Individual-specific environmental influences common to depression explained only 11% of the individual-specific environmental variance in PTSD.

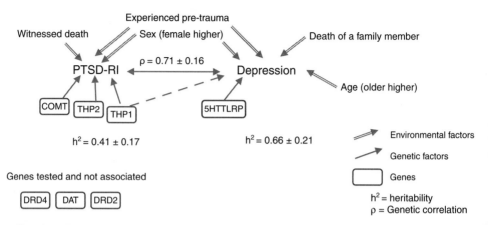

**Figure 8.2** Shared and unique genetic and environmental risk factors for PTSD and depression in the Spitak Earthquake Genetic Study. (A black- and- white version of this figure will appear in some formats. For the color version, please refer to the plate section.)
COMT = catechol-O-methyltransferase; TPH = tryptophan hydroxylase; 5HTTLRP = serotonin-transporter-linked polymorphic region; DRD4 = dopamine receptor D4; DAT = dopamine transporter; DRD2 = dopamine receptor D2.

In the Spitak Earthquake Genetic Study (SEGS), bivariate analyses were performed to assess whether the genetic components of PTSD, depression, and anxiety were shared. The bivariate phenotype (the correlation between two phenotypes, e.g., PTSD symptoms and depressive symptoms) is modeled as a linear function of the individual's phenotypic values, population means, and additive genetic and environmental correlations (Lange and Boehnke, 1983). The significance of the additive genetic correlation between the two phenotypes tests pleiotropy (shared genetic vulnerability) by comparing the likelihoods of the model. Controlling each variable for respective confounders, the genetic correlation between PTSD and depression was $\rho_g = 0.71$ (Figure 8.2), significantly different from 0 ($p < 0.01$), indicating substantial sharing of genes, and 1 ($p < 0.0001$), indicating that not all genes are shared. We also assessed the genetic correlation of anxiety (using the Beck Anxiety Inventory) to PTSD and depression. The heritability of anxiety was 61% ($p < 0.001$), and genetic correlation anxiety and PTSD was 0.75, significantly different from 0 ($p < 0.001$) and 1 ($p < 0.0001$). The genetic correlation of anxiety and depression was 0.54, significantly different from 0 ($p < 0.04$) and 1 ($p < 0.0001$). These findings indicate that PTSD shares genes with depression and anxiety symptoms.

In summary, the heritability study indicated that the genetic make-up of some individuals renders them substantially more vulnerable than others to develop symptoms of PTSD and depression, and PTSD and anxiety. A large proportion of genes for these phenotypes are shared. The findings offered promise for identifying susceptibility genes for these phenotypes.

## 8.6 Localizing the Genetic Cause

Heritability estimates only tell us that a disorder has a genetic component. They do not tell us how many genes are involved or where they are located in the genome, i.e., the complete set of genes or genetic material present in a cell or organism. We often say that we are looking for "genes for PTSD." What is meant by that is "variants or mutations of genes that confer susceptibility to PTSD." This distinction is important because it means that individuals with PTSD do not have different genes than other people; they have different variants of specific genes that are producing some biological function that is rendering them vulnerable to experiencing PTSD when exposed to trauma. There might be many susceptibility genes with many variants, and individuals may have the same phenotype for many differing genetic reasons (called heterogeneity). Also, most variants in susceptibility genes are harmless. The challenge is to determine which specific variant causes disease under which circumstances.

There are different ways to localize genes that cause susceptibility to PTSD. Candidate gene studies are hypothesis-driven based on *a priori* evidence from animal or human models. Genome-scans thoroughly search the entire genome.

There are different genetic epidemiology study designs that can be used to localize genes, including multi-generational family studies, twin studies, and case/control studies. These study designs can all be used in both candidate genes as well as genome scans, albeit with different power (i.e., the ability to detect the gene). There tends to be a trade-off – family studies are more powerful, but case/control studies are easier to collect subjects and could gain power by increasing sample size. However, genetics studies among unrelated individuals (as in case-control studies) are always problematic because there is no *a priori* assumption that they share the same causal genes as in family studies.

## 8.7 Candidate Genes

The most intuitive way to look for susceptibility genes is to look at genes that code for molecules that play an obvious function in psychiatric disorders, such as brain neurotransmitters. Not surprisingly, the candidate genes that have been studied among those with PTSD were genes related to brain chemistry, mostly neurotransmitters or receptors. Most of the studies that have focused on the dopaminergic and serotonergic systems and used case-control methodology which could not control for confounding variables, have relied heavily on how well the control groups matched. The power of a study to detect genes depends on the size and scope of the study. While rarely presented in the literature, the power of these studies can be calculated from their sample sizes. Calculations have shown that many of these studies are underpowered. Another confounding problem with case-control studies is the lack, or inadequacy, of exposure information among the control groups. For example, if the exposure of the control group was mild while the case group was severe, comparing the outcomes without stratifying based on severity and timing of the event may lead to erroneous conclusions.

The SEGS used a family-based variance method to study candidate genes while adjusting for significant covariates (Almasy et al., 1999). Power calculations demonstrated that the cohort had 80% power to detect variants that accounted for at least a tenth of the overall trait variance using these methods. Candidate genes seen in brain chemistry were studied.

## 8.7.1 Dopaminergic System

Dopaminergic pathways in the brain synthesize and release the neurotransmitter dopamine. This system is involved in many functions, including executive, learning, reward, motivation, and neuroendocrine control. Dysfunction of these pathways and nuclei may involve disorders such as Parkinson's disease, attention deficit hyperactivity disorder, tardive dyskinesia, and addiction. In the dopaminergic system, the candidate gene studies of PTSD have focused on dopamine receptors, transporters, and metabolizers, e.g., DAT,

DRD2, DRD4, COMT. The "DAT" (dopamine transporter) gene, also known as SLC6A2, codes for the regulation of dopamine levels. Most individuals have one of two alleles ("9" or "10"). The association with PTSD was initially found with the "9" allele in a study with 102 cases and 104 matched combat and trauma-exposed controls (Noble et al., 1991). In the Spitak Earthquake Genetic Study, the dopamine transporter "9" repeat allele of the DAT gene was not associated with PTSD (Bailey et al., 2010). DAT pumps the dopamine out of the synaptic cleft back into the cytosol. DAT is implicated in several dopamine-related disorders, including attention deficit hyperactivity disorder, bipolar disorder, clinical depression, alcoholism, and substance-use disorder.

Comings et al. (1996) found an association of PTSD and the dopamine receptor D2 (DRD2) TaqA1/A2 allele system in a cohort of subjects on an addiction treatment unit who had been exposed to severe combat conditions in Vietnam. The findings were replicated by Young et al. (2002).

In the Spitak cohort, the DRD2 TaqA1/A2 allele system was not associated with PTSD (Bailey et al., 2010). The association was also not replicated in another cohort by Gelernter et al. (1999). DRD2 is the main receptor for most antipsychotic drugs. The dopamine receptor DRD2 functions to regulate the synthesis, storage, and release of dopamine. Mutations in the DRD2 gene can inhibit dopamine production and activity, leading to psychiatric and psychotic effects as well as an increased risk for addiction and neuropsychiatric diseases.

The dopamine receptor D4 (DRD4) is activated by dopamine. It is linked to many neurological and psychiatric conditions, including schizophrenia and bipolar disorder, ADHD, addictive behaviors, Parkinson's disease, and eating disorders. In the SEGS cohort the "long" allele of DRD4 was not associated with PTSD (unpublished). However, there was a trend of an association between DRD4 rs16122917C and depression ($p = 0.08$).

Dopamine is metabolized by catechol-O-methyltranferase (COMT). To study if the COMT gene was influential on PTSD in the SEGS cohort, we studied eight single nucleotide polymorphisms (SNPs) in the COMT gene and found a positive association with allele rs4633C with PTSD ($p < 0.03$) (Goenjian, 2015). This was the first implication of COMT in PTSD and needs to be further studied. Prior studies have found an association of variants of COMT Val allele and depression, anxiety, and PTSD.

## 8.7.2 Serotonergic System

Serotonin, 5-hydroxytryptamine (5HT), is a small molecule that functions both as a neurotransmitter in the central nervous system and as a hormone in the periphery. The serotonergic system has been shown to play a role in controlling arousal, sleep, anxiety, and depression. Serotonin has been the target of various types of antidepressants, including tricyclics and serotonin reuptake inhibitors (SSRIs). These medications have been effectively used to treat both depression and PTSD symptoms. Tryptophan hydroxylase (TPH) gene and serotonin transporter (5HTT) gene (SLC64A) have been the focus of many mood disorder studies. The TPH gene encodes tryptophan, the rate-limiting enzyme in serotonin synthesis. The 5-HTTLPR (serotonin-transporter-linked polymorphic region) is in the SLC6A4 gene that codes for the serotonin transporter. Since the polymorphism was identified in the middle of the 1990s, it has been extensively investigated, e.g., in connection with neuropsychiatric disorders. The polymorphism produces long/short (L/S) alleles. These alleles have been associated with psychiatric disorders including PTSD and depression. An association with the "S" allele and PTSD was found (Grabe et al., 2009) but not replicated

(Mellman et al., 2009; Thakur et al., 2009). Li et al. (2021) studied the 5-HTTLPR genotype among 963 participants in a longitudinal study and used a quantitative measure of PTSD; they demonstrated that the "S" allele predicted the symptom severity and recovery rate.

Post-traumatic stress disorder was not associated with 5HTTLPR in the SEGS, but depressive symptoms were significantly associated with the "S" allele (p = 0.03). This gene explained 4% of the phenotypic variance seen in depression. A meta-analysis by Karg et al. (2011) found that 5-HTTLPR moderated the relation between stress and depression.

## 8.7.3 Tryptophan Pathway

Tryptophan hydroxylase (TPH) genes have been the focus of many mood disorder studies (Zill et al., 2004; Van Den Bogaert et al., 2006). The TPH gene encodes tryptophan, the rate-limiting enzyme in serotonin synthesis. There are two isomorphisms of this compound, TPH1 and TPH2, which are located on different chromosomes. In the SEGS, after adjusting for age, sex, exposure, and environmental variables, there was a significant association of PTSD symptoms with the "t" allele of the TPH1 SNP rs2108977 (p < 0.004), which explained 3% of the phenotypic variance, and there was a significant association of PTSD symptoms and the "t" allele of TPH2 SNP rs11178997 (p = 0.03), explaining 4% of the variance (Figure 8.2) (Goenjian et al., 2012). The SEGS study was the first published report showing that variants in TPH1 and TPH2 genes constitute risk factors for PTSD symptoms. This allele in TPH2 also showed a non-significant trend for an association with depressive symptoms (p = 0.08), indicating it could be one of the pleiotropic (shared) genes of PTSD and depression.

## 8.7.4 Candidate Gene Summary

Candidate gene studies of PTSD show replication in some cohorts, implying that there are shared and different genes in different cohorts. Non-replication of a candidate gene association does not necessarily mean false results (false-positive), nor does it negate the importance of that gene in other cohorts, as genes act differently in different ethnic populations. Non-replication could also be due to an insufficient sample size lacking enough power to detect a true positive result. False results may also occur when genetically vulnerable candidates who have not been exposed to trauma (who may otherwise develop PTSD upon exposure to trauma) are classified as controls. This can lead to false results because their "PTSD genes" will be incorrectly included in the control group. There may also be differences in the cohorts under study with regard to the severity of their exposures or varying time-of-exposure to the time-of-assessment interval, or the use of different instruments to measure PTSD symptoms, resulting in false-negative or positive results. These various methodological problems may explain why many PTSD studies do not replicate findings.

The case-control studies suggest that the dopaminergic and the serotonergic systems play a role in developing PTSD. They explain a small portion of the variance of PTSD, which is a polygenic disorder as are most psychiatric disorders, i.e., influenced by more than one gene. Candidate gene studies are limited because they focus on genes already suspected. An agnostic method for localizing susceptibility genes is to study markers using genome scans.

# 8.8 Genome Scans

Scanning the genome (the complete set of genes or genetic material present in a cell or organism) means assessing genetic markers that have a known location spaced evenly over the genome. Markers used include restriction fragment length polymorphisms (RFLP) and single nucleotide polymorphism (SNPs). Genetic markers exploit the variations in DNA sequences, known as polymorphisms, between individuals to pinpoint the locations of genes within a genomic sequence. Genes can be tested through linkage analysis, whereby fragments of DNA that harbor susceptibility genes can be identified/localized, or through association analysis, where markers are tested for statistical association with the piece of DNA and a trait. Not all study designs can do both types of analyses. Linkage analysis is more accurate but requires related individuals; case/control cohorts may be more powerful but are only suitable for association (and not linkage) studies (e.g., GWAS) (Terwilliger and Göring, 2000).

## 8.8.1 Genome-Wide Association Studies

Genome-wide association studies (GWAS) is an approach used in genetics research to associate specific genetic variations with particular diseases. The method involves scanning the genomes from many different people and testing genetic markers for a significant increase of particular variants in affected vs. unaffected individuals.

There have been several GWAS of PTSD with no consistency of findings (Guffanti et al., 2013; Logue et al., 2013; Xie et al., 2013; Almli et al., 2015; Ashely-Koch et al., 2015; Duncan et al., 2018; Gelernter et al., 2019; Nievergelt et al., 2019). The most interesting genome-wide association finding with a Bonferroni-corrected level of significance was RS8042149 located in the RORA gene on 15q22.2 (Logue et al., 2013). The RORA gene is a key regulator of embryonic development, cellular differentiation, immunity, circadian rhythm, as well as lipid, steroid, xenobiotics, and glucose metabolism. In a small number of studies, RORA has been associated with depression (Garriock et al., 2010) and autism (Nguyen et al., 2010).

Xie et al. (2013) found another gene in the Tolloid-Like 1 gene (TLL1) at 4q32.3. Studies in mice suggest that this gene plays multiple roles in the development of the mammalian heart. Other different target genes that merit further investigation revealed in a large consortium study of over 30,000 PTSD cases include PARK2, which plays a role in the dopaminergic system and is associated with Parkinson's disease; PODXL, which is involved in neural development and synapse formation; SH3RF3, which is associated with neurocognition and dementia; and KAZN, which is expressed in the brain (Nievergeit et al., 2019). These genes have been identified because they are located in or near SNPs, which showed statistical significance, and actual studies on the genes remain to be carried out.

Association analyses tests for either a particular variant or a particular genetic marker in linkage disequilibrium with a causal variant resulting from a mutation. If there are enough cases that share that particular variation, an association can be detected. If there were multiple mutational events in a gene among the cases, or if mutations in different genes are involved, then the power to detect any particular variant will be lowered. Lack of replication for association studies of PTSD is not surprising given that a large number of less common alleles is likely to be involved in the etiology of complex disease with individually trivial attributable fractions (Terwillinger and Goring, 2000). Other methods, like those that directly look at the sequence, are more promising to elicit genes.

## 8.8.2 Whole Genome Sequencing and Whole Exome Sequencing

Due to the advances in technology, we can affordably sequence the genome, which allows us to look directly at genetic variation so we can explicitly study causal variants. Whole genome sequencing (WGS) is the process of determining the complete DNA sequence of a person's genome. The genome, the genetic material of an organism, includes both the coding regions (exons) and the non-coding regions (introns). An alternative way of sequencing, known as whole exome sequencing (WES), includes only the exons, which are the coding regions or the DNA parts that get translated to RNA and transcribed to protein.

In the SEGS, we performed WES in fifteen individuals from three families. These individuals were selected based on quantitative PTSD scores and relationship in the pedigree, maximizing genetic distances or meiosis to make the analyses most informative. After bioinformatic analyses, all the affected participants shared three variants: olfactory receptor 4C3 (OR4C3), which is putative; a variant in MUC16, which is not putative because it has a minor allele frequency over 5%; and a variant in MIR548F5, which is not putative because MIR548F5 is a microRNA only expressed in heart muscle. The OR4C3 gene codes for an olfactory receptor that interacts with odorant molecules in the nose and shares a domain structure with many neurotransmitters. It is an interesting putative gene for PTSD.

In a study among war veterans, Dileo et al. (2008) found veterans with PTSD exhibited significant olfactory identification deficits compared to controls, despite uncompromised performance on cognitive measures. In another study among veterans with and without PTSD, Vermetten et al. (2007) found PTSD patients rated noxious olfactory stimulus as distressing, resulting in increased PTSD symptoms and anxiety and an increase in regional blood flow (rCBF) in the amygdala, insula, and medial prefrontal cortex (mPFC), suggesting the involvement of neural circuitry that shares olfactory elements and memory processing regions when exposed to trauma-related stimuli. With regard to the OR4C3 gene, further testing of the variant is necessary to determine if it meets the rigorous criteria for being "implicated" in PTSD.

Using WES, we were able to show that the SEGS cohort did not have causal variants in the exomes of the candidate genes APOE, CNR1, HTR2A, HTR2A, FKBP5, NR3C1, RGS22, CNR1, TLL1, CRHR1, GABRA2, ADCYAP1R1, or DTNBP1. We also did not find any causal variants in the candidate regions from the GWAS areas on 4q32.3 nor 4p15.1. These results support the contention for heterogeneity in PTSD indicating that different genes are "more" causal in different populations. Alternatively, the findings were chance occurrences.

## 8.9 Summary

The genetics of PTSD may be considered to be in its infancy. It is a difficult disorder to study due to the complexity of the trauma component, which is a precondition of the disorder. Besides the different types of traumatic events (e.g., violence, earthquake), the timing of the measurements after the trauma and the intensity of the trauma may vary among genetic studies. Normalizing these variables for analysis is not trivial. Analyses of the data from the Spitak Earthquake Genetic Studies (SEGS) have demonstrated the heritability of vulnerability of PTSD, depression, and anxiety severity. They have also identified the association of two serotonergic genes (TPH1 and TPH2) and one dopaminergic gene (COMT) with PTSD (Figure 8.2). The analyses have also replicated the association of the serotonin transporter promoter gene, 5HTTLPR and depression among multi-generational families. The WES demonstrated an association between OR4C3 (the gene for olfactory receptors) and PTSD.

We expect many other genes will be found in the future, including a unique gene for PTSD and depression. The current genes explain a small proportion of the estimated variance for PTSD. Genes that have been found to be influential in other samples (DRD4, DAT, DRD2) were not significantly associated in our studies. Heterogeneity (i.e., different genetic mechanisms that produce the same or similar phenotypes) is expected. Dissimilar findings in different studies suggest that there may be additional genes working in different populations, and that there are probably many genes involved in these complex psychiatric disorders.

The Spitak earthquake provided a unique opportunity to contribute to the understanding of the genetic inheritance of vulnerability to PTSD and depression and their genetic correlation. The similarities in the type and severity of the traumatic events and the contemporaneous measurements for the study enabled the minimization of confounding non-genetic environmental factors. The multigenerational family study design reduced genetic heterogeneity, which is also a confounder in genetic research. This powerful study design enabled identification of a number of shared and unique genetic and environmental risk factors of PTSD and depression.

Figure 8.2 shows the complex relationship between genetic and non-genetic risk factors for PTSD and depression. Environmental risk factors for PTSD included female sex, experiencing pre-earthquake traumatic experiences, and witnessing death during the earthquake. For depression, the risk factors included age (older), sex (female), pre-earthquake traumatic experience, and death of a nuclear family member related to the earthquake. The figure also shows the three genes (TPH1, TPH2, and COMT) associated with PTSD and one gene (5HTTLPR) associated with depression. The two traits, PTSD and depression, were not correlated after adjusting for the genetic and environmental factors.

## 8.10  Recommendations

Still, much work needs to be done before genetic findings such as these can be translated into therapeutic and preventive approaches. Different cohorts need to be assessed to determine the range of heterogeneity. Gold standard instruments should be used to measure cumulative variables and allow for coding into various diagnostic categories. Additionally, blood samples should be taken to allow for more complex genetic studies, e.g., RNA for expression studies, DNA for methylation studies. After establishing that a gene or set of genes are associated with a disorder, the next step is to demonstrate how the gene(s) contribute to the disorder by studying normal and disrupted functions *in vitro* and *in vivo*. This will provide a better understanding of how and why people get PTSD after trauma and will lead to better treatments and cures.

## References

Almasy, L. A., Williams, J. T., Dyer, T. D., & Blangero, J. (1999). Quantitative trait locus detection using combined linkage/disequilibrium analysis. *Genetic Epidemiology*, 17 (Suppl. 1), S31–S36.

Almli, L. M., Stevens, J. S., Smith, A. K., Kilaru, V., Meng, Q., Flory J., Abu-Amara, D., . . . & Ressler, K. J. (2015). A genome-wide identified risk variant for PTSD is a methylation quantitative trait locus and confers decreased cortical activation to fearful faces. *American Journal of Medical Genetics B Neuropsychiatric Genetics*, 168B (5), 327–336.

Ashley-Koch, A. E., Garrett, M. E., Gibson, J., Liu, Y., Dennis, M. F., Kimbrel N. A., . . . & Hauser, M. A. (2015). Genome-wide association study of posttraumatic stress disorder in a cohort of Iraq-Afghanistan era veterans. *Journal of Affective Disorder*, 15 (184), 225–234.

Bailey, J. N., & Almasy, L. A. (1995). A brute force dichotomization approach to quantitative trait linkage analyses. *Genetic Epidemiology*, 12, 719–722.

Bailey, J. N., Goenjian, A. K., Noble, E. P. , Walling, D. P., Ritchie, T., & Goenjian, H. A. (2010). PTSD and dopaminergic genes, DRD2 and DAT, in multigenerational families exposed to the Spitak earthquake. *Psychiatry Research*, 178 (3), 507–510.

Comings, D. E., Muhleman, D., & Gysin, R. (1996). Dopamine D2 receptor (DRD2) gene and susceptibility to posttraumatic stress disorder: a study and replication. *Biological Psychiatry*, 40 (5), 368–372.

Daley, J. (2019). Gene therapy arrives. *Nature*, 576, S12–S13.

Davidson, J., Swartz, M., Storck, M., Krishnan, R. R., & Hammett, E. (1985). A diagnostic and family study of posttraumatic stress disorder. *American Journal of Psychiatry*, 142 (1), 90–93.

Davidson, J., Smith R., & Kudler, H. (1989). Familial psychiatric illness in chronic posttraumatic stress disorder. *Comprehensive Psychiatry*, 30 (4), 339–345.

Dierker, L. C., & Merikangas, K. R. (2001). Familial psychiatric illness and posttraumatic stress disorder: findings from a family study of substance abuse and anxiety disorders. *Journal of Clinical Psychiatry*, 62 (9): 715–720.

Dileo, J. F., Brewer, W. J., Hopwood, M., Anderson, V., Creamer, M. (2008). Olfactory identification dysfunction, aggression and impulsivity in war veterans with posttraumatic stress disorder. *Psychological Medicine*, 38, 523–531.

Duncan, L. E., Ratanatharathorn, A., Aiello A. E., Almli, L. M., Amstadter, A. B., Ashley-Koch, A. E., . . . & Koenen, K. C. (2018). Largest GWAS of PTSD (N=20 070) yields genetic overlap with schizophrenia and sex differences in heritability. *Molecular Psychiatry*, 23 (3), 666–673.

Garriock, H. A., Kraft, J. B., Shyn, S. I., Peters, E. J., Yokoyama, J. S., Jenkins, G. D., . . . & Hamilton, S. P. (2010). A genome-wide association study of citalopram response in major depressive disorder. *Biological Psychiatry*, 67 (2), 133–138.

Gelernter, J., Southwick, S., Goodson, S., Morgan, A., Nagy, L., Charney, D. S. (1999). No association between D2 dopamine receptor (DRD2) "A" system alleles, or DRD2 haplotypes, and posttraumatic stress disorder. *Biological Psychiatry*, 45, 620–625.

Gelernter, J., Sun, N., Polimanti, R., Robert, P., Levey, D. F., Bryois, J., . . . & Stein, M. B. (2019). Genome-wide association study of post-traumatic stress disorder reexperiencing symptoms in >165,000 US veterans. *Nature Neuroscience*, 22 (9), 1394–1401.

Goenjian, A., Najarian, M., Pynoos, R. S., Steinberg, A. M., Manoukian, G., Tavosian, A., & Fairbanks, L. (1994a). Posttraumatic stress disorder in adults and elderly after the 1988 earthquake in Armenia. *American Journal of Psychiatry*, 151, 895–901.

Goenjian, A., Najarian, L. M., Pynoos, R. S., Steinberg, A. M., Petrosian, P., Setrakyan, S., & Fairbanks, L. A. (1994b). Posttraumatic stress reactions after single and double trauma. *Acta Psychiatrica Scandinavia*, 90, 214–221.

Goenjian, A. K., Pynoos, R. S., Steinberg, A. M., Najarian, L. M., Asarnow, J. R., Karayan, I. . . . & Fairbanks, L. A. (1995). Psychiatric co-morbidity in children after the 1988 earthquake in Armenia. *Journal of the American Academy of Child and Adolescent Psychiatry*, 34, 1174–1184.

Goenjian, A. K., Karayan, I., Pynoos, R. S., Minassian, D., Najarian, L. M., Steinberg, A. M., & Fairbanks, L. A. (1997). Outcome of psychotherapy among early adolescents after trauma. *American Journal of Psychiatry*, 154(4), 536–542.

Goenjian, A. K, Najarian, L. M., Steinberg, A. M., Fairbanks, L. A., Tashjian, M., & Pynoos, R. S. (2000). A prospective study of post-traumatic stress, anxiety, and depressive reactions after earthquake and violence. *American Journal of Psychiatry*, 157, 911–916.

Goenjian, A. K., Molina, L., Steinberg, A. M., Fairbanks, L. A., Alvarez, M. L., Goenjian, H. A., & Pynoos R. S. (2001). Post-traumatic stress and depressive reactions among Nicaraguan adolescents after Hurricane Mitch. *American Journal of Psychiatry*, 158, 788–794.

Goenjian, A. K., Noble, E. P., Walling, D. P., Goenjian, H. A., Karayan, I. S., Ritchie, T., & Bailey, J. N. (2008). Heritabilities of symptoms of posttraumatic stress disorder, anxiety and depression in earthquake-exposed Armenian families. *Psychiatric Genetics*, 18, 261–266.

Goenjian, A. K., Bailey, J. N., Walling. D. P., Steinberg A. S., Schmidt, D., Dandekar, U., & Noble, E. P. (2012) Association of TPH1, TPH2, and 5HTTLPR with PTSD and depression. *Journal of Affective Disorders*, 140, 244–252.

Goenjian, A. K., Noble, E. P., Steinberg, A. M., Walling, D. P., Stepanyan S. T., Dandekar, S., & Bailey J. N. (2015). Association of COMT and TPH-2 genes with DSM-5-based PTSD symptoms. *Journal of Affective Disorders*, 172, 472–478.

Goenjian, A. K., Steinberg, A., Walling, D., Bishop, S., Karayan, I., & Pynoos, R. S. (2020). 25-year follow-up of treated and not-treated adolescents after the Spitak earthquake: course and predictors of PTSD and depression. *Psychological Medicine*, 14, 1–13. Advance online publication. https://doi.org/10.1017/S0033291719003891.

Grabe, H. J., Spitzer, C., Schwahn, C., Marcinek, A., Frahnow, A., Barnow, S. , . . ..& Rosskopf, D. (2009) Serotonin transporter gene (SLC6A4) promoter polymorphisms and the susceptibility to posttraumatic stress disorder in the general population. *American Journal of Psychiatry*, 166, 926–933.

Guffanti, G., Galea, S., Yan, L., Roberts, A. L., Solovieff, N., Aiello, A. E., . . . & Koenen, K. C. (2013). Genome-wide association study implicates a novel RNA gene, the lincRNA AC068718.1, as a risk factor for post-traumatic stress disorder in women. *Psychoneuroendocrinology*, 38 (12), 3029–3038.

Karg, K., Burmeister, M., Shedden K., & Sen, S. (2011). The serotonin transporter promoter variant (5HTTLPR), stress, and depression meta-analysis revisited. *Archives of General Psychiatry*, 68, 444–454.

Koenen, K. C., Lyons, M. J., Goldberg, J., Simpson, J., Williams, W. M., Toomey, R., . . . & Tsuang, M. T. (2003). A high-risk twin study of combat-related PTSD comorbidity.

*Twin Research*, 6 (3), 218–226. https://doi.org/10.1375/136905203765693870.

Koenen, K. C. , Fu, Q. J. , Ertel, K., Lyons, M. J., Eisen, S. A., True, W. R., Goldberg, J., & Tsuang, M. T. (2008). Common genetic liability of major depression and posttraumatic stress disorder in men. *Journal of Affective Disorders*, 105, 109–115.

Lange, K., & Boehnke, M. (1983). Extensions to pedigree analysis. IV. Covariance components models for multivariate traits. *American Journal of Medical Genetics*, 14 (3), 513–524.

Li, G., Wang, L., Cao, C. , Fang, R. , Hall, B. J. , Elhai, J. D. , & Liberzon, I. (2021). Post-traumatic stress symptoms of children and adolescents exposed to the 2008 Wenchuan earthquake: a longitudinal study of 5-HTTLPR genotype main effects and gene-environment interactions. *International Journal of Psychology*, 56 (1), 22–29.

Logue, M. W., Baldwin, C., Guffanti, G., Melista, E., Wolf, E. J., Reardon, A. F., . . . & Koenen, K. (2013). A genome-wide association study of post-traumatic stress disorder identifies the retinoid-related orphan receptor alpha (RORA) gene as a significant risk locus. *Molecular Psychiatry*, 18 (8), 937–942.

Logue, M. W., Miller, E. J., Wolf, E.J., et al. (2020). Traumatic Stress Brain Study Group. An epigenome-wide association study of posttraumatic stress disorder in US veterans implicates several new DNA methylation loci. *Clinical Epigenetics*, 12 (1), 46.

Lyons, M. J., Goldberg, S. A., Eisen, S. A, et al. (1993). Do genes influence exposure to trauma? A twin study of combat. *American Journal of Medical Genetics*, 48 (1), 22–27.

Mellman, T., Alim, D. D., Brown, E., Gorodetsky, B., et al. (2009). Serotonin polymorphisms and posttraumatic stress disorder in a trauma-exposed African American population. *Depression and Anxiety*, 26, 993–997.

Nguyen, A., Rauch, T. A., Pfeifer, G. P., et al. (2010). Global methylation profiling of lymphoblastoid cell lines reveals epigenetic contributions to autism spectrum disorders and a novel autism candidate gene, RORA,

**Figure 2.1** A group of Psychiatric Outreach Program therapists in front of the Gumri clinic. On the far right (with bow tie) is Dr. Louis M. Najarian, and on the far left of the third row is Dr. Armen Goenjian. (A black and white version of this figure will appear in some formats. For the color version, please refer to the plate section.)

**Figure 2.2** Students in a makeshift classroom with their teacher in Gumri (Leninakan) in 1989. (A black and white version of this figure will appear in some formats. For the color version, please refer to the plate section.)

**Figure 2.3.** "Yogi Bear's Help After the Earthquake" (a Hanna-Barbera Production, 1989). (A black and white version of this figure will appear in some formats. For the color version, please refer to the plate section.)

**Figure 3.1** Students in a makeshift school classroom in Leninakan, 1990. (A black and white version of this figure will appear in some formats. For the color version, please refer to the plate section.)

**Figure 3.3** Psychiatric Outreach Program therapists, Dr. Madeline Tashjian and Dr. Angela Boghosian, shown walking among the poorly insulated small makeshift homes in Gumri, 1990. (A black and white version of this figure will appear in some formats. For the color version, please refer to the plate section.)

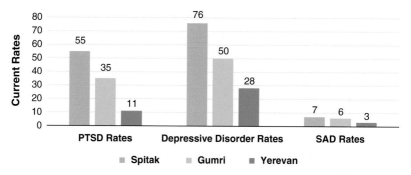

**Figure 3.4** Rates of PTSD, depressive disorder, and separation anxiety disorder across three differentially exposed cities 1.5 years after the Spitak earthquake. (A black and white version of this figure will appear in some formats. For the color version, please refer to the plate section.)

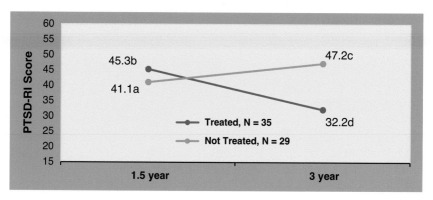

**Figure 3.5** PTSD-Reaction Index (PTSD-RI) scores at 1.5 and three years after the Spitak earthquake among treated and not treated early adolescents in Gumri. (A black and white version of this figure will appear in some formats. For the color version, please refer to the plate section.)
  Data from the *American Journal of Psychiatry* 1997; 154: 536–542.
  a ≈ b (p-value not significant)
  c > a (t = 3.12, df =59, p < 0.01)
  d < b (t = -6.69, df = 59, p < 0.01)
  d < c (t = -7.64, df = 59, p <0.01)

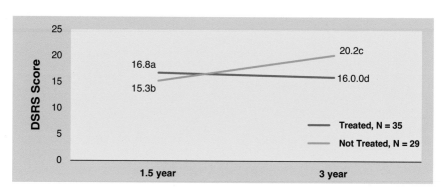

**Figure 3.6** Depression Self-Rating Scale (DSRS) scores at 1.5 and three years after the Spitak earthquake among treated and not treated early adolescents in Gumri. (A black and white version of this figure will appear in some formats. For the color version, please refer to the plate section.)
  Data from the *American Journal of Psychiatry* 1997; 154: 536–542.
  a ≈ b (p-value not significant)
  d < c (t = –4.09, df = 59, p < .01)
  c > b (t = 4.08, df = 59, p < .01)

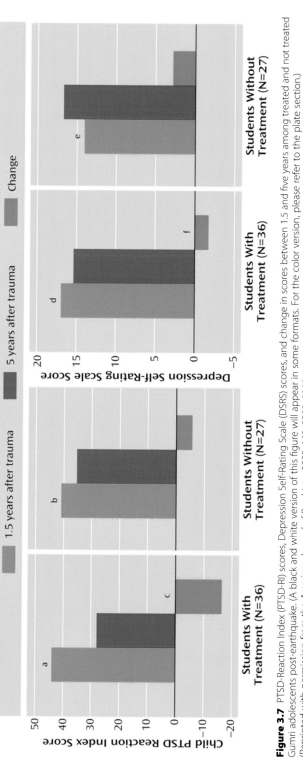

**Figure 3.7** PTSD-Reaction Index (PTSD-RI) scores, Depression Self-Rating Scale (DSRS) scores, and change in scores between 1.5 and five years among treated and not treated Gumri adolescents post-earthquake. (A black and white version of this figure will appear in some formats. For the color version, please refer to the plate section.) (Reprinted with permission from the *American Journal of Psychiatry* 2005; 162: 2302–2308.

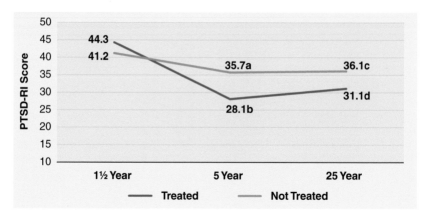

**Figure 3.8** The PTSD-Reaction Index (PTSD-RI) scores at 1.5, five, and twenty-five years after the 1988 Spitak earthquake for treated and not treated participants from Gumri. (A black and white version of this figure will appear in some formats. For the color version, please refer to the plate section.)

At five years: mean PTSD-RI score: treated group (b) < not treated group (a) ($p < 0.01$).

At twenty-five years: mean PTSD-RI score: treated group (d) < not treated group (c) ($p < 0.05$).

Between five and twenty-five years: no significant change of mean PTSD-RI scores for either group.

At 1.5 years: no significant difference in the PTSD-RI scores between the two groups.

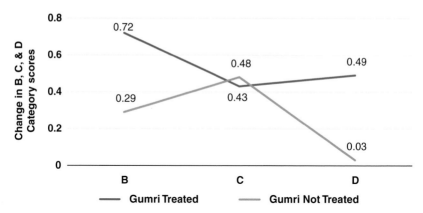

**Figure 3.9** Changes in mean B, C, and D category scores among treated and not treated subjects from Gumri between 1.5 and twenty-five years after the Spitak earthquake. (A black and white version of this figure will appear in some formats. For the color version, please refer to the plate section.)

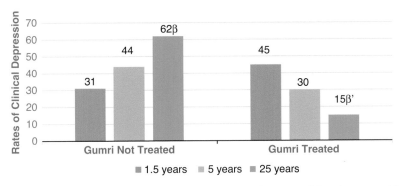

**Figure 3.10** Estimated rates of clinical depression among treated and not treated Gumri groups at 1.5, five, and twenty-five years post-earthquake. (A black and white version of this figure will appear in some formats. For the color version, please refer to the plate section.) At 25 years the not treated group ($\beta$) > the treated group ($\beta'$) (X2 = 7.41; p = .006).

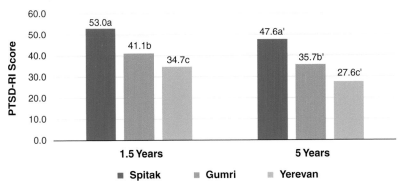

**Figure 4.1** Mean PTSD-RI scores at 1.5 and five years after the Spitak earthquake among differentially exposed not treated adolescents. (A black and white version of this figure will appear in some formats. For the color version, please refer to the plate section.)
Data from the *American Journal of Psychiatry*, 2005.
At 1.5 years, between-city comparisons: a > b > c (*P* < 0.001).
At five years, between-city comparisons: a' > b' > c' (*P* < 0.001).
Within-city comparisons (between 1.5 and five years): a > a', b > b', c > c'(all ps < 0.05).

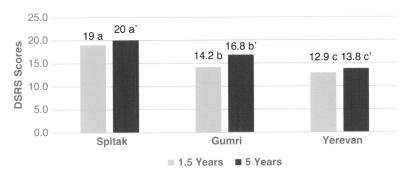

**Figure 4.2** Mean DSRS scores at 1.5 and five years post-earthquake among differentially exposed not treated adolescents. (A black and white version of this figure will appear in some formats. For the color version, please refer to the plate section.)
At 1.5 years, between-city comparisons of DSRS scores: a > b > c (*P* < 0.001).
At five years, between-city comparisons of DSRS scores: a' > c' (*P* < 0.001).
Within-city by time comparison of DSRS scores: b' > b (*P* < 0.05).

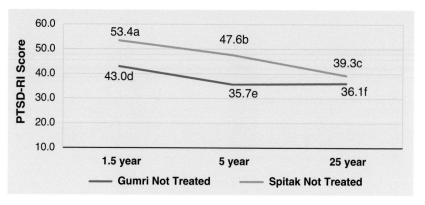

**Figure 4.3** PTSD-RI scores at 1.5, five, and twenty-five years post-earthquake among not treated subjects from Gumri and Spitak. (A black and white version of this figure will appear in some formats. For the color version, please refer to the plate section.)

Within-group comparisons of PTSD-RI scores: a > b ($P = 0.01$); b > c ($P = 0.01$); d > e ($P = 0.005$); e ≈ f (n.s.); a > c ($P < 0.001$); d > f ($P = 0.002$).

Between-group comparisons of PTSD-RI scores: a > d ($P < 0.001$); b > e ($P < 0.001$); c ≈ f (n.s.).

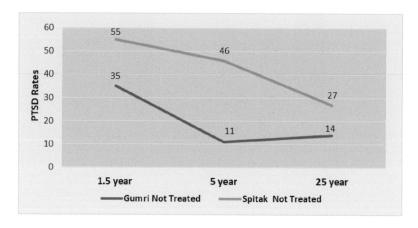

**Figure 4.4** Estimated PTSD rates, based on PTSD-RI, among not treated groups from Gumri and Spitak at 1.5, five, and twenty-five years. (A black and white version of this figure will appear in some formats. For the color version, please refer to the plate section.)

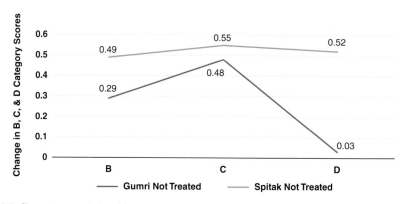

**Figure 4.5** Change in mean B, C, and D category scores between 1.5 and twenty-five years post-earthquake among not treated participants from Spitak and Gumri. (A black and white version of this figure will appear in some formats. For the color version, please refer to the plate section.)

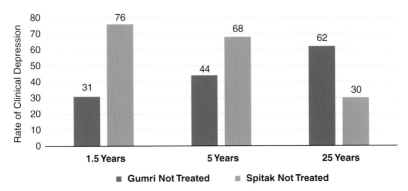

**Figure 4.6** Estimated rates of clinical depression among not treated groups from Gumri and Spitak at 1.5, five, and twenty-five years post-earthquake. (A black and white version of this figure will appear in some formats. For the color version, please refer to the plate section.)

**Figure 4.7** Gumri 1997, a destroyed building, one of many, next to makeshift homes. (A black and white version of this figure will appear in some formats. For the color version, please refer to the plate section.)

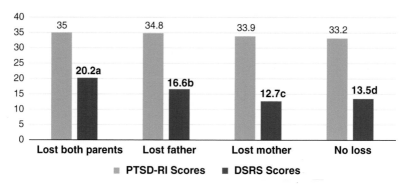

**Figure 4.8** Mean PTSD-RI and DSRS scores for not treated early adolescents who lost one or both parents during the earthquake and the control group without parental loss 6.5 years after the Spitak earthquake. (A black and white version of this figure will appear in some formats. For the color version, please refer to the plate section.)
Data from the *Journal of Affective Disorders*, 2008.
Bonferroni post-hoc test results: *a* > *b*, *c*, and *d* scores (all *P*s < 0.001);
*b* > *c* and *d* scores (*P* < 0.002).

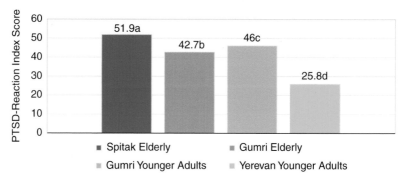

**Figure 7.1** Mean PTSD-Reaction Index scores 1.5 years after the 1988 Spitak earthquake among elderly and younger adults from differentially exposed groups. (A black and white version of this figure will appear in some formats. For the color version, please refer to the plate section.)
a > b ~ c > d (F = 53.8, df = 3, 175, *P* <0.001)
Data from Goenjian et al., *American Journal of Psychiatry*, 1994a.

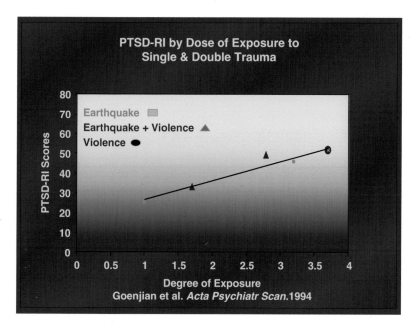

**Figure 7.2** Mean PTSD-Reaction score by degree of exposure to earthquake, violence, or both. (A black and white version of this figure will appear in some formats. For the color version, please refer to the plate section.)

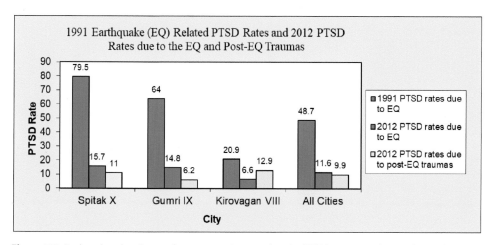

**Figure 7.3** Earthquake-related rates of post-traumatic stress disorder (PTSD) in 1991, and rates of PTSD due to the earthquake and post-earthquake traumas in 2012. (A black and white version of this figure will appear in some formats. For the color version, please refer to the plate section.)
Intensities of the earthquake on the Medvedev-Sponheuer-Karnik-64 scale are indicated by roman numerals next to the names of the cities. The rates were calculated among participants with valid responses to all variables presented in the figure (N = 717).
EQ = earthquake.
Reprinted from the *Journal of Traumatic Stress* (2018), 31, 47–56.

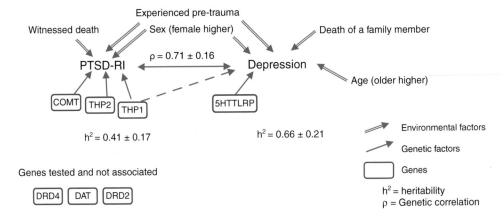

**Figure 8.2** Shared and unique genetic and environmental risk factors for PTSD and depression in the Spitak Earthquake Genetic Study. (A black and white version of this figure will appear in some formats. For the color version, please refer to the plate section.)

COMT = catechol-O-methyltransferase; TPH = tryptophan hydroxylase; 5HTTLRP = serotonin-transporter-linked polymorphic region; DRD4 = dopamine receptor D4; DAT = dopamine transporter; DRD2 = dopamine receptor D2.

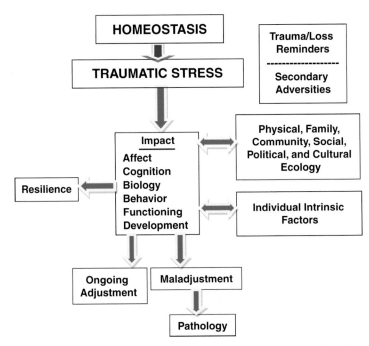

**Figure 10.1** Developmental model of child traumatic stress. (A black and white version of this figure will appear in some formats. For the color version, please refer to the plate section.)

whose protein product is reduced in autistic brain. *The Journal of the Federation of American Societies for Experimental* Biology, 24 (8), 3036–3051.

Nievergelt, C. M., Maihofer, A. X., Klengel, T., et al. (2019). International meta-analysis of PTSD genome-wide association studies identifies sex- and ancestry-specific genetic risk loci. *Nature Communications*, 10 (1), 4558.

Noble, E. P., Blum, K., Khalsa, M. E. (1991). Allelic association of the D2 dopamine receptor gene with receptor binding characteristics in alcoholism. *Archives of General Psychiatry*, 48, 648–654.

Ruskin, J., Rasul, R., Schneider, S., et al. (2018). Lack of access to medical care during hurricane Sandy and mental health symptoms. *Preventive Medicine Reports*, 10, 363–369. https://doi.org/10.1016/j.pmedr.2018.04.014.

Segman, R. H., Cooper-Kazaz, F., Macciardi, F., et al. (2002). Association between the dopamine transporter gene and posttraumatic stress disorder. *Molecular Psychiatry*, 7 (8), 903–907.

Sharma, A., & Kar, N. (2019). Posttraumatic stress, depression, and coping following the 2015 Nepal earthquake: a study on adolescents. *Disaster Medicine and Public Health Preparedness*, 13, 236–242.

Stein, M. B., Jang, K. L., Taylor, S., Vernon, P. A., Livesley, W. J. (2002). Genetic and environmental influences on trauma exposure and posttraumatic stress disorder symptoms: a twin study. *American Journal of Psychiatry*, 2002; 159 (10): 1675–1681.

Steinberg, A. M, Brymer, M. J., Kim, S., Ghosh, C., Ostrowski, S. A., Gulley, K., Briggs, E. C., & Pynoos, R. S. (2013). Psychometric properties of the UCLA PTSD Reaction Index: Part 1. *Journal of Traumatic Stress*, 26, 1–9.

Terwilliger, J. D., & Göring H. H. (2000). Gene mapping in the 20th and 21st centuries: statistical methods, data analysis, and experimental design. *Human Biology*, 72 (1), 63–132.

Thakur G. A., Joober, R., & Brunet, A. (2009). Development and persistence of posttraumatic stress disorder and the 5-HTTLPR polymorphism. *Journal of Traumatic Stress*, 22, 240–243.

True, W. J., Rice, J., Eisen, S. A., Heath, A. C., Goldberg, J., & Lyons M. J. (1993). A twin study of genetic and environmental contributions to liability for posttraumatic stress symptoms. *Archives of General Psychiatry*, 50, 257–264.

Van Den Bogaert, A., Sleegers, K., De Zutter, S., Heyrman, L., Norrback, K. F., Adolfsson, R., Van Broeckhoven, C., & Del-Favero, J. (2006) Association of brain-specific tryptophan hydroxylase, TPH2 with unipolar and bipolar disorder in a northern Swedish, isolated population. *Archives of General Psychiatry*, 63, 1103–1110.

Vermetten, E., Schmahl, S., Southwick, S. M., & Bremner, J. D. (2007). A positron tomographic emission study of olfactory induced emotional recall in veterans with and without combat-related posttraumatic stress disorder. *Psychopharmacology Bulletin*, 40 (1), 8–30.

Wurtman, R. J. (2005). Genes, stress, and depression. *Metabolism*, 54 (5 Suppl. 1), 16–19.

Xie, P., Kranzler, H. R., Yang, C., Zhao, H., Farrer, L. A., & Gelernter, J. (2013). Genome-wide association study identifies new susceptibility loci for posttraumatic stress disorder. *Biological Psychiatry*, 74 (9), 656–663.

Young, R. M., Lawford, B. R., Noble, E. P., Kann, B., Wilkie, A., Ritchie, T., Arnold, L., & Shadforth, S. (2002). Harmful drinking in military veterans with post-traumatic stress disorder: association with the D2 dopamine receptor A1 allele. *Alcohol and Alcoholism*, 37 (5), 451–454.

Zill, P., Baghai, T. C., Zwanzger, P., Schüle, C., Eser, D., Rupprecht, R., Möller, H. J., Bondy, B., & Ackenheil, M. (2004). SNP and haplotype analysis of a novel tryptophan hydroxylase isoform (TPH2) gene provide evidence for association with major depression. *Molecular Psychiatry*, 9, 1030–1036.

# Chapter 9

# Epidemiology of Disasters and the Spitak Earthquake

Vahe Khachadourian and Haroutune K. Armenian

## 9.1 Introduction

Acute response to public health emergencies has been at the core of early epidemiologic activity. Over the past decades, however, the field of epidemiology has been additionally concerned with chronic disease, and as a result, newer methods have been developed to study population-level disease and health longitudinally. More recently, epidemiologic methods have been used to study the longer-term effects of natural disasters.

In the acute phase after a disaster, the primary attention of health and mental health professionals has been to provide humanitarian relief. As such, epidemiologic strategies have been employed to assist disaster relief efforts and to conduct research that can contribute to preventing morbidity and mortality. Public health concerns dictate that epidemiology aims at:

1. Preventing morbidity and mortality caused by disasters.
2. Providing timely and accurate health information for decision-makers.
3. Improving prevention and mitigation strategies for future disasters.

In achieving these objectives for disaster situations, the field of epidemiology has developed:

1. Strategies and methodologies for conducting needs assessments and ongoing surveillance to provide information for public policy and decision-making.
2. Disease control strategies for well defined emerging health problems.
3. Post-disaster assessments for use by health and mental health professionals.
4. Etiologic research on factors associated with morbidity and mortality after disasters.

## 9.2 Developments in the Epidemiology of Disasters

One of the earliest innovations in the epidemiology of disasters was the application of epidemic or outbreak investigative methods. Introduced in the late 1950s, this approach improved disaster epidemiology at the operational level. In one of the earliest reviews of the application of epidemiology in response to disasters, Saylor and Gordon (1957) proposed epidemiologic terminology and methods for solving problems in disaster situations. For them, a single impact disaster can be studied like a point epidemic, and in general, medical problems during and following disaster can be studied according to distributions of time, place, and persons. Following a similar perspective, we have highlighted the following in our work after the Spitak earthquake (Armenian, 2009):

1. In most disasters, we are dealing with an *urgent situation* where the epidemiologist needs to be professionally trained to plan the methods and metrics of an investigation.

2. In these investigations, decisions have to be made at every step based on data that is often rudimentary. The possibility of making mistakes and for methodological biases in such decisions is high.

3. In order to understand relationships and determinants of variables, a spectrum of investigative tools must be used, including clinical examinations, environmental inspections, surveys, special laboratory analyses, short-term case-control, and long-term cohort studies.

4. The process of such an investigation is very dynamic. The epidemiologist working under such conditions may have to assess the situation continuously and redirect the investigation, particularly when there are changing patterns of morbidity and mortality.

5. Investigation needs to be conducted with the objective of applying prevention and control measures as soon as possible. Thus, following initial data gathering, identifiable actions have to be implemented to mitigate disability and morbidity. There is no need to wait until the completion of all investigations or until all the results are reported before taking action.

6. A number of other problems may hamper the investigation, including the inability to conduct tests for laboratory investigation because of a lack of resources and, frequently, a lack of timely collection of specimens.

Michel Lechat (1976) introduced multidimensional models in disaster epidemiology. He proposed a model for organizational planning and the long-term evaluation of disaster prevention public health programs. Lechat classified the timeframe for studying disasters as during impact, post-impact, and long-term. A special unit at the Pan American Health Organization, under the leadership of Claude de Ville de Goyet, produced important literature dealing with various aspects of disasters, including the use of epidemiologic methods. As proposed by de Ville de Goyet (1979), epidemiology needs to be involved at all levels of disaster relief operations.

Epidemiological approaches focusing on disasters can have a number of objectives. One of the main objectives is to offer data for decision-making in order to prevent or reduce the number of deaths, illnesses, and injuries caused by disasters, while also informing prevention and mitigation strategies. Depending on the focus of the epidemiological approach, available resources, as well as the specific outcomes and exposures of interest, and the choice of methodological and practical tools may vary. The next section provides an overview of some of the commonly used study designs and methods for conducting disaster-related needs assessment, surveillance, and etiological research.

# 9.3 Methods and Tools in the Epidemiology of Disasters

## 9.3.1 Needs Assessment

Needs-assessment strategies have been used to identify the impact across differentially exposed populations and current needs. The information from such assessments provides guidance in regard to the allocation of resources, decision-making, and plans for action aimed at response and recovery. The ample literature on the methodology and application of needs assessment broadly (e.g., Tutty and Rothery, 2001; Sleezer et al., 2011) and in the aftermath of disasters specifically (e.g., Guha-Sapir and Lechat, 1986; Coker et al., 2006) documents the utility of needs assessment in planning post-disaster recovery efforts (Sleezer et al., 2011). A number of attempts have been made to use epidemiologic field survey methods to assess the need for planning and distribution of services. De Ville de Goyet (1979) and Western (1982) have provided comprehensive guidelines for such surveys in disaster situations. These large-scale assessments at the population level have provided a broader perspective on the issues in such situations and their management. Both of these authors have emphasized the need to use systematic population-based needs assessment and surveillance methods in the context of disaster.

One of the classics in population-based assessments of a major disaster is the study of the East Bengal cyclone of 1970 by Sommer and Mosley (1972), where two needs assessments were conducted. The first was a rapid eighteen-site survey focusing on the adequacy of water supply and post-cyclone morbidity, while the second survey was wider in scope and was carried out two months after the cyclone. Although most needs assessment strategies are based on quantitative approaches, the use of qualitative assessments should not be over-looked (Hayward et al., 1993). Qualitative methodology offers key advantages, and the results from such assessments provide valuable direction for developing interventions. Qualitative needs assessment often provides better insight into the gaps and requirements in situations where constructing a predefined set of needs is difficult (Ochieng, 2009). Such instances might occur during unique disasters (e.g., the 9/11 World Trade Center attacks) or disasters affecting specific population groups with unique characteristics and needs. When combined with quantitative assessment, qualitative assessment can paint a more comprehensive picture of the situation and needs (Hayward et al., 1993; Reviere et al., 1996).

One of the readily available and commonly used tools for conducting a needs assessment in the aftermath of disasters is the Community Assessment for Public Health Emergency Response (CASPER) developed by the Centers for Disease Control and Prevention (2019). CASPER is a rapid needs assessment tool that uses valid statistical methods to collect household-level data, informing allocation of resources and allowing prioritization of responses regarding the community's needs. CASPER, a relatively inexpensive and reliable tool, along with the continuous training conducted for public health and emergency management staff in the United States, remains a useful, accessible choice for needs assessment in the aftermath of disasters (Schnall et al., 2017).

The United Nations Development Group, the World Bank, and the European Union have also developed a set of guidelines for conducting Post Disaster Needs Assessments (PDNA) (Global Facility for Disaster Reduction and Recovery, 2013). One of the key advantages of these comprehensive guidelines is the prevention of duplication of effort, which is of great importance considering the limited resources typically available for disaster response measures.

## 9.3.2 Surveillance

Surveillance remains one of the essential strategies for public health practitioners. Despite variations in the language used to define it, most definitions include the idea that surveillance requires systematic data collection and processing (e.g., management, analysis, interpretation, and dissemination) for decision-making (World Health Organization, 2001; Centers for Disease Control and Prevention, 2012). Passive and active surveillance are the two most common types of surveillance. Passive surveillance has become the most common type of surveillance since fewer resources are required. It relies on health professionals' periodic or incidence-based reporting to local or national health authorities. This type of reporting usually includes pre-defined sets of variables and measures, and therefore might not necessarily contain all the needed details that are important under different circumstances. Another potential disadvantage of passive surveillance is the timeliness of information for decision-making. Although the wide use of electronic reporting systems has decreased processing time and made the lag time between reporting and access to the information minimal, it can still result in significant delays.

In active surveillance, instead of waiting for the reporting of information, authorities actively seek and collect the required data. This allows for more flexibility in terms of the variables and measures collected, as well as more control over the timelines of the processes. Nevertheless, the resources required to implement active surveillance are greater than for passive surveillance. Therefore, the decision between using active vs. passive surveillance depends on the weight given to methodological considerations and resource requirements.

## 9.3.3 Epidemiological Investigation with Examples from the Spitak Earthquake

Although acute injuries and fatalities may have more direct causative pathways during a natural disaster, some of the emergencies in disaster situations may require a multifaceted approach to determine etiology, particularly for some of the longer-term effects of the disasters where there may be a complex web of causation. Etiological research is a specific type of epidemiological investigation that aims to identify causal risk factors and the underlying mechanisms for health and mental health outcomes.

The range of available tools and methodologies for such studies is wide, broadly including those used in controlled experimental and observational studies. Considering the logistical challenges, as well as the nature of the trauma and loss exposures studied in the aftermath of disasters, controlled experimental studies are often neither feasible nor ethically acceptable. Nevertheless, experimental studies, either randomized or non-randomized, are well suited to evaluating interventions and other measures, including those among disaster-affected populations.

Case-control studies offer a rigorous methodological basis for assessing the relationship between levels of disaster exposure and outcomes. The major advantages of case-control studies are their efficiency and informativeness (Armenian, 2009). Within hours of the occurrence of the disaster, one may be able to design and implement a case-control investigation and provide the results of the analysis within a few short days. Case-control studies are distinct in their flexibility and are considered to be the method of choice for studying rare outcomes. Case-control studies allow for the study of multiple exposures; however, their susceptibility to recall bias (due to differential reporting, remembering of exposure, and other covariates) can be a limitation. While the selection of controls from a source population that gave rise to cases is theoretically straightforward, it can be practically challenging. Damaged infrastructure and displacement of people in disaster situations impose significant difficulties for executing random selection of cases and controls. The use of pre-disaster sampling frames, preferably containing information on characteristics of the potential participants, can be a valuable source for comparing respondents and non-respondents in terms of their characteristics as presented in the sampling frame. Knowing the characteristics of respondents and non-respondents could also be used for evaluation of, and adjustment for, potential selection biases.

In December 1988, following the massive earthquake in Northern Armenia, the Soviet Union opened up to Western assistance. As part of the Armenian diaspora's assistance group, our group was in Yerevan within three weeks of the earthquake. While much of the assistance was focused on the delivery of humanitarian aid, in the absence of any effective health monitoring system in the earthquake zone, our colleagues from the Computer and Information Services of the Ministry of Health of Armenia, together with our team, focused on a surveillance and monitoring system of the health of survivors of the disaster. This was also an opportunity to introduce a number of modern epidemiologic methods to a country in the Soviet Union where epidemiology had a traditional infectious disease-microbiology base. As part of assessing the health status of the survivors, we initiated a rapid case-control study in Leninakan (Gyumri) among patients hospitalized due to injuries. As a result, we were able to identify protective behaviors during the earthquake and determinants of serious injuries (Armenian et al., 1992). One of the methodological challenges in this study was the selection of controls. Comparing the sociodemographic characteristics of the cases and controls with those of the total population provided a way of assessing selection bias, which was estimated to be minimal.

Cohort studies, mainly prospective cohort studies, remain one of the top study designs for etiological research. The possibility of selecting the study population in cohort studies by exposure status makes it an efficient tool for examining rare exposures. Although cohort studies allow for studying multiple outcomes, the nature of the exposure can often restrict the investigation's focus to one major outcome. The greater period of time required to establish a cohort and follow participants makes cohort studies more resource-demanding than case-control studies. Nevertheless, digitization of medical records and the growing number of population-based registries over the past decades have offered opportunities for conducting population-based cohort studies and have decreased the cost associated with primary data collection. The availability of individual-level pre-disaster health data in electronic databases and registries also allows for more accurate identification of the population at risk at the time of the disaster, while minimizing potential errors in measurements of pre-disaster covariates and health conditions.

War and its long-term impact on human health have catalyzed interest in longitudinal methods in the epidemiology of disasters. The most studied cohort of a population exposed to a disaster is the longitudinal cohort study of the Atomic Bomb Casualty Commission in Hiroshima and Nagasaki. Other longitudinal studies of the long-term health effects of war include research involving concentration camp survivors and psychological studies of different subgroups exposed to severe war trauma and other types of violent experiences (Eitinger and Storm, 1973).

In addition to the case-control study after the Spitak earthquake (Armenian et al., 1992), several longitudinal studies have evaluated mental health and other outcomes among populations differentially exposed to the Spitak earthquake. In a prospective study among children and adolescents after the Spitak earthquake, Goenjian et al. (1995, 2000) surveyed students from Spitak located 6.6 miles from the epicenter, Gyumri, at 16.6 miles, and Yerevan, the control group, 47 miles from the epicenter. The study demonstrated a dose-response relation for PTSD, depression, and separation anxiety, with participants from Spitak experiencing the most severe symptoms commensurate with the severity of exposure, followed by the Gyumri and Yerevan groups respectively.

The most extensive longitudinal cohort investigation of the Spitak earthquake survivors included 33,000 people differentially exposed to the earthquake (Armenian et al., 1997,

1998). The baseline wave collected data on sociodemographic characteristics, health outcomes, and disaster experience) and the cohort was followed for four years. Studies based on these data showed a positive association between building height and risk of earthquake-related deaths as well as non-fatal injuries. These findings have important implications for pre-earthquake planning and post-earthquake response.

The follow-up of the earthquake survivors also revealed excess long-term mortality and morbidity, a pattern that had also been described following earthquakes in Thessalonica in Greece (Katsouyanni et al., 1986) and Naples in Italy (Trevisan et al., 1986, 1992). During the six-month period after the earthquake, survivors experienced an increased incidence of cardiovascular disease, arthritis, and diabetes. The elevated morbidity was strongly associated with material loss, loss of a family member, and injury of family members caused by the earthquake. Similarly, the survivors had overall excess mortality as well as cardiovascular disease-specific mortality. Nevertheless, unlike morbidity, the study did not provide evidence for associations between mortality and earthquake-related exposures. These findings provided clinicians and public health practitioners with the means to delineate subpopulations at risk for adverse health outcomes that can be targeted for prevention and treatment. Additionally, the findings were used to guide the allocation of resources and planning for necessary health care services.

In a follow-up of a geographically stratified sub-sample of 1,785 adults from the initial cohort of the Spitak earthquake survivors, a psychiatric questionnaire was administered to assess mental health problems about two years after the earthquake. This longitudinal cohort approach was wholly unique, not just for Armenia and the Soviet Union, as it had not been done on such a large scale elsewhere after earthquakes. During the two years following the earthquake, about 49.6% of this adult population had symptoms that met diagnostic criteria for PTSD and 50.2% for major depression. To avoid conflation of results and minimize the risk of misclassification, the analyses for investigating risk factors of depression included only cases with depression who did not have any other psychopathology and compared them to those who did not meet the criteria for any psychiatric disorder. A similar approach was applied for identifying factors associated with PTSD incidence. The risk of PTSD and depression was higher in areas with more destruction and was associated with the amount of material loss. Protective factors for mental illness included having a higher level of education, sharing the experience at the time of the disaster with someone else, receiving support from family and friends early on, and making new friends after the earthquake (Armenian et al., 2000, 2002). Another follow-up of this population began in April 2012 (almost twenty-one years after the baseline study). In addition to the psychological assessment, this follow-up collected data on several physical health outcomes, including measures of self-rated health and quality of life and a wide range of non-communicable diseases (Khachadourian et al., 2016). The availability of detailed primary and secondary contact information of participants and their relatives collected during the earlier phases of the study was key to achieving high rates of follow-up conducted more than two decades after the earthquake and the baseline assessment.

Findings from the longer-term follow-up of survivors did not suggest an association between earthquake exposure and self-reported health twenty-three years after the earthquake (Demirchyan et al., 2015). Nevertheless, material loss due to the earthquake was found to be associated with a standardized measure of the quality of life of survivors (Khachadourian et al., 2015). The study highlighted the importance of continuous monitoring of individuals who have experienced severe earthquake damage and material losses.

Additionally, the study provided insights into a more effective allocation of resources and aid distribution among affected populations.

Advances in psychiatric diagnosis have implications for the conduct of long-term prospective studies. For example, after introducing PTSD in DSM-III, its diagnostic criteria have been updated in subsequent editions. The baseline and most recent follow-up survey of Spitak earthquake survivors in Armenia in the 1990s and 2012 spanned various diagnostic criteria of PTSD (Khachadourian et al., 2016). In our studies, for each phase, we included the psychometric instruments based on the then-current DSM criteria. Additionally, we also used baseline instruments and measures to allow for comparability with previous measures and depiction of the trajectory of psychiatric conditions over time. Even in the absence of changes in diagnostic criteria, revisions in widely used mental health assessment scales might result in similar challenges (e.g., CES-D (Radloff, 1977). Chapter 7 in this book, "The Long-term Course of PTSD and Depression among Adults," provides further details about the trajectory of mental health outcomes in the aftermath of disasters.

## 9.4 Recent Developments and Directions

Over the past few decades, the field of causal inference has advanced significantly. Nevertheless, its application in disaster research and other fields lags. Although association studies can identify high-risk groups and help with planning for health services, their findings often have limitations for developing targeted interventions for prevention and intervention. Accessibility and implications of scientific findings remain a challenge for policymakers (Pearl, 2014).

Mediation analysis examines the possible causal relation between two correlated variables by positing a third intervening variable and testing for mediating pathways and causal mechanisms in both experimental and observational studies (MacKinnon et al., 2013). A mediation analysis framework offers evidence and more accessible information for policy-making. The results of mediation analysis combined with simulations can provide quantitative estimates of the effects of potential interventions on outcomes. Mediation analysis can also guide the targeting of specific pathways, refining existing interventions (Vanderweele, 2015). Knowledge of mediating mechanisms of the exposure-outcome effect can provide alternative options to target causal risk factors associated with disaster exposure.

Disasters – especially earthquakes – are sudden and unexpected. Therefore, minimizing their immediate impact requires advanced planning and significant financial and scientific investment in infrastructure and disaster preparedness. Lack of such developed infrastructure in low-income, middle-income, and even many high-income countries makes populations more vulnerable to the adverse effects. Since affected communities inevitably experience some level of negative impact, it is crucial that researchers and policymakers gain a better understanding of how pre- and post-disaster factors can affect the impact and course of recovery. Such knowledge can help policymakers develop targeted strategies to mitigate negative consequences for disaster-affected communities.

Post-disaster experiences have received growing attention. Early studies have shown that the effect of loss on certain health outcomes is moderated by the amount of aid in the aftermath. As discussed above, even two decades after the earthquake in Armenia, the severity of loss was associated with poorer quality of life among the survivors in Spitak. However, this association was significantly attenuated among a subgroup of people who had severe losses but received financial aid in the aftermath of the event (Khachadourian et al.,

2015). A parallel pattern was observed for the effect of disaster loss on PTSD. Those with severe losses who received aid after the earthquake demonstrated a significantly lower risk for PTSD compared to those with severe losses who did not receive aid (Armenian et al., 2000; Goenjian et al., 2018).

In the past few years, researchers on disasters have formally applied the mediation analysis framework (e.g., Khachadourian, 2019; Shiba et al., 2020) by identifying specific pathways through which disasters affect health outcomes and associated targets for intervention. In such an analysis (Khachadourian, 2019), longitudinal data from the Spitak earthquake was used to evaluate the impact of disaster exposure and the mediating role of post-disaster experiences on the risk for diabetes. Destruction of housing was found to be associated with a higher incidence of diabetes, while there was no evidence of an association between the death of a family member and severe earthquake-related injury, and increased risk for diabetes. As to the possible role of receiving permanent housing and post-disaster job loss in mediating the effect of housing damage on diabetes, job loss mediated a portion of the total effect of housing damage. Further computer simulations can be used to quantify the projected impact of hypothetical interventions targeting job loss on the risk for diabetes. Such analyses can provide further insights for prioritization of resource allocation and evaluation of the cost-effectiveness of different interventions.

Bridging the gap between novel methodologies and applied research can further fuel advancements in the field. Targeted studies answering policy-relevant questions can also improve translating research findings into relevant policies and interventions. The discussion in this chapter is by no means exhaustive in covering the tools and methodologies available to epidemiologists. Other approaches such as case-cohort and case-crossover and system science methods, including agent-based modeling, are among many other methods that can further advance the field of disaster epidemiology and our understanding of the health consequences of disasters and strategies for their prevention and mitigation.

# References

Armenian, H. K. (2009). *The Case-Control Method: Design and Applications*. New York, NY: Oxford University Press.

Armenian, H. K., Noji, E. K., & Oganesian, A. P. (1992). A case-control study of injuries arising from the earthquake in Armenia, 1988. *Bulletin of the World Health Organization*, 70 (2), 251–257.

Armenian, H. K., Melkonian, A., Noji, E. K., & Hovanesian, A. P. (1997). Deaths and injuries due to the earthquake in Armenia: a cohort approach. *International Journal of Epidemiology*, 26 (4), 806–813.

Armenian, H. K., Melkonian, A. K., & Hovanesian, A. P. (1998). Long term mortality and morbidity related to the degree of damage following the 1988 earthquake in Armenia. *American Journal of Epidemiology*, 148 (11), 1077–1084.

Armenian, H. K., Morikawa, M., Melkonian, A. K., Hovanesian, A. P., Haroutunian, N., Saigh, P. A., Akiskal, K., & Akiskal, H. S. (2000). Loss as a determinant of PTSD in a cohort of adult survivors of the 1988 earthquake in Armenia: implications for policy. *Acta Psychiatrica Scandinavia*, 102 (1), 58–64.

Armenian, H. K., Morikawa, M., Melkonian, A. K., Hovanesian, A., Akiskal, K., & Akiskal, H. S. (2002). Risk factors for depression in the survivors of the 1988 earthquake in Armenia. *Journal of Urban Health*, 79 (3), 373–382.

Centers for Disease Control and Prevention (CDC). (2012). Principles of epidemiology in public health practice. In *An Introduction to Applied Epidemiology and Biostatistics*. Atlanta, GE: U.S. Department of Health and Human Services.

Centers for Disease Control and Prevention (CDC). (2019). *Community Assessment for*

*Public Health Emergency Response (CASPER) Toolkit: Third edition.* www.cdc.gov/nceh/casper/default.htm

de Ville de Goyet, C. (1979). Communicable diseases and epidemiological surveillance in relation to natural disasters. *Bulletin of the World Health Organization,* 57 (2), 153–165.

Demirchyan, A., Petrosyan, V., Armenian, H. K., & Khachadourian, V. (2015). Prospective study of predictors of poor self-rated health in a 23-year cohort of earthquake survivors in Armenia. *Journal of Epidemiology and Global Health,* 5 (3), 265–274.

Eitinger, L., & Storm, A. (1973). *Mortality and Morbidity after Excessive Stress.* New York, NY: Humanities Press.

Global Facility for Disaster Reduction and Recovery. (2013). *Post-Disaster Needs Assessment Guidelines.* Available at: www.undp.org/content/undp/en/home/librarypage/crisis-prevention-and-recovery/pdna.html.

Goenjian, A. K., Pynoos, R. S., Steinberg, A. M., Najarian, L. M., Asarnow, J. R., Karayan, I., Ghurabi, M., & Fairbanks, L. A. (1995). Psychiatric comorbidity in children after the 1988 earthquake in Armenia. *Journal of the American Academy of Child & Adolescent Psychiatry,* 34 (9), 1174–1184.

Goenjian, A. K., Steinberg, A. M., Najarian, L. M., Fairbanks, L. A., Tashjian, M., & Pynoos, R. S. (2000). Prospective study of posttraumatic stress, anxiety, and depressive reactions after earthquake and political violence. *American Journal of Psychiatry,* 157 (6), 911–916.

Goenjian, A. K., Khachadourian, V., Armenian, H. K., Demirchyan, A., & Steinberg, A. M. (2018). Posttraumatic stress disorder 23 years after the 1988 Spitak earthquake in Armenia. *Journal of Traumatic Stress,* 31 (1), 47–56.

Guha-Sapir, D., & Lechat, M. F. (1986). Information systems and needs assessment in natural disasters: an approach for better disaster relief management. *Disasters,* 10 (3), 232–237.

Hayward, P., Peck, E., & Smith, H. (1993). Qualitative and quantitative approaches to needs assessment in mental health: creating a common currency. *Journal of Mental Health,* 2 (4), 287–294.

Katsouyanni, K., Kogevinas, M., & Trichopoulos, D. (1986). Earthquake-related stress and cardiac mortality. *International Journal of Epidemiology,* 15 (3), 326–330.

Khachadourian, V., Armenian, H., Demirchyan, A., et al. (2015). Loss and psycho-social factors as determinants of quality of life in a cohort of earthquake survivors. *Health and Quality of Life Outcomes,* 13, 13. https://doi.org/10.1186/s12955-015-0209-5.

Khachadourian, V., Armenian, H. K., Demirchyan, A., Melkonian, A., & Hovanesian, A. (2016). A post-earthquake psychopathological investigation in Armenia: methodology, summary of findings, and follow-up. *Disasters,* 40 (3), 518–533.

Khachadourian, V. (2019). Effect of earthquake-related losses and post-earthquake events on morbidity and mortality: causal mediation analysis of the prospective cohort data of the 1988 earthquake survivors in Armenia. University of California, Los Angeles.

Lechat, M. F. (1976). The epidemiology of disasters. *Proceedings of the Royal Society of Medicine,* 69 (6), 421–426.

MacKinnon, D. P., Kisbu-Sakarya, Y., & Gottschall, A. C. (2013). *Developments in Mediation Analysis,* in *The Oxford Handbook of Quantitative Methods,* edited by T. D. Little. New York, NY: Oxford University Press.

Ochieng, P. A. (2009). An analysis of the strengths and limitations of qualitative and quantitative research paradigms. *Problems of Education in the 21st Century,* 13, 13–18.

Pearl, J. (2014). Is scientific knowledge useful for policy analysis? A peculiar theorem says: no. *Journal of Causal Inference,* 2 (1), 109–112.

Radloff, L. S. (1977). The CES-D Scale: a self-report depression scale for research in the general population. *Applied Psychological Measurement,* 1 (3), 385–401.

Reviere, R., Berkowitz, S., Carter, C. C., & Ferguson, C. G. (eds.). (1996). *Needs Assessment: A Creative and Practical Guide*

*For Social Scientists*. Abingdon: Taylor & Francis.

Saylor, L. F., & Gordon, J. E. (1957). The medical component of natural disasters. *The American Journal of the Medical Sciences*, 234 (3), 342–362.

Schnall, A., Nakata, N., Talbert, T., Bayleyegn, T., Martinez, D., & Wolkin, A. (2017). Community Assessment for Public Health Emergency Response (CASPER): an innovative emergency management tool in the United States. *American Journal of Public Health*, 107 (S2), S186–S192.

Shiba, K., Aida, J., Kondo, K., Nakagomi, A., Arcaya, M., James, P., & Kawachi, I. (2020). Mediation of the relationship between home loss and worsened cardiometabolic profiles of older disaster survivors by post-disaster relocation: a natural experiment from the Great East Japan earthquake and tsunami. *Health & Place*, 66, 102456.

Sleezer, C. M., Russ-Eft, D. F., & Gupta, K. (eds.) (2011). *A Practical Guide to Needs Assessment* (3rd ed.). New York, NY: John Wiley & Sons.

Sommer, A., & Mosley, W. (1972). East Bengal Cyclone of November, 1970. *Lancet*, 299 (7759), 1030–1036.

Trevisan, M., Celentano, E., Meucci, C., Farinaro, E., Jossa, F., Krogh, V., Giumetti, D., Panico, S., Scottoni, A., &

Mancini, M. (1986). Short-term effect of natural disasters on coronary heart disease risk factors. *Arteriosclerosis*, 6 (5), 491–494.

Trevisan, M., Jossa, F., Farinaro, E., Krogh, V., Panico, S., Giumetti, D., & Mancini, M. (1992). Earthquake and coronary heart disease risk factors: a longitudinal study. *American Journal of Epidemiology*, 135 (6), 632–637.

Tutty, L. M., & Rothery, M. A. (2001). Needs assessments. In *The Handbook of Social Work Research Methods*, edited by B. A. Thyer (pp. 160–175). London: SAGE Publications, Inc.

Vanderweele, T. J. (2015). *Explanation in Causal Inference: Methods for Mediation and Interaction*. New York, NY: Oxford University Press.

Western, K. A. (1982). Epidemiology surveillance after a natural disaster. Washington, DC: Pan American Health Organization.

World Health Organization. (2001). Protocol for the assessment of national communicable disease surveillance and response systems: guidelines for assessment teams. Available at: https://apps.who.int/iri s/bitstream/handle/10665/66787/WHO_ CDS_CSR_ISR_2001.2_eng.pdf? sequence=3&isAllowed=y.

# Traumatic Stress Conceptual Framework

Alan Steinberg, Robert Pynoos, and Armen Goenjian

## 10.1 Introduction

This chapter provides a theoretical underpinning to explicate the multi-dimensional parameters that guided the implementation of the Psychiatric Outreach Program and research conducted over three decades after the Spitak earthquake in Armenia. In the intervening years, many of the concepts have benefitted from increased scientific clarification and elaboration, as well as accumulating scientific evidence from a wide range of studies after disasters and mass violence. We will review each layer of the conceptual model, highlighting the critical features, some of which were only implicit when our studies began but have become more explicit over time. We hope that in doing so, we can provide a modern comprehensive conceptual framework for the future of disaster psychiatry.

As the Psychiatric Outreach Program began, we had been working on a comprehensive developmental psychopathology model of childhood traumatic stress which we subsequently published, featuring discussion of the intersection of trauma with related anxiety disorders over the lifespan (Steinberg and Ritzmann, 1990; Pynoos, Steinberg, and Wraith, 1995; Pynoos, Goenjian, and Steinberg, 1998). A developmental psychopathology model recognizes the centrality of traumatic experiences within an intricate matrix of child, adolescent, and adult intrinsic factors, developmental maturation, and evolving physical, family, community, and social ecologies that contribute to proximal and distal outcomes.

This framework posits a continuum from adaptive to maladaptive outcomes that reflect ongoing adjustments or maladjustments in a variety of developmental domains that weigh outcomes within a framework of normality – pathology. It recognizes multiple sources that contribute to acute post-trauma sequelae and involves a multipronged approach that includes concepts of resistance, resilience, vulnerability, strengths, adjustment, maladjustment, and pathology. It places equal importance on proximal developmental disturbances and proximal psychopathology and highlights their interactive dynamics. It also incorporates a life trajectory perspective that invites examination of distal health and mental health outcomes, again, as dynamically interactive with distal developmental consequences. The model is depicted in Figure 10.1.

In developing metrics for both the clinical and research efforts in Armenia, we characterized earthquake-related circumstances of traumatic stress in terms of situations in which a child, adolescent, or adult was exposed to a directly life-threatening event during the earthquake or in the immediate aftermath, had sustained serious injury, witnessed serious injury or death, as well as having learned about traumatic details of the injury or death of a loved one. In addition, we included such factors as seeing someone trapped or buried in the rubble, separation from a family member during the earthquake, loss/destruction of home, immediate loss of income, and earthquake-related subjective distress. One

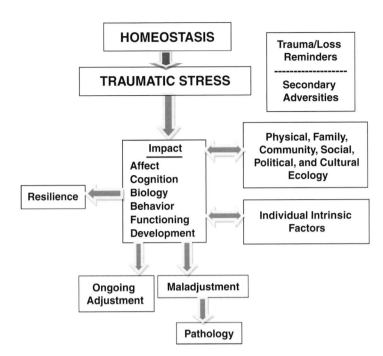

**Figure 10.1** Developmental model of child traumatic stress. (A black and white version of this figure will appear in some formats. For the color version, please refer to the plate section.)

overarching finding from our studies has been that, for children, both objective and subjective features of exposure make independent contributions to the severity and persistence of post-disaster sequelae (Goenjian et al., 2001).

Early on, we recognized that many of the constructs that fall within the impact of traumatic stress, and importantly the metrics used to operationalize them, are often amalgamations or hybrids of items from the categories of cognition, affect, behavior, biology, functioning, and development. For example, the construct of PTSD includes items of affect (e.g., psychological reactivity to reminders, extreme negative emotions such as guilt and shame); cognition (e.g., intrusive thoughts, distorted cognitions, difficulty concentrating or paying attention, inability to recall); biology (e.g., exaggerated startle, physiological reactivity to reminders); behavior (e.g., avoidance of reminders, diminished participation, reckless behavior), and impairment in functioning. We also learned that traumatic stress had a significant impact on child and adolescent development. Developmental sequelae include effects on emotional regulation, attachment, autonomous strivings, future planning, learning and memory, schematizations of risk, danger, safety, security, and protection, and moral development (Goenjian et al., 1999).

Based on the clinical work and studies in Armenia after the earthquake, we recognized that post-earthquake salient ecological features included a host of post-disaster stresses and adversities: (e.g., the devastation of physical infrastructure; the pervasiveness and persistence of trauma and loss reminders; impairment in caregiver, family, and community functioning; disturbances in family, peer, and interpersonal relationships; and, in the case of physical injury, continued disability and rehabilitation.

The traumatic stress pathway is embedded in a surrounding physical, family, community, social, political, and cultural ecology, and also considers individual intrinsic factors. The literature is replete with examples of adjustment resources that include a variety of ecological and individual intrinsic factors. These factors need to be considered in terms of their contribution to a range of outcomes. Each of these factors may operate differently, depending on the specific outcome under consideration. While many of these factors are themselves affected by traumatic stress, they also constitute potential outcome variables for investigation.

Our framework considered a wide range of individual intrinsic factors that bear on the impact of traumatic stress, including biological factors, life history, psychological traits, social and developmental competencies, and interpersonal functioning. Over the years, the disaster literature has increasingly identified and investigated numerous intrinsic factors that moderate outcomes, (e.g., age, sex, biology, coping repertoire, prior trauma history, secure attachment, self-regulation, and executive function). Of special importance, we were aware that after the earthquake, the nature and course of grief was strongly influenced by family, cultural, and religious beliefs and rituals related to mourning. In this regard, we found that inter-current trauma and loss are important factors that adversely influence the course of recovery (Goenjian et al., 1993).

We understood the term *resilience* to refer to the capacity for early, effective adjustment and recovery. This is contrasted with ongoing adjustment, which we understood to refer to the use of effective efforts to contend with the impact and to adequately recover over time. On the other hand, maladjustment involves the failure of efforts to adjust that do not adequately remediate the impact, often leading to pathology. Pathology is the product of a failure of adjustment that can take the form of medical (Filetti et al., 1998; Anda et al., 2006) and psychiatric disorders. Psychiatric disorders have been found to include acute stress disorder, PTSD, depressive disorder, somatization disorder, phobic disorder, separation anxiety disorder, substance abuse, sleep disorder, adjustment disorder, and what is now termed "prolonged grief disorder."

An important concept falling under traumatic stress within this conceptual framework is the "signature of the event."

## 10.2 Signature of the Event

The signature of the event focusses on a number of objective features regarding the nature of the event, including its magnitude and intensity; the affected populations; the extent of the destruction, morbidity, and mortality; the nature and extent of immediate psychological consequences; and the impact on infrastructure and critical community leadership. These factors also include the number, nature, and severity of injuries (including emergency and hospital treatment and rehabilitation course and needs) and the extent of personal material losses. The signature of the event introduces the epidemiological concept of "dose of exposure" as an organizing principle (Susser, 1973). With sufficient early information, characterization of the signature allows for an estimate of the overall public disaster mental health challenges, the severity of the expected responses within and across affected populations, estimation of the acute demand for services, and the likely length of the community and societal recovery process.

In the case of Armenia, the signature included that the 6.8 magnitude earthquake was transmitted by the hard ground that exacerbated its destructive force and whose shock wave was preceded by an exceedingly loud sound wave. The epicenter was nearby; a small mountainous city, Spitak, built with construction not designed to withstand an earthquake of this magnitude. There was barely a house that was left standing, let alone habitable. The earthquake occurred at 11:41 a.m., when many of the children were in school, and nearly all school buildings collapsed, resulting in an overwhelming loss of life within the school community. As our studies revealed, there was barely a family that did not suffer the loss of an immediate or extended family member. The rural infrastructure was basically destroyed, local leadership was depleted, and outside access severely impeded.

Gumri, the second-largest city in Armenia, was within the highly affected earthquake zone, and suffered extensive physical damage to major buildings and residences, and even though the rate of mortality was 50% of that in Spitak, this represented a much larger number of traumatized and bereaved families. Despite the influx of families evacuating from Spitak, the infrastructure in Gumri had also been severely disrupted, while the political leadership remained intact. The capital city of Yerevan was spared, with minor physical damage, a small number of injuries, and fully functioning infrastructure and local, regional, and national leadership intact.

The signature of the event across the affected cities from a population epidemiological vantagepoint presented a natural dose of exposure cohort design that governed both the implementation of interventions within the Psychiatric Outreach Program and its research arm. Some of the original cohort data from the three city comparisons were provided to the political leadership to better govern the allocation of limited resources in light of these population-based findings and to influence the wider international Armenian diaspora to direct donor funding to maximize disaster recovery.

In contradistinction, the Chi-Chi earthquake in Taiwan (Chen et al., 2002; Chen and Wu, 2006) was characterized by a different signature. The epicenter was also in a difficult-to-access mountainous rural community. However, it occurred in the middle of the night. Even though many schools were seriously damaged, there was far less loss of life involving children and school personnel. Most families lived upstairs from their family businesses, and even though many second floors collapsed to the first floor, causing injury and some death, most of the population was spared by not having been shopping at the time.

In contrast to Armenia, the earthquake in Haiti destroyed much of the capital city of Port-au-Prince, and in so doing, disrupted long-term the infrastructure that was needed to undertake a national response, along with having a major impact on political and social key leadership.

An earlier disaster study that used a cohort design after the collapse of the Buffalo Creek Dam (Green et al., 1990), with flooding on one bank while the other remained intact, led to a descriptive psychiatric and sociological longitudinal finding of its differential impact. In addition, Erikson (1978) described the longitudinal adverse impact of disruption of community connectedness on community and individual recovery.

This modeling of the signature of the event must also be put in the context of two other concepts, as over time, we expanded our conceptual framework to take account of additional categories that need to be included in developing a comprehensive conceptual framework, as listed below.

# 10.3 Pre-Event Ecology of the Community/Pre-Event Individual and Community Experiences

As work in Armenia progressed, we became aware that a comprehensive approach to understanding the impact and recovery after a disaster must consider the pre-disaster community ecology and individual and community pre-disaster experiences as the setting in which the disaster occurred. The pre-event ecology of the community in Armenia included population demographics and socioeconomic status, physical infrastructure (including pre-earthquake unsafe housing and school construction), and prevailing political turmoil. These factors bear on various aspects of the impact of the disaster, and importantly on struggles over issues of responsibility and accountability related to the death toll among students in poorly constructed school buildings. One of the major aspects of pre- and post-earthquake community influences was the challenge of the transition from being within the communist satellite sphere of the USSR to an independent nation. The mistrust of the central communist government led to a widespread belief that the earthquake had been caused by an undeclared nuclear explosion that influenced causal attributions within the recovery community.

## 10.4 Mapping Categories of Disaster Experiences and Inventory of Traumatic Details

Pre-event community experiences can prime the nature, severity, and course of initial response and recovery. This includes both immediate individual and family experiences, sub-population experiences, and the influence of cultural/historical trauma. In our studies, we chose to examine a sub-population who had moved to the earthquake zone from Azerbaijan where they had recently suffered horrific political violence and were seeking safety and protection, only to be exposed to the catastrophic earthquake. The violence in Azerbaijan, directed at the Armenian enclave, also served as a powerful historic reminder of the 1915 Armenian Genocide to the general population in the earthquake zone. We were able to include a study that examined the impact of dual exposure to recent political violence and subsequent exposure to the earthquake, where we found that those who had come from Azerbaijan (after exposure there to political violence) and had then been exposed to the earthquake, showed more severe PTSD symptoms than expected for their level of exposure to the earthquake (Goenjian et al., 1994).

Mapping categories of disaster experiences and inventory of traumatic details allows for another level of refinement to better delineate potential mental health consequences among subpopulations across and within cohorts of exposure. From our earliest studies, we identified four major categories of disaster experiences: (1) life-threatening experiences including injury; (2) witnessing threat to life or injury; (3) experiences of traumatic deaths and personal material losses, and; (4) experiences of worry about a significant other. The first two parallel current central DSM-5 exposure risk criteria for PTSD. The third is less tied to direct witnessing and expands the disaster mental health consideration to include grief, complicated by the traumatic circumstances of the death, a feature that is not bound by the physical perimeter of threat to life or destruction, but extends far and beyond, including to relatives and friends who reside outside the disaster zone. Worry about a significant other tends to receive less attention. However, a more recent study of ours from the mass violence event at Virginia Tech (Hughes et al., 2011) documented that, while it may be a less potent factor than the first three, it can be widespread and of sufficient intensity and duration to be responsible for a significant fraction of cases of PTSD within the expanded community of those affected. Within the mapping of disaster experiences, we would also include attention to the perceived effectiveness or failure of protective interventions at the personal, family, community, and societal levels. On the personal level, it can identify traumatic features that are prone to elicit immediate and intense guilt, a critical risk factor in the immediate aftermath, and over time that can increase the level of severity and duration of PTSD reactions within an exposure cohort. In escaping a collapsing building, the risks of falling debris after violent earthquakes are well described, beginning with Pliny the Younger's description of the eruption of Mt. Vesuvius in 70 AD. This is well illustrated by one adolescent boy in Gumri, who blamed himself for the death of his mother who was crushed by a collapsing building. He claimed that if had he run one way instead of in the opposite direction, then his mother would not have died. His unjustified self-blame was a more bearable thought than his overwhelming feeling of helplessness to save his mother from destruction.

Within each subcategory of disaster experience, we would further delineate features and traumatic details that carried potential importance for a disaster mental health program. For example, in our Los Angeles Unified School District study after the Northridge earthquake, only 2%–3% of the population at the epicenter described being trapped. However, those who reported being trapped carried an 85% risk of PTSD at five months compared to a much lower risk among the general population in the epicenter. In the case of Spitak, where nearly all the schools collapsed, many of the children died, and the surviving children heard cries of distress, witnessed death and injury, and had to be rescued from the rubble, it is not surprising that they had a high level of PTSD even at 1.5 years post-earthquake. Even more so, in our study of adolescents who were among the most severely exposed group in Nicaragua after Hurricane Mitch, 90% suffered from PTSD (Goenjian et al., 2001). In Hurricane Hugo, where there was large-scale evacuation before the hurricane hit, there were only mild to moderate levels of PTSD and, as a predictive factor, prior anxiety disorder was associated with more moderate and prolonged responses.

In addition to this mapping and detailing, we would include two additional concepts that may also shape the disaster experience.

## 10.5 Cultural Beliefs/Personal Attitude Toward Disaster/ Immediate Pre-Disaster Personal Context

Firstly, cultural attitudes and personal beliefs, including religious and spiritual values, may directly influence the disaster experience as it is happening. Secondly, the immediate context, including the temporal pairing of the disaster event with other significant community or personal life events, may play the same role. In addition, we gathered information from across and within exposure groups to better understand the nature and range of high-risk disaster-related experiences. Combining the signature of the event with mapping categories of disaster experiences provides information for planning disaster mental health response, including types and level of interventions needed, location (e.g., hospitals, clinics, schools, community outreach), and staffing of disaster relief and recovery efforts, required levels of supervision, and anticipated costs and duration of the program. Dr. Goenjian was effective in providing this information to local officials which resulted in better decision-making regarding allocation of resources between Spitak and Gumri.

We also found that it was important to understand the immediate context of the earthquake, for example one child's birthday was on the day of the earthquake. The family had gathered in the house for the birthday party where multiple family members were killed. The child struggled with guilt that, if it were not for the birthday party that day, family members would have been spared.

## 10.6  Resource Loss/Resource Replenishment/Gain/Social Vulnerability Index

At the time we began our research, a new dimension to the study of traumatic stress was emerging. It was developed by Stevan Hobfoll and was referred to as the conservation of resources theory (1989). Although this approach has gone through extensive empirical investigation and refinement over the years, its basic principles have influenced our studies through the decades and were a key consideration in our research. This theory posits (as a complementary model to the one presented) that resource loss, replenishment, and resource gain in the recovery environment powerfully influence the course of population recovery over time. It places importance on resource loss as a major ingredient in the generation and debilitating effects of traumatic stress. Resource loss includes the loss of parental resources to a child (e.g., availability or quality of time) for example, due to parental efforts to meet the increased demands of daily living and rebuilding or from parental PTSD or depression, as well as compromises in community resources as measured in terms of adverse economic changes, material losses, reduced social services, and disruptions of societal infrastructure that interfere with daily activities, the meeting of basic needs, and social cohesion.

Conservation of resource theory contributed to the design of our twenty-five-year Armenian follow-up studies, where we examined not only the effect of resource loss, but differences in the societal infusion of resources across the cohort of cities that may have beneficially affected the course of recovery and outcome for both health and mental health indices. Many of the objective indices were identified in the early stage of this work, for example residential damage, rates of unemployment, loss of educational opportunities, infrastructure damage, and demands on parenting. These analyses were not just confined to material measures but recognized that improvement in infrastructure, for example in public transport, can contribute to the restoration of social connectedness (getting to work, visiting family and friends, and attending religious services). Restoring public playgrounds and parks provided opportunities for children to play together, make new friends, and participate in sports. For adolescent boys in Armenia, an important developmental resource was the opportunity to participate in soccer leagues.

We would add to this discussion that our initial studies of the sustained mental health effects on children and adolescents, for example, in rates of PTSD, depression, and separation anxiety, raised a larger issue of resource loss when, as a result of a disaster of this proportion, a large segment of the next generation over an entire region is affected by such mental health insults. We would argue that the sustained improvements in mental health outcome, as demonstrated by the twenty-five-year follow-up of intervention during adolescence, represents an important indicator of "resource replenishment," that has major import to the future of the region. Most recently, Gibbs et al., (2019) have documented the region-wide delayed impact on academic performance among primary school children affected by massive bush fires in Australia, indicating another important developmental domain that can be adversely affected by large-scale disasters, but one that in other studies of child traumatic stress, is also amenable to effective trauma-grief-focused school-based interventions.

The Social Vulnerability Index of the US Center for Disease Control (Center for Disease Control, 2020) is becoming an increasingly utilized tool for identifying communities that need support before, during, and after disasters. The balance of resource loss and resource gain after a single disaster serves as a major metric to enhance the use of US Census variables to identify the vulnerability of communities to respond to future hazardous events as a result of the impact of already experienced disasters within communities. This process becomes particularly important in localities or regions that face multiple disasters over time.

# 10.7 Trajectories of Ongoing Adjustment

The literature is replete with studies of the course of recovery after disasters, although there is no consensus concerning a typology of recovery profiles. For example, Lai et al. (2017) reviewed studies of PTSD symptom trajectories among children after natural disasters, identifying "resilience," "recovery," and "chronic" patterns. Mixed evidence was found for a "delayed recovery" pattern (see La Greca et al., 2013). Across broad types of trauma, Galitzer et al., (2018) reviewed fifty-four studies of the nature and prevalence of trauma response trajectories, with the most consistently observed trajectories being resilience, recovery, chronic, and delayed. For the future, more refined trajectory models are needed that identify patterns of response referenced to a broad range of outcome domains to investigate trajectories of adjustment and associated mediating and moderating factors more fully. For example, Layne and Hobfoll (2020) recently proposed a more differentiated typology of adjustment trajectories – including stress resistance, resilient recovery, prolonged recovery, growth, decline, delayed decline, phasic adjustment, severe decline, and chronic maladaptive functioning.

# 10.8 Seamless Data Model

As our dynamic modeling of disaster psychiatry interventions has progressed, we have proposed the importance of a seamless data collection system, one that relies on a set of measurements that can incorporate added features to serve more complex purposes over time. We contrast this approach to one too often found that uses different instruments at different time periods, making it hard not only to evaluate the data but making for a far less efficient methodology to conduct ongoing planning, to identify factors in the ecology of recovery that are changing courses of recovery, and to refine or revise to reflect ongoing assessment and outcome parameters. We include the following components in a seamless data collection system:

1. *Pre-disaster surveillance* – trauma history, distress, behavior, functioning
2. *Acute impact* – trauma/loss, objective features of exposure, distress, behavior, functioning
3. *Needs assessment* – trauma/loss exposure, adversities, abbreviated measures of distress and functioning
4. *Screening* – brief measures of exposure, distress, behavior, and functioning
5. *Ongoing surveillance* – monitoring of psychosocial recovery and of the recovery environment
6. *Clinical evaluation* – full-scale self-report and structured clinical interviews
7. *Treatment outcome* – use of instruments sensitive to therapeutic change
8. *Program evaluation* – data collection strategies and metrics to assess overall effectiveness of the program

Pre-disaster surveillance can be systematically carried out through periodic national representative surveys to track demographically related rates of various types of exposure to trauma and loss, symptom response, and functional impact. Such data is valuable in providing population-based baseline information for statistical comparison in interpreting findings from data collection efforts post-disaster. Collection of acute post-disaster triage data can be effectively used to obtain early information about the impact of the event and its population distribution, and also link survivors early on with available services. Needs assessment involves systematic data collection from a representative sample of an affected population to determine the scope and impact of the event. Such data can be used for planning needed response strategies and resources. Ongoing surveillance is used to monitor the course of recovery among an affected population and the impact of new events and adversities. Screening more systematically targets members of an affected population for linkage with available recovery resources. Clinical evaluation and intervention outcome data focuses on the rigorous evaluation of affected individuals and the contribution of interventions to the course of recovery. Program evaluation data is gathered to evaluate the effectiveness of interventions and services provided in the aftermath. Using this seamless data collection system, we have also developed with our collaborators over the years a disaster tiered intervention model that relies on these metrics to match trajectories of recovery with a continuum of care.

## 10.9  Stages of Disaster Response and Tiered Intervention Model

A modern public mental health approach to the post-disaster recovery of children, adolescents, adults, and families recognizes the importance of conceptualizing stages of disaster response. Although the timing, setting, and service providers for delivery of acute, intermediate, and longer-term post-disaster services will vary by type of disaster and post-disaster ecology, different levels of intervention are needed for each of these stages. For children and families, schools represent a major setting for many modalities of intervention (e.g., individual, classroom, group, family). Acute interventions are typically brief and are provided in the days and weeks post-event, while intermediate-stage interventions are offered over the first eighteen months following a disaster. Children and adolescents who continue to experience difficulties for months after a disaster can benefit from longer-term, more comprehensive trauma-grief-focused treatment that also addresses concomitant comorbid conditions and rehabilitation of developmental disruptions.

These different stages of intervention represent more in-depth and extended efforts that encompass similar objectives so that the main foci of intervention remain constant. For example, although post-disaster stresses and adversities may evolve over time, a focus on these remains an integral component across all stages of recovery. The same may be said for a focus on reactivity to trauma and loss reminders, despite the fact that the nature and frequency of exposure to reminders may vary over time. In this model (Pynoos, Goenjian, and Steinberg, 1998), Tier 1 interventions concentrate on providing broad-based mental health education and informational support. Tier 2 strategies focus on screening, education, and providing emotional support to higher-risk individuals, while Tier 3 focuses on providing direct mental health services to individuals in need.

## 10.10  Treatment

There have been many advances in the continuum of care for child traumatic stress and bereavement since the Psychiatric Outreach Program initiated its therapeutic interventions in Armenia. Many of the essential ingredients of this continuum of care were already embedded in the intermediate treatment approach that was the bedrock of the treatment outcome studies. The previously described foci (the complexity of the traumatic experience; the interplay of traumatic stress and grief reactions; the ecology of the recovery environment, trauma and loss reminders; and developmental progression) were incorporated into the treatment protocol.

The Psychiatric Outreach Program staff provided treatment in the Gumri schools during school hours. The intervention was designed to take advantage of using the school classroom to initiate a group intervention as the most efficient means to reach a large, affected population of children and adolescents. The classroom sessions were complimented by individual sessions for students with the most severe trauma and loss experiences and supplemented by short-term family interventions with students and parents to increase support and understanding of the child, and to address parental distress that was disturbing their parental functioning. The treatment consisted of six sessions, of ninety minutes each, completed within a six-week period. Therapy included addressing five major areas related to trauma that included the following:

1. Reconstruction of earthquake-related experiences immediately before, during, and after the earthquake. This entailed co-construction of a trauma narrative reviewing features of the earthquake experience, with clarification of distortions and misattributions. The reconstruction and repeated recounting of the most traumatic experiences were coupled with relaxation methods, such as deep breathing relaxation deep breathing.

2. Identification of trauma reminders, with links made to aspects of traumatic experiences. The students were assisted with increasing tolerance for anticipated reactivity to reminders, increasing support-seeking behavior during and after exposure to reminders, and avoiding unnecessary exposure to distressing reminders.

3. Identification of post-disaster stresses and adversities. The students received guidance to help them cope better with changes and losses at home and at school. They were assisted in decreasing maladaptive and avoidant behaviors and in the promotion of adaptive problem-solving for ongoing challenges.

4. Assistance with grief resolution by helping bereaved students reconstitute a non-traumatic mental representation of a deceased person so as to be able to engage in positive reminiscing. The students were helped to identify and engage other individuals who could provide advice, counseling, or companionship. Special attention was given to identifying, managing, and gaining additional support in response to loss reminders.

5. Identification of missed developmental opportunities due to loss of family members or traumatic avoidance. The students were assisted in re-engaging in activities that promoted normal developmental progression.

# 10.11 Modernizing Disaster Public Mental Health

The modernization of disaster mental health has developed a continuum of acute, intermediate, and more intense interventions that continue to employ the same foci, with increasing levels of depth and duration of treatment. The two most accepted and empirically supported acute and intermediate interventions are Psychological First Aid (PFA) (Watson, Brymer, and Bonnano, 2011), and Skills for Psychological Recovery (SPR) (Berkowitz et al., 2010). PFA is an evidence-informed skill-based approach to reduce acute post-disaster distress and promote adaptive functioning. A widely used PFA approach was developed by the National Center for Child Traumatic Stress (NCCTS) and the National Center for PTSD (Brymer et al., 2006). Based on the principles of fostering safety, calm, hope, connectedness, and self-efficacy (Hobfoll et al., 2007), it includes eight core actions: (1) contact and engagement; (2) safety and comfort; (3) stabilization; (4) information gathering; (5) practical assistance; (6) connection with social supports; (7) information on coping; and (8) linkage with collaborative services. Randomized controlled trials have yet to be conducted, although providers have rated PFA as appropriate (Allen et al., 2010). PFA is designed for use by non-mental health personnel in a variety of settings. PFA has been adopted by the Medical Reserve Corps of the United States for training and use by this national volunteer force, adapted for use by community religious professionals, and specially tailored for use in school settings. The World Health Organization (WHO) has incorporated these principles and specific intervention skills into their WHO disaster response plans, with demonstrated cross-cultural efficacy.

Skills for Psychological Recovery (SPR) is another model also developed by the NCTSN and NCPTSD (Berkowitz et al., 2010). SPR is designed to be implemented after the period when PFA has been utilized or when more intensive intervention is needed. Like PFA, SPR was designed to be appropriate for all ages, and can be delivered in a range of settings. SPR includes a set of skill-building modules that include: (1) gathering information about current needs and concerns (psychological and non-psychological), and prioritizing assistance; (2) building problem-solving skills; (3) promoting positive activities; (4) managing reactions; (5) promoting helpful thinking; and (6) rebuilding healthy social connections. SPR also incorporates motivational enhancement principles, guidelines for prioritizing problems, and strategies for addressing barriers to skill implementation. SPR is a promising evidence-informed intervention, although it awaits controlled studies to be considered evidence-based. SPR is designed for use by paraprofessionals under mental health supervision, as well as mental health professionals themselves. Studies are now emerging that demonstrate the efficacy of this intermediate level of care.

The Armenian intervention outcome studies were the first of their kind in child disaster mental health, using a protocol with specific intervention foci and a validated PTSD and depression measure for children and adolescents after a major disaster (Goenjian et al., 1997, 2005). The remarkable sustained outcome advantages to the treatment arm at twenty-five-year follow-up supports the underlying therapeutic centricity and power of these foci. It demonstrated that even when adverse post-disaster circumstances are so extreme that there is a substantial delay in establishing a system of post-disaster intervention, it is not too late to achieve substantial and sustainable gains.

The following case presentation from the initial outcome study initiated at 1.5 years post-disaster illustrates the capability of severely traumatized and bereaved youth to participate in partnership with a therapist in their own treatment, with courage and their own personal striving, and to benefit from such a challenging task of recovery.

## 10.12 Case Presentation (From Goenjian et al., 1997)

*Anna was 12 years old at the time of treatment. She had experienced extreme life-threat during the earthquake and lost her mother and brother. During the first classroom session, she appeared detached, with a fixed and incongruous smile. She did not participate in drawing or describing her earthquake experiences, stating, "I don't want to talk about the earthquake.*

*Why did you have to come so long after, just to remind us about what happened?"* At the end of the session, she accepted the therapist's invitation to meet individually.

During the individual session, Anna began to talk about her earthquake experiences. On the day of the earthquake, her grandmother had come to their house to help her mother bake a cake for Anna's birthday. Suddenly, "the earth shook," and the house collapsed on top of them. Anna and her grandmother held on to each other under the collapsed building for two days. She remembered her grandmother's constant prayers to God to save her grandchild. In recounting this, Anna said, "God, why didn't you take me away? Is it because I am not good enough? You made me live and suffer and remember everything. God, I love my mother. I was teasing her when it happened, telling her that I loved grandmother more than her."

After sharing what had been important to her about her experience and the initial reconstruction of her trauma narrative, Anna began to talk about her current feelings and concerns. She described her difficulty in falling asleep, her nightmares about the earthquake, her problem with bedwetting, her recurrent stomachaches, and her difficulty in paying attention in the classroom and concentrating on homework. She described the onset of her menstruation as a "bad" event that she wished she could talk about with her mother. She described her ambivalence about her father's plan to remarry and how she saw herself as an obstacle to his finding a new wife. She confided in the therapist that she felt obliged to keep smiling for the benefit of her father.

During the following sessions, Anna was able to describe some of her worst traumatic moments and their associated catastrophic emotions. She recollected being embraced in her grandmother's arms and hearing her grandmother's cries grow weaker until she died. She remembered how much it hurt to have the weight of her grandmother's dead slumping body on top of her and how she felt desolate, terrified, and fearful that, in addition to her grandmother, her mother and baby brother were also dead.

The therapist gave special attention to clarifying distortions and misattributions. In regard to Anna's numerous self-attributions of guilt, the therapist assisted Anna in clarifying the relationship of her guilt feelings to excessive self-blame in reaction to her experience of extreme helplessness during the earthquake. The therapist assisted Anna in resolving feelings about having teased her mother just before her death about something as important as her love for her and identified her recurrent discomfort over angry feelings toward her mother for no longer being there to care for her. The therapist clarified that another key source of guilt that had been imparted by surviving family members—who had told Anna that if it were not for her birthday, the family might not have been home that day—stemmed from their own grief reactions.

As Anna improved, the therapist actively engaged her in adopting more effective strategies to cope with current stresses and adversities. While Anna was in treatment, the therapist met with Anna's father to address some of his trauma- and grief-related problems and suggested ways to be more responsive to his daughter, including specific ways to improve communication with her. Over the course of psychotherapy, Anna's affect became more animated, she exhibited less estrangement, and her nightmares subsided. She resumed the dance lessons that she had ceased after the earthquake. She and her father became closer, and, for the first time, in a moment of poignant mutual grief, she joined him to visit the grave of her mother.

The reconstruction and reappraisal of her traumatic experiences, in reducing her conflict over traumatic helplessness, appeared to facilitate suspended grief work. As a result, Anna was able to 1) reconstitute a nontraumatic mental representation of her mother, one that was less contaminated by images and emotions associated with the traumatic lethal circumstances of *the death, and 2) repair the artificial estrangement that had been created by the teasing exchange in her last contact with her.*

## 10.13 Further Discussion of the Conceptual Model

Our studies began with a healthy respect for the importance of an overarching conceptual model that, on the one hand, used these concepts to organize what to examine, and, on the other hand, used the data as they emerged to refine the conceptual model. This disaster mental health program utilized an overarching conceptual model that over time has become more sophisticated with more fully defined causal concepts and a better framework to understand their complex and temporal interactions. The field has moved beyond a simplistic mediating and moderating model, and some of these additional features were already present in a rudimentary form in our long-term studies. In addition to the major domains included in the conceptual model, over time, we recognized the need for clarification and definitions of key causal concepts that constitute basic building blocks that underlie the model. We subsequently have described a set of definitions that were implicit in conceptualizing our research (Layne, Steinberg, and Steinberg, 2014). These are presented below.

## 10.14 Definitions of Key Causal Concepts

- A *partial or contributory cause* plays a limited role in the cause/effect relation.
- A *necessary cause* is a causal agent without which the effect cannot occur.
- A *sufficient cause* is a causal agent whose presence/occurrence ensures the effect.
- A *sole cause* is a causal agent that is both necessary and sufficient for the effect to occur.
- A *conjunctive cause* is a causal agent that must be jointly present with one or more other causal agents for the effect to be produced.
- A *disjunctive cause* is a causal agent among a number of other causal agents, any of which may produce the same effect.
- A *reciprocal causal relation* occurs when two entities are causes and effects of one another.
- A *causal chain* or *multi-step causation* occurs when there are a number of successive causal agents that collectively produce an effect.
- A *moderator* interacts with a causal agent so that its effect on a given outcome varies as a function of the moderator. Moderators can be classified as *not therapeutically modifiable* (e.g., age, sex) vs. *therapeutically modifiable* (e.g., social support, help-seeking behavior).
- A *vulnerability factor* is a type of moderator whose presence or level is associated with an exacerbation of the adverse effect(s) of a causal risk factor on an outcome.
- A *protective factor* is a type of moderator variable whose presence or level is associated with attenuation of the adverse effect(s) of a causal risk factor on an outcome.
- A *facilitative factor* is a type of moderator whose presence or (increasing) level is associated with an intensification of the beneficial effect(s) of a promotive factor on an outcome.
- An *inhibitory factor* is a type of moderator whose presence or level is associated with an attenuation of the beneficial effect(s) of a promotive factor on an outcome.
- A *mediator* is a link (B) in a causal chain that transmits the effects of a prior cause (A) to a subsequent cause (C), such that A→B→C, where B is both an effect of A, and a cause of C.

- *A fully mediated relationship* occurs when the effect of a causal agent is fully transmitted via the mediator.
- *A partially mediated relationship* occurs when the effect of a causal agent is transmitted both by a direct pathway and via the mediator.
- A *risk marker* is a factor associated with a significant increase in the likelihood of a focal outcome.
- A *causal risk factor* is a causal precursor to a focal outcome.

These intervening factors need to be considered against a broad range of outcomes, many of which are beginning to be intensively investigated, as each factor may operate differently depending on the specific outcome under consideration. In addition, many of these factors may themselves be affected by traumatic stress, and as such, may be conceived as potential outcome variables. To date, in addition to factors that relate specifically to the onset and severity of PTSD, outcomes of trauma in children and adolescents that have been studied have been quite varied and cover a range of psychological reactions and psychiatric disorders, as well as biological alterations, behavioral disturbances, functional impairments, alterations in a sense of safety and protection, alteration in expectations and aspirations for the future, cognitive and emotional development, physical health and well-being, and disturbances in moral development and conscience functioning (Goenjian et al., 1999; Fairbank, Putnam, and Harris, 2007).

The following are selected examples from our longitudinal research that illustrate how we improved our conceptual thinking regarding the impact and recovery related to this catastrophic disaster in Armenia.

1. In examining causal pathways, our conceptual model assumed that pre-disaster history, disaster exposure, adversities, and the recovery environment may each contribute in a complex way to the findings from the regional assessments of PTSD, depression, and separation anxiety and their interplay. One of the refinements in conceptual thinking grew out of the results from the 1.5-year post-disaster treatment outcome study. Up until then, we had considered the purpose of the intervention was primarily directed at reducing symptom severity and cases meeting diagnostic criteria. What we learned is that in an environment with such ongoing adverse recovery ecology, the prevention of depressive reactions progressing to clinical levels (Goenjian et al., 2020; see also Chapter 4 in this book) can be an equally important outcome of intervention.

2. Another conceptual improvement was in our understanding of the promotive value of social support. Typically, social support has been conceptualized as a moderating factor in relation to symptom severity. The twenty-five-year follow-up suggests that social support also serves to promote improved long-term health outcomes. Using a broader conceptual model can be especially helpful in understanding the mechanism by which important cultural influences are at work in determining personal and family recovery.

3. Especially regarding the concept of a facilitative factor, the area of bereavement provided some of the strongest examples of how to understand findings that emerged which, on the surface, did not have an obvious explanation. For example, the loss of a father, even for young children, had more deleterious developmental outcomes than the loss of a mother. In Armenian culture, the extended family mobilized to provide sustained substitute maternal caregiving that did not occur in a similar fashion in the death of a father.

# References

Allen, B., Brymer, M., Steinberg, A., Vernberg E., Brymer, M. J., Jacobs, A., Speier, A., & Pynoos, R. (2010). Perceptions of psychological first aid among providers responding to Hurricanes Gustav and Ike. *Journal of Traumatic Stress*, 23, 509–513.

Anda, R. F., Felitti, V. J., Bremner, J. D., Walker, J. D., Whitfield, C. H., Perry, B. D., . . . & Giles, W. H. (2006). The enduring effects of abuse and related adverse experiences in childhood. *European Archives of Psychiatry and Clinical Neuroscience*, 256 (3), 174–186.

Berkowitz, S., Bryant, R., Brymer, M., Hamblen, J., Jacobs, A., Layne, C., Macy, R., Osofsky, H., Pynoos, R., Ruzek, J., Steinberg, A., Vernberg, E., & Watson, P. (2010). National Center for PTSD and National Child Traumatic Stress Network, Skills for psychological recovery: field operations guide. Available at: www.nctsn.org and www.ptsd.va.gov.

Brymer, M., Jacobs, A., Layne, C., Pynoos, R., Ruzek, J., Steinberg, A., Vernberg, E., & Watson, P. (2006). Psychological First Aid Field Operations Guide, National Child Traumatic Stress Network and National Center for PTSD.

Center for Disease Control Agency for Toxic Substances and Disease Registry, Social Vulnerability Index. (2020). Available at: https://www.atsdr.cdc.gov/.

Chen, S. H., Lin, Y., Wu, Y. (2002) Posttraumatic stress reactions in children and adolescents one year after the 1999 Taiwan Chi-Chi earthquake. *Journal of the Chinese Institute of Engineers*, 25 (5), 597–608. https://doi.org/10.1080/02533839.2002.9670734.

Chen, S. H., & Wu, Y. C. (2006). Changes of PTSD symptoms and school reconstruction: a two-year prospective study of children and adolescents after the Taiwan 921 earthquake. *Natural Hazards*, 37, 1–2, 225–244.

Coker, A. L., Hanks, J. S., Eggleston, K. S., Risser, J., Tee, P. G., Chronister, K. J., Troisi, C. L., Arafat, R., & Franzini, L. (2006). Social and mental health needs assessment of Katrina evacuees. *Disaster Management & Response*, 4 (3), 88–94.

Erikson, K. T. (1978). *Everything in its Path: Destruction of Community in the Buffalo Creek Flood*. New York, NY: Simon & Schuster.

Fairbank, J. A., Putnam, F. W., & Harris, W. W. (2007). The prevalence and impact of child traumatic stress. In M. J. Friedman, T. M. Keane, & P. A. Resick (eds.), *A Handbook of PTSD: Science and Practice* (pp. 229–251). New York, NY: Guilford Publications.

Felitti, V. J., Anda, R. F., Nordenberg, D., Williamson, D. F., Spitz, A. M., Edwards, V., & Marks, J. S. (1998). Relationship of childhood abuse and household dysfunction to many of the leading causes of death in adults: The Adverse Childhood Experiences (ACE) Study. *American Journal of Preventive Medicine*, 14 (4), 245–258.

Frankenberg, E., Friedman, J., Gillespie, T., Ingwersen, N., Pynoos, R. S., Umar Rifai, L., Sikoki, J., Steinberg, A. M., Sumantri, C., Suriastini, W., & Thomas, D. (2008). Mental health in Sumatra after the tsunami. *American Journal of Public Health*, 98, 1671–1677.

Galatzer, I. R., Huang, S. H., & Bononno, G. A. (2018). Trajectories of resilience and dysfunction following potential trauma: a review and statistical evaluation. *Psychology Review*, 63. 41–55.

Gibbs, L., Nursey, J., Cook, J., Ireton, G., Alkemade, N., Roberts, M., Gallagher, H., Bryant, R., Block, K., Molyneaux, R., & Forbes, D. (2019). Delayed disaster impacts on academic performance of primary school children. *Child Development*, 90, 1402–1412.

Goenjian, A. K. (1993) A mental health relief programme in Armenia after the 1988 earthquake: implementation and clinical observations. *British Journal of Psychiatry*, 163, 230–239.

Goenjian, A., Najarian, L. M., Pynoos, R. S., Steinberg, A. M., Petrosian, P., Sterakyan, S., & Fairbanks, L. A. (1994). Posttraumatic stress reactions after single and double trauma. *Acta Psychiatrica Scandinavia*, 90, 214–221.

Goenjian, A. K., Karayan, I., Pynoos, R. S., Minassian, D., Najarian, L. M., Steinberg, A. M., & Fairbanks, L. A. (1997). Outcome of psychotherapy among early adolescents after trauma. *The American Journal of Psychiatry*, 154 (4), 536–542. https://doi.org/10.1176/ajp.154.4.536.

Goenjian, A. K., Stilwell, B. M., Steinberg, A. M., Fairbanks, L. A., Galvin, M., Karayan, I., & Pynoos, R. S. (1999). Moral development and psychopathological interference with conscience functioning among adolescents after trauma. *Journal of the American Academy of Child and Adolescent Psychiatry*, 38, 376–384.

Goenjian, A., Molina, L., Steinberg, A., Fairbanks, L., Alvarez, M., Goenjian, H., & Pynoos, R. (2001). Posttraumatic stress and depressive reactions among Nicaraguan adolescents after Hurricane Mitch. *American Journal of Psychiatry*, 158, 788–794.

Goenjian, A. K., Walling, D., Steinberg, A. M., Karayan, I., Najarian, L. M., & Pynoos, R. (2005). A prospective study of posttraumatic stress and depressive reactions among treated and untreated adolescents 5 years after a catastrophic disaster. *American Journal of Psychiatry*, 162 (12), 2302–2308. https://doi.org/10.1176/appi.ajp.162.12.2302.

Goenjian, A., Steinberg, A., Walling, D., Bishop, S., Karayan, I., & Pynoos, R. S. (2020). 25-year follow-up of treated and not-treated adolescents after the Spitak earthquake: course and predictors of PTSD and depression. *Psychological Medicine*, 51 (6), 1–13. Advance online publication. https://doi.org/10.1017/S0033291719003891.

Green, B., Grace, M., Jacob, D., Lindy, G., Gleser, A., Leonard, A., & Kramer, T. (1990). Buffalo Creek survivors in the second decade: comparison with unexposed and nonlitigant groups. *Journal of Applied Social Psychology*, 13, 1033–1050.

Hobfoll, S.E., (1989) Conservation of Resources: A New Attempt at Conceptualizing Stress. American Psychologist, 44: 513–524.

Hobfoll, S., Watson, P., Bell, C., et al. (2007). Five essential elements of immediate and mid-term mass trauma intervention: empirical evidence. *Psychiatry Interpersonal & Biological Processes*, 70, 283–315.

Hughes, M., Brymer, M., Chiu, W. T., Fairbank, J. A., Jones, R. T., Pynoos, R. S., Rothwell, V., Steinberg, A. M., & Kessler, R. C. (2011). Posttraumatic stress among students after the shootings at Virginia Tech. *Psychological Trauma: Theory, Research, Practice, and Policy*, 3 (4), 403–411.

La Greca, A. M., Lai, B. S., Labre, M. M., Silverman, W. K., Vernberg, E. M., & Prinstein, M. J. (2013). Children's post-disaster trajectories of PTS symptoms: predicting chronic distress. *Child & Youth Care Forum*, 42 (4), 351–369.

Lai, B. S., Lewis, R., Livings, M. S., La Greca, A. M., & Esnard, A. (2017). Posttraumatic stress symptom trajectories among children after disaster exposure: a review. *Journal of Traumatic Stress*, 30, 571–582.

Layne, C. M., Steinberg, J. R., & Steinberg, A. M. (2014). Causal reasoning skills training for mental health practitioners: promoting sound clinical judgment in evidence-based practice. *Training and Education in Professional Psychology*, 8, 292–302.

Layne, C. M., & Hobfoll, S. E. (2020). Understanding posttraumatic adjustment trajectories in school-age youth: supporting stress resistance, resilient recovery, and growth. In E. Rossen (ed.), *Supporting and Educating Traumatized Students: A Guide for School-Based Professionals* (2nd edn.) (pp. 75–97). New York, NY: Oxford University Press. Available at: https://global.oup.com/academic/product/supporting-and-educating-traumatized-students-9780190052737.

Pynoos, R. S., Steinberg, A. M., & Wraith, R. (1995). A developmental model of childhood traumatic stress. In: D. Cicchetti and D. J. Cohen (eds.), *Manual of Developmental Psychopathology*. New York, NY: John Wiley & Sons, 72–93.

Pynoos, R. S., Goenjian, A. K., & Steinberg, A. M. (1998a). Children and disasters: a developmental approach to posttraumatic stress disorder in children and adolescents. *Psychiatry and Clinical Neurosciences*, 52 (Supplement), S129–S138.

Pynoos, R. S., Goenjian, A. K., & Steinberg, A. M. (1998b). A public mental health approach to the post-disaster treatment of children and adolescents. *Psychiatric Clinics of North America*, 7, 195–210.

Pynoos, R. S., Steinberg, A. M., & Piacentini, J. C. (1999). Developmental psychopathology of childhood traumatic stress and implications for associated anxiety disorders. *Biological Psychiatry*, 46, 1542–1554.

Pynoos, R. S., Steinberg, A. M., Layne, C. M., Liang, L., Vivrette, R., Briggs, E. C., & Fairbank, J. A. (2014). Modeling constellations of trauma exposure in the National Child Traumatic Stress Network core data set. *Psychological Trauma: Theory, Research, Practice, and Policy*, 6 (Suppl.1), S9–S17. https://doi.org/10.1037/a0037767.

Steinberg, A. M., & Ritzmann, R. F. (1990. A living systems approach to understanding the concept of stress. *Behavioral Science*, 35, 138–146.

Steinberg, A. M., Pynoos, R. S., Goenjian, A. K., Sossanabadi, H., & Sherr, L. (1999). Are researchers bound by child abuse reporting laws? *Child Abuse and Neglect*, 23, 771–777.

Steinberg, A. M., Brymer, M. J., Kim, S., Ghosh, C., Ostrowski, S. A., Gulley, K., & Pynoos, R. S. (2013). Psychometric properties of the UCLA PTSD Reaction Index: Part 1. *Journal of Traumatic Stress*, 26 (1), 1–9. https://doi.org/10.1002/jts.21780

Susser, M. (1973). *Causal Thinking in the Health Sciences: Concepts and Strategies of Epidemiology*. Oxford: Oxford University Press.

Watson, P., Brymer, M., & Bonnano, G. (2011). Post-disaster psychological intervention since 9/11. *American Psychologist*, 66, 482–494.

# Memoirs of the Spitak Earthquake

## Pavagan Petrosyan, Ida Karayan, and Liana H. Grigorian

## 11.1  How the Earthquake Changed my Life

Pavagan Petrosyan was the lead psychotherapist of the Psychiatric Outreach Program's Spitak clinic for two decades. In this memoir, she vividly describes her traumatic experiences and losses and her arduous journey as a widowed mother who chose to become a psychotherapist after the earthquake to help other survivors with their psychological difficulties.

Up until the Spitak earthquake, we lived quite comfortably. I graduated from Yerevan State Pedagogical University's Department of Psychology and subsequently got a job in the village of Jrashen near Spitak where my family lived. There, I became the principal of a kindergarten with 120 children and twenty-six employees. A short time later, I met my husband, who also worked at the school as a language instructor. We lived with his family after getting married, but we dreamed of having our own home. My husband had already bought land to build a house by himself. Every day, he would work on the floor plans. When my son Pargev was born, my husband was ecstatic. He used to say that he was destined to have four sons. Meanwhile, the Karabagh Movement began in February of 1988. My husband started organizing meetings for volunteers to help the army. He said he was ready to free Karabagh.

The evening before the earthquake, we were sitting in the living room. Pargev was one-and-a-half years old. To our delight, he had recently begun to walk. He stepped into his father's shoes and was staring at us from across the room. We were laughing at the spectacle. Suddenly, a powerful jolt shook the house. My husband ran over and grabbed Pargev, saying, "This is terrifying! I feel like the house might collapse any minute." I laughed dismissively, though, and said, "Why would it collapse? It's only an earthquake." There had been earthquakes before. The house had shaken, and nothing bad had happened. But we had no idea what was coming next.

On the morning of December 7, my husband came and woke Pargev up and kissed him before going to work. He had never done anything like that before. He said, "If the Turks attack us, take the child and flee to the mountains." I laughed at what he said. He then started to walk away. But then he paused, turned around, and stared at us for a long time before turning around and leaving.

Later that morning, my son Pargev, my husband's five-year-old nephew who was living with us after the parents' divorce, and I went to the kindergarten in Jrashen. I dropped the children off at the school and continued to go to the neighboring city of Vanadzor to buy a few items for the school. Suddenly, the ground shook violently. It would not stop. Everyone panicked and ran out of the building. I heard a crashing sound coming from the chemical factory nearby. That loud, roaring noise created by the earthquake still haunts me to this day.

My sister lived close by, so I then ran to her house. Once I confirmed that she and her family were still alive, I rushed to the bus stop to go to Jrashen where I heard people saying that Spitak was buried. This paralyzed me. I could not think or move. I felt sick to my stomach. My heart raced.

I boarded the bus for Yerevan that made stops at Spitak and Jrashen. As I sat on the bus, it seemed like time had frozen. I was restless and crying. When we finally approached Spitak, I saw the destruction close-up. The enormous bread factory where my sister worked had collapsed entirely. I was beside myself at the site of the rubble. I started screaming, "Where is my sister?" People were trying to calm me down, but I could not control myself as the bus continued to its next stop. When we arrived at Spitak, I saw that the buildings on both sides of the street where I had grown up were in ruins. Those who survived were running aimlessly, not knowing what to do, crying and screaming. I felt as if I was in a nightmare and that I would surely wake up at any minute. My father, mother, and brother's family all lived on that street. The thought crossed my mind that they were "not going to be there." But I could not bring myself to get off of the bus. I wanted to find my child and my husband.

I don't remember arriving at the village of Jrashen. The school where my husband worked was in ruins. The kindergarten where Pargev was supposed to be was also demolished. I saw people running, screaming, looking for their loved ones, and I, too, began to look for my husband and Pargev. I grabbed people on the street and asked them desperately about the whereabouts of the children.

Then, I saw my sister-in-law holding Pargev in her arms, his clothes covered in blood, a sight that made me feel like they had just handed me my world. I cried and held him tight. I kissed him. I was told I was lucky: he was the only child who survived the collapse of the building because the electrician had saved him! I had hired the electrician to renovate the kindergarten's lighting system, so when the earthquake hit, he was in my office, along with my husband's nephew, my son Pargev, and their teacher. When he felt the shaking start, he grabbed Pargev and jumped out of the office's window. He left Pargev in a safe location before running home to make sure his family was safe. My mother-in-law, who had rushed to the school to find Pargev, found him there, soaked in the electrician's blood. Except for Pargev and the electrician, those who had remained in my office had died, including my husband's nephew.

Some of the school employees who survived told me that they had seen my husband exiting the building alive but that he had gone back in to save the children who were trapped in a classroom. At that moment, a strong aftershock hit and demolished the already damaged building, and my husband was no more. He died with the rest of the children. Rescuers found his lifeless body the next day, holding children in his arms. Once he was found, my husband's father and a few others started gathering wood from the buildings that had crumbled to fashion a casket to bury him in. Those images are my most painful memories.

During the week or so that followed the earthquake, we lived in a tent. Eventually, we built a shack and lived in it until my brother's friend came from neighboring Georgia to take us to Batumi. At the time, I was four months pregnant. I was devastated, downtrodden, and had almost nothing left. I had lost my husband, my home, and my life as I knew it. I had no job and no income. The stress was overwhelming, and the thought of going to a strange place among strangers was the final blow, one that resulted in one more tragedy: I lost my baby. This was another added trauma for me.

We lived in Batumi for a month before returning to Spitak, where we lived in tents until they took us to Moscow. There, they gave us a house in the neighboring city of Vladimir. But I yearned for Spitak, my city, my home. Even though Spitak was in ruins, I didn't want to live anywhere else. I knew I could not stay in Vladimir for long, so five months after relocating there, my brother picked us up and took us back to Spitak, where we moved into a small, prefabricated house he had bought from Moscow. We lived in it with my parents and my brother's family.

The earthquake also killed my beautiful niece, an eleven-year-old named Meline. After being buried alive under the Russian school ruins in Spitak for days, she was rescued by my brother and other workers. Her kidneys were severely injured. So she was transferred to a well-known hospital in Moscow. The doctors were unable to save her. She died fifteen days after being admitted there. Just before she died, she told her mother, "Mom, don't cry. I'll come back. Take good care of my piano."

Because of her grief, my sister was unable to function for six months. She was admitted to a hospital in Moscow, where she slowly recovered. For the following two years, she was unable to have children until she finally gave birth to baby Mary on Meline's birthday. Mary and Meline resembled each other like two drops of water. She gave joy to our family. When Mary was two years old, my sister had a dream in which her departed daughter asked her, "Why have you named my sister Mary? She was born on my birthday. She is me." So, my sister changed Mary's name to Meline, but to this day, none of us are able to call her by that name. Mary changed our lives. She was our consolation.

In 1989, the Soviet Union had not yet collapsed. The demolished city had turned into an "open arena" where relief workers from the Soviet Republics and other countries from all over the world came to rebuild Spitak. However, instead of placing the new prefabricated homes in the city, they were placed five to six miles outside the city center, mostly accommodating those who had lost family members. This distance separated families who, until the earthquake, had always lived close to each other. The newly constructed region was also divided into districts named after the nationalities of the people who built them, such as Italian, Estonian, Uzbek, German, and Swiss. Meanwhile, the central region of old Spitak remained in ruins. The authorities claimed that it was not possible to rebuild in the old city because the ground was unstable.

What followed were many more dreadful years. The Soviet Union collapsed, and the Karabagh War began. Not only did people lose their homes, but there was no electricity, gas, or bread. We faced an existential crisis. For hours, we would stand in line just to buy dough because there was no bread. My father would walk several kilometers before sunrise simply to buy a small amount of dough for the entire family that would typically feed one adult. The dough was dark grey, and the bread we made from it tasted awful. The winters were also freezing without any form of heating, and by 5 o'clock, it was already dark. My only source of happiness was Pargev. All I seemed to dream of was having a house.

During these trying times, we didn't have any visitors or assistance from anyone outside of Spitak. Our hope that there were people who cared for us was finally realized when members of the Psychiatric Outreach Program, like Dr. Najarian, Dr. Karayan, and others from the United States, visited us.

In all honesty, when I look back on those years now as a therapist myself and see the road we plodded, I feel terrified and ask myself, "Was it real?" And if Dr. Goenjian and the other team members had not been there to help us financially and psychologically, I don't know what would have become of us. The work carried out by the clinic meant a great deal not only to me but to the entire city. Even today, when I run into former clinic patients or students of mine, they tell me, "Had you not been there, I don't know what would have happened to us."

When I first started as a therapist, it was difficult for me to conduct sessions because the visitors would talk about similar issues that I was having. On multiple occasions, not knowing my personal history, my clients would talk about my husband and how he died in the classroom along with many children during the earthquake. It was from one of them that I found out that he continued to call out my name before he died. I did not know what to do when patients mentioned him during sessions. All I could do was stay quiet and wait until the visit ended. I would then close the door and cry for an hour. I was tempted to quit my work. But I loved it too much to quit. I have always practiced my profession with pride and love. If they would ask me today what specialty I would choose if I had to start all over again, I would say unequivocally that I would pick psychotherapy and nothing else.

Even though the Armenian Relief Society stopped supporting the center after doing so for two decades, the clinic is still operating. Patients continue to visit, not only from Spitak but from Vanadzor and other neighboring regions. They come to me with different problems, such as depression, phobias, anxieties, and family problems. I always help them and they get better.

During the last few years, Spitak has begun to recover. The construction of Central Square and the rebuilding of the schools were very important for the residents of Spitak. These positive changes have improved the morale of the people. The main square has been very important for the townsfolk of Spitak, especially for their psychological recovery. Additionally, almost all of the schools have been rebuilt, and they have also played an important part in the recovery of the children. Nevertheless, there are still families who do not have homes and live in makeshift dwellings.

The generation that witnessed the earthquake has lived two lives – one that was before the earthquake, which was nice and comfortable, and the other that was after the earthquake, filled with sorrow and hardship. Having lived through years of terrifying events, our generation has become overemotional and detached. They fear that something ominous will happen, especially the fear of losing loved ones and ending up alone. Even during the happiest occasions, they tend to withdraw. During celebrations, they may be happy for a brief period, and then they huddle and talk about the earthquake, recounting events and memories of those who have perished. The new generation, for its part, bears the imprint of the earthquake as well, even though they had not experienced it. They grew up during turbulent times, facing the hardships following the earthquake, which they can describe in detail. This new generation tends to be somewhat more aggressive and less compromising.

Every year, when we get close to December, people become sad and withdrawn. Inadvertently, without thinking, I feel that way too. I refrain from talking to others and cry over the smallest mishap. I feel gripped by anxiety, as if something terrible is about to happen. People around me notice these changes and ask me, "What happened?" Only I know the reason. I want very much to get rid of these feelings, but I am unable to. They happen spontaneously. I feel I have no control over them. Almost everyone who experienced the earthquake talks about going through similar experiences around that time. For ten years after the earthquake, no music was played during weddings. When revelers from other towns or villages passed through Spitak after a wedding, they would stop playing music out of respect. Mourning still goes on every December.

Presently, I am working as a therapist for a new project designed to help formerly hospitalized psychiatric patients who have been abandoned. I help them adjust to living with minimal supervision as independently as possible. The project is called Khnamki Dun ("Home for Caring"). I feel sorry for them for being abandoned by their families, so I want to do everything possible to ensure that they feel happy and are not transferred to a mental hospital. Now, my greatest wish is to see my son get married and have children.

## 11.2 Working in the Trenches after the Spitak Earthquake

Comment from the editors: Since the inception of the Psychiatric Outreach Program in 1989, Dr. Karayan had traveled to Gumri (formerly Leninagan) and Spitak, working for two decades in schools, treating patients, training therapists, consulting hospital staff, and conducting research. Her diaries take the reader to the heart of the earthquake zone and acquaint them with the daily challenges and rewards of working with the survivors. She reveals to the reader with absolute candor the emotional impact of working with the survivors. She also describes the importance of empowering survivors in therapy. The poignant stories of Sahak and Gagik are remarkable examples of how a caring and competent therapist can help deep wounds to heal.

## 11.2.1 Excerpts from the Diaries of Ida Karayan, PsyD, LMFT

In horror, I watched the news of the earthquake on TV from my home in Pasadena, California. My people, who had endured so many tragedies, now were suffering in the aftermath of a horrifying natural disaster. My prayers for some way to lessen their pain were answered when Dr. Armen Goenjian, a clinician and research professor of psychiatry at UCLA with expertise in trauma psychiatry, invited me to join a group of mental health workers traveling to the earthquake zone. Four months after the disaster, I finally boarded the Lufthansa plane and headed to Armenia.

After traveling through Germany and Russia, we arrived in Armenia and headed to Leninagan (now Gumri). I was shocked by the extensive destruction. A haze of dust hung in the air. There was the odious stench of the dead bodies buried under the ruins. The government didn't have the equipment to remove the debris. We were surrounded by collapsed buildings.

Our first stop was a hospital, or what was left of it. We had lunch with the Deputy Minister of Health and the Chiefs of Medicine and Surgery. Each told of their story of loss. The Chief of Surgery had been treating the injured since the first day after the earthquake. He looked haggard, preoccupied, and seemed easily irritated. He had seen thousands of patients. The most shocking experience for him was one day at work, when he was examining two severely injured bodies. He did not recognize them at first. But then he realized that they were his wife's and son's. His only way to cope with the unbearable pain was to keep working. He had no time for grief. The Deputy Minister of Health had lost his married daughter and all of her family. The Chief of Medicine had his share of tragedy. He had finished having lunch with his ten-year-old son and had stepped outside the front door to go back to work when the earthquake struck. His house collapsed. He ran back but could not reach his boy, whose body was recovered from the rubble days later.

We did not have a place to stay in Leninagan because the usable buildings were filled to capacity and the water supply was contaminated. We drove to the town of Artik, twenty minutes away from Leninagan, only to find the hotel there closed because it was unsafe. While asking at a tavern for lodging, a drunk man invited us to his home. We tried to ignore him, but as we couldn't find anywhere else to stay, we accepted his invitation. Our host, Fiodor, had been a policeman before he quit his job in protest against the Soviet regime. He, his wife, and their two children welcomed us as honored guests. They gave us the entire house and stayed with Fiodor's parents. Their unselfishness and hospitality were heartwarming.

The next morning, driving back to Leninagan, we passed two schools. In school number 9, about half of the students had died, and in school number 10, three-quarters had died. When the earthquake tremors began, both school principals feared that Leninagan was being invaded by Azerbaijan, so they locked the entrance doors against the suspected invaders. Both schools had many recent Armenian refugees from Sumgait, a city in Azerbaijan where there had been pogroms against Armenians.

As we drove, we saw the severely damaged, famous State Academy of Fine Arts. We saw a destroyed factory where the majority of the employees had died. Many preschools, a maternity hospital, and a home for the disabled had been destroyed. I was in such a state of shock that I could barely move. I could not bring myself to take pictures of this unbelievable horror. Finally, we arrived at school number 16, now held in tents. We were invited into a tent by Rima, the Headmistress. She welcomed us with a sad smile. After introducing ourselves and discussing our purpose, we made plans for the next day.

The following morning, we arrived early at the school comprised of grades 1 through 10, with about 750 students, thirty-five teachers, and the Headmistress. Before the earthquake, it was a large, well equipped, two-story building. Now the classrooms were tents scattered throughout the ruins. The salvaged chairs and desks were twisted and dented remnants, grim reminders of the former school.

Everyone knew we were coming; a group had assembled in the office. Some of the teachers were anxious to talk to me, and some were very defensive, asking, "Why did you come here? What do you think you can do for us?" The men were either protective or aggressive. The women shared their feelings more easily. All had lost someone close. There was a lot of crying. A teacher called Sahak didn't speak at all. He stared at me with sad eyes the whole time. He was probably in his early thirties. He was the dean of students. The classic signs of trauma were everywhere.

After discussing confidentiality and the ethics of group therapy, teachers recounted their experiences of the earthquake. It was a very emotional and draining experience. After the session, Sahak gingerly asked, "Why are you here? What is your goal? Will you leave soon?" I told him I came to help them cope with their pain and grief and lessen their burden by talking with them. He shook his head and walked away.

After the session with the teachers, I went to the classroom of the first-grade children who were excited about a visitor from America. Their faces lit up with smiles. They were beautiful. We sat and talked, and I played with them. With their teacher's help, I screened them to decide who needed therapy. I promised to return the next day. I visited a total of five classrooms, evaluated each student, and made arrangements to begin counseling groups the following morning.

When teachers greeted us the next day, I felt a change in their attitude. They were eager to work with me. Sahak was there, looking detached and cold, quietly watching what I was doing.

We chatted a little, and then one of the first-grade teachers started talking. She had been in the classroom with the children rehearsing a Christmas song, "Gaghant Baba (Santa Clause), come to us, we love you, you bring us happiness." Then the earthquake struck. The children tried to hold on to her. She didn't know who to hold. They were crying, "Mama, Mama, Mama." A section of the wall collapsed, and she and sixteen of the children were trapped. They kept hearing the screams of the ten other children from the separated area.

Most of the teachers had not shared their stories until now, four months after the earthquake. They knew little of each other's experiences. One teacher spoke of how helpless she felt because she couldn't help many of her students. She felt guilty about how fright-ened she was. It was a very emotionally charged, challenging session. As other teachers began talking, I looked at Sahak. He covered his face with his hands and stared at the floor. We wrapped up the session by acknowledging how painful it was to think about those experiences.

After the meeting with the teachers, Sahak and I went to a classroom to screen the children for counseling. During the screenings, he stayed close to me. He was bitter and angry. I knew he had a background in psychology and wanted to learn what I was doing, but he would not express his thoughts except for periodic negative comments. He seemed bitter and angry, and dismissive of the importance of recalling the earthquake.

There were thirty children in the third-grade tent classroom. They were sitting in chairs which they had pulled from out of the ruins. They were proud of saving parts of their classroom and setting up a new one under the tent. I told them that I had come from the United States to see them. They asked me many questions. One read me a poem she had written for her mother who died in the earthquake. Most of the children seemed more mature than their chronological age. Many had died, but these survivors had lost their childhood.

The children talked about thoughts that bothered them, memories, beliefs, fears, and activities – things they avoided talking about at home to protect their families from more pain. They shut off their feelings at home. At school, with their classmates, they were open and able to share their experiences, some speaking, some drawing, and some writing. Susana read a poem about her mother:

> My lovely Mom, I miss you.
> Why did you leave me?
> God, why did you take my Mom?
> I am too young to be alone. I need my Mom.
> I need her hugs. I need her care.
> I miss my Mom! I miss my Mom!
> I don't know what to do . . .

While reading, Susana started crying, and suddenly others in the room were crying too. I looked at Sahak, and I saw tears in his eyes. Then he stood up and approached the girl and told her not to cry anymore, that it was enough. Later that day, I met with Susana individually to help her cope with losing her mother.

At lunchtime, Sahak suggested we go for a walk. As we stepped through the mud, he asked me whether I thought the children were exaggerating their feelings to get some attention, as it was four months since the earthquake. I explained that different people have different reactions and that many people need to talk and have someone listen to them. For the first time, it seemed, Sahak realized that it was okay to express emotions in front of others. I said that it was more difficult for some to share their grief with others, especially with people they don't know well, and that it was not a sign of weakness to show or to share one's emotions. Sahak was beginning to understand better what my role was. In traditional Armenian culture, individuality is frowned upon.

It became clear to me that food meant love to these people. They expressed their appreciation by inviting me to their homes. I started to decline the daily invitations for lunch and dinner. They invited me even if they had to borrow money to buy food from their neighbors to feed me. I was embarrassed by their gracious generosity. Each day I met new people, each with a sad story. As much as I wanted to, I could not help every person I met. I couldn't possibly help more than twenty people a day. As time went on, I started getting worn out. It became harder for me to set limits. That Saturday, I awoke after sleeping poorly. I had had a nightmare in which people were hanging onto me and choking me. In my dream, I was unable to move and felt overwhelmed by their need.

One afternoon, I stayed after school to meet with the parents of the students. I finished work at about 6:00 p.m., tired and sad, but I felt gratified. I was proud to see the strength and determination of a nation that has survived countless tragedies, massacres, and political turmoil and still keeps going. Despite my fatigue, I thanked God for giving me this opportunity to help others.

On Monday, everybody looked more at ease, less somber. They had more energy and appeared hopeful. Perhaps, I thought, we were making an impact. I went into the tent of the Headmistress Rima. She was alone. I offered her some American coffee. She had been reluctant to talk about her experiences, so I described to her my past fears and insecurities when I used to be the director of a school in Glendale, California, during an earthquake. As

I spoke, she started crying and then told me how, when the trembling started, she stood still, scared, not knowing who to help first. She had found some children above a collapsed stairway, hanging from the side of the school building, crying and calling for help. She got as close as possible but became scared that adding her weight would collapse the remaining structure. She kept on shaking and crying as she recounted how she tried to help them, but it was impossible. Then suddenly, the stair railing broke, and the children fell to their deaths. I gave her a hug and let her continue the outpour of her pent-up emotions, and I thanked her for sharing her story. She said she felt like a heavy burden came off of her back and thanked me.

The following day, I met with the teachers in our morning group and asked them to help me organize a space for play therapy. They got excited with the idea of planning for the future. Sahak offered his classroom, a tent where he taught classes on communism. I set the toys on benches. The teachers were inquisitive; they had never seen such toys. I found a wooden box among the ruins near the tents and used it for sand tray therapy. I also set up some water in a pan. We covered the tent floor with plastic that a teacher brought for me. The caretaker of the school came in with some jasmine flowers and said, "You know, you are making a difference." Hearing those words was so gratifying. Then Sahak came in and looked around the tent where he used to teach. He told me, with anger in his voice, that it was good he didn't have to work anymore, that now that I was here, he could just watch me and do nothing.

While we were setting up the play tent, I explained to the teachers how different therapy modalities helped children process traumatic experiences, including play therapy and sand tray therapy, which were based on the work of Carl Jung. [In sand tray therapy, a child (or adult) starts with a flat box of sand and selects small toys or objects to create a "world" that will often depict or reflect the child's conflicts and struggles. The therapists simply watch, though they may discuss or interpret at the end.] As the teachers were playing with the toys, one asked if I thought that the children working one-on-one would handle the newness and strangeness of the therapy. We talked more and decided to conduct play therapy in small groups of children. The teachers were eager, each asking to have their students first. I asked them to make a schedule with Sahak, who was in charge of the play tent.

The teachers had explained to the group of first-graders that they would play with me in a tent full of toys. They stood in the middle of the tent and looked around with wide eyes. Four of the five children had lost both parents in the earthquake. The fifth child, Gagig, had not lost either parent but showed severe symptoms of separation anxiety and PTSD symptoms. He wanted to stay next to his mother and did not fully enter the tent with his classmates. He had a forced smile on his face. He couldn't concentrate well. When the wind blew, he would yell, jump, and run out of the tent. At home, he couldn't sleep alone. He had a twin who was doing well, but Gagig was a big problem for his teachers and his mother.

For fifteen minutes, the children sat, not touching the toys. Staying close to his mother, Gagig watched from the door with a fixed smile. Eventually, the children began to play "earthquake," knocking down the blocks, building new structures, knocking them down again. They started talking about the earthquake and sharing the toys. I had not given them instructions or guidelines; they decided to play "earthquake" and chose what to do them-selves. Gagig continued to stay by the door and watch the others play.

After the children left, Sahak took some blocks and stacked them on top of each other. He knocked them down and stacked them again. And then again. He became angrier and angrier. He did this for quite a long time, and then he picked them up, stacked them, and almost lovingly – with tears in his eyes – put them away. He was restraining himself, but it was becoming more difficult for him to contain his sadness. He came to me with a guarded faint smile on his face and said, "It is lunchtime." I said, "Yes, it is." Then he left the tent. I was worn out and needed some "quiet time." I told Sahak, "I would like to walk alone after lunch and think a little." He asked me if he had done something wrong. I asked him why he thought that, and he said, "Because you want to be alone." I told him that I needed space to think. He couldn't understand and left with a puzzled look.

I walked for a while in the fresh air, wondering, "God, is there any way to help these people? What I am doing is just a drop in a bucket." When I got back to the tent, the teachers were waiting for me. During our meeting, they asked, "How can we help our students?" One teacher suggested that if they help themselves, they would automatically help their students.

The teachers shared more about their experiences. One teacher who was stoic during previous meetings opened up and told how he found the body of his wife. After trying for over ten years, she had become pregnant. He came home and found her sitting in her chair, holding a gown that she had been sewing for the baby. He said that he couldn't forget the sweet smile she had on her face and was sure she had been thinking about their unborn baby when she died. Once again, I felt overwhelmed. I could identify with the story of the pregnant woman. Almost everyone had sad stories to fill a book. We did some role-plays, including a therapeutic exercise to express grief, fears, and difficulties at school and at home. We discussed ways for teachers to support one another without being critical and wrapped up our group.

Sahak went back to the play tent before me. A new group of children came to the tent and had almost the same reactions as the previous group. After they finished the play therapy and left the tent, I was picking up toys and playing with them as I cleaned. Sahak stood there for a while, then went to the blocks and again began to stack them. He stacked them higher and higher, and then he kicked them. He repeated this several times. It was interesting how play therapy can engage adults, too. He picked up some dolls, buried them under the sand in the sandbox, then took them out. His eyes were full of rage, but I could sense the grief underneath. He asked, "Are you angry at me? Is it childish to play with the toys? I am an adult; I am not supposed to play with toys." I said that I played with toys all the time and that my office back home was filled with toys. He reminded me that I was a woman, implying that it was okay for me to play with toys. I explained that play is a form of relief for me and that it helps some people. He asked me not to tell anybody that he touched the toys. I said that I would not. We both smiled. He was trusting me more.

The next morning at school, I sat with Rima for coffee, and she shared more about her life. During the teacher's group meeting, more people opened up. Eventually, it was time to go to the play tent again. It was cold and damp inside. When the children came in, they knew where the toys were. They started to play right away. For the first time, Gagig came to the play tent without his mother but stayed standing next to the entrance door. Soon he asked if he came in and an earthquake happened, would I rescue him? I told him I would do my best to save him if that happened. He said that if I would hold his hand, then he would come inside the tent. I took his hand, and we sat down together. After looking at the toys for a short while, Gagig asked me to hold his knee instead of his hand so that he would be able to play. He made a tall building with toys and blocks, played a while, and then went to the sand tray, still needing me to hold his knee. We must have been quite a sight, crawling along like that! He put two little cars and one medium-sized car together and then took a big truck and smashed those three cars. He said, "The big truck is attacking the little cars. They are so small; they cannot do anything. The 'Mama car' cannot do anything. The big car will kill everybody; he is so strong. He is so strong; little cars should like the big car." Next, he put a gas pump beside the big truck and said that when the truck has too much gas, he gets powerful and smashes the little cars. He took the gas pump and buried it. He put lots of sand on top of it and said, "Nobody can find it now." Then he said, "The little car is broken, and no one can fix it, not even you." I told him maybe I would be able to help him fix it, maybe we could fix it together. He just sighed and said that I didn't know how to and started talking about how he fights with his twin brother. I pointed out that the session was ending soon, and he smiled and told me he would tell me about his brother tomorrow and went to play with the other children.

At last, Sahak started to participate in children's play. Two of the children created a scene of dead bodies, wounded people, ambulances, and rescue workers. They had no need for imagination now; their memories were enough. After a while, one of them said, "Let's make an American building." The other children got excited and used Lego and bristle blocks stacked together to make a building. I said to them, "Let's see if it will break," and they said "No, it is American. It is strong!" They tried to break it, but it was sturdy. They continued the building with Sahak's help and decided to leave it standing. Gagig smiled and, for the first time, it was a real smile. It was beautiful. After the children left, Sahak remained alone in the play tent while I went out to meet the teachers.

When I returned, Sahak was standing next to the sand tray. He asked me if he could play for a while longer. "Of course," I told him, "Why not?" Once again, he wondered if it was too childish for a grown man to play. I explained that we always have our "inner child" with us, so I think that makes it okay to play, even if you are a grown-up man. Again, he reminded me not to tell anyone. Then he gathered twenty-one of the little dolls – babies, women, men, and children – and buried them in the sand. He put crosses he had made from wooden matchsticks and a small stone at each "grave." He lit twenty-one "candles" (matches) and then knelt beside the sand tray. He started crying and talked as he cried. When he finished, I offered him some tissue and, with a gentle smile, he said, "These are too soft for a man."

Sahak wanted to know why I hadn't asked him what happened to him during the earthquake. I told him that I thought he would tell me when he was ready. He told me how in forty-eight hours he had buried twenty-one people by himself. All were members of his family. He did not sleep, he did not eat, he did not change his clothes for days. He just searched for their bodies, found coffins, and buried his loved ones. Afterwards, he collapsed and slept for two days. I felt drained after listening to Sahak's story. Each person has a story about loss and the horror inflicted by the earthquake, but each story is unique, painful, and personal. I needed to walk by myself for a while. The needs and expectations of so many were wearing me down.

That afternoon I met with Gagig's mother. She told me about Gagig and her husband. Gagig's father was an alcoholic who beat her and the children when he was drunk. Since the earthquake, Gagig had been bed-wetting, had difficulty sleeping, was jumpy, and fearful of being alone. When I asked how she felt, she said, "I do not exist. I live only because of my children. I've put up with his abuse for years because of the children." I asked if she had ever thought about getting a divorce. She told me that in Armenia, when a woman gets divorced, people treat her poorly as if she is a criminal. She had never told anyone about his abuse. When I asked how she tolerated her husband's behavior, she just shook her head. Suddenly, she blurted out, "God forgive me, but I wish he were dead! I wish he had been killed in the earthquake." She stopped abruptly and expressed remorse for her wishes.

On the way back that evening, I was too tired to talk with anyone. I just wanted to sleep. I woke early the next morning and admitted to myself (finally) that I could not help everyone by myself. My task was to help empower them to take responsibility for their well-being. During the morning coffee break, I shared my thoughts with Rima. She responded with excitement that she wanted to create a plan to help herself first, then the teachers and the children. I described what I had done after the earthquake at my school in Glendale. We discussed implementing a similar earthquake preparedness plan, a teachers' support group, and a children's support group. We ended by expressing our goal of empowering everyone at the school to become more self-sufficient. Rima seemed content and relieved.

After another long day of meetings with teachers, children in the play tent, and teenagers, I arrived back late. I needed to talk with my colleagues to sort out my feelings of inadequacy.

They too spoke of their experiences and of feeling overwhelmed. I remembered the advice Dr. Goenjian had given me prior to leaving Los Angeles. He said that I should be aware of my physical and emotional needs and limitations and that I should pace myself accordingly. I had pushed myself beyond my limits and needed to take a break. Together, we decided to go to Yerevan for the weekend. I knew it would not be easy to take a day off, but I had to take care of myself and address the secondary traumatic stress.

The next day, I told Rima and Sahak that we would leave for the weekend a day earlier than planned. I explained that the other counselors and I were exhausted and needed the extra day. Rima protested that I was being selfish. I explained that everyone's first responsibility was to take care of themselves. Otherwise, we do not have the strength to care for others. After a little discussion, they agreed. The separation was difficult for them, but I knew this would be beneficial for all of us.

At the teachers' meeting, we reiterated the necessity of taking care of ourselves in order to take care of others. As a group, we proposed a project for them while I was gone: the teachers would meet briefly with the children before class to discuss daily problems and ways to handle them. I encouraged the teachers to continue with their group meetings, and we chose Sahak to lead the group meeting on Friday.

Next, I met with the younger students, telling them that they would have a special project to write a song about anything they wanted. Gagig was to be their leader, and Sahak would guide the project. I met with Gagig, and he completed another sand tray. He then depicted the fantasy that his father had died in the earthquake and admitted to feeling guilty because of it. When he finished the meeting, he told me, "You know, you are a magician. You know children's secrets."

We left for Yerevan the next morning. I took my first bath in over a week. What a joy it was to bathe in hot water! I actually felt that some of the stress had washed away. From my hotel room, I could see Mt. Ararat – with the ever-present cloud at its peak – I'd never seen a more beautiful mountain. I started thinking about my family for the first time in two weeks. I had been away from my home for two weeks. Now I missed them deeply: my daughter's hugs, my son's gentle and loving comments, and my husband's support.

When I returned to Leninagan on Monday, I visited Rima, and started on the plans for emergencies, such as another earthquake or a fire. We agreed that she should have a self-care plan with a "go-to" support person, whom she trusts. We decided that teachers should have weekly (or twice weekly) group meetings and made guidelines on active listening and constructive problem-solving. We thought that teachers should conduct a "circle time" every morning before class to "check-in" with their students. Rima offered to write up a plan of action for us to review.

The teachers told me it was difficult for them to talk together on Friday without my being there; however, once Sahak began talking, the rest joined in. I was glad to hear that they shared some things they could not share with me. After an hour, they had to force themselves to stop because time had run out. They agreed that they are the ones who must overcome their hurt and that they need each other's support and care. They discussed talking about feelings in class with their students and identifying coping strategies to address their problems. All but a couple of teachers agreed that it was good talking about feelings and that if they did it every morning, they would make real progress.

When I met with the teens, they told me they could not meet with me right then, but they could meet the following day. It seemed that they were taking responsibility for their well-being. I admit I was feeling sad that I was not needed anymore. At times, I found myself not wanting to let go of some people. It's human nature to feel good when we are needed. I had to be content with the knowledge that they were adapting, healing, and moving forward.

Gagig came over to me and announced, "I will meet with you now." We went to the play tent, he walking in front of me, without asking for my hand. He went directly to the sand tray and started playing. He made a mountain and put a tree on top of it, then put two little boys and a mother under the tree. He said they were having a picnic. Far away from the small group, he had placed a closed garage with a big truck full of sand and a gas pump. The two places were divided by a river with no bridge, wholly separated. Gagig asked me, "Have you ever wished somebody died?" I told him that when I was younger, sometimes I would wish my teacher would die because she was mean to me. He asked what had happened when I wished that. "Nothing," I told him, "I just felt relieved. Using my imagination helped me with my anger." Gagig asked if anyone ever died because someone wished they would die. I said, "No. Humans don't have the power to kill someone with their thoughts." I suggested we try to kill a fly by wishing it will die. After a few minutes, he said, "Nothing happened to the fly." It seemed to help. He smiled, hugged me, and said, "I did not wet my bed for three days." Gagig told me that he and the class had a surprise for me the next day, then added, "By the way, this small car is not broken anymore; we fixed it."

When I arrived at the school the following day, Rima was ready with "the big plan." She had written a three-month schedule for herself, the teachers, and the students. We reviewed it, and I told her it was perfect. I knew we could not give the people homes or food or restore what they had lost. We could not satisfy their physical needs, but we may have helped them deal with their fears, thoughts, and behaviors.

I met with Gagig's mother. She was seriously considering giving her husband an ultimatum to stop drinking, or else she would divorce him. She said Gagig was much better and now had tools to cope with his fears. Now, when he gets scared, he'd say, "I am scared. I need to talk about it, or I need to draw a picture of the wind or my bad dreams."

The next day was our last in Leninagan for this trip. I arrived at the school and had coffee with Rima, Sahak, and the school caretaker. We talked about their plans. Rima showed me the preparedness plan in case of another earthquake. There were no typewriters or copy machines in Leninagan. So, she had handwritten the plans and used carbon paper to copy it. I promised to have it typed and sent back to her. They told me they were planning to have a room for play therapy in their new school. The room would be named "The Pasadena Playroom."

After I left Rima, I met with the teachers, and we went over their plans. They were very good. I then met with the teens, who gave me some photographs of their city before the earthquake. They also wrote a poem about their friends and family members who had died. A few had written short stories about their loved ones and included their pictures. The teens gave me some beautiful red and white carnations. They were full of hope for the future.

Finally, I went to the play tent. The children were making tall buildings with Legos and blocks. Sahak was standing with Gagig. The play tent had become a beautiful city with cars, trees, people, streets, and strong buildings. As I entered the tent, they started singing:

> We are not afraid of you, earthquake,
> We are stronger than you, earthquake,
> We know how to build, earthquake,
> We have plans for you, earthquake!

I stood there, unable to hold back my tears. Sahak and the teachers were crying. Gagig and the children gathered around me and gave me a paper with the words to their song, another bouquet of flowers, and several beautiful drawings. I hugged and thanked each one. Gagig came close and kissed me and asked, "May I keep this car?" I told him he could, and he said, "I can fix it when it gets broken, and I will keep it clean, and I will shine it inside and out." I knew he would, too. Gagig was healing.

Sahak came with us when we left Leninagan for Yerevan. When it was time to say goodbye, we shook hands, and he looked at me with a smile on his face and tears in his eyes. He said, "Men can cry, men can have feelings, men are human beings, and they can feel.

It is okay to cry and to be sad. It is okay to get mad. It is okay to have a wife and child, even though your brother has lost his. It is okay if your father lost his brother or your cousin is lonely in this world." He hugged me, and we cried. He asked me, "Is it okay to hug a woman?" and we laughed.

The people were so special, so courageous, and so resilient. I would miss each one. I had learned Armenian history and culture through songs, poems, and stories from my teachers and my family, but I no longer needed a museum or a book to know where I come from. Living here, I had found my past, my family, my people, and my country. I had gotten in touch with my real feelings and my inner self. After I returned home to the United States, I struggled for several weeks. Despite using the tools to deal with secondary traumatic stress, I spent days unable to eat more than a few bites. I was angry at everyone for having plenty to eat, for being comfortable, and for being alive. I was plagued with nightmares, anxiety, and a depressed mood. I struggled to connect with my family. I had pushed myself beyond my boundaries to create safe spaces for the people of Leninagan to share their pain. Yet, there was so much more to do. I felt I had done too little.

To address my vicarious traumatization symptoms, I became involved with *Bioenergetic Analysis* (IIBA), a form of therapy that involves addressing psychological issues, physical tension, and relational concerns. It alleviated my distress substantially. Consequently, I trained to become a bioenergetic analysis therapist. Six months after leaving Leninagan, I returned. Although I was disappointed to find the city still covered in rubble and not rebuilt, it was a joy to see that the groups for teachers and students were still running. The people had tools to address their emotional and mental health, even though they struggled to keep warm and have food on the table.

I used my IIBA therapy training to help the people of Leninagan and to handle my secondary traumatic stress better. I returned to Armenia with many of my colleagues, year after year, and tried to add "a few more drops in that bucket," hoping they will have a ripple effect. While this account came from the journals I kept at the time and reflects my thoughts and experiences in 1989, I could fill several books with the painful experiences of the wonderful people I met.

Last year, in 2019, I went back for the twenty-second time to Armenia's devastated region with Dr. Goenjian's group to memorialize the thirtieth anniversary of the earthquake. Many of the teachers with whom I had worked, with the help of our clinicians, had become child therapists. I met with adults who had been children when I first arrived and now had children of their own. They told me that they didn't remember much about what I had said or done. Only three things stood out to them: my hands, my smell, and my calm.

In offering me the opportunity to go to Armenia, Dr. Goenjian gave me a priceless, life-changing gift. My time in Armenia allowed me to understand and accept the tragedy, but more, it taught me to value connection – and feeling common humanity – with other people. I also learned so much about being a clinician from Dr. Goenjian, from his heart, his presence, and his humanity. He demonstrated that presence during tragedy was one of the most important things; that if you are "there" with your heart, you can make a difference. These experiences made me a better therapist; they deepened how I work with people.

I remember the first time I walked onto the school grounds in Leninagan. The air was cold, and there were collapsed buildings all around. As we arrived, in the middle of the rubble, a teacher was playing the piano with icy fingers with a choir of pale children singing to welcome us. To me, that was the spirit of these people: a spirit of strength, survival, and resilience.

# 11.3   Earthquake Memories

Liana H. Grigorian is a housewife from Spitak. She was nine years old when the earthquake struck in 1988. The following year she received psychotherapy at her school by a Psychiatric Outreach Program therapist. She wrote these memoirs in 2018.

On December 7, 1988, I was a third-grader at school. We were in a physical education class. My two friends and I were sitting together when suddenly the earth started shaking violently. The wall beside us cracked, came loose in one piece, and fell on us. It went completely dark, and we were covered in dust. Children were screaming. My friends Gevorg and Varduhi, who were beside me, died instantly. I was pinned between them, unable to move. I yelled and screamed, but no one responded. My classmates were lying beside me; they were dead, but I did not comprehend that they were no longer there.

I lay immobile, covered with dust and rubble, for four hours. Suddenly, someone lifted the tin roof. I heard a man's voice. The entire concrete wall had fallen on me, and he could see my head and arms. Still, he could not help me. He left, swearing he would return, but he never came back. I lost all hope. I laid trapped in the rubble for a few more hours. My voice was hoarse and almost inaudible from screaming. I was spent.

Then I heard a voice. It was my mother's. She was frantically searching for my brother and me and yelling out our names, "Liana! Hamayak!" I felt as if a supernatural strength overtook me. I started crying out, "Mama! Mama! I'm here!" My mother raised the tin roof and saw me, and she began to cry with happiness. After some struggle, she managed to come near me, slowly removed the rocks from behind my back, and wiped the dust off my mouth. She kept crying and kissed me over and over.

I was exhausted and drained. I felt faint, but my mother kept me alert as she called for help. Not only was my body buried under the concrete wall, but also my leg was trapped under a table. After a while, it became numb, and I could not feel anything.

My mother managed to call some people over to help, but they also could not raise the concrete wall. Then foreign rescue team workers arrived, over twenty of them. Using a crane, they were able to lift the wall and save me. I escaped that deadly place.

I was hospitalized for a long time because I could not put pressure on my leg. I lost hope that I would ever walk again. However, after months of therapy, I was able to walk.

Now, I am grown and married and have two marvelous children, a boy and a girl. Yet, the physical signs of the earthquake remain. There is a scar on my leg. I have intolerable pain at times, especially when the weather changes, and I have problems with my thyroid and blood pressure.

And the fears remain. Ever since the earthquake, I have been afraid to stay at home alone. I am fearful that the walls are about to come crumbling down. The dread seems so deep. I cannot escape it. Every little thing upsets me. I get easily dispirited. I become irritated and feel dejected at minor problems. When I think about the earthquake, my mood changes. I remember how my classmates died. I smell the dust, I see the terror on people's faces, I hear the screams, the cries. I visualize those moments like a horror movie.

Sitting at home, I am waiting for the walls to collapse. Walking in Yerevan, I am afraid to pass by tall buildings, and I won't spend even one night there. The reminders of the earthquake have affected my ability to live and be at peace. I cannot forget those moments that turned my lovely city into hell and stole so many of our loved ones. I worry that my fears will accompany me for the rest of my life.

# Lessons Learned from the Spitak Earthquake and Other Catastrophic Disasters

Armen Goenjian, Alan Steinberg, and Robert Pynoos

## 12.1 The Psychiatric Outreach Program after the Spitak Earthquake: Lessons Learned

The Psychiatric Outreach Program (POP) mental health clinicians from the diaspora who worked in Armenia shared the same language and religion as the earthquake survivors. Despite these similarities, there were many differences in traditions, customs, religious practices and rituals, and cultural values. For example, some of the survivors in Armenia were atheists, unlike the great majority from the diaspora. To optimize the effectiveness of therapy, it was important for therapists to recognize and respect those cultural and religious differences and not impose their own views. Also, it was important to remain focused on providing mental health care and refrain from political activism. For example, up to the end of 1991, Armenia was a communist country and many of the therapists from the diaspora opposed communism.

We commenced work by first establishing a working relationship with the Ministers of Health and Education and their proxies, the Chief of Psychiatry and the Deputy Minister of Education. Once their support was secured, we moved down the ladder to the principals of schools and teachers. Working with the hierarchy of administrators accomplished two things. First, the potential resistance by local school authorities and principals was minimized. They saw us as allies and not intruders. Second, in instances where we ran into problems, the leaders were available to help us. For example, two applicants who had important government posts wanted their relatives to be accepted to the POP teaching/training program. Because these individuals were not qualified, they were not enrolled in the program. Several allies of these applicants got together and filed a complaint against us with the mayor of the city. The manager of the clinic and I met with the deputy Minister of Education, who realized that the complaints had no basis and were acts of retaliation. He intervened and resolved the matter with one telephone call.

In another instance, by-passing the headmaster of a school in Spitak (who was not present at the school for our appointment) and working with the teachers proved to be an organizational glitch. When the principal joined the meeting with the teachers, he became disruptive. During the break, he opened up and discussed his personal problems. His needs were addressed, and from then on, he was cooperative with our therapists. Had we met and discussed his problems before meeting with the teachers, most probably he would not have intruded in the meeting with the teachers.

*Lesson learned*: Had we not established a relationship with the hierarchy, including the Health and Education Ministry personnel, and not agreed on a plan for intervention with local school administrators or headmasters, we would not have been able to operate effectively with the students and teachers. This is especially true in authoritarian countries.

With regard to treatment, in general survivors did not present with a circumscribed set of symptoms that fit a specific diagnostic category, such as PTSD or depression. Most were having multiple symptoms of PTSD, depression, anxiety, and grief reactions. Additionally, they had to deal with post-earthquake challenges and adversities such as poverty, homelessness, lack of food, electricity, and disturbed interactions with family members, peers, and teachers. Among those therapists who acknowledged the complexity of the clinical presentations and secondary stresses and adjusted treatment to the survivors' needs, their patients responded better and dropped out of therapy less frequently.

*Lesson learned*: The therapists' flexibility, not insisting on a fixed therapeutic approach when treatment was not effective, improved outcomes and reduced early termination of treatment and drop-outs.

Two experienced highly educated mental health workers did not have the opportunity of pre-departure preparation. Once in the trenches, both were highly distressed and unable to work effectively. Although over-identification with the victims' plight was a problem that many were able to overcome, these therapists were not able to do so. Another problem was anxiety related to a lack of self-confidence in dealing with the multiplicity and severity of the difficulties survivors experienced.

*Lesson learned*: Selection of appropriate candidates to provide mental health services was a challenge. Two senior psychologists or psychiatrists interviewed the applicants to assess their temperament and commitment to work in the earthquake zone under challenging conditions. Pre-departure preparations included bi-monthly meetings with past and future candidates. The past candidates shared their experiences. Video footage was used to show the destruction, living conditions, and conditions at the schools, hospitals, etc. Diagnoses and treatment modalities were discussed, with a review of assessments and treatments of commonly occurring disorders. The few who were unable to perform well were among those who were not adequately vetted and who had not gone through the pre-departure preparation. To minimize burn-out and fatigue of the diaspora therapists, we had them work with a peer at each location (e.g., school, hospital) and meet regularly with the team leader to debrief and consult about difficult cases or other problems (e.g., travel arrangements, housing).

*Lesson learned*: An early lesson taught by patients occurred when I was asked to see adults who were experiencing significant distress. Two unrelated survivors expressed their anger toward psychiatrists and psychologists who had rushed from Yerevan and Moscow universities soon after the earthquake, allegedly to help them. They gathered data for their research and then left without informing the survivors. This was perceived by the survivors as betrayal and exploitation. They indicated that they did not want to deal with us if we were going to do the same. I assured them that it was not our purpose. Accordingly, we refrained from conducting studies for the first year after the earthquake. In general, the POP therapists were very well received and appreciated by the survivors.

## Summary

- Working with the hierarchy of education and mental health systems of the country (starting from the Ministries) gave us the necessary support to implement the outreach program.

- Guidelines for the therapists included sensitivity to local traditions, customs, religious practices and rituals, and the cultural ethos of the local population.
- Therapists were instructed to refrain from political activism while in the host country.
- Most victims experienced symptoms of various diagnostic categories (e.g., PTSD, depression, anxiety, and grief reactions) and adversities (e.g., poverty, homelessness, lack of food, electricity, dysfunctionality in family, peer relations, etc.).
- Effective therapists were those who were flexible and adjusted treatment according to the most pressing psychosocial needs of survivors.

**Measures to Minimize Burn-Out or Incapacity of Therapists**

- Vetting of potential candidates based on their incentive, motivation, and willingness to work with colleagues, and pre-departure preparations for the psychological (e.g., vicarious traumatization, depression, anxiety) and physical challenges (e.g., cold temperatures, housing shortages, transportation problems) in the earthquake zone reduced the likelihood of being incapacitated to carry out their responsibilities.
- Pre-departure preparation of therapists included reviewing commonly occurring psychosocial problems and their treatments. These included a review of trauma literature, testimonials by therapists who had worked in the earthquake zone, and video presentations depicting the people and conditions in the earthquake zone.

# 12.2 Annotated Bibliography of Key Articles that Provide Important Additional Lessons Learned and Recommendations for Disaster Preparedness, Response, and Recovery

## 12.2.1 Pfefferbaum, Shaw, and the AACAP Committee on Quality Issues (2013): Practice Parameters on Disaster Preparedness

This article presents an overview of practice parameters for assessing and managing children and adolescents across all phases of disaster recovery. It was prepared by the Committee of the American Academy of Child and Adolescent Psychiatry.

### Clinical Guidelines

Delivered within a disaster system of care, many intervention approaches are considered appropriate for implementation in the weeks and months after a disaster. These include: (1) screening, (2) psychological first aid, (3) family outreach, (4) psychoeducation, (5) social support, and (6) anxiety reduction techniques. Additionally, clinicians should assess, monitor, and address risk and protective factors across all phases of a disaster. Schools are considered a natural site for conducting screening, assessments, and delivering services to children. Multimodal approaches using social support, psychoeducation, and cognitive behavioral techniques have the strongest evidence. Psychopharmacologic interventions are not generally used, but may be necessary as an adjunct to other interventions for children with severe reactions or coexisting psychiatric conditions.

## 12.2.2 Schoenbaum et al., (2009): Promoting Mental Health Recovery after Hurricanes Katrina and Rita: What Can Be Done at What Cost?

### Administrative/Fiscal Considerations

The authors used examples from Hurricane Katrina and Rita to propose a model for evidence-based mental health intervention after major disasters. They quantified the potential costs and benefits of large-scale implementation of such a model and considered its logistical and human resource requirements. They focused on a medium-term response, i.e., from seven months post-disaster, when new mental disorders can be diagnosed, through to twenty-four months, when more permanent service delivery strategies might be implemented. Three age groups were considered: 5–14 (17% of the total), 15–19 (9%), and 20 and older (75%). The extent of services required (e.g., such as duration, number of prescriptions) was assigned, assuming that treatment for mild/moderate illness was equivalent to about two out of three of the requirements for a course of cognitive behavioral therapy (eight to ten sessions) and/or several months of medication management; and that severe illness faced a known risk of short-term hospitalization and required both psychotherapy and medication, more visits, consultation and/or supervision, and case management. In addition, they assumed that successful population-level implementation would also require outreach efforts, provider training, particularly for the care of children, and the development of a management, communication, and accountability infrastructure.

Based on the assumptions, they estimated the cost of providing an evidence-based mental health intervention model to the population affected by a disaster such as the 2005 Gulf storms would cost $1,133 per capita across the affected population in months 7–24 post-disaster, with nearly half of this spending in months 7–12. In turn, it was estimated that the services would reduce the number of six-month episodes of storm-attributable mental health problems by 35%, corresponding to a per capita average of two extra months spent free of mental illness for each person in the disaster-affected area.

These findings suggest that population-level implementation would almost certainly exceed local provider capacity. While disaster preparedness may help motivate some expansion of local capacity, it is unlikely to be feasible or efficient for each geographic area to have adequate local reserve resources to meet post-disaster needs. Response to future disasters may be substantially enhanced if it could draw on a pre-established national "ready reserve" of providers trained in evidence-based treatments, along with a logistical infrastructure to deploy them effectively – in-person and via telehealth – and to coordinate their work. Disaster preparedness should be considered a public health requirement, and national mental health preparedness will likely require federal sponsorship for financing, as well as the establishment of parameters for a national mental health response, and development of rules under which it would operate, activate/deploy the response infrastructure, and monitor outcomes.

Telehealth through available large, managed care companies seems like a natural fit with the goal of achieving a nationally distributed network of "reserve" providers. Other methods to consider for increasing supply rapidly may include retooling of providers for different kinds of health or social services and/or training and deployment of non-professional/lay providers, including community religious professionals. More generally, these authors have taken a medical perspective on ameliorating the mental health consequences of disasters. Comprehensive disaster response requires intervention across multiple domains, including short- and long-term efforts to ensure meeting survivors' mental health, physical, social, and economic needs.

## Summary

- The article provides an example of how to estimate the costs for early and mid-term intervention as implemented after the Gulf storms.
- Local reserve resources may not meet post-disaster needs. For that reason, disaster preparedness should consider federal assistance to draw on a pre-established national "ready reserve" of trained providers.

# 12.2.3 Hoyer et al., (2009): Lessons from the Sichuan Earthquake

### Organizational/Administrative and Leadership Considerations

On May 12, 2008, a powerful earthquake struck China's Sichuan province, killing 87,500 people and causing the displacement of 14.4 million. According to a recent Department for International Development (DFID) report, the earthquake drove an estimated ten million people below the poverty line, with overall poverty in badly affected areas increasing from 11% to 35% of the population.

Unlike disasters in many other countries, very little international assistance was provided in China. The response was state led. In their day-to-day work, it became clear that the overall success of the government's response was made possible by its authoritarian position, its experience in managing large population movements and natural disasters, and the rapid deployment of the military. These elements enabled the government to avoid or minimize many of the problems common to disaster response. Mitigation strategies included an immediate emphasis on controlling infectious disease through widespread medical care and surveillance, the provision of tents for shelter (albeit insufficient in number at the outset and eventually upgraded to temporary, prefabricated structures), maintenance of security, and the rule of law through substantial police and military deployments, traffic, and supply-chain management at the regional and local level, as well as triage of patients, deployment of qualified volunteers, and the efficient management of in-kind donations. For example, as large quantities of unsolicited foreign medicines and supplies accumulated in airport warehouses (donated primarily by organizations without a physical presence in Sichuan), the provincial health bureau coordinated with the government in charge of volunteers to assign pharmacology students to sort, translate, and test these donations.

Additionally, the movement of people was strictly regulated in the affected areas. For months, police and military roadblocks prevented non-essential personnel from entering the disaster zone (personnel sprayed traffic passing through with disinfectant in the belief that this would reduce the risk of disease). These authoritarian measures largely succeeded in saving lives and reducing the secondary disasters of disease, flooding, and damage from strong aftershocks. However, these results came at the expense of personal liberties, limited access to affected areas, and, in some cases, the unquestioned acceptance of sub-standard living conditions.

Affected populations worked to reconstruct markets and establish a home in their government-issued tents. While awaiting further instructions from the local authorities, millions of people affected by the Sichuan earthquake, even those living in mountainous rural areas, stayed in close proximity to their destroyed homes. This differs from the experience in the North-West Frontier Province (NWFP) in Pakistan following the 2005 earthquake, where there was an elevated sense of anxiety, especially in remote rural areas. For example, in the Allai Valley of NWFP (population approximately 100,000), insufficient assistance saw virtually every family electing to migrate to camps at a lower elevation.

A coordinated response in China was achieved through the government's hierarchical approach, and decisions followed the chain of command from national to provincial and down to the prefecture and county levels. Unlike the direction eventually chosen by the government of Pakistan following the earthquake, the Chinese authorities did not immediately establish a parallel relief agency. Instead, relief activities were partitioned along with the formation of working groups roughly corresponding with government agencies – an important approach for ongoing coherence in policy and practice.

Another partnership strategy used in the aftermath of the earthquake, which may prove a model for long-term recovery, was the "twinning" of several badly affected counties and cities with other Chinese provinces and municipalities. These partnerships assisted affected areas with resources, personnel, and practical support for recovery. Teams of doctors, public health professionals, and sanitation and disease control experts were immediately dispatched to the affected partner county. The government's approach to the emergency response was effective in several respects. The setting of clear criteria and appropriate restrictions on unsolicited in-kind medical or other supplies led to the more efficient use of resources and eased the supply-chain bottlenecks common in other disasters of similar magnitude. Overall the response was crucial in saving many lives.

In the health sector, little attention was paid to psychosocial and mental health programs, especially among older adults who may have benefited from specialized support from the humanitarian community. Finally, although the state deserves praise for its handling of the response, a lack of transparency in terms of specific data and details of the response may have concealed many of these successes, as well as obscured areas for improvement.

## Summary

- China's success in mitigating post-disaster adversities was due to the authoritarian government's response based on past experiences in managing large population movements and natural disasters and the military's rapid deployment.
- The government's hierarchical approach and decisions that followed the chain of command from national to provincial and down to the prefecture and county levels made the implementation feasible.
- Emphasis was put on infection control, provision of shelters, maintaining security, the flow of necessary supplies, and triaging patients.
- Providing shelters, tents, followed by prefabricated structures, and keeping the victims in the proximity of their destroyed homes helped the recovery.
- 'Twinning' of several badly affected counties and cities with other Chinese provinces and municipalities was also beneficial in the recovery.
- A purported shortcoming was in the behavioral health sector, as little attention was paid to psychosocial and mental health programs, especially for those directed at the elderly population.

## 12.2.4 Ren et al., (2017): Experiences in Disaster-Related Mental Health Relief Work: An Exploratory Model for the Interprofessional Training of Psychological Relief Workers

### Clinical Considerations

This report details the response to the 2008 China earthquake in Wenchuan in Sichuan province. The authors note that services provided by psychologists, psychological counselors, and social workers were new to China, as these services were mostly unavailable before the earthquake. Additionally, many of the disaster-related psychological intervention techniques and practices used in Sichuan were newly implemented. They tended to gravitate towards individualism. Many relief workers quit disaster relief work because they neither received enough supervision nor emotional support. Many of the participants complained of "burn-out" and other psychosocial disturbances related to their relief work. Their experiences exposed a common theme: training systems have not been developed to address relief workers' wellness adequately, and they lack sensitivity to their psychological needs. Many mental health disaster relief workers reported that most of their training was conducted during short-term courses and often lacked any follow-up, making it hard to put what they learned into practice in their clinical encounters. The relief workers suggested the importance of providing culturally informed services.

This study identified progressive and interactive core elements, including building and effectively regulating training content, including the quality of teachers, ethical guidelines, cultural-awareness, and empirical evidence standards. The most important step was to empower health providers to take proper actions based on their local situations rather than apply foreign methodology mechanically. Foreign methods may not solve the problems of the local population and may even sometimes cause adverse effects. Empowerment requires relief workers to recognize that any disaster mental health service will focus not only on the use of the disaster survivor's resources such as self-capacity, but also on their social-cultural resources (e.g., community support, networks, agencies, and cultural resources).

### Summary

- Wenchuan's mental health workers experienced "burn-out" and other psychosocial disturbances related to their relief work and quit working due to their distress.
- Difficulties in dealing with the emotional challenges were attributable to a lack of adequate supervision and emotional support.
- Therapists stressed the importance of cultural awareness and recommended refraining from "mechanical application of foreign methodology" to solve local problems.
- Recommendations included empowering relief workers to participate in the decision-making process and using culturally informed practices.

## 12.2.5 Tanisho et al., (2015): Post-Disaster Mental Health in Japan: Lessons and Challenges

### Organizational Considerations

Following this triple disaster in Japan, one of the worst disasters in the last 100 years, a fundamental re-think was required by Japanese authorities to create a comprehensive and flexible response system capable of dealing with a variety of disaster scenarios that take into account Japan's unique cultural character. Fundamental to this was addressing inter-agency, inter-organization, and chain-of-command issues, which proved highly problematic after the disaster.

The authors emphasized the importance of distress caused by the dislocation of people crowded into evacuation shelters and small temporary housing units where survivors faced a variety of socio-economic stresses, including loss of social status, loss of livelihood, and an enormous shift in their long-term outlook for the future. Although evacuees did have direct access to health care, frequently reported symptoms included those associated with dementia, medication interruption, neglect, isolation, and continued stress. The number of long-term care applications from the elderly in communities near Tohuku's nuclear facilities jumped from 150% to 400% between 2010 and 2012. This increase was attributed to fear of what the future held, loss of property and community, and increased psychological stress from prolonged shelter-living.

Another important preventable problem noted was the effect of stigma (as occurs in many other societies) associated with psychological problems. Stigma was a barrier to accessing mental health services in the hard-hit Tokohu region. The authors stressed the need to increase mental health services by including more trained personnel other than psychiatric specialists, such as social workers or public health nurses.

The authors recommended that authorities need to establish basic principles, including training (e.g., in psychological first aid) for first responders and volunteers that can then be delivered to the general public. In this way, these individuals can learn how to properly assess disaster survivors and make the best use of available resources. Additionally, volunteers, selected community members, and primary health workers have to be empowered to assist with critical outreach activities and refer to psychiatrists only when needed.

### Summary

- At-risk groups included those who were relocated, isolated from their communities, and suffered socio-economic losses (e.g., housing and financial).
- Stresses included neglect, isolation, medication interruptions, especially among those with dementia.
- Recommendations included the provision of basic training (e.g., psychological first aid) to first responders, volunteers, and NGOs.
- Recommendations also included the provision of mental health services by nurses and social workers in addition to psychologists and psychiatrists.

## 12.2.6 Jonathan Patrick (2011): Haiti Earthquake Response: Emerging Evaluation Lessons

### Organizational Considerations

This report was organized around the evaluation criteria of the Development Assistance Committee (DAC), as adapted for the humanitarian community by Active Learning Network for Accountability and Performance (ALNAP).

An earthquake registering 7.0 on the Richter scale struck Haiti on January 12, 2010, at a shallow depth of 13 kilometers. The epicenter was near Léogane, about 25 kilometers from the capital Port au Prince. Approximately 220,000 people died (or one in fifty of the population); 300,000 were injured; two million (one in five) were suddenly made homeless; and 1.3 million were relocated to spontaneous settlements. These depressing figures were partly due to the earthquake occurring in a highly urban area with underlying vulnerabilities. The very actors who would normally be expected to lead and manage the response were themselves victims of the earthquake. Many national and municipal government buildings were destroyed, and many civil servants died, were injured, or were absent caring for their own families.

Emerging lessons included that it is better to have moderately reliable information and "good enough" analysis on time than "perfect" information and analysis that comes too late. Late analysis, no matter how good, is of little use in designing immediate life-saving humanitarian interventions. The limited inclusion of Haitians in needs assessments and analyses missed an opportunity to build relationships with Haitian partners. Inclusiveness is not necessarily a barrier to speed.

Recovery strategies should have been articulated from day one and integrated into humanitarian programming. Such strategies should have included serious consideration of establishing shelter in, or close to, former settlements and supporting the community and individual efforts to provide shelter in-situ, thereby maintaining family and social groupings and support networks. Better capacity assessments of Haitian political and civil leadership should have been undertaken early after the earthquake. Support and empowerment of affected government and civil society, however incremental, would have played a central role in the humanitarian response.

### Summary

- Leaders traumatized and incapacitated may need psychological assistance.
- Outside agencies should include local leaders to plan and implement recovery efforts.
- Establish shelter in or close to former settlements and support the community and individual efforts to maintain family and social networks.

## 12.2.7 Telford et al., (2004): Learning Lessons from Disaster Recovery: The Case of Honduras

### Organizational Considerations

Hurricane Mitch hit Honduras and other areas of Central America, notably Nicaragua, from October 25 to November 1, 1998. The hurricane remained static over the Isthmus for days, resulting in the most destructive natural disaster experienced in Honduras in recent memory. The Hazard Management Unit (HMU) of the World Bank provided proactive leadership in integrating disaster prevention and mitigation measures into the range of activities designed to improve emergency response. This report summarizes the findings of a Honduras country case-study, which is part of a ProVention Consortium initiative aimed at learning lessons from recovery efforts following major natural disasters.

The article recommends that criteria be set to determine who has been affected by the disaster, to what degree, and therefore who might be eligible for state and/or international assistance. The authors stress that a demand-driven process would have been preferable to an "all aid is welcome" policy. Competition and duplication of efforts were evident among international agencies. Competition for donor visibility resulted in rushed projects. Conditions set for some major international loans were often excessive.

Development principles should not be dropped because the recovery phase is considered to be responding to an emergency. Projects remained unfinished. Aims to bring about major socio-economic, cultural, and political changes during a post-disaster recovery process are probably over-ambitious. The focus should be recovery from the disaster and not the pursuit of a political agenda. Recovery aid should be provided in a fair, transparent, and balanced manner. This requires the inclusion of remote areas and vulnerable sectors where the disaster's impact may not have been as visible or dramatic as in more accessible locations. Donors should limit conditions associated with recovery funds, particularly on multilateral loans. Goals should be realistic. Donors should integrate their international aid structures, instruments, and approaches (e.g., emergency, rehabilitation, and development). Stable government posts were a key to recovery. Risk and disaster management should not be subject to political rotation. A balance should be achieved between centralizing certain tasks and resources and decentralizing others. For instance, broad, flexible standards and guidelines for recovery need to be set and enforced at a central level. These should then be adapted at regional, municipal, and community levels according to local conditions.

Community leaders and local mayors should be trained and equipped to manage decentralized resources (to allow them to assess and plan, to establish local databases, to implement recovery activities with their communities, etc.). Building the capacity of local communities can be a source of employment generation and development of new skills that should be encouraged as an alternative to a massive influx of foreign personnel. Legislation is required to regulate and hold accountable NGOs regarding cases of incomplete or substandard projects.

Arrangements should be made with national radio and television stations to facilitate national public information campaigns regarding recovery program entitlements and procedures for accessing support. Relocation of communities or individual groups should be seen as an extreme option due to the negative impact it can have on those communities and groups.

## Summary

- Competition and duplication were evident among international aid agencies. Competition for donor visibility resulted in rushed projects.
- Broad, flexible standards and guidelines for recovery need to be set and enforced by a central government. These should then be adapted at regional, municipal, and community levels according to local demands.
- Needs should be prioritized and aid by donors should be need-driven.
- Assistance should not be politicized.
- Unreasonable demands by donors should not be tied to loans.
- Post-recovery completion of projects should be agreed upon from beginning.
- The use of local workers is preferable to bringing in outsiders.
- Aid should be provided in a fair and transparent way.

## 12.2.8.  Madrid and Grant (2008): Meeting Mental Health Needs Following a Natural Disaster: Lessons Learned From Hurricane Katrina

### Organizational Considerations

In 2005 Hurricane Katrina struck the Gulf of Mexico region, causing 1,800 deaths and the displacement of one million people. Homes were destroyed, jobs were lost, family members were separated. Federal and local disaster relief agencies had underestimated the need for mental health preparedness and interventions. Mental health services were inadequate to meet post-disaster needs. Community officials and care providers experienced burn-out.

The authors recommend that treatment by professionals skilled in psychotherapy and psychopharmacology be prioritized and integrated into disaster relief programs. They also suggested that city, state, and federal governments, as well as the insurance industry, should adopt short-term and long-term solutions that facilitate accessible care and reimbursement with parity between physical health and mental health services. People's safety must first be secured with adequate shelter, food, medications, and clothing to begin the process of recovery from psychological trauma. Similarly, family reunification is essential for the well-being of children and parents.

Recovery can be fostered in the aftermath of a disaster such as Hurricane Katrina by planning and meeting the ongoing needs of those affected. A recurrent finding was the importance of meeting the needs of those responsible for children, including parents, guardians, and teachers. The authors recommend that psychologists and other mental health professionals and pediatricians become advocates for their patients' ongoing needs. Ongoing services will be required to help evacuees adjust to their new communities or their prior communities if and when they return. Finally, it is critical that mental health considerations become an integral part of disaster preparedness, response, and recovery, especially with regard to children and vulnerable populations.

## Summary

- People's safety must first be secured with adequate shelter, food, medications, and clothing in order to begin the process of healing from psychological trauma.
- The reunification of displaced families should be a priority.
- Assistance should be given to those who care for children.
- Resilience may be fostered by planning ahead.
- Health care workers should advocate for their patients' needs.
- Mental health considerations should be an integral part of disaster preparedness, response, and recovery.

## 12.2.9 Daw (2002): What Have We Learned Since 9/11: Psychologists Share their Thoughts on Lessons Learned and Where to Go from Here

### Clinical Considerations

Contributors to this article included several prominent psychologists who were involved in relief efforts after the 9/11 terrorist attacks. Housing, jobs, and other instrumental needs had to take priority over mental health needs. Ongoing psychological problems emerged slowly as other more pressing needs were met. Among many who developed PTSD, years passed before they became desperate enough to seek out mental health services. Prominent symptoms of PTSD were avoidance symptoms. There were lasting psychological effects of indirect exposure to mass violence (for example, seeing it in real-time or repeatedly on TV or knowing someone indirectly who was lost or who suffered). Exposed therapists had to deal with their feelings of vulnerability. They were uncertain how to reassure their traumatized patients that they were safe when they themselves didn't feel safe. A cautionary observation was that there is some evidence from controlled studies that psychological debriefing soon after a traumatic event can impede recovery.

## Summary

- Post-disaster housing, jobs, and other instrumental needs take priority over mental health needs.
- Ongoing psychological problems will emerge slowly as other more pressing needs are met.
- Traumatized therapists may not be effective.

## 12.2.10 McFarlane and Williams (2012): Mental Health Services Required after Disasters: Learning From the Lasting Effects of Disasters

### Clinical Considerations

After major disasters, the health services required differ markedly according to the nature of the disaster and the geographical spread of those affected. Epidemiological studies have shown that services need to be equipped to deal with major depressive disorder and grief, not just PTSD, and not only for victims of the disaster itself but also for emergency service workers. The challenge is for specialist advisers to respect and understand the existing health care and support networks of those affected, while also recognizing their limitations.

In the initial aftermath of these events, a great deal of effort goes into developing early support systems, but the longer-term needs of these populations are often underestimated. These services need to be structured, taking into consideration the pre-existing psychiatric morbidity within the community. Disasters provide an opportunity for improving services for patients with post-traumatic psychopathology in general and later can be utilized for improving services for victims of more common traumas in modern society, such as accidents and interpersonal violence.

There is growing professional consensus and increasing evidence that a series of psychosocial interventions should be applied immediately after disasters. This approach is based on the principles of psychological first aid. Recently, the World Health Organization published its guidelines on PTSD for field workers. The philosophy for the psychosocial and mental health interventions is the PIES (Performance, Image, Exposure) model, developed from the military, that services provided should be based on their proximity, immediacy of response, expectancy of recovery, and simplicity. It is critical to make people feel safe and decrease their anxiety immediately after a disaster. This involves providing information and dealing with immediate survival, welfare, and humanitarian needs. Survivors should be provided with reassurance and physical comfort. Those suffering pain from injuries should be given adequate pain relief. However, providing immediate counseling risks creating a false belief that there will be no long-term morbidity. Furthermore, counseling immediately after disasters has not been shown to be effective.

## Summary

- In the immediate recovery phase, intervention should be employed to provide information and efforts to deal with immediate survival, welfare, and humanitarian needs.

- Victims of disasters also include emergency service workers.
- Mental health workers should be prepared to deal with PTSD, depression, and grief.
- There is emerging information that a series of psychosocial interventions applied soon after disasters may be beneficial.
- Services provided should be based on their proximity, immediacy of response, and expectancy of recovery.
- It is critical to make people feel safe and to assist in decreasing their anxiety immediately after a disaster.

## 12.2.11   Reifels et al., (2010): Lessons Learned about Psychosocial Responses to Disaster and Mass Trauma: An International Perspective

### Organizational Considerations

At the thirteenth meeting of the European Society for Traumatic Stress Studies in 2013, a symposium was held that brought together international researchers and clinicians involved in psychosocial responses to disaster. One of the presentations was in reference to the 2012 Northern Italian earthquake in Emilia Romagna, which affected 14,350 people. It caused twenty-six deaths, damaged 33,600 buildings, and resulted in the widespread evacuation of affected community members. Doctors Gabriel Prati and Luca Pietrantoni described the lessons learned from the disaster recovery efforts. First, earthquake preparedness programs were needed: most individuals were at risk of injuries and fatalities due to inappropriate or unsafe behavioral responses during the shocks, such as moving to another room. Second, psychosocial intervention should focus more on resilience factors at the family, organization, and community levels. For example, given the protective role of social integration and social support, interventions should mobilize social support networks (e.g., family, friends, and community members) and promote collective action, participation, and empowerment. Third, psychosocial interventions were more effective when they focused on promoting networking between different institutions and NGOs.

Another presentation was on the 2011 Great East Japan earthquake, tsunami, and nuclear disaster by Dr. Yoshiharu Kim. Major challenges included the evacuation of psychiatric hospitals and obtaining psychiatric drugs to ensure treatment and service continuity in affected areas. Another challenge was the coordination among many different organizations involved in the mental health response, underscoring the importance of having comprehensive national guidelines, a central information portal, regular provider briefings, and cross-professional work in mental health care teams.

### Summary

- The authors stress the importance of earthquake preparedness that could have avoided injuries and fatalities.
- Psychosocial interventions should focus on resilience factors at family, organization, and community levels.
- Psychosocial interventions were more effective when they focused on the promotion of networking between different organizations.
- A major challenge was the evacuation of psychiatric patients from hospitals and securing their medications.

- The importance of having comprehensive national guidelines, a central information portal, and cross-professional working in mental health care teams.

## 12.2.12 United States Department of Homeland Security (2019): National Response Framework, Fourth Edition

The National Response Plan provides a framework for all types of threats and hazards, ranging from accidents, technological hazards, natural disasters, and human-caused incidents. Implementation of the National Response Framework (NRF) allows for a scaled response, delivery of the specific resources and capabilities, and a level of coordination appropriate to each incident. The response mission area includes capabilities necessary to stabilize an incident, save lives, meet basic human needs, restore community lifeline services and community functionality, and establish a safe and secure environment to facilitate recovery activities. The NRF sets out fundamental principles for disaster response to support local-, state-, and federally funded disaster operations. These principles include: (1) engaged partnership; (2) tiered response; (3) scalable, flexible, and adaptable operational capabilities; (4) unity of effort; and (5) readiness to act. These principles reflect the history of emergency management and the distilled wisdom of responders and leaders across the whole community.

### Engaged Partnership

Those who lead emergency response efforts must communicate and support engagement with the whole community by developing shared goals and aligning capabilities to reduce the scope and duration of impact. Mutually supporting capabilities of individuals, communities, the private sector, NGOs, and governments at all levels allow for coordinated planning in times of calm and effective response in times of crisis. Engaged partnership and coalition building include ongoing clear, consistent, accessible, and culturally and linguistically appropriate communication to ensure an appropriate response.

### Tiered Response

Most incidents begin and end locally and are managed and executed at the local level. Incidents require a unified response from local agencies, the private sector, and NGOs. Some may require additional support from neighboring jurisdictions or state governments and federal support. National response processes are structured to provide tiered levels of support when additional resources or capabilities are needed.

### Scalable, Flexible, and Adaptable Operational Capabilities

As incidents change in size, scope, and complexity, response efforts must adapt to meet evolving requirements. The number, type, and source of resources must be able to expand rapidly to meet the changing needs associated with a given incident and its cascading effects. As needs grow and change, response processes must remain nimble, adaptable, and resilient. The structures and processes must be able to apply resources from the whole community to support disaster survivors and stabilize the community. As incidents stabilize, response efforts must be flexible to facilitate the integration of recovery activities.

### Unity of Effort through Unified Command

Unified command maximizes response efforts while integrating and respecting the roles, responsibilities, and capabilities of all participating organizations. The Incident Command

System (ICS) is important to ensuring interoperability across multijurisdictional or multia-gency incident management activities. Unified command enables unity of effort when no single jurisdiction, agency, or organization has primary authority and/or the resources to manage an incident on its own. The use of unified command enables jurisdictions and those with authority or responsibility for the incident to jointly manage and direct incident activities through the establishment of common incident objectives, strategies, and a single incident action plan.

## Readiness to Act

From individuals and communities to businesses, non-profit, faith-based, and voluntary organizations and all levels of government, the national response depends on the ability to act decisively. A forward-facing outlook is imperative for incidents that may expand rapidly in size, scope, or complexity, as well as incidents that occur without warning. Decisive action is often required to save lives and protect property and the environment. Although some risk to responders may be unavoidable, all response personnel are responsible for anticipat-ing and managing risk through proper planning, organizing, equipping, training, and exercising.

# References

Daw, J. (2002), What have we learned since 9/11. Psychologists share their thoughts on lessons learned and where to go from here. *Monitor Psychology*, 33 (8). Available at: www.apa.org/monitor/sep02/learned.

Hoyer, B. (2009). Lessons from the Sichuan earthquake. *Humanitarian Exchange*, 43, 14–17. Available at: https://odihpn.org/wp-content/uploads/2009/07/humanitarianexchange043.pdf.

Madrid, P., & Grant, R. (2008). Meeting mental health needs following a natural disaster: lessons learned from Hurricane Katrina. *Professional Psychology: Research and Practice*, 39, 86–92.

McFarlane, A. C., & Williams, R. (2012) Mental health services required after disasters: learning from the lasting effects of disasters. *Depression Treatment and Research*, 1–13. https://doi.org/10.1155/2012/970194.

United States Department of Homeland Security. (2019). National Response Framework, Fourth Edition, 1–57. Available at: www.fema.gov/emergency-managers/national-preparedness/frameworks/response.

Patrick, J. (2011). Haiti earthquake response emerging evaluation lessons. *Evaluation Insights*, 1, 1–14. Available at: www.alnap.org/help-library/haiti-earthquake-response-emerging-evaluation-lessons

Pfefferbaum, B., Shaw, J., & AACAP Committee on Quality Issues. Practice parameters on disaster preparedness. (2013). *Journal of the American Academy of Child and Adolescent Psychiatry*, 52 (11), 1224–1238.

Reifels, L., Pietrantoni, L., Prati, G., Kim, Y., Kilpatrick, D. G., Dyb, G., Halpern, J., Olff, M., Brewin, C. R., & O'Donnell, M. (2013). Lessons learned about psychosocial responses to disaster and mass trauma: an international perspective. *European Journal of Psychotraumatology*, 4, 10.3402/ejpt.v4i0.22897. https://doi.org/10.3402/ejpt.v4i0.22897.

Ren, Z., Wang, H. T., & Zhang, W. (2017). Experiences in disaster-related mental health relief work: an exploratory model for the interprofessional training of psychological relief workers. *Journal of Interprofessional Care*, 31 (1), 35–42. https://doi.org/10.1080/13561820.2016.1233097

Schoenbaum, M., Butler, B., Kataoka, S., Norquist, G., Springgate, B., Sullivan, G., . . . & Wells, K. (2009).Promoting mental health recovery after hurricanes Katrina and Rita: what can be done at what cost. *Archives of*

*General Psychiatry*, 66 (8), 906–914. https://doi.org/10.1001/archgenpsychiatry.2009.77.

Tanisho, Y., Smith, A., Sodeoka, T., & Murakami, H. (2015). Post-disaster mental health in Japan: lessons and challenges. Washington, DC: Center for Strategic & International Studies, pp. 1–8.

Telford, J., Arnold, M., Harth, A., with ASONOG. (2004). Learning lessons from disaster recovery: the case of Honduras. International Recovery Platform. *Disaster Risk Management Paper Series*, 8, 1–31. Available at: www.recoveryplatform.org/assets/publication/honduras_wps.pdf.

# Index